THE NEW COLD WAR
AND THE REMAKING
OF REGIONS

THE NEW COLD WAR AND THE REMAKING OF REGIONS

T.V. PAUL AND
MARKUS KORNPROBST, EDITORS

GEORGETOWN UNIVERSITY PRESS / WASHINGTON, DC

© 2025 Georgetown University Press. All rights reserved. No part of this book may be reproduced or utilized in any form or by any means, electronic or mechanical, including photocopying and recording, or by any information storage and retrieval system, without permission in writing from the publisher.

The publisher is not responsible for third-party websites or their content. URL links were active at time of publication.

Cataloging-in-Publication Data is on file with the Library of Congress.

ISBN 978-1-64712-586-8 (hardcover)
ISBN 978-1-64712-587-5 (paperback)
ISBN 978-1-64712-588-2 (ebook)

EU GPSR Authorised Representative
LOGOS EUROPE, 9 rue Nicolas Poussin,
17000, LA ROCHELLE, France
E-mail: Contact@logoseurope.eu

26 25   9 8 7 6 5 4 3 2   First printing

Cover design by Jeremy John Parker
Interior design by Westchester Publishing Services

CONTENTS

List of Illustrations   vii

Preface   ix

1. Introduction: The New Cold War, Regional Orders, and Peaceful Change   1
   T.V. Paul and Markus Kornprobst

2. Regional Orders and Great Power Rivalry in a Multiplex World   28
   Manjeet S. Pardesi and Amitav Acharya

3. Norms in Great Power Competition: Peaceful Change in a Spheres of Influence World   53
   Anders Wivel

4. The Ideological Sources of Great Power Competition in the Regions   75
   Thierry Balzacq and Vera Grantseva

5. Great Power Competition and Regional Orders: A Neoclassical Realist Interpretation   96
   Mark Brawley and Jonathan Paquin

6. Status Competition in the Regions: Past, Present, and Future   121
   Xiaoyu Pu

7. New Institutional Economic Statecraft beyond the Border: Technology Competition in the Asia-Pacific   141
   Vinod K. Aggarwal and Andrew W. Reddie

8. The United States and Changing Regional Orders in Europe and Asia   170
   Deborah Welch Larson

9. China and the Changing Regional Order in East Asia   189
   Selina Ho
10. Russia and the Shaping of the Regional Order in Eurasia   211
    Seçkin Köstem
11. Conclusion: Rethinking Great Powers, Regions, and Peaceful Change in the New Cold War Era   231
    Andrej Krickovic and Jaeyoung Kim

Index   253

List of Contributors   263

ILLUSTRATIONS

FIGURES

Figure 4.1　The Russian-led regional order: institutional dimension　85

Figure 7.1　The determinants of state intervention　146

Figure 7.2　Explaining institutional change　151

TABLES

Table 1.1　Great Power Conflicts and Regional Orders　10

Table 1.2　Regional State Strategies　12

Table 4.1　A Typology of Policies in Grand Strategy Competition　82

Table 5.1　Second-Tier States' Strategic Selection　102

Table 5.2　Second-Tier States' Strategic Interaction and Regional Outcomes　103

PREFACE

The international order is currently undergoing major changes, especially in the sphere of great power relations along with alterations in regional orders. The great powers, both rising and declining, are working hard to obtain or preserve their spheres of influence, while the second-ranking states are attempting to maintain their sovereignty and territorial integrity. The great power-led order is aimed at bringing back polarity, while the second-ranking states want to create a multiplex order where they have greater agency. In the globalized world order, the latter have more agency in choosing their paths than they had during the Cold War–era bipolar order. Both global order and regional orders affect each other while generating a hybrid, multiplex-multipolar order and the effort in this volume is to unravel these dynamics in different regions and critical countries. It is the outgrowth of a major collaborative project launched by the Global Research Network on Peaceful Change (GRENPEC), a grouping consisting of numerous scholars and institutions from different parts of the world who share an interest in advancing scholarship on this subject. GRENPEC originated from the 2017 International Studies Association (ISA) annual conference theme, "Change in World Politics," during the presidency of T.V. Paul. The emerging international and regional orders are of special interest to us, in our efforts to understand how and why conflict or its opposite, peaceful relations, emerge globally. Our contributors specially deserve our thanks for working with us assiduously and patiently. We acknowledge the research assistance provided by Alice Chessé, Viktor Vucic, Jaeyoung Kim, Muhammed Yusuf Yilmaz, Moges Zewiddu Teshome, and Lauren Kook. The initial papers were presented at the two roundtables that were held at McGill University in March and October 2023, which were followed by another roundtable at the International Studies Association (ISA) annual meeting in San Francisco in April 2024. We appreciate the comments at these meetings by Amitav Acharya, Michael Byers, Ferry De Kerckhove, Eric Haney, David Haglund, Kai He, Juliet Johnson, Andrej Krickovic, Erik Kuhonta, Benjamin Miller, Krzysztof Pelc, Lisa Shapiro, David A. Welch, Jennifer Welsh, Anders Wivel, and Alexandra Zeitz, in addition to the suggestions by the three anonymous readers of the book manuscript, which helped us in improving the chapters. We are much grateful for the support of Georgetown University Press editor, Don Jacobs. We acknowledge the financial support of MINDS program of the Department of National Defense, Canada, Social Sciences and Humanities Research Council Canada (SSHRC), McGill's James McGill Chair, Centre for International Peace and Security Studies (CIPSS), Faculty of Arts, and the Department of Political Science, and the Vienna School of International Studies. Finally, we thank our respective families for their moral support.

T.V. Paul, Montreal, Canada
Markus Kornprobst, Vienna, Austria
May 2024

CHAPTER 1

Introduction

The New Cold War, Regional Orders, and Peaceful Change

T.V. Paul and Markus Kornprobst

The Russian offensive against Ukraine that began in February 2022 signaled the end of three decades of great power peace and an acceleration of great power competition. In the early 2010s the great power peace that followed the collapse of the Soviet Union in 1991 began to erode amid deteriorating relations between an increasingly belligerent Russia (especially in its neighborhood but also in the Middle East and Africa), a more and more assertive China in East Asia and the world under Xi Jinping, and a United States internally divided about how to uphold its international status. The competition encompasses security and economic rivalries but extends into other areas such as science and technology, especially digital innovation. We contend that the world is in the first stages of a New Cold War, albeit with significant differences from the previous one.

This book conceptualizes the New Cold War as a power contest, in which several contenders, including great powers, rising powers, and pivotal regional actors, all vie for power and influence without placing their security and prosperity fully in the hands of one or the other great power or a bloc. The New Cold War, in other words, is multipolar and multiplex at the same time. On the one hand, there are three great powers—that is, the United States, China, and Russia—who contend for spheres of influence. On the other hand, there are more rising powers and middle powers with plenty of regional agency. These range from Saudi Arabia to Brazil, from South Africa to Indonesia, and from India to the United Arab Emirates. This has important analytical repercussions. Making sense of the New Cold War necessitates scrutinizing not only global powers but also increasingly assertive regional powers.[1] A large part of this is caused by the increased material and ideational capacities acquired by the regional actors thanks to globalization and new norms that emerged in the post–Cold War era. They thus have more agency than before while conversely the great power contestants want to push the world order into a new form polarity where spheres of influence matter the most. This rising power and middle power agency is reflected in their choosing somewhat independent policies of strategic autonomy by not binding or bandwagoning with any of the great powers too closely. Structures created by the distribution of power among great powers matter, but not to the extent prevalent during the bipolar Cold War or US unipolarity that followed the Cold War.

We investigate what this New Cold War means for regional orders. More precisely, we examine how the former impacts on propensities of regional orders to bring about peaceful change or its opposite, violence. Thus, this book makes two key contributions to the existing literature: First, we compare how the New Cold War affects different regions, ranging from the Middle East to Central Asia, and from South Asia to Europe. The New Cold War does not manifest itself in the same fashion in every region. There is considerable variation. Second, our regional accounts, taken together, amount to a nuanced view of world order. Staying away from assumptions of a monolithic world order that can be explained by looking at great power relations only, our findings provide crucial insights into how the interaction of multiple actors—global and regional—shapes the evolving international order. State and non-state actors other than great powers are not mere bystanders, and constellations of relations among actors vary significantly across regions. In some regions, great powers have more reach and influence than in others. Europe and the Indo-Pacific are two such regions.

This introduction is organized into eight sections. First, we conceptualize the New Cold War. Second, we elaborate on the rationale of this volume. Third, we discuss competing great power strategies. Fourth, we move on to how these strategies shape international regions. Fifth, we examine the strategies of non-great powers. Sixth, we investigate the prospects for peaceful change in regions. Seventh, we develop a vocabulary for studying how great powers shape regional orders. Finally, we provide an overview of the chapters of this edited volume.

THE NEW COLD WAR

In the last decade, more and more scholars have written about a New Cold War when they attempt to characterize today's global order.[2] But what actually are the features of this New Cold War? What is reminiscent of the post–Second World War superpower confrontation? And what is new?[3]

Even before the Second World War, the expression "cold war" was already used as shorthand for a constellation in which states are locked into enmity relations but stop short of confronting each other directly on the battlefield. In France in the mid-1930s, Franco-German relations were described with the metaphor *guerre froide* (cold war). In the mid-1940s, Bernard Swope made sense of the concept in similar ways, juxtaposing a "shooting war" to a "cold war." At the same time, this absence of direct combat was linked to nuclear weapons. George Orwell, for instance, hoped for a "tacit agreement" among nuclear weapons states not to use these weapons. To Orwell, this amounted, in 1945 already, to an existential question: "Two or three monstrous super-states, each possessed of a weapon by which millions of people can be wiped out in a few seconds, dividing the world between them."[4]

When we speak about a New Cold War today, it is no longer just a metaphor. It is a historical analogy. On the one hand, there are at least three notable similarities between the Cold War and the New Cold War. First, direct combat between the great powers is absent. A "cold war" is different from "hot war" (where actual force is used destructively) as there is no imminent war but parties prepare for active conflict, if necessary, by engaging in intense arms racing and holding zero-sum and worst-case assumptions of each other's intentions and capabilities. Orwell still has a point when it comes to the sources of this absence of direct war among the great powers. Today, nuclear weapons underpin great power relations. There is a strategic convergence across great powers that using nuclear weapons is prohibitively costly. This constitutes, up to now at least and despite a new arms race that is bound to change strategic calculations, a similarity in the relations between the United States and the Soviet Union in the past as well as those among the United States, China, and Russia in the present.

Second, this absence of a direct great power war—this is where the metaphor has its shortcomings—comes at the expense of escalating conflicts in regions. The Cold War was an enduring superpower rivalry characterized by recurrent crises with high escalation possibilities, and parties did not make serious efforts to resolve their conflict once and for all. On the contrary, the superpowers used force in regions and supported their client states to signal protection of their spheres of influence.[5] The Soviet Union and the United States, in other words, fought proxy wars but no direct wars. Similarly, the United States, China, and Russia are not fighting a hot war against one another. The New Cold War remains cold. But, at the same time, they are involved in interstate and intrastate conflicts in various regions of the world. The war between Russia and the Ukraine happens against the background of escalating great power tensions between Russia and the United States. The civil war in Sudan, pitting Hemeti and al-Burhan against one another, is intricately linked to the war in the Ukraine because gold, mined in Sudan helps Russia finance its war in the Ukraine.

Third, great powers fail to play their role in comanaging international crises that the United Nations Charter ascribes to them. Even though the permanent members of the Security Council are meant to be the custodians of collective security and peace, the great powers deadlock the Council. This happened during the Cold War, and it happens now in the nascent stages of the New Cold War. Reactions to this problem by middle and smaller powers are comparable, too. In 1950, the General Assembly tried to circumvent deadlock in the Security Council by introducing the Uniting for Peace resolution (A/RES/377 A). Long dormant, the provision was used again in 2022 as a reaction to Russia's war in the Ukraine (A/RES/ES-11/1). Yet, the General Assembly, struggling to move beyond declarations, has not proven capable of overruling vetoes at the Security Council and taking matters firmly into its own hands. In the last decade, the Security Council, due to increasing great power competition, has failed over and over to de-escalate crises together. Hamas's terrorist attack on Israel on October 7, 2023, Israel's subsequent heavy-handed invasion of Gaza, and the threat of escalation of long-standing conflicts in the region (involving Iran, Lebanon, and Syria) notwithstanding, the Security Council hardly managed to pass any resolutions on resolving the crisis.

However, there are notable differences between the Cold War and the New Cold War. The "New" amounts to an important qualification. Overall, the New Cold War is more diffuse. At least three differences are worth emphasizing: First, ideological dividing lines between the two great powers were very clear cut during the Cold War. The Cold War was, among other things, an ideological battle between capitalism and communism as well as democracy and authoritarianism. Strategy and interests mattered, of course. But so did beliefs about what is good and what is bad.[6] Ideology, as Balzacq and Grantseva demonstrate in this volume, still plays an important role. But it is, for the time being at least, much more difficult to make out a clear-cut dividing line between two entirely irreconcilable camps. For one, there are no longer just two camps. There are three great powers and many rising powers (see below). Furthermore, the old dichotomy of capitalism versus communism does not seem to be a major motivating force anymore. Juxtaposing democracy and authoritarianism may be more of a contender for future ideological battles between the great powers.

Second, compared to the Cold War, there is a much higher degree of economic interconnectedness in today's world. While economic markers of globalization flows hit rock bottom in the early stages of the Cold War, they are still at a very high level in the nascent stages of the New Cold War. Yet, many of these indicators have plateaued in recent years amid neo-mercantilist tendencies and trade wars. Great powers compete not only in the military realm but also very much in the economic one. To what extent the competition will end up fueling deglobalization is something that remains to be seen.[7] Some scholars sketch future scenarios that are not all that different from the early stages of the Cold War—plenty of economic interdependence within blocs but significantly less of it between blocs.[8]

Third, there are many pivotal regional states—such as India, Brazil, Saudi Arabia, and Indonesia—that have gained more autonomy and agency than what they possessed during the old Cold War era thanks to their material, especially economic, advancements.[9] Most of them have not joined any military alliances or bandwagoning coalitions as many did during the previous Cold War era. Cross-cutting institutional structures characterize the times—with international institutions such as G-20; Brazil, Russia, India, China, South Africa (BRICS, by now also encompassing Iran, Egypt, Ethiopia and the United Arab Emirates); and Shanghai Cooperation Organisation (SCO), all having memberships of a variety of states. Even those informal groupings led by the United States, such as Quadrilateral Security Dialogue (QUAD, including Australia, India, Japan, and the United States), are yet to form a proper institutional structure. There is a considerable amount of hedging by the second-ranking states relying on soft balancing, limited hard balancing, and institutional engagement, both at the multilateral and mini-lateral levels.[10] Many second-ranking states are members of the China-led Belt and Road Initiative (BRI), largely for economic as opposed to geopolitical reasons. For instance, several Association of Southeast Asian Nations (ASEAN) states are participants in BRI as well as regional trading arrangements, such as the Regional Comprehensive Economic Partnership (RCEP), that include China as well, even while they oppose Chinese hegemonic efforts in the Indo-Pacific.

Much of this diffuse nature of the New Cold War can be captured by the concept of multiplexity.[11] Even during the Cold War, smaller powers mattered a great deal. They could escalate conflicts further. Cuba during the Cuban Missile Crisis is a case in point. Or they could participate in working toward détente, as Austria, Finland, and Switzerland did by facilitating diplomatic efforts that would culminate in the 1975 Helsinki Final Act. In our days, the agency of smaller powers, and, even more so, rising powers, is considerably more pronounced. Regional players have become significantly more powerful and with many of them sitting on the fence and blurring the boundaries of spheres of influence, great powers find it even more difficult to lay down the rules of the game. At the same time, it is all too obvious that great power politics still matters a great deal. The United States, China, and Russia retain dominant status in terms of military and institutional structures. Furthermore, the United States and China are mighty global economic players. Thus, the New Cold War is not just about multiplexity. It is also about multipolarity. In this *multiplex multipolarity*, the great powers seek to retain or acquire spheres of influence, while the second-ranking actors wish not to succumb to great power dominance and retain their agency—that is, sovereignty, territorial integrity, and strategic autonomy.

WHY STUDY THE NEW COLD WAR, REGIONAL ORDERS, AND PEACEFUL CHANGE?

Historically, imperial powers and the modern-day great powers largely determined the fate of regions and regional orders. As colonial empires waned in the aftermath of World War II and decolonization, direct control of imperial powers declined, but their indirect role persisted in almost all regions of the world. The great power conflict during the Cold War shaped and reshaped regional orders as the superpowers and their alliances competed globally in every region for allies and allegiances. Proxy wars were common, although regional allies fought wars and played security games expecting support from one great power or another. Several million people died in proxy wars in the Global South.[12] The end of the Cold War in 1991 produced a short period of relative peace in many regions of the world. Several conflicts in Southern Africa, Southeast Asia, and Latin America came to an end, and there was a short period of optimism in settling the Israeli-Palestinian conflict. However, the emergence of the United States as the near-unipolar power produced a period of US activism in the regions, only scantily challenged by other great powers. US interventions in Iraq in 1991 and later in 2003 showed the power of Washington to upset regional orders and engage in military intervention with impunity. The United States–led war on terrorism produced immense violence in states like Iraq and Afghanistan, even though some Islamic extremist groups were eventually suppressed.[13] Instead of bringing peace and stability, US hegemony seemed to have brought much disorder to regions such as the Middle East and South Asia. The US failures in Iraq and Afghanistan to bring lasting peace showed the limitations of great power hegemony, and in the case of Afghanistan the return of the repressive Taliban regime was the outcome. According to one estimate, the post–Cold War wars that the United States waged generated some 900,000 deaths and cost $8 trillion during the twenty-year period.[14] Through its military interventions, the norm of territorial integrity, which is codified in the UN Charter and had grown stronger as a behavioral standard during the Cold War, was violated by the United States, but other great powers did not contest American policies directly.[15] Russia followed regional intervention through its active participation in the Syrian civil war in support of the discredited Assad regime. The territorial integrity norm at present is violated by all great powers, especially Russia. More importantly, proxy war has returned to great power contestation as the Ukraine and Syrian cases illustrate.

The peak of the US hegemony came to an end in 2009 when the global financial crisis brought about new centers of power. The rise of China as a serious contender since 2014 has once again produced a round of great power activism in the regions. Since 2012, Russia under Vladimir Putin has also been more active in regional conflict zones in the Middle East and Central Asia. The Russian offensive against Ukraine in 2022, the annexation of Donetsk, Kherson Luhansk and Zaporizhzhia, as well as its earlier annexation of Crimea in 2014 are the most powerful challenges yet posed by Russia to regional and global orders. Russia is indeed challenging the norm of territorial integrity while defending exclusive spheres of influence, although it is doing so in response to the humiliating strategy of the United States and its Western allies to extend NATO to erstwhile Soviet areas.

The Chinese strategy has centered around developing geo-economic links with all regions through its BRI network. This has generated criticism as a new form of colonialism spread to Africa and Asia among weak states. The United States has not been able to come up with effective counter programs to the Chinese strategy of gaining spheres of influence through massive economic and infrastructural programs. Yet, in the security domain, the United States retains a leading position, especially in the Indo-Pacific. Increasingly, the security games with China in particular have become too subtle for the United States to employ past strategies effectively. Containment in a new format may be the choice strategy for the United States and the West, but many regional states such as India and Brazil appear to be buck-passing while maintaining their links with both Russia and the West.

COMPETING GREAT POWER GRAND STRATEGIES

The strategies of key great powers of the day matter for global and regional orders, especially in producing different outcomes, be it positive or negative. It is worth noting that the grand strategic visions that the contemporary great powers, the United States, China, and Russia, hold are not all that conducive to sustained order or peaceful change in the regions.

The *US* strategy appears to be maintaining its hegemony in key regions including Europe, the Indo-Pacific, and the Middle East. After emerging as the lead power in the near-unipolar order, the United States supported deepened globalization and the integration of key countries such as China and India in the economic order. Since the late 2010s, however, the strategy has become much less accommodating. Trump's national security strategy was all about great power competition: "China and Russia challenge American power, influence, and interests, attempting to erode American security and prosperity."[16] This had effects on regions, including those traditionally very much outside of Washington's sphere of influence. The United States, for instance, sought "Central Asian states that are resilient against domination by rival powers."[17] The Biden strategy does not constitute a paradigm shift in this regard. It, too, writes about "the contest for the future of the world" and singles out China and Russia (as well as "autocrats" more generally) as the main competitors.[18] The Biden strategy discusses regions in much detail. In Central Asia, it attempts to institutionalize greater US influence: "We will continue to work through the C5 + 1 diplomatic platform (Kazakhstan, Kyrgyz Republic, Tajikistan, Turkmenistan, Uzbekistan and the United States)."[19]

China's strategy is aimed at replacing the United States as the world's leading power, particularly in the Indo-Pacific. In his opening remarks at the Chinese Communist Party Congress in October 2022, Xi pledged that by the middle of the twenty-first century, China "leads the world in terms of composite national strength and international influence," by boosting per capita incomes to the level of a middle-income country and fully modernizing its armed forces and economy by 2035.[20] This aim underpins the BRI. In recent years, statements about rejuvenating the nation and its peaceful rise in world affairs have given way to a much more competitive language.[21] As Xi Jinping put it at the twentieth Party Congress, "We have put our national interests first, (...) and maintained firm strategic resolve. We have shown a fighting spirit and a firm determination to never yield to coercive power."[22] This resolve is most apparent in its neighborhood, especially with how Beijing pursues its territorial claims to Taiwan and in the South China Sea. These, in turn, sour relations with a number of important players in the region, including India and Japan. Yet, China has long ceased to be a power preoccupied with its own neighborhood. Reaching out across the globe, it implements, *inter alia*, a comprehensive Africa strategy. Xi visits Africa frequently and has institutionalized a number of summit diplomacy fora such as the China-Africa Leaders' Dialogue.[23]

Russian strategy initially accepted the post–Cold War order. There were efforts during the times of Yeltsin and early Putin to join the Western-led international order. However, the decision by the United States and NATO partners to expand their membership to the erstwhile Soviet sphere led to a rethinking on Russia's part, especially under Vladimir Putin. The joining of several Eastern European and Baltic states in NATO and the EU generated vehement criticism from Russia. The military and foreign policy doctrines of Russia have undergone key changes in the last decade. Moscow's vision of the world is about multipolarity, with Russia forming one of the poles or "leading centres," as the recent Foreign Policy Doctrine puts it. This involves— and the doctrine is very clear about this—Russia's involvement in regional affairs across the globe. Yet, even though the document lists no less than ten "regional tracks," the first three that are mentioned, close to home, are discussed in greater detail than the others: Near Abroad, the Arctic, and Eurasia. While interaction with China on the world level and also on the regional level in the Asia-Pacific is addressed several times, the "US and other Anglo-Saxon states" feature almost at the very bottom of the list of "regional tracks" (only Antarctica does worse). They are, given their striving for global hegemony and supporting of the Ukraine, portrayed as the enemies of Russia.[24]

GREAT POWER COMPETITION IN THE REGIONS TODAY

Great powers and non-great powers today do not look through the same lens when they orient themselves in international politics. There is a polarization of paradigms. On the one hand, great powers increasingly rely on a geopolitical paradigm, built around spheres of influence. Russia and China, as rising powers, are at the forefront of regaining lost or acquiring new spheres of influence, while the United States as the reigning hegemon, is attempting to retain its sphere of influence in Europe and expand it into former Soviet territories. On the other hand, most secondary states seek to uphold (oftentimes select) elements of the international rule of law, most importantly sovereign equality and territorial integrity. Ukraine has emerged as the lead actor for maintaining and protecting the territorial integrity norm from direct great power interventions, but it is paying a steep price. The challenge for frontline second-ranking states such as Ukraine is that the clashing paradigms could produce more violent outcomes, especially as a result of responses by great powers that experienced status decline yet want to resurrect it through coercive means.

Table 1.1 summarizes the different historical eras since the onset of the intense Cold War in 1949, the end of the Cold War in 1991, and the

Table 1.1: Great Power Conflicts and Regional Orders

Historical eras	Leading norms	Instruments of contestation	Institutional structures	Impact on regional orders
Cold War 1949–1991	• Sphere of influence • Territorial integrity	• Hard balancing • Proxy wars • Direct interventions • Containment/global/regional • Selective military and economic aid	• UN • Military alliances	• Exacerbation of regional conflict/rivalries • Negative impact on economic development
Immediate Post–Cold War 1991–2014	• Partial territorial integrity • Limited multilateralism	• Limited bilateral/multilateral cooperation • Soft balancing, limited hard balancing • Globalization mechanisms • War on Terror	• UN • EU, ASEAN • New forums—BRICS/G-20	• Reduction in regional tensions except transnational terrorism • Some attention to collective action problems • United States–led unilateral interventions
New Cold War 2014–present	• Spheres of influence • Partial territorial integrity	• Hard balancing • Soft balancing • Economic statecraft technological denial/expansion (e.g. cyber, AI)	• Weakened UN • Weakened EU/ASEAN • G-20 • BRICS	• Selected military interventions • Economic sphere contestation • Less attention to collective action problems

beginning of the New Cold War in 2014. The changing norms of the times, especially on spheres of influence, territorial integrity, and sovereignty, and the leading instruments of contestations, such as hard balancing, proxy wars, direct interventions, containment, and their variations, offer a way to capture the differences in regional orders. The different institutional structures, be it the UN or military alliances, as well as their impact on regional orders, have not often produced the desired stabilizing effects.

During the past two hundred years since the Congress of Vienna, geopolitical ambitions and commitments to uphold territorial integrity have been colliding. The latter has been a reasonable success story as the idea got progressively well entrenched as a pillar of the postwar settlement in 1945.[25] Yet, great powers periodically used extraordinary violence to assert their status and superiority, and their victims in the nuclear era have largely been weaker powers in the regions. Even though the great powers have lost several asymmetrical wars, they have inflicted enormous damage and extraordinary suffering on the weaker challengers. The US failures in Vietnam, Iraq, and Afghanistan, and the Russian failures in Afghanistan show that weaker actors can win wars against great powers, despite the latter's immense material superiority. These wars have not produced much functional learning for the great powers as they repeat their violent behavior periodically hoping to assert themselves, particularly in their regional spheres of influence. They often intervene without a proper exit plan, or their strategy inevitably falls victim to the complex realities of the target state and its domestic ethnic and power structures. The interventions are often enabled by the great power's advantages in military technologies, such as precision-guided munition and hybrid warfare. They are also driven by short war illusions.

NON-GREAT POWER STRATEGIES

Secondary states are often portrayed as objects of great power politics with little or no agency, especially in systemic perspectives. This is not accurate, especially in today's world order. Often secondary states attempt to navigate systemic conflicts, even when great power conflicts constrain their choices.[26] However, sometimes great power conflicts can be used by secondary states to advance their strategic and territorial goals. The active use of alliances by regional states such as Israel, Egypt, India, Pakistan, Turkey, and the Koreas during the Cold War era to compete with their rivals suggests that great powers often fell for secondary allies' strategies, especially over territorial conflicts with their neighbors.

Secondary states aligned with great powers can navigate and even prosper under some circumstances. The level of rivalry and the capacity of the elite matter for the strategic choices of second-ranking states in the regional contexts, whether they succeed or fail in making use of the great power competition to their advantage. In the current era, some have been pursuing hedging strategies, using bilateral and multilateral engagements in institutional forums, limited hard balancing, soft balancing, buck-passing, and in rare cases, bandwagoning.[27] Table 1.2 summarizes non-great power strategies as they evolved from the Cold War to the New Cold War today.

Although many regional states have made use of the opportunities provided by the new great power competition to further their security and economic interests, it is difficult to predict how long it is possible to continue their trajectories. Regional orders are affected negatively by the resurgent great power rivalries, as we are witnessing in the increased conflict in

Table 1.2: Regional State Strategies

Historical eras	Strategies	Institutional mechanisms	Outcomes
Cold War 1949–1991	• Alignments • Non-alignment • Bandwagoning • Soft balancing	• UN General Assembly • NAM & G-77 • Alliances—NATO/Warsaw Pact	• Intense regional conflicts • Proxy wars • Skewed economic development
Immediate Post–Cold War 1991–2014	• Hedging • Diplomatic engagements • Soft balancing • Economic liberalization • War on Terror	• UN General Assembly • EU/ASEAN • New forums (e.g., BRICS, SCO) • Regional economic grouping	• Increase in regional tensions in Middle East/South Asia • General economic growth • Some attention to collective action problems
New Cold War 2014–present	• Hedging • Limited hard balancing coalitions • Seeking strategic autonomy	• G-20 • BRICS • QUAD • ASEAN forums • BRI	• Intense conflicts in select regions • Decline in economic growth • Increasing instability • Less attention to collective action problems

the post-Soviet region, especially in Ukraine, the Middle East, East Asia, and South Asia. Some conflicts such as Syria and Yemen are persisting partly thanks to great power inactivism, while the botched US withdrawal from Afghanistan in August 2021 caused the resurgence of extreme violence and deprivation for millions in that beleaguered country.

The responses of second-ranking states to great power violence, particularly Russia's military actions, have been muted. Many second-ranking states have failed to unequivocally criticize Russia's invasion, and some such as India have even been actively trading with Russia, in particular oil and gas, dampening Western economic sanctions. These states seem to want to keep Russia as an important actor, as they worry about Western dominance hurting their interests. They desire to preserve their strategic autonomy against possible assertive policies by the resurgent West. They also seem sympathetic to Russia's grievances, in particular NATO's expansion toward its former territorial sphere.

More systematic work is needed on the differences between today's great power competition from the Cold War era when the US-Soviet rivalry defined the contours of many regional orders. Is the scholarship on systemic/regional interactions mainly developed during the Cold War era sufficient to understand these new dynamics? What does the past tell us of the present and the future? What new tools do we need in order to explain patterns of regional orders and the impact of systemic rivalries on these orders and vice versa? Before addressing these questions, we clarify some conceptual issues.

REGIONAL ORDERS AND PEACEFUL CHANGE

We define a region as a "cluster of states that are proximate to each other and are interconnected in spatial, cultural and ideational terms in a significant and distinguishable manner."[28] We define a regional order as *a pattern of regularized interactions among states and between states and key non-state actors in a regional domain characterized by conflict, cooperation, peace, or mixed patterns.* From a systemic perspective, the international system is the most prominent unit of analysis to examine both global and regional orders. However, regional subsystems can be formed with the larger system affecting it and vice versa. In the aftermath of the end of the Cold War, the topic of regional order gained much prominence in International Relations (IR) scholarship, and all theoretical perspectives have something to say about regional order.[29]

Existing IR paradigms cannot explain well the emerging international or regional orders. They seem to be presenting one dimension of the orders as they are idealized patterns. Complex world orders require complex analysis, which the IR discipline is yet to develop rigorously. For instance, *realism*, both classical and structural, gives extreme importance to systemic and structural factors, especially the distribution of power among great powers. The emerging order cannot be called bipolar, multipolar, or unipolar. Here the agency of secondary states constrains neat classification as made in structural theories. Complex interdependencies and rapidly changing economic and technological fortunes also generate challenges for the theories in this category. Realist schools, be it the classical, structural, or neoclassical varieties, privilege systemic variables as primary shapers of regional orders, although the latter pays attention to domestic and individual factors as intervening variables in their formations.[30]

Realism of various hues considers proper balance of power as essential to obtain stable regional orders. Perpetual peace is impossible to achieve as the system remains anarchic and self-help is the primary operating mode. Regional hegemony is often sought by powerful states, be it by an outside power or a regional power, but it will hurt the sovereign existence of weaker states.[31] Balance of power is achieved either thorough internal arms buildup or external alignment of like-minded states. Structural realists like Waltz imply systemic variables as the most implicitly important, suggesting that regional order—if it exists—is a function of the global balance of power. A more stable order is a bipolar distribution of power, and a less stable order is multipolar power distribution.[32]

There is indeed debate as to whether states balance against power or against threats as well as if states balance against or bandwagon with a powerful state that may be threatening.[33] There is also debate as to whether states balance using less coercive mechanisms as discussed by soft-balancing theorists.[34] Going by balance of power, the emerging power transition in key regions like East Asia and the larger Indo-Pacific in general will produce turbulent outcomes if Chinese power is not balanced by established powers in combination with like-minded regional actors.

Regional orders from the hegemonic perspective are the functions of a hegemonic power assuming a leadership role as opposed to balancing power. It is only when the hegemonic power declines that instability occurs globally as the rising power may attempt to accelerate its progress through violent means. Power transition theories of various hues also consider the preponderance of a dominant state as essential to maintain peace.[35] This is because as Douglas Lemke states: "So long as the dominant state is preponderant it is able to defend the status quo against all dissatisfied states. The weak dissatisfied states realize that they do not have the wherewithal to successfully challenge the dominant state for control of the international system, and *cold peace* [albeit not harmony or *deep peace*] is likely to prevail."[36] The United States, as the prevailing hegemon, can offer order and stability in regions such as the Indo-Pacific. Conversely, to adherents of this perspective, the US decline would spell disaster for regional order. A rising China challenging US hegemony will produce conflict, potentially violent. However, from the Chinese perspective, a new tributary system or *tianxia* (a derivative of hegemonic stability) is necessary to achieve peace.[37] The transition from one hegemony to another, however, can be violent going by the historical record. The smaller actors could fall victim to the hegemonic transition conflicts. The US dominance, however, produced much violence in regions such as the Middle East and South Asia, where Washington engaged in a war on terror often ignoring the territorial integrity norm. This experience challenges the core of hegemonic stability theory on regions.

Both the balance of power and hegemonic stability perspectives ignore the many contextual factors that can determine and shape regional orders. Three of these factors are particularly important. First, the type of rivalry among the regional states, between great powers and regional states concerned, matters. If the great power rivalry is systemwide and well entrenched, it can hurt regional orders profoundly. Conversely, if the rivalry is mellowed, regions can have greater autonomy and may have different patterns of order and stability. Second, different regional orders are characterized by different degrees of openness to great power competition. Prospects for peaceful change—even just a cold peace—have been dashed by the superpower rivalry at the Horn of Africa during the Cold War, and the New Cold War does not bode well for the region either. Other regions, even those located in Africa, have a better track record of avoiding some of the most destructive manifestations of great power competition. West Africa is among them. Third, the realist literature on great powers and regional orders all too often ignores that regional players have agency too. Research should analyze the relations of regional and extra-regional actors, including great powers, instead of simply assuming that the latter entirely trumps the former.

Key *liberal* approaches, such as liberal institutionalism, commercial liberalism, and democratic peace, offer diverse explanations for the prevalence of peace or conflict in a region. The focus here is on transformative peace, as the presence of the three mechanisms brings peaceful regional order while their absence means conflict or disorder. The role of the great power is performed by a hegemonic liberal state with a benign strategy to transform regions in its image.[38] Liberalism is equally weak in explaining present-day world politics as the world order is not becoming more liberal. Even the liberal hegemon, the United States, is showing many illiberal tendencies, both domestically and internationally.[39] Europe remains the only place with strong liberal characteristics. Yet, even there, right-wing populism is reappearing in different manifestations. A pure Kantian world, as sought by liberals, is unlikely to emerge anytime soon, given that the new players, China and India in particular, seek to emerge as civilizational great powers, attempting to resurrect their so-called glorious yesteryears.

Similarly, *constructivism* has constraints, although its emphasis on identity could be useful in understanding the world order. Constructivism also draws from liberal notions of institutional peace, but ideas and identities matter more in these perspectives.[40] "Distribution of identity" has been suggested as an alternative to "distribution of power."[41] Increasingly, constructivist literature has focused on the social sources of power[42] and uncovering deeply seated hierarchical relations among actors.[43] Yet, all too often, the deeply seated context analyzed by constructivists does not go much beyond non-Western identities, knowledge, and practices. Much more research on these, especially how they shape the world's regional orders, would be warranted.[44] More eclectic theorizing linking realism and constructivism explore great power hierarchies and hegemonic orders in the context of power transitions maybe of some use.[45]

English school scholars emphasize regional orders as creations of historical great power politics.[46] The Copenhagen school also emphasizes the clout of great powers. By definition, they have the capabilities to reach beyond their neighborhoods and into different world regions. Even though they are extra-regional actors, they are pivotal players in creating regional security complexes.[47] Others have focused on plural international orders, beyond the Western order, based on cultural diversities.[48] *Critical perspectives*, such as postcolonial and post-structural theories, focus also on the legacies of colonialism and power structures created by hegemonic orders that have done enormous damage to regional architectures through their lingering legacies.[49] These perspectives may explain one or more dimensions of regional orders, but we are yet to find a clear answer to why some regions develop *stability-instability, warm/stable peace, normal peace, cold peace, cold war,* and *hot war*.[50] The role that great powers play in regional transformation is yet to receive full critical evaluation in these perspectives. Some overemphasize while others underplay great power politics and its role in order building in the regions. The traditional paradigms tend to focus on a limited number of critical variables that need not be equally applicable in diverse regional contexts, especially in explaining different types of conflict, cooperation, peace, and peaceful change.

For peaceful change, we draw upon the definition used in the *Oxford Handbook of Peaceful Change in International Relations*, as a continuum involving a minimalist and a maximalist understanding. The minimalist version posits a *"change in international relations and foreign policies of states, including territorial or sovereignty agreements that take place without violence or coercive use of force"*; while in the maximalist perspective, peaceful change is a *"transformational change that takes place non-violently at the global, regional, interstate, and societal levels due to various material, normative and institutional factors, leading to deep peace among states, higher levels of prosperity and justice for all irrespective of nationality, race or gender."* The maximalist definition focuses on "not only the absence of war, but also the achievement of sustained non-violent cooperation for creating a more just world order." There are also mixed varieties such as the one offered by Karl Deutsch: "The resolution of social problems mutually by institutionalized procedures without resort to largescale physical force." In this framework, states resolve disputes not by war but through institutional channels and diplomacy.[51]

Great powers have indeed attempted peaceful change in regions within a minimalist framework, especially in the aftermath of major systemic events like the end of the world wars or the end of the Cold War, or major regional wars such as the 1973 Arab-Israeli conflict. However, they tend to produce partial minimalist outcomes unless regional states themselves make strong efforts in this regard. The deteriorating security situation in the aftermath of the October 2023 Hamas attack on Israeli civilians and the retributory offensive operation by Israel showed that permanent peace or even a minimum of stability is not attainable unless regional actors themselves take concrete steps toward rapprochement. Both Europe and Southeast Asia attest to the role of regional states in attempting to create somewhat maximalist peaceful orders through institutions they devised and developed over time.

Since the 2000s, we have been witnessing the great powers' abandonment of attempts to move toward maximalist notions of peaceful change. The 1990s may be remembered for advancing a human rights–inspired agenda, and for a series of peaceful changes in states located in regions otherwise as different as central and Eastern Europe, Southern Africa, Southeast Asia, and Central America. More recently, even the minimalist reading of peaceful change has come under severe pressure. Great powers have forsaken their roles as custodians of peace as P-5 members of the Security Council, relegating the UN to a nonfunctioning collective security entity. Further, their recent actions in Ukraine and elsewhere have put in jeopardy many advancements the Global South countries have made in recent years, including economic and social development. In fact, Global South countries are creating their own institutions in conjunction with established powers or abandoning existing ones as key pillars of international and regional orders. They seem more interested in strengthening G-20, BRICS, SCO, ASEAN, and so on, even though China has been able to exert more influence in some of them. Still, they cannot be characterized as dominated by any single great power in the contemporary era.

EMERGING ORDER IN THE REGIONS

As the power capabilities and diplomatic strategies of various actors, both great and non-great powers, evolve, one thing is increasingly becoming clearer: world order is unlikely to be a replica of the past, as the international system is no longer led by European-era great powers or Cold War–era superpower-led blocs. The main reasons are: First, great power–led alliances are not easy to form as bandwagoning coalitions are not emerging as in the past. The key rising power, China, despite its activism in the South China Sea, is yet to follow the behavioral traits of past rising powers in the European or Japanese cases. China is seeking hegemony through indirect means, and until and unless it seeks direct aggrandizement, thereby threatening the sovereign existence of secondary states, these secondary states have little incentive to form military alliances directed against China. Beijing is also not attracting many takers to its version of regional hegemony even when they are participating in the Chinese-led infrastructure project, the Belt and Road Initiative. In the face of limited Chinese threats, they are developing soft balancing and limited balancing coalitions.

Second, although US-China economic interdependence has weakened in recent years, the dependence of many countries on China's market and products makes it difficult for them to break the relationship. The costs and vulnerabilities of interdependence of this nature are complex, and China's trading partners realize that cold war–type military alliances will hurt all states, big and small alike. Third, the agency of the non-great powers has increased partly due to economic growth in many of these countries and the presence of intensified globalization, which give them more capacity to negotiate with great powers. Most of the pivotal states, the likely candidates for alliance and bloc formations, are pursuing strategic autonomy and have been somewhat successful in this pursuit. Most of them have not jumped on the Western bandwagon against Russia or the Chinese hegemonic project.

India, Brazil, Turkey, and South Africa are cases in point. Third, institutional architectures at the global and regional levels are crosscutting, and membership is not narrowly constructed along cold war lines.

Hence, the emerging world order is likely to be polycentric for some time to come. In the economic arena, the order fast emerging is multipolar while in military domains a kind of bi-multipolarity may emerge if China and the United States manage to keep up their dominance in key military hardware and technologies of the future. In the economic sphere, by 2030 some three countries—India, Indonesia, and Brazil—are very likely to overtake existing lead economies such as Japan, Germany, and France. In October 2022, India overtook the United Kingdom as the fifth largest economy in the world.[52] Hybrid and multiplex patterns will continue until the distance between powerful states and secondary states widens and the powerful ones once again seek alignments and spheres of influence through direct aggrandizement or indirect strategies. Possible military conflicts in Taiwan, the South China Sea, or more Russian neighbors such as the Baltic states could be the harbingers of such a transition.

CHAPTER OVERVIEW

The ten chapters of this book start with exploring the repercussions of the New Cold War for regional orders, first by focusing on key concepts constituting this New Cold War and its regional manifestations. Then, we zoom in on the global protagonists of the New Cold War—that is, the United States, China, and Russia. Taken together, the chapters address all world regions, focusing especially on those that have become already major theaters of the New Cold War, such as Eurasia, Central Asia, and Asia-Pacific.

Each conceptual chapter, employing different theoretical traditions, focuses on a key concept that constitutes the New Cold War and helps us understand its manifestations in regional orders: multiplexity, spheres of influence, ideology, strategy, status, technology, and statehood. Pardesi and Acharya show that the New Cold War is a *multiplex* order. Studying the Indo-Pacific region—that is, a theater where the Sino-US rivalry plays out—they contend that the new multiplex world order is composed of open regional orders that are pluralist and not simply hierarchical all the way down. It will not do, therefore, to simply look at great powers while researching prospects for peaceful change in regional orders. These prospects are shaped but not determined by the great powers. Regional agency very much matters, too. *Spheres of influence* amount as much to a key aspect of the New Cold War as they did during the Cold War. But in our days, Wivel submits, there is much more contestation. Whether regions can peacefully change amid this contestation depends on how regional hegemonies are negotiated given similarities and differences across repertoires of expectations of great and regional powers. *Ideology*, Balzacq and Grantseva argue, was not just a key component of the Cold War but remains to be one during the New Cold War. Although no longer as explicit as during the Cold War, ideologies remain a compass for great powers to orientate themselves vis-à-vis one another. Regional actors have three options open to them to place themselves in the ideological contests among the great powers: balancing, subversion, and usurpation. What options they embark on shapes prospects for peaceful change in regions. The authors illustrate their argument by studying Central Asia.

Strategy was an important concept to make sense of Cold War dynamics, and it remains just as salient for the New Cold War. Brawley and Paquin model strategic outcomes to grasp how amenable regional orders are to peaceful change. They apply their neoclassical realist framework to Cold War and New Cold War cases, demonstrating important parallels of how great power competition (used to) shape regional orders. They deal with the cases of East Asia and Eastern Europe in depth. Great power competition is, among other things, about *status*. Drawing parallels between the Cold War and the New Cold War, Pu argues that status competition fuels wars by proxy, thus disrupting processes of peaceful change in regional orders. He illustrates his contention with cases from the post-Soviet space and East Asia. *Technology*, too, is a major shaper and breaker of great power competition. Technological innovation played a critical role during the Cold War. With the New Cold War gaining momentum in times of fundamental technological changes linked to ever-more rapid advances in digital technology, technology is likely to play an even greater role for great power competition in years to come. Aggarwal and Reddie write about the new economic statecraft, geared toward competing in high- and low-technology sectors. The authors compare readings of economic statecraft embraced by the United States, China, and the EU, and investigate how these interpretations reshape regional orders.

In addition to focusing on these concepts specifically, more conceptual explorations criss-cross these chapters. These range from power to interest and from norms to legitimacy. Different authors put emphasis on different dimensions of these concepts. Wivel's conceptualization of *power*, for instance, rests on tangible capabilities that structure actors in horizontal (great powers) or vertical (great powers vis-à-vis regional actors) ways. Likening power to status, Pu emphasizes the less tangible aspects of the concept.

Interest features prominently in Brawley and Paquin's as well as in Balzacq and Grantseva's chapters. The former exogenies preference formation in order to model strategic interaction while the latter endogenizes interests by linking them to ideologies. Since no political order can exist purely by coercion, *legitimacy* requires careful analytical scrutiny. This is an important point that Pardesi and Acharya make for regional orders. Aggarwal and Reddie echo it when they write about the legitimacy of foreign policy objectives. Several authors stress the salience of *norms*. Wivel links norms to spheres of influence. Pu makes a similar point when he writes about "norms-spheres of influence." Balzacq and Grantseva remind us that it is not only international norms but also domestic ones that require our analytical attention. Norms for how a nation is to conduct itself internationally are ingrained in the identity narratives of states, and whether there are prospects of regional peaceful change or not has a lot to do with the directions in which these norms point.

The chapters on the United States, China, and Russia, putting to use these concepts, discuss how great powers and their competition with one another shapes and reshapes processes of peaceful and violent change in the regions. Focusing on the *United States*, Larson analyzes US-Russian competition in Europe as well as Sino-US competition in East Asia. On the one hand, she differentiates between the New Cold War and the Cold War. Echoing Pardesi's and Acharya's multiplexity argument, she contends that alignment patterns in the New Cold War are more fluid. On the other hand, she finds that, similar to the Cold War, great power politics deeply permeates regional orders in the New Cold War. Making sense of the dynamics that link great power competition to prospects of peaceful change in regions, she puts strong emphasis on the concept of status. This makes for an interesting parallel between her findings and those of Pu. Ho submits that *China*, thus far, is somewhat less global in its ambitions than the United States. While Beijing under Xi aims for a global reach, it is only in East Asia where China is actively involved in building its own sphere of influence. China seeks to rebuild the region as a vertical regional order. This hegemonic design clashes with US interests in the region. While China realizes that the United States is an important extra-regional actor that cannot be made to withdraw from the region entirely, it is determined to keep US influence at bay and get Washington's recognition that East Asia is China's sphere of influence. Analyzing *Russia*, Köstem's chapter mirrors Ho's in some interesting ways. He contends that while Russia seeks to assert itself globally, it also focuses first and foremost on one region, and that is Eurasia. Unlike China, however, Russia faces more adversity in defending what it sees as its traditional sphere of influence. Köstem contends that Russia's hegemonic designs are doomed to fail.

Relying too much on coercion and aggression, Moscow pushes states away instead of closer into its orbit. This provides openings for China, the United States, and the European Union.

Finally, Krickovic and Kim summarize and discuss the findings of the book. They do so by exploring how the New Cold War reconfigures great powers, regions, and change. Similarities between the Cold War and the New Cold War notwithstanding, what makes for a great power, how regional orders are delineated and constituted, and how these orders change in violent or peaceful ways have to be reconsidered. The authors underline that taking multiplexity seriously is the key for getting at these new dimensions of the New Cold War. Krickovic and Kim postulate a research agenda that helps us study these dimensions in depth. Two items are on the very top of this agenda: analytically, to study material and intersubjective drivers of the evolving New Cold War; and, normatively, to sketch pathways of peaceful change that do not rely too much on great powers but take smaller, regional actors seriously, too.

This is a very warranted point, indeed. Ushering into a new era, we need to reconsider the analytical and normative tools available to international relations. Overhauling the toolbox amounts to an important leitmotif of this book.

NOTES

1. The concept of multiplexity, coined by Acharya, is highly useful to describe the agency of regional actors in the current world order. Yet, this book stays away from a binary understanding of multipolarity and multiplexity. In the New Cold War, the two interact with one another. On Acharya's conceptualization of multiplexity, see chapter 2 of this book as well as Amitav Acharya, *The End of American World Order* (Cambridge: Polity, 2014) and, more recently, Amitav Acharya, Antoni Estevadeordal, and Louis W. Goodman, "Multipolar or Multiplex? Interaction Capacity, Global Cooperation and World Order," *International Affairs* 99, no. 6 (2023): 2339–65.
2. David E. Sanger, *New Cold Wars: China's Rise, Russia's Invasion, and America's Struggle to Defend the West* (New York: Crown, 2024); Robin Niblett, *The New Cold War: How the Contest Between the US and China Will Shape Our Century* (London: Atlantic Books, 2024); Jim Sciutto, *The Return of Great Powers: Russia, China, and the Next World War* (New York: Dutton, 2024); Richard Sakwa, "'New Cold War' or Twenty Years' Crisis? Russia and International Politics," *International Affairs* 84, no. 2 (2008): 241–67; Edward Lucas, *The New Cold War: Putin's Russia and the Threat to the West* (London: Macmillan, 2014); Robert Legvold, "Managing the New Cold War: What Moscow and Washington Can Learn from the Last One," *Foreign Affairs* 93, no. 4 (2014): 74–84. Samuel Charap and Jeremy Shapiro, "Consequences of a New Cold

War," *Survival* 57, no. 2 (2015): 37–46. Marvin Kalb, *Imperial Gamble: Putin, Ukraine, and the New Cold War* (Brookings Institution Press, 2015); Sergey Karaganov, "The New Cold War and the Emerging Greater Eurasia," *Journal of Eurasian Studies* 9, no. 2 (2018): 85–93. Minghao Zhao, "Is a New Cold War Inevitable? Chinese Perspectives on US–China Strategic Competition," *Chinese Journal of International Politics* 12, no. 3 (2019): 371–94. Seth Schindler, Jessica DiCarlo, and Dinesh Paudel, "The New Cold War and the Rise of the 21st-century Infrastructure State," *Transactions of the Institute of British Geographers* 47, no. 2 (2022): 331–46. Ho-fung Hung, *Clash of Empires: From 'Chimerica' to the 'New Cold War'* (Cambridge: Cambridge University Press, 2022). Hal Brands and John Lewis Gaddis, "The New Cold War: America, China, and the Echoes of History," *Foreign Affairs* 100 (2021): 10–21.
3. The following draws from a framework on how to scrutinize analogous reasoning, developed in Markus Kornprobst, "Comparing Apples and Oranges? Leading and Misleading Uses of Historical Analogies," *Millennium* 36, no. 1 (2007): 29–49.
4. All cited in Lawrence D. Freedman, "Frostbitten: Decoding the Cold War, 20 Years Later," *Foreign Affairs* 89 (2010): 137.
5. For a somewhat similar characterization of Cold War, see Benjamin Miller, *States, Nations and the Great Powers: The Sources of Regional War and Peace* (Cambridge: Cambridge University Press, 2007), 45.
6. John Lewis Gaddis, "The Cold War, the Long Peace, and the Future," *Diplomatic History* 16, no. 2 (1992): 234–46.
7. Markus Kornprobst and T.V. Paul, "Globalization, Deglobalization and the Liberal International Order," *International Affairs* 97, no. 5 (2021): 1305–16.
8. John M. Owen, "Two Emerging International Orders? China and the United States," *International Affairs* 97, no. 5 (2021): 1415–31; Jon-Arild Johannessen, *Deglobalization: China-US Rivalry in the Innovation Economy* (London: Routledge, 2023).
9. We can learn a lot from studying bilateral competition patterns between the United States and Russia as well as between the United States and China. See, for example, Michael Beckley and Hal Brands, *Danger Zone: The Coming Conflict with China* (New York: Norton, 2022); Rush Doshi, *The Long Game: China's Grand Strategy to Displace American Order* (Oxford: Oxford University Press, 2021); Angela Stent, *Putin's World: Russia against the West and with the Rest* (London: Hachette, 2019); John Mearsheimer, *The Great Delusion: Liberal Dreams and International Realities* (Cambridge: Yale University Press, 2018); Evan Medeiros, ed., *Cold Rivals: The New Era of US-China Strategic Competition* (Washington, DC: Georgetown University Press, 2023). At the same time, however, studying the New Cold War requires going beyond a mere great power focus. There are simply too many pivotal regional players that critically affect regional orders and even world order.
10. On this, see T.V. Paul, *Restraining Great Powers: Soft Balancing from Empires to the Global Era* (New Haven, CT: Yale University Press, 2019).
11. Acharya, "After Liberal Hegemony."
12. Odd Arne Westad, *The Global Cold War: Third World Interventions and the Making of Our Times* (Cambridge: Cambridge University Press, 2007); Paul Rogers, "A Century on the Edge: From Cold War to Hot World, 1945–2045," *International Affairs* 90, no. 1 (2014): 93–106; Lorenz M. Luthi, *Cold Wars: Asia, the Middle East and Europe* (Cambridge: Cambridge University Press, 2020).

13. Others, such as Al Shabaab, are more difficult to defeat, and even ISIS, which appeared to have ceased to be a force to be reckoned with by the early 2020s, seems to have regrouped. In January 2024, ISIS-Khorasan targeted Iran and in March Russia. The latter attack, killing at least 150 people at Crocus Hall in Moscow, was the worst terrorist attack on Russia in two decades.
14. Costs of War Project, Watson Institute, Providence, Brown University, September 1, 2021. https://www.brown.edu/news/2021-09-01/costsofwar.
15. Mark W. Zacher, "The Territorial Integrity Norm," *International Organization* 55, no. 2 (2001): 15–50.
16. White House, National Security Strategy 2017, 2. Accessed October 25, 2023. https://trumpwhitehouse.archives.gov/wp-content/uploads/2017/12/NSS-Final-12-18-2017-0905.pdf.
17. White House, National Security Strategy 2017, 60.
18. White House, National Security Strategy 2022, 3. Accessed October 25, 2023. https://www.whitehouse.gov/wp-content/uploads/2022/10/Biden-Harris-Administrations-National-Security-Strategy-10.2022.pdf.
19. White House, National Security Strategy 2022, 39.
20. BNN Bloomberg, October 26, 2022. https://www.bnnbloomberg.ca/xi-s-vow-of-world-dominance-by-2049-sends-chill-through-markets-1.1837448.
21. Feng Zhang, "The Xi Jinping Doctrine of China's International Relations," *Asia Policy* 14, no. 3 (2019): 7–24.
22. Xi Jinping, *Hold High the Great Banner of Socialism with Chinese Characteristics and Strive in Unity to Build a Modern Socialist Country in All Respects*. Report to the 20th National Congress of the Communist Party of China, October 16, 2022, 3. https://www.fmprc.gov.cn/eng/zxxx_662805/202210/t20221025_10791908.html.
23. Keynote speech by H.E. Xi Jinping, president of the People's Republic of China at China-Africa Leaders' Dialogue, Johannesburg, August 24, 2023.
24. The Concept of the Foreign Policy of the Russian Federation, Decree of the President of the Russian Federation, no. 229, March 31, 2023. https://mid.ru/en/foreign_policy/fundamental_documents/1860586/.
25. Mark Zacher, "The Territorial Integrity Norm." Even more so, there was a move toward a territorial status quo norm—that is, the thought that existing borders must not be changed in principle: Markus Kornprobst, *Irredentism in European Politics: Argumentation and Compromise* (Cambridge: Cambridge University Press, 2007). See also Boaz Atzilli, *Good Fences, Bad Neighbors: Border Fixity and International Conflict* (Chicago: University of Chicago Press, January 2012). Others argue that even though such a norm has been existing, territorial incursions have replaced large-scale wars in contemporary times. See Dan Altman, "The Evolution of Territorial Conquest after 1945 and the Limits of the Territorial Integrity Norm," *International Organization* 74, no. 3 (2020): 490–522.
26. Kai He, ed., "Navigating International Order Transition in the Indo-Pacific," special issue, *The Pacific Review*, 36, no. 2 (March 2023).
27. T.V. Paul, "Strategies for Managing China's Rise," *Harvard Asia Quarterly* 16, no. 2 (Summer 2014): 11–18.
28. The definition is from T.V. Paul, "Regional Transformation in International Relations," In *International Relations Theory and Regional Transformation*, ed. T.V. Paul (Cambridge: Cambridge University Press, 2012), 4.

29. Several IR books have emerged since the 1990s on regional orders. Examples include: David A. Lake and Patrick M. Morgan, eds., *Regional Orders: Building Security in a New World* (University Park: Pennsylvania State University Press, 1997); Barry Buzan and Ole Waever, *Regions and Powers: The Structure of International Security* (Cambridge: Cambridge University Press, 2003); Peter J. Katzenstein, *A World of Regions: Asia and Europe in the American Imperium* (Ithaca, NY: Cornell University Press, 2005); Amitav Acharya, *Constructing a Security Community in East Asia in Southeast Asia: ASEAN and the Problem of Regional Order* (London: Routledge, 2001); Miller, *States, Nations and the Great Powers*; Paul, ed., *International Relations Theory and Regional Transformation*.
30. Kenneth Waltz, *Theory of International Politics* (New York: Random House, 1979); John J. Mearsheimer, *The Tragedy of Great Power Politics* (New York: W. W. Norton, 2001); Norrin M. Ripsman, Jeffrey Taliaferro, and Steven E. Lobell, *Neoclassical Realist Theory of International Politics* (Oxford: Oxford University Press, 2016). See also Nina Graeger, Bertel Heurlin, Ole Waever, and Anders Wivel, eds., *Polarity in International Relations: Past, Present, Future* (London: Palgrave Macmillan, 2022).
31. For classical balance of power theory, see Inis L. Claude, *Power and International Relations* (New York: Random House, 1964); Michael Shaheen, *The Balance of Power: History and Theory* (London: Routledge, 1996); Henry Kissinger, *World Order* (New York: Penguin, 2014); Richard Little, *The Balance of Power in International Relations: Metaphors, Myths and Models* (Cambridge: Cambridge University Press, 2007); T.V. Paul, James J. Wirtz, and Michel Fortmann, eds., *Balance of Power: Theory and Practice in the 21st Century* (Stanford, CA: Stanford University Press, 2004).
32. Waltz, *The Theory of International Politics*, 127.
33. Stephen Walt, *The Origins of Alliances* (Ithaca, NY: Cornell University Press, 1987).
34. Paul, *Restraining Great Powers*.
35. A.F.K. Organski. *World Politics*, 2nd ed. (New York: Alfred A. Knopf, 1968), 364–66; Jacek Kugler and Douglas Lemke, eds., *Parity and War* (Ann Arbor: University of Michigan Press, 1996).
36. Douglas Lemke, *Regions of War and Peace* (Cambridge: Cambridge University Press, 2002), 25.
37. For differing perspectives on this, see Sinan Chu, "Whither Chinese IR? The Sinocentric Subject and the Paradox of Tianxia-Ism," *International Theory* (2020): 1–31; Huiyun Feng and Kai He, eds., *China's Challenges and International Order Transition: Beyond "Thucydides's Trap"* (Ann Arbor: University of Michigan Press, 2020); Feng Zhang, *Chinese Hegemony: Grand Strategy and International Institutions in East Asian History* (Stanford, CA: Stanford University Press, 2015); Roland Paris, "The Right to Dominate: How Old Ideas about Sovereignty Pose New Challenges for World Order," *International Organization* 74, no. 3 (2020): 453–89; Colin Chia, "Social Positioning and International Order Contestation in Early Modern Southeast Asia," *International Organization* 76, no. 2 (2022): 305–36.
38. See for instance, David A. Lake, *Hierarchy in International Relations* (Ithaca, NY: Cornell University Press, 2009).
39. See Freedom House, *Freedom in the World 2023*. https://freedomhouse.org/country/united-states/freedom-world/2023.
40. Markus Kornprobst, "The Management of Border Disputes in African Regional Subsystems: Comparing West Africa and the Horn of Africa," *Journal of Modern African Studies* 40, no. 3 (2002): 369–93; Aarie Glas, "Habits of Peace: Long-term Regional

Cooperation in Southeast Asia," *European Journal of International Relations* 23, no. 4 (2017): 833–56.

41. Bentley B. Allan, Srdjan Vucetic, and Ted Hopf, "The Distribution of Identity and the Future of International Order: China's Hegemonic Prospects," *International Organization* 72, no. 4 (2018): 839–69.

42. On the social sources of power, see Simon Reich and Richard Ned Lebow, *Good-Bye Hegemony! Power and Influence in the Global System* (Princeton, NJ: Princeton University Press, 2014); Christian Reus-Smit, "Power, Legitimacy, and Order," *Chinese Journal of International Politics* 7, no. 3 (2014): 341–59.

43. On this, see Ayse Zarakol, *Before the West: The Rise and Fall of Eastern World Orders* (Cambridge: Cambridge University Press, 2022); Feng Zhang and Richard Ned Lebow, *Taming Sino-American Rivalry* (Oxford: Oxford University Press, 2020); Richard Ned Lebow, *The Rise and Fall of Political Orders* (Cambridge: Cambridge University Press, 2018).

44. Exceptions are Amitav Acharya's works on Southeast Asia. For instance, see Acharya, "Ideas, Norms and Regional Orders," in *International Relations Theory and Regional Transformation*, ed. T.V. Paul, (Cambridge: Cambridge University Press, 2012), 183–209.

45. Daniel H. Nexon and Iver B. Neumann, "Hegemonic-Order Theory: A Field-Theoretic Account," *European Journal of International Relations* 24, no. 3 (2017): 662–86; Alexander Cooley, Daniel Nexon, and Steven Ward, "Revising Order or Challenging the Balance of Military Power? An Alternative Typology of Revisionist and Status-Quo States," *Review of International Studies* 45, no. 4 (2019): 689–708; Stacie E. Goddard, Paul K. MacDonald, and Daniel H. Nexon, "Repertoires of Statecraft: Instruments and Logics of Power Politics," *International Relations* 33, no. 2 (2019): 304–21.

46. Cornelia Navari, "Peaceful Change in English School Theory: Great Power Management and Regional Order," in *The Oxford Handbook of Peaceful Change in International Relations*, eds. T.V. Paul, D.W. Larson, H.A. Trinkunas, A. Wivel, and R. Emmers (New York: Oxford University Press, 2021), 191–204; Shunji Cui and Barry Buzan, "Great Power Management in International Society," *Chinese Journal of International Politics* 9, no. 2 (2016): 181–210; Barry Buzan and Yongjin Zhang, eds., *Contesting International Society in East Asia* (Cambridge: Cambridge University Press, 2014).

47. The "regional security complex" approach captures the role of great powers in determining the regional order in the security domain. Barry Buzan, *People, States and Fear: An Agenda for International Security Studies in the Post-Cold War Era*, 2nd ed. (Boulder, CO: Lynne Rienner, 1991); Buzan and Weaver, *Regions and Powers: The Structure of International Security*, ch. 3.

48. Andrew Phillips and Christian Reus-Smit, eds., *Culture and Order in World Politics: Diversity and Its Discontents* (Cambridge: Cambridge University Press, 2020); Barry Buzan and George Lawson, *The Global Transformation: History, Modernity and the Making of International Relations* (Cambridge: Cambridge University Press, 2015).

49. For earlier works on this, see Johan Galtung, *Peace by Peaceful Means: Peace and Conflict, Development and Civilization* (Oslo: International Peace Research Institute and Sage Publications, 1996); Johan Galtung, *Pax Pacifica: Terrorism, the Pacific Hemisphere, Globalisation and Peace Studies* (London: Pluto Press, 2005). Notably, some critical scholars challenge the notion of regions and regional boundaries. See, for instance, the various chapters in Paul J. Kohlenberg and Nadine Godehardt, eds., *The Multidimensionality of Regions in World Politics* (London: Routledge, 2020).

50. These concepts are developed in Miller, *States, Nations and the Great Powers*, 42–47.
51. T.V. Paul, "Introduction: The Study of Peaceful Change in World Politics," in *The Oxford Handbook of Peaceful Change in International Relations*, eds. T.V. Paul, D.W. Larson, A. Wivel, H. Trinkunas, and R. Emmers (Oxford: Oxford University Press, 2022), 4; Karl Deutsch, *Political Community and the North Atlantic Area* (Princeton, NJ: Princeton University Press, 1957), 5.
52. "GDP (current US$)," *World Bank*, September 1, 2023, https://data.worldbank.org/indicator/NY.GDP.MKTP.CD.

CHAPTER 2

Regional Orders and Great Power Rivalry in a Multiplex World

Manjeet S. Pardesi and Amitav Acharya

The American World Order (AWO), also known as the Liberal International Order (LIO), is coming to an end whether or not the United States itself is declining.[1] The emerging world order will not be defined by the hegemony of any single actor, neither the United States nor China, or by their duopoly. At the same time, the emerging world order will not reflect the dominance of any single idea, whether liberal or otherwise. The concept of the LIO associated with scholars such as John Ikenberry, or simply "liberal hegemony," is often invoked to mean the world order created by the United States after 1945.[2] This world order, whose nature and duration have always been contested, seems to be finally passing. Many analysts believe the next world order will be multipolar. Paul Kennedy, one of the most influential scholars of the rise and fall of the great powers, has identified "six great powers—or slightly-less-than great powers" in this multipolar configuration: the European Union (EU), Japan, Russia, India, China, and the United States.[3] However, in this chapter, we argue that the emerging world order is more than just multipolar because there are other actors and forces at play, not just the above-mentioned great powers and their interactions. Among the most important such forces are regions.

While the other great and almost-great powers are likely to pursue their own forms of globalization, regions are emerging as the locus of order-making.[4] However, these regional worlds will not be isolated tectonic plates, but will continue to interact with each other because the world will remain deeply interconnected and interdependent, albeit configured differently compared to the eras of American (and Western) dominance.[5] At the same time, these regions are themselves reorganizing—re-regionalizing—as they are reflective of the power and ideas of the actors that constitute these (re-)regions.[6] While these new regional formations may have echoes of the regional worlds that existed during the eras of American/Western dominance, and even the periods that preceded the rise of the West, they are dynamic configurations and are reflective of the "competing strategic imaginaries"[7] of the great powers as well as the regional (or non-great) powers. It is the contemporary processes of global and regional interactions that are enabled and constrained by underlying norms and ideas of these multitudes of actors that are shaping the contours of these (re-)regions themselves as well as the connections between the different regional worlds.

In other words, it is the combination of these three features: the passing of America's "liberal hegemony" and the emergence of multiple great and rising powers, the regionalization of world politics, and the interregional connections between these regional worlds is heralding the rise of a multiplex world.[8] Like multipolar worlds, multiplex worlds also contain multiple great powers.[9] However, multiplex worlds are worlds of regions, and it is these regions—as opposed to the identity and number of poles (or polarity[10])—that are the basic building blocks of this world order. Furthermore, these regions are not simply the creations of the great powers but are generated from within with the active agency of the "lesser" or the non-great powers. Consequently, the processes of connectivity within and across regions then emerge from the interaction of material power and the normative agency of several large and small players. A multiplex world order is therefore non-hegemonic as it is a multiregional world order without a global hegemon. It is also a "decentered" world despite the presence of several great and regional powers because the active agency of the non-great powers is crucial to these regional worlds. Finally, the constituent regions of multiplex world orders are non-bounded and "open" given their interconnections with other regional worlds.[11]

We argue that the passing of AWO is giving rise to such a multiplex or multiregional world order. Drawing on the concept of multiplexity, we contend that regions will play an increasingly important role, not just as theaters of great power rivalry but as relatively autonomous entities in shaping its intensity and scope. The primary purpose of such orders will be to prevent system breakdown. More specifically, we analyze the emerging regional order in the Indo-Pacific—that is witnessing the re-regionalization of the eastern Indian Ocean and the Western Pacific—to empirically demonstrate the formation of such a multiplex order. This Indo-Pacific region—or the primary theater of the United States-China rivalry—is seeing the emergence of a non-hegemonic, decentered, and open regional order. This Indo-Pacific order is being proactively shaped and legitimized by the weaker regional powers in Southeast Asia that are ideologically plural. The Indo-Pacific regional order will be connected with its neighboring regions in the Middle East, Europe, and the Americas. While some powers—notably the United States, India, Japan, and Australia as members of the Quad (Quadrilateral Security Dialogue)—are pushing the Indo-Pacific idea primarily as a geopolitical-strategic construct, its future development or survival requires this broader, pluralistic, and more inclusive framing provided by Southeast Asian nations.[12]

The rest of this chapter is divided into three sections. First, we explain the idea of multiplex orders. More specifically, we dismiss other possibilities, especially the emergence of hegemonic orders (whether America-led or China-led) as well as bipolar/multipolar power balances. Although a multiplex world will have several power centers, it will be a multiregional world order. Consequently, we also focus on the processes related to region (trans) formation here and highlight the active agency of the regional/weaker powers. Next, we empirically demonstrate the emergence of a non-hegemonic, decentered, and open regional order in the Indo-Pacific with its connections to the world beyond. We pay attention to the dynamics of the United States-China rivalry and show how the normative agency of the weaker powers of Southeast Asia is making and shaping the regional order in the Indo-Pacific. In the third and final section, we briefly compare the roles of regions and regional institutions in Europe/the North Atlantic and the Indo-Pacific. We conclude after noting that the Indo-Pacific regional order may be better suited to manage the complexities of our emerging multiplex reality than its European/North Atlantic counterpart.

MULTIPLEX WORLD: A MULTI-REGIONAL WORLD ORDER

American unipolarity is dissipating with the diffusion and dispersion of power to other parts of the world, especially Asia. Almost two decades ago, the US National Intelligence Council (NIC) had noted that US unipolarity in the post–Cold War period was unusual because a "world with a single superpower is unique."[13] The NIC report also added that the "likely emergence of China and India, as well as others" is similar to "the advent of a united Germany in the 19th century and a powerful United States in the early 20th century," and "will transform the geopolitical landscape, with impacts potentially as dramatic as those in the previous two centuries."[14] The passing of American unipolarity and the world order that the United States had created is understandably raising concerns about the fate of the world and what comes next.

It is hardly surprising that the proponents of the LIO fear the passing of American hegemony. Although they elide the coercion entailed in the creation of this ostensibly "liberal" order,[15] the future is painted in dark and forbidding terms. For Ikenberry, one of the main proponents of the LIO, the options are the United States being "at the center of a one-world system" or "less-desirable alternatives familiar from history: great-power balancing orders, regional blocs, or bipolar rivalries."[16] Although Ikenberry seldom makes the link, and even as his theory focuses on multilateral institutions to manage and maintain it, Ikenberry's LIO is clearly built upon the idea of hegemonic stability.[17]

Similarly, for Charles Krauthammer, who coined the term "unipolar moment" after the end of the Cold War, America's "abdication" of its global role would mean "insecure sea lanes, impoverished trading partners, exorbitant oil prices, [and] explosive regional instability."[18] In a similar vein, Richard Haass, the former president of the Council on Foreign Relations who was also the head of the Policy Planning Bureau of the US State Department under George W. Bush's first presidential term, flatly asserts: "With U.S. hegemony waning but no successor waiting to pick up the baton, the likeliest future is one in which the current international system gives way to a disorderly one with a large number of power centers acting with increased autonomy, paying less heed to U.S. interests and preferences."[19]

We argue that all these visions are misleading. First, the future will not be hegemonic, neither a reestablished American hegemonic order nor will the baton of hegemony be passed on to China, the most likely contender for hegemonic status in these debates. To begin with, the nature of hegemony is imprecise and contested in the international relations literature. According to Gilpin, a "single powerful state controls or dominates the lesser states" in an imperial or hegemonic system.[20] This material power-centric approach is also shared by Wohlforth for whom hegemony obtains when power is "sufficiently concentrated in one state to permit it to 'lay down the law' to others."[21] In other words, hegemony requires "extraordinary asymmetry in power capabilities"[22] between the potential hegemon and the next most powerful state in the system. However, the rise of China has diminished the power asymmetry with the United States.[23] Consequently, maritime Asia has become a "contested zone" where the United States is unlikely to be able to exercise "command" or "primacy."[24]

Other conceptions of hegemony moved it beyond material capabilities. The most important reformulation relies on the Gramscian notion, which rejected traditional Marxism's emphasis on coercion while focusing on consent and went beyond economic/material factors to ideological ones. According to Cox, hegemony means "dominance of a particular kind where the dominant state creates an order based ideologically on a broad measure of consent, functioning according to general principles that in fact ensure the continuing supremacy of the leading state."[25] The liberal institutionalist view of hegemony developed by Ikenberry applies this Gramscian and Coxian notion of hegemony to LIO but leaves out coercion altogether.

The key to any normative understanding of order is legitimacy that also depends upon the preferences of weaker states and the wider international system.[26] Consequently, Barnett argues that world orders "are created and sustained not only by great power preferences but also by changing understandings of what constitutes a legitimate international order."[27] However, the global transformation underway means that such *global* hegemony is no longer seen as legitimate. While material power asymmetries will persist, the United States (and the West more generally) "will need to get used to the fact that they do not own the future."[28] Although the United States may continue to have "a restricted constituency of support"[29] among its allies, American hegemony has already eroded.[30] Similarly, Foot has argued that China's rise is not fostering "a hegemony based on generating negotiated acceptance of its leading role and normative vision," and therefore, its "coalitions of support remain restricted and will probably remain so."[31] To put in the words of Buzan and Lawson, "it is not going to be 'China's turn' next."[32] In other words, a hegemonic (or Thucydidean) transition between the United States and China is not in the offing despite the popularity of this idea.[33]

Second, a bipolar order led by the United States and China is also not in the making. Tunsjø has argued that a US-China bipolarity is emerging in contemporary Asia because of the massive power gap between these two great powers, on the one hand, and the players in the next rung of the capabilities hierarchy: Russia, India, Japan, and others, on the other.[34] While this materialist view ignores the normative dimension discussed above, others like Kennedy noted at the start of this chapter foresee a multipolar world in the making. Given these issues related to unipolarity/hegemony, bipolarity, and multipolarity, Wohlforth, who earlier wrote about "the stability of the unipolar moment,"[35] now downplays the concept of polarity. "Polarity matters less than it used to because of the diffusion of power."[36]

This is not to argue that there will be no great powers in the emerging world order. In fact, the relative decline of the United States and the rise of

China and others means that the international system will remain stratified when it comes to material power capabilities even as power dynamics are changing. However, the United States is likely to be the last superpower.[37] While regional and trans-regional great powers will certainly exist, no truly *global* superpower will, and the degree of American dominance in the world is also declining.[38] Given the salience of this regional dimension, the emerging international order will be one of multiple great powers and almost-great powers. However, it will also need to account for "more actors, factors, and vectors than the concept of polarity can capture."[39]

We argue that such an order is best understood as multiplex. As power shifts from the United States (and the West) to the rest, we are entering a world without a *global* hegemon. While power asymmetries will continue, most of the other great and rising powers will largely focus on their own regions and on adjacent regions instead of becoming truly *global* in *all* functional areas: military power, economics, and cultural/ideational authority. The United States will continue to remain important, but it will become just one of many such centers of authority. Although power politics will hardly be absent from such a world, it will also be shaped by the norms and ideas of other actors, including the non-great powers and the international institutions (both regional and global institutions). In the absence of a global hegemon and with polarity mattering less, a multiplex world will be a decentered world in which no single actor will emerge as the *center* that radiates its power and ideational influence across the system. Nor will two or more such *centers* be able to coordinate and run the system.[40] Such orders will be legitimized only through the active representation and participation of the local actors. In other words, regions will become the sites of order-making.

It is noteworthy that even the LIO was not a truly *global* order.[41] It was closed to rival powers during the Cold War and was denied to recalcitrant states after the end of the Cold War. Moreover, many large players, especially those outside of the West such as China, Russia, and India, engaged with the LIO only selectively. The claim that "a unitary 'liberal order' prevailed and defined international relations is both ahistorical and harmful."[42] As observed by Kissinger, "No truly global 'world order' has ever existed."[43] All orders have finite geographical scope, and this scope also varies over time. Similarly, despite claims of a historical "Chinese World Order" that extended to "All-Under-Heaven," it was rather limited in its geographic spread.[44] Furthermore, it coexisted and overlapped with other orders,[45] and historical China's foreign relations also exhibited modes of interaction not captured in the practices of the tributary system of this "Chinese World Order."[46]

In other words, our thinking about *global* orders should not exclude considerations of *regional* order. Bull defined international order as "a pattern of activity that sustains the primary goals of the society of states" that include stability, the maintenance of independence, peace, and limitation of violence among others.[47] However, note that the emphasis is on relative peace. Order does not mean the absence of war, conflict, or competition. Deutsch and Singer define stability, a key element of order, in terms of the absence of system-destroying conflict (and not in terms of the absence of conflict per se).[48] Beyond this minimalist definition, we also contend that viable orders cannot ignore considerations of legitimacy that emerge from broad representation and participation. Consequently, we emphasize the role of ideas and norms in order-making rather than simply viewing them as a by-product of military and economic factors that privilege the role of the great and established powers. As such, order emerges from "rule-governed interaction"[49] in pursuit of common goals related to limiting conflict, inducing cooperation, and expanding legitimacy.

The norms and ideas underpinning these "rules" are not supplied by the great powers alone. Regional actor agency is constitutive of these rules, and therefore crucial to the functioning and legitimacy of regional orders. The idea of the LIO has neglected the role of regions and regional constructions of order outside Europe.[50] There is a tendency to associate regional orders and regionalism with "regional blocs" rather than a building bloc of world order. But regions are not simply created by the great powers to "run" the world nor do they exist in isolation from other regional worlds. Regions are dynamic configurations of social and political identities and are neither wholly self-contained entities nor purely extensions of global dynamics. Regions emerge from "purposeful social, political, cultural, and economic interactions,"[51] and any conceptualization of region must also pay attention to the region "as a cognitive construct shared by persons in the region themselves."[52]

As such, regions are dynamic constructions that are made from within. However, they are emergent from interactions with the wider world. "Multiple regions overlap and contradict one another to form complex webs of power, interaction, and imagination that are constantly in motion."[53] Consequently, regions are not "hermetically sealed."[54] In fact, they are "open" entities in constant dialogue with each other.[55] Openness is a function of material and ideational interaction capacity in the system, and the global transformation of world politics over the past two centuries has intensified such interactions.[56] Although strategic rivalries and patterns of economic interdependence may be reconfiguring contemporary world regions, they remain intertwined. In the following section, we show that the Indo-Pacific *regional* order is being actively made and shaped by the normative agency of the "lesser" powers of Southeast Asia. Even as it is being (re-)made from within, it is an open order entwined with the world outside and is therefore an important building block of the emerging *global* order. At the same time, we also explore the possibility of peaceful change (defined as the absence of a system-destroying conflict) in the process of transition toward such a multiregional global order.

A MULTIPLEX INDO-PACIFIC: DECENTERED, OPEN, AND CONNECTED TO OTHER REGIONS

The rise of Asia has made the Indo-Pacific the primary theater of the United States-China great power rivalry. As a region, the Indo-Pacific is a dynamic entity that is emerging from the connections between the subregions of South Asia, Southeast Asia, and (North)East Asia as well as the maritime space connecting them. However, there is nothing natural about the *region-ness* of any of these spaces. All three of these regional spaces that we take for granted as ontological truths "out there" in world politics only emerged during the Cold War (especially in the 1960s).[57] These "smaller" Asias had themselves formed out of a larger pan-Asian "system" that was in the making after the Second World War.[58] While the contemporary re-regionalization of these spaces as the Indo-Pacific is certainly driven by America's discursive and material power, local actor agency (or endogenous dynamics) is equally important, if not more.[59]

According to Buzan and Wæver, Northeast Asia and Southeast Asia had already merged, both economically (by the 1980s) and politico-militarily (by the 1990s).[60] However, the Association of Southeast Asian Nations (ASEAN), whose membership had not yet been extended to Vietnam, Laos, Myanmar, and Cambodia, had launched the ASEAN Regional Forum (ARF) in 1994. By the end of that decade, the ARF had become the first truly multilateral security forum covering all parts of Asia. In other words, it went beyond East Asia (Northeast Asia and Southeast Asia) and included India, Australia, New Zealand, Russia, the United States, and even the EU among other actors. Moreover, it did so in the face of open hostility from the administration of George Bush Sr. in the United States that had dubbed it as a "solution in search of a problem."[61] The aim of the ARF was to co-engage both, the United States and China, and to discourage the United States from preemptive containment of China. It was also seen as a mechanism to preclude the emergence of an independent Japanese security role in the region while giving all other major powers a stake in regional affairs, thereby keeping the region "open."

In the meanwhile, India had also launched its "Look East" policy after the end of the Cold War.[62] At the same time, given their own dependency on the Indian Ocean for trade routes and energy security, Chinese analysts were already asserting in the 1990s that they "were not prepared to let the Indian Ocean become India's Ocean."[63] By 2005, Singapore's Goh Chok Tong was talking about "reconceptualizing East Asia" because the simultaneous rise of China and India meant that it will be "increasingly less tenable to regard South Asia and East Asia as distinct strategic theaters interacting only at the margins."[64] Later that year, when the ASEAN-led East Asia Summit (EAS) was established, it included the ten ASEAN states, three countries in Northeast Asia (China, Japan, and South Korea), one in South Asia (India), and two in Oceania (Australia and New Zealand). The United States and Russia were admitted only in 2011 after they signed the Treaty of Amity and Cooperation (TAC), a legally binding code that is deemed by Southeast Asia as crucial for the peaceful management of interstate relations.

In other words, ASEAN-led institutions have allowed the smaller Southeast Asian powers to exercise normative leadership in regional affairs encompassing not only East Asia but all the major powers bordering East Asia as well the system's great powers. The inclusion of several powers beyond East Asia as well as China and the United States' "growing strategic interests and imperatives in abutting regions"[65] beyond East Asia demonstrate that Asian region was *re-regionalizing* even before the rise of the Indo-Pacific nomenclature/concept in more recent years. Furthermore, local initiative of the weaker Southeast Asian players has been fundamental to the strategic contours of this space, both in the cognitive making and remaking of this space, through institutional membership, and normative leadership. Although the burgeoning Sino-American strategic rivalry is driven by its own logic, it is being actively influenced and shaped by regional norms and institutions spearheaded by Southeast Asia.

THE SINO-AMERICAN RIVALRY

The US-China contest seems primarily motivated neither by traditional security concerns nor by trade-related issues per se. Instead, it seems to be rooted in the ideational issues related to prestige and status at the apex of the international system.[66] For Wertheim, America's quest of armed primacy that began during the Second World War was "intended to outlive the circumstances of its origination and shape the distant, perhaps perpetual, future."[67] According to Singapore's Lee Kuan Yew, Chinese leaders want to "share this century as co-equals with the U.S."[68] It is these status/positional dynamics that are at play in the US-China maritime contest in the Indo-Pacific region.

By 2001, the Pentagon had come to define the "east Asian littoral . . . as the region stretching from south of Japan through Australia and into the Bay of Bengal."[69] The "expansion" of the definition of maritime East Asia to include Australia and the Bay of Bengal in 2001—even before the term "Indo-Pacific" became common—was to some degree a tacit acknowledgement of the fact that China's power was rapidly rising, and that a newer approach was needed to maintain American primacy.[70] However, China's military-technological transformation centered on anti-access and area denial (A2/AD) strategies, and long-range precision-guided munitions have transformed maritime East Asia into a contested zone.[71] The creation and militarization of China's artificial islands in the South China Sea have also contributed to this. Indeed, the general prognosis is that China will be increasingly able to challenge the United States at greater distances from the Chinese coast.[72] Although there is no doubt that the United States remains the strongest naval power in the world, it is the *primus inter pares* as opposed to hegemonic.

The US-China strategic competition then centers on two interconnected politico-military and politico-economic facets. First, as leading economic powers, the United States and China are developing their navies "to protect and expand [their] trade" as they vie for the *position* at the apex of the international system.[73] The second dimension in their naval rivalry revolves around the geopolitics of access. The United States is determined to maintain continued access to regions around China given China's growing A2/AD capabilities. In the meanwhile, China faces the "Malacca dilemma" in accessing the Indian Ocean given the overall maritime superiority of the United States in the Indo-Pacific. While the United States is seeking to prevent (and perhaps reverse) its relative naval decline in the Indo-Pacific, China is also keen to prevent the emergence of American (or Indian) hegemony in the Indian Ocean. None of this means that China is on its path toward regional hegemony.

America's Strategy

There are three strands in America's emerging strategy. First, the United States is transforming its postwar hub-and-spokes pattern of alliances into various bilateral and minilateral alignments.[74] The United States is not only deepening some of its full-fledged alliances (with Japan and Australia, for example) but it is also pursuing security relationships beyond such alliances with partners like Vietnam and India. Furthermore, America's various security partners are also forging defense and security relationships with each other instead of creating such links with the United States only. Scholars are referring to such relationships as "networks"[75] and "patchworks."[76]

The Quad is perhaps the most prominent of such groupings in the Indo-Pacific. Japan's proactive diplomacy with its other three partners (the United States, Australia, and India)—in bilateral and trilateral settings—was crucial to the formation of the Quad. However, China is not unduly worried as the Quad falls short of a full-fledged alliance. Since India does not have an alliance with the United States (or with the other Quad members), Beijing thinks of the Quad as "an uneasy 3 + 1 rather than a monolithic quartet."[77] India's quest for strategic autonomy along with the others' reluctance to fight alongside India against China in the Himalayas means that such alliances are unlikely.

Second, and relatedly, the United States is promoting the rise of India. The underlying logic behind this strategy is the belief that the rise of India will help balance China's power in the region, as India has reasons independent of the United States to do so as a consequence of the Sino-Indian rivalry. In other words, the simultaneous presence of Sino-American and Sino-Indian rivalries and the absence of such a strategic rivalry between the United States and India enables the United States to accommodate the slow rise of India. Not surprisingly, China's leading scholars of India have noted that the United States was "promoting India from the periphery of the Asia-Pacific region to the core of the Indo-Pacific region."[78] While this is likely to exacerbate the Sino-Indian rivalry,[79] China's primary concern is to prevent the emergence of a hegemonic power in the Indian Ocean that could deny access to China. Given India's overall naval inferiority vis-à-vis China, there is little fear of India's ability to do so by itself. Furthermore, the absence of an alliance between the United States and India implies that a joint bid by them to deny China access to the Indian Ocean is also unlikely.

The third component of the United States' strategic approach to the Indo-Pacific includes the involvement of its extra-regional partners and allies in regional affairs. Biden's Indo-Pacific strategy specifically calls for engaging with allies and partners from "outside of the region," especially the EU and the North Atlantic Treaty Organization (NATO).[80] While NATO's engagement with the Indo-Pacific is in its early stages, individual European powers are already engaging with the region. The United Kingdom has teamed up with the United States and Australia through the AUKUS security pact that aims to provide Australia with nuclear powered submarines.[81] Similarly, France is also looking toward the Indo-Pacific, especially given its island territories in the Indian Ocean and the South Pacific. The engagement of these extra-regional powers in the Indo-Pacific is pointing toward an "open" regional order that is not bounded to the countries of the Indo-Pacific only.

Consequently, America's three-pronged approach to the region centered on networks/patchworks like the Quad, India, and the involvement of the extra-regional powers is in fact pointing toward a complex order that cannot be captured by the concept of multipolarity that pays insufficient attention to the quality of relations between the different powers. For example, Australian analysts worry that "growing Indian naval power may not always reinforce Canberra's interests unless it can be coordinated with Australian or U.S. activity."[82] Unlike Australia, which is seeking to augment America's power and position in the Indo-Pacific, a rising India will probably use its power "to maximise India's influence, not America's."[83] This patchworked multipolarity of multiple powers with different strategic interests, with different relationships with China, and in multiple fora (from the Quad to AUKUS) that are the sites of cooperation in different functional areas means that America's own approach toward the Indo-Pacific is pointing toward a non-hegemonic multiplex region.

China's Strategy

China's navy is officially striving to emerge as a two-ocean navy—in the Indian and Pacific Oceans—even if China does not use the Indo-Pacific lexicon.[84] According to Garver, "Unless China can secure its interests in the SA-IOR" or South Asia-Indian Ocean Region, "China will remain a regional East Asian power and fall short of its aspiration of being a global power."[85] However, China cannot emerge as hegemonic in the Indian Ocean unless the United States and India "make major strategic mistakes" or "suffer a sharp decline in their national power."[86] These developments are not very likely, especially simultaneously. Therefore, China's naval modernization is largely about the quest to cement its great power credentials and to ensure the security of its maritime routes.[87] China is pursuing a three-pronged approach in pursuit of these interests, neither of which imply Chinese hegemony.

First, even as China is determined to emerge as a maritime power, China is not putting all its "eggs in the maritime basket."[88] China is seeking access to the Indian Ocean directly via maritime routes and indirectly via continental routes through Myanmar and Pakistan. "Strategically, Myanmar is China's link to the Indian Ocean."[89] Similarly, plans are also underway to connect western China with the Persian Gulf via Pakistan. Chinese analysts are under no delusion that the energy pipelines through Myanmar or Pakistan will remove China's dependence on the Strait of Malacca. Nevertheless, these options are still being pursued as a "form of effective hedging in order to prevent other countries from blackmailing China" given its maritime vulnerabilities.[90]

Second, China's Belt and Road Initiative (BRI) also builds up on this land-sea complementarity. Although the BRI has been critiqued as a unilateral Chinese initiative that seeks to mimic the US hub-and-spokes model in Asia, its overland component is also seen as a lifeline "in case of supply disruptions at sea or economic isolation."[91] It is also significant that many of these overland routes (like the one via Pakistan into the Persian Gulf) traverse way beyond the eastern Indian Ocean. Similarly, the maritime component of the BRI also aims to go beyond Southeast Asia via the "China + ASEAN + X" model into South Asia, East Africa, the Middle East, and beyond.[92] Not surprisingly, China's supply routes and the BRI—analogous to America's support for extra-regional powers in the Indo-Pacific discussed above—are also pointing toward an "open" order in the Indo-Pacific that will be deeply connected with the world beyond.

Third and finally, China is pursuing its own minilateral initiatives. The Lancang-Mekong Cooperation (LMC) mechanism that held its first summit in 2016 is "the first Chinese-built Southeast Asian institution."[93] The LMC includes China and the countries of mainland Southeast Asia (Cambodia, Laos, Myanmar, Thailand, and Vietnam), and focuses on sustainable development, regional infrastructure, and nontraditional security issues. Furthermore, China, Laos, Myanmar, and Thailand have been conducting joint patrols on the Lancang-Mekong River since 2011.[94] China does not seem to be pursuing sea control or naval hegemony even as it has attenuated America's post–Cold War regional predominance through its growing power projection capabilities.

SOUTHEAST ASIAN NORMATIVE LEADERSHIP AND "THE ASEAN WAY" IN THE INDO-PACIFIC

The Southeast Asian states, whether individually or collectively, are not mere spectators in the US-China contest in the Indo-Pacific. Southeast Asia is actively shaping great power engagement with the region. As noted by Stuart-Fox almost two decades ago, the Southeast Asian states "want the United States to remain a powerful presence [in the region] . . . but they do not want to be part of any balance-of-power coalition. At the same time, they also want to make room for China."[95] More specifically, it is the regional norms embedded in the so-called ASEAN Way that are being projected into the Indo-Pacific. The ASEAN Way refers to the regional norms that emerged in Southeast Asia during the Cold War that sought conflict avoidance while preventing great power domination in the region.[96] Importantly, the Southeast Asian states have also rejected binary (balance-of-power) thinking, and there is a powerful regional norm against collective defense (or binding multilateral security alliances) in Southeast Asia.[97] Focusing on informality, consultation, and consensus, "the ASEAN Way" emerged from the region's search for staying strategically relevant in the context of great power rivalry.

After the end of the Cold War, "the ASEAN Way," with its emphasis on cooperative security (or security for all as opposed to "security against") and "open" regionalism were promoted in the wider Asian region. The aim of this normative framework was to co-engage all the major powers while promoting strategic restraint and responsible conduct, including among rivals. Some of these ideas spread through institution-building in the form of soft regionalism such as the ARF. Others were embodied in ASEAN's Treaty of Amity and Cooperation (TAC) that has been signed by all the members of the EAS. While there is no need to overstate the amplification of these norms from Southeast Asia into the wider Indo-Pacific, they have come to constitute a regional "cognitive prior."[98]

The region rejects hegemonism and wants to avoid a zero-sum rivalry between the United States and China. The regional states have chosen "to work selectively with China and the United States, rather than siding entirely with one or the other."[99] Southeast Asian states are "ambivalent about the United States" and the role it "should play in the region,"[100] as the United States often appears "distracted, arrogant, condescending, fickle, and self-preoccupied."[101] At the same time, the region's unity over China has also frayed, and on certain issues such as the South China Sea, Beijing appears as a bully. Southeast Asia has adopted a three-pronged approach to manage this rivalry by keeping both China and the United States engaged in the region in addition to working with other external powers.

First, Southeast Asian states have been the initiators of many of the changes in the regional order, and "regional states have widened the composition of this order."[102] Importantly, Southeast Asian states are setting their own discourse on the Indo-Pacific.[103] Indonesia sees itself at the center of the Indo-Pacific region, a "Global Maritime Fulcrum" that connects the Indian and Pacific Oceans. Furthermore, Indonesia's approach to the Indo-Pacific had a major influence on the ASEAN Outlook on Indo-Pacific (AOIP). The AOIP emphasized its "open" and "inclusive" nature and avoided the term "free" as used in the American articulation of it as it was seen as directed toward China. Similarly, while none in the region reject China's BRI, they also keep their exposure to the BRI limited as shown in pushback by the second Mahathir government in Malaysia.[104]

Additionally, there are latent ideas such as the Indonesian initiative for an "Indo-Pacific wide treaty"[105] modeled on ASEAN's TAC that may imply the amplification of ASEAN's norms and ideas at the level of the Indo-Pacific in the future. ASEAN-led institutions such as EAS and the ARF are the only Indo-Pacific-wide regional institutions, and they include both the United States and China, in addition to other important powers despite the past and ongoing rivalries among many of them. Along with the AOIP that is concerned with "regional architecture in Southeast Asia *and the surrounding regions*,"[106] ASEAN's initiatives, like those of the United States and China discussed above are also pointing toward an "open" regional order.

Second, the Southeast Asian states are also establishing their own minilaterals that are not ASEAN-led. Singapore, Indonesia, Malaysia, and Thailand have been conducting the Malacca Straits Patrols (MSP) that include coordinated naval patrols, coordinated air patrols, and intelligence-sharing. In fact, they are even allowed "hot pursuit rights of five nautical miles into the sovereign waters of the other members."[107] These littoral states were wary of any attempt by the external great powers to dominate the Malacca Strait. "For Singapore, Indonesia, and Malaysia, the key to preventing other powers from controlling access to the region is to find the resources to control it themselves."[108] Similarly, maritime attacks by the Abu Sayyaf Group led to the launch of the Sulu-Sulawesi Sea Patrols (SSSP) by Indonesia, Malaysia, and the Philippines in 2017. Notably, these patrols are modeled on the MSP and include coordinated naval and air patrols as well as intelligence-sharing (but without hot pursuit rights). In part, this initiative emerged after concerns in Indonesia and Malaysia that China would send its ships to patrol these waters at the behest of the Philippines.[109] The MSP and the SSSP point toward local security initiatives backed by the great powers. In other words, they demonstrate the collective—as opposed to hegemonic—provision of regional public goods in the absence of any binding alliances.

Third and finally, the Southeast Asian states are also actively engaging India in the eastern Indian Ocean although they remain suspicious of the Quad with its balance of power undertones. While India is not a member of the MSP, India does engage in bilateral coordinated patrols with all three of its maritime neighbors in the eastern Indian Ocean: Indonesia, Thailand, and Myanmar.[110] Furthermore, India also has reciprocal naval logistics agreements with Vietnam and Singapore.[111] Indian military facilities on the Andaman and Nicobar Islands allow New Delhi to project its power into the Strait of Malacca as well as the South China Sea.[112]

In other words, the cumulative American, Chinese, Southeast Asian, and Indian strategic approaches to the Indo-Pacific are in the process of creating a complex order that cannot be captured through simplistic formulations such as hegemonic, bipolar, or multipolar. In fact, trends point toward a non-hegemonic and multiplex order that will be decentered and open despite the presence of several great and rising powers. The region's smaller players are actively contributing to the regional order, especially by providing normative leadership. Together, these approaches are also ensuring that the Indo-Pacific will remain an "open" region that is actively connected with the world beyond.

The prospects for peaceful change from the AWO to the multiplex order as emergent in the Indo-Pacific is more likely than is sometimes believed. Since the contest between the United States and China is centered on prestige and status at the apex of the international system, a hegemonic global war is unlikely. An all-out system-destroying Sino-American war is not in the offing. Although the United States and China may compete for regional hegemony in the Indo-Pacific, it should be noted that such hegemony is not seen as legitimate in that region, and the ASEAN Way also supports co-engagement of all regional and great powers. While the maritime facet of the Sino-American rivalry in the Indo-Pacific does raise the possibility of "limited warfare" in the region, "a major war remains unlikely" for several reasons including continued complex economic interdependence (despite some "decoupling"), the presence of nuclear weapons, and absence of a zero-sum ideological rivalry between them.[113] Given this larger context, ASEAN's normative agency will likely facilitate a negotiated (if contested) transition from the AWO toward a multiregional world order.

CONCLUSION

The passing of the AWO is not producing disorder or instability. As the United States and China compete for relative position and maritime access, Southeast Asia is co-engaging both the major powers while rejecting hegemony. A hegemonic navy exercising sea control is not in the offing in the Indo-Pacific. Along with the ASEAN-led institutions and the regional norms embodied in the ASEAN Way, Southeast Asian states are beginning to provide the regional public goods for the safe transit of trade. They are doing so individually and collectively with each other, and with all the consequential players in the region. The United States is likely to be last naval superpower to command the seas.[114]

Southeast Asia's active participation along with others such as India, Japan, and Australia in addition to the United States and China in the making of the regional order has added depth and resilience to the emerging regionalism that has become "thick" and legitimate with the participation of multiple actors. In other words, a multiplex and non-hegemonic order is in the making in the Indo-Pacific even in the absence of a grand design although the process is being actively influenced by ASEAN's normative framework. The decentralized choices of several large and small actors are collectively producing the regional order in the Indo-Pacific. Furthermore, this is an "open" order with multiple linkages with actors in regions beyond.

While the proponents of the LIO tend to be dismissive of regional orders in general, especially those outside of Europe, Asia's regional institutions have arguably done a better job of dealing with a rising China than have Europe's in dealing with Russia. Southeast Asia-led regionalism has not only discouraged any America-led containment of China, but it has also softened the region's balance-of-power geopolitics by making space for China in regional affairs. Asia, which has long-rejected a NATO-like alliance and collective defense, has avoided the type of provocation to China that NATO expansion represented for Russia. Furthermore, while the EU has employed its normative power to shape the preferences of the smaller players in the European periphery, ASEAN's normative role has been concerned with engaging and socializing the great powers of Asia and the international system.

In other words, the ideologically plural countries of Southeast Asia provide a better model of regionalism for coping with the complexities of the emerging world order than the ideologically similar liberal democracies of Europe. Therefore, Europe does not hold a monopoly over successful pathways to regionalism and regional-order building. In Europe, the principal multilateral security arrangement, NATO, represents a form of hegemonic regionalism under American predominance. Speaking the language of normative power while sticking to an expanding NATO allowed the EU members to speak moralpolitik while practicing realpolitik. By contrast, ASEAN's principles and practices such as "open regionalism" and consensus-building foster a more accommodationist and communitarian regional order in which the great and rising powers live in a world of the smaller and weaker powers. The contemporary Indo-Pacific regional order that is being actively shaped by Southeast Asia is perhaps one of the most important examples of a decentered regional world that remains deeply connected with other world regions and defines our emerging multiplex reality.

NOTES

1. Amitav Acharya, *The End of American World Order*, 2nd ed. (Cambridge: Polity Press, 2018).
2. G. John Ikenberry, *Liberal Leviathan: The Origins, Crisis, and Transformation of the American World Order* (Princeton, NJ: Princeton University Press, 2011).
3. Paul Kennedy, "The Rise and Fall of the Great Powers redux," *The New Statesman*, September 20, 2023, https://www.newstatesman.com/ideas/2023/09/rise-and-fall-of-great-powers-redux-paul-kennedy.
4. Barry Buzan and Ole Wæver, *Regions and Power: The Structure of International Security* (New York: Cambridge University Press, 2003); Peter J. Katzenstein, *A World of Regions: Asia and Europe in the American Imperium* (Ithaca, NY: Cornell University Press, 2005); Amitav Acharya, "The Emerging Regional Architecture of World Politics," *World Politics* 59, no. 4 (2007): 629–52; and T.V. Paul, ed., *International Relations Theory and Regional Transformation* (New York: Cambridge University Press, 2012).
5. Amitav Acharya, Antoni Estevadeordal, and Louis W. Goodman, "Multipolar or multiplex? Interaction capacity, global cooperation and world order," *International Affairs* 99, no. 6 (2023): 2339–65.
6. On "re-regionalization" form a historical perspective, see Cemil Aydin, "Regions and Empires in the Political History of the Long Nineteenth Century," in *An Emerging Modern World, 1750–1870*, eds. Sebastian Conrad and Jürgen Osterhammel (Cambridge, MA: The Belknap Press, 2018), 35–247. Also see Martin W. Lewis and Kären E. Wigen, *The Myth of Continents: A Critique of Metageography* (Berkeley: University of California Press, 1997).
7. Evelyn Goh, "Competing strategic imaginaries in Asia," SDSC Public Lecture, Australian National University, Canberra, July 21, 2021, https://youtu.be/EWAK631cFDw?si=s_BCW0l_Jq1I3Mik. Also see Evelyn Goh, "The Asia-Pacific's 'Age of Uncertainty': Great Power Competition, Globalisation, and the Economic-Security Nexus," *RSIS Working Paper No. 30*, June 10, 2020, https://www.rsis.edu.sg/rsis-publication/rsis/the-asia-pacifics-age-of-uncertainty-great-power-competition-globalisation-and-the-economic-security-nexus/.
8. See chapter 1 in Acharya, *The End of American World Order*.
9. On the dominant perspectives in the international relations literature on great power status and polarity, see Jack S. Levy, *War in the Modern Great Power System, 1495–1975* (Lexington: The University Press of Kentucky, 1983); Kenneth N. Waltz, *Theory of International Politics* (Reading, MA: Addison-Wesley, 1979).
10. For a comprehensive overview on the literature on polarity, see Barry Buzan, *The United States and the Great Powers: World Politics in the Twenty-First Century* (Cambridge: Polity Press, 2004), 31–45.

11. On the attributes of such decentered and open orders, see Manjeet S. Pardesi, "Decentering Hegemony and 'Open' Orders: Fifteenth-Century Melaka in a World of Orders," *Global Studies Quarterly* 2, no. 4 (2022), https://doi.org/10.1093/isagsq/ksac072.
12. Amitav Acharya, "Flawed Geopolitics: Turning the Idea of the Indo-Pacific into Reality," *East Asia Forum Quarterly* 16, no. 1 (2024): 21–22.
13. National Intelligence Council, "Mapping the Global Future," December 2004, 63, https://www.dni.gov/files/documents/Global%20Trends_Mapping%20the%20Global%20Future%202020%20Project.pdf.
14. National Intelligence Council, "Mapping the Global Future," 9.
15. For details, see Jeanne Moorefield, "Crashing the Cathedral: Historical Reassessments of Twentieth-Century International Relations," *Journal of the History of Ideas* 81, no. 1 (2020): 131–55; and Stephen Wertheim, *Tomorrow, the World: The Birth of U.S. Global Supremacy* (Cambridge, MA: The Belknap Press, 2020).
16. Ikenberry, *Liberal Leviathan*, 32.
17. Also see G. John Ikenberry, "Liberal Internationalism 3.0: America and the Dilemmas of Liberal World Order," *Perspectives on Politics* 7, no. 1 (2009): 71–87; and Daniel Deudney and G. John Ikenberry, "Liberal World: The Resilient Order," *Foreign Affairs* 97, no. 4 (2018), https://www.foreignaffairs.com/articles/world/2018-06-14/liberal-world.
18. Charles Krauthammer, "The Unipolar Moment," *Foreign Affairs* 70, no. 1 (1990/1991): 27.
19. Richard N. Haass, "The Unraveling: How to Respond to a Disordered World," *Foreign Affairs* 93, no. 6 (2014): 73.
20. Robert Gilpin, *War and Change in World Politics* (New York: Cambridge University Press, 1981), 29.
21. William Curti Wohlforth, *The Elusive Balance: Power and Perceptions During the Cold War* (Ithaca, NY: Cornell University Press, 1993), 13. On the other hand, Mearsheimer argues that hegemony is only possible at the regional level and not at the global level due to the "stopping power of water" and the difficulty of clear-cut nuclear superiority. See John J. Mearsheimer, *The Tragedy of Great Power Politics* (New York: W. W. Norton, 2014), 69. As explained subsequently, neither the United States nor China is hegemonic in the Indo-Pacific region.
22. T.V. Paul, "The Rise of China and the Emerging Order in the Indo-Pacific Region," in *China's Challenges and International Order Transition: Beyond Thucydides's Trap*, eds. Huiyun Feng and Kai He (Ann Arbor: University of Michigan Press, 2020), 73.
23. Stephen G. Brooks and William C. Wohlforth, "The Rise and Fall of the Great Powers in the Twenty-First Century: China's Rise and the Fate of America's Global Position," *International Security* 40, no. 3 (2016): 7–53.
24. Barry Posen, "Command of the Commons: The Military Foundations of U.S. Hegemony," *International Security* 28, no. 1 (2003): 7.
25. Robert W. Cox, *Production, Power, and World Order: Social Forces in the Making of History* (New York: Columbia University Press, 1987), 7.
26. Amitav Acharya, *Constructing Global Order: Agency and Change in World Politics* (Cambridge: Cambridge University Press, 2018).
27. Michael Barnett, "Social constructivism," in *The Globalization of World Politics*, 8th ed, eds. John Baylis, Steve Smith, and Patricia Owens (New York: Oxford University Press, 2020), 201.

28. Barry Buzan and George Lawson, *The Global Transformation: History, Modernity, and the Making of International Relations* (Cambridge: Cambridge University Press, 2015), 298.
29. Ian Clark, *Hegemony and International Society* (New York: Oxford University Press, 2011), 123.
30. Simon Reich and Richard Ned Lebow, *Good-Bye Hegemony: Power and Influence in the Global System* (Princeton, NJ: Princeton University Press, 2014).
31. Rosemary Foot, "China's Rise and US Hegemony: Renegotiating Hegemonic Order in East Asia?," *International Politics* 57, no. 2 (2020): 163.
32. Buzan and Lawson, *The Global Transformation*, 298.
33. See Graham T. Allison, *Destined for War: Can America and China Escape Thucydides's Trap?* (Boston: Houghton Mifflin Harcourt, 2017). For an excellent critique of this "trap" and the associated power transition theory, see Steve Chan, *Thucydides' Trap? Historical Interpretation, Logic of Inquiry, and the Future of Sino-American Relations* (Ann Arbor: University of Michigan Press, 2020).
34. Øystein Tunsjø, *The Return of Bipolarity in World Politics: China, the United States, and Geostructural Realism* (New York: Columbia University Press, 2018).
35. William C. Wohlforth, "The Stability of a Unipolar World," *International Security* 24, no. 1 (1999): 5–41.
36. William C. Wohlforth, "Polarity and International Order: Past and Future," in *Polarity in International Relations: Past, Present, Future*, eds. Nina Græger, Bertel Heurlin, Ole Wæver, and Anders Wivel (Cham: Palgrave Macmillan, 2022), 413.
37. Barry Buzan, "The Inaugural Kenneth N. Waltz Annual Lecture—A World without Superpowers: Decentered Globalism," *International Relations* 25, no. 1 (2011): 3–25.
38. Acharya, *The End of American World Order*. On the difference between "great powers" and "superpowers" see Barry Buzan, "Great Powers" in *The Oxford Handbook of International Security*, eds. Alexandra Gheciu and William C. Wohlforth (Oxford: Oxford University Press, 2020), 639–52.
39. Evelyn Goh, "Policy Forum—Introduction," *The Georgetown Journal of International Affairs* Volume 9, August 2023, 8, https://repository.library.georgetown.edu/handle/10822/1084990.
40. On the interplay of structure and agency in decentered worlds, see Pardesi, "Decentering Hegemony and 'Open' Orders."
41. Acharya, *The End of American World Order*.
42. Patrick Porter, "A World Imagined: Nostalgia and Liberal Order," *Policy Analysis*, CATO Institute, Number 843, June 5, 2018, 1, https://www.cato.org/sites/cato.org/files/pubs/pdf/pa-843.pdf.
43. Henry Kissinger, *World Order* (New York: Penguin, 2014), 2.
44. John King Fairbank, ed., *The Chinese World Order: Traditional China's Foreign Relations* (Cambridge, MA: Harvard University Press, 1968).
45. There were "three distinct worlds" in historical Inner and East Asia—Chinese, Mongol, and Tibetan-Buddhist—that patterned inter-polity relations. See Timothy Brook, Michael van Walt van Praag, and Miek Boltjes, eds., *Sacred Mandates: Asian International Relations since Chinggis Khan* (Chicago: The University of Chicago Press, 2018). Similarly, the Persian cosmopolis intersected and overlapped with the Chinese world order in certain periods in historical Southeast Asia. See Pardesi, "Decentering Hegemony and 'Open' Orders."

46. There was "no systematic tributary system" in practice. See Peter C. Perdue, "The Tenacious Tributary System," *Journal of Contemporary China* 24, no. 96 (2015), 1002.
47. Hedley Bull, *The Anarchical Society: A Study of Order in World Politics*, 3rd ed. (New York: Palgrave, 2002), 8.
48. Karl W. Deutsch and J. David Singer, "Multipolar Power Systems and International Stability," *World Politics* 16, no. 3 (1964): 390–91.
49. Muthiah Alagappa, "The Study of International Order," in *Asian Security Order: Instrumental and Normative Features*, ed. Muthiah Alagappa (Stanford, CA: Stanford University Press, 2003), 39.
50. Acharya, *The End of American World Order*.
51. Emmanuel Adler and Beverley Crawford, "Normative Power: The European Practice of Region-Building and the Case of the Euro-Mediterranean Partnership," in *The Convergence of Civilizations: Constructing a Mediterranean Region*, eds. Emmanuel Adler, Federica Bicchi, Beverley Crawford, and Raffaella A. Del Sarto (Toronto: University of Toronto Press, 2006), 14.
52. Iver B. Neumann, "A Region-Building Approach to Northern Europe," *Review of International Studies* 20, no. 1 (1994): 57.
53. Sita Ranchod-Nilsson, "Regional Worlds: Transforming Pedagogy in Area Studies and International Studies," Regional Worlds, University of Chicago, 2000, 8, http://regionalworlds.uchicago.edu/transformingpedagogy.pdf.
54. We have borrowed this phrase from Matthew Fitzpatrick, "Provincializing Rome: The Indian Ocean Trade Network and Roman Imperialism," *Journal of World History* 22, no. 1 (2011): 47.
55. On the concept of "open regionalism" that was developed in East Asia, see Amitav Acharya, *Whose Ideas Matter? Agency and Power in Asian Regionalism* (Ithaca, NY: Cornell University Press, 2009), 101–108. On "open orders," see Manjeet S. Pardesi, "Interconnected Asian History and 'Open' World Orders," *Oxford Research Encyclopedias, Politics*, April 17, 2024, https://doi.org/10.1093/acrefore/9780190228637.013.2161.
56. Barry Buzan and Richard Little, *International Systems in World History: Remaking the Study of International Relations* (New York: Oxford University Press, 2000), 404.
57. On the making of "South Asia," see Nicholas B. Dirks, "South Asian Studies: Futures Past," in *Autobiography of an Archive: A Scholar's Passage to India*, ed. Nicholas B. Dirks (New York: Columbia University Press, 2015), 265–290. On the making of "Southeast Asia," see Donald K. Emmerson, "'Southeast Asia': What's in a Name?," *Journal of Southeast Asian Studies* 15, no. 1 (1984): 1–21. On the making of "East Asia," see Paul Evans, "The Concept of Eastern Asia," in *Eastern Asia: An Introductory History*, 3rd ed., ed. Colin Mackerras (Frenchs Forest, NSW: Longman, 2000), 7–13.
58. For example, Brecher clubbed China along with South and Southeast Asia into the "Southern Asian System" in the early 1960s. Michael Brecher, "International Relations and Asian Studies: The Subordinate State System of Southern Asia," *World Politics* 15, no. 2 (1963): 213–35. He also felt that China and Pakistan were members of other "systems," thus keeping his systems/regions "open."
59. Manjeet S. Pardesi, "The Indo-Pacific: A 'New' Region or the Return of History?," *Australian Journal of International Affairs* 74, no. 2 (2020): 124–46.
60. Buzan and Wæver, *Regions and Power*, 144.
61. Amitav Acharya, *Constructing a Security Community in Southeast Asia: ASEAN and the Problem of Regional Order* (London: Routledge, 2001), 182.

62. Isabelle Saint-Mézard, *Eastward Bound: India's New Positioning in Asia* (New Delhi: Manohar, 2006).
63. China's General Zhao Nanqi made this statement in 1993 that is quoted in J. Mohan Malik, "China-India Relations in the Post-Soviet Era: The Continuing Rivalry," *China Quarterly*, no. 142 (June 1995): 328.
64. Goh Chok Tong, "Reconceptualizing East Asia," Keynote address by Senior Minister Goh Chok Tong at the official launch of the Institute of South Asian Studies (ISAS) on Thursday, 27 January 2005 at 8:00 P.M. at Orchard Hotel, Singapore Government Press Release, https://www.nas.gov.sg/archivesonline/data/pdfdoc/2005012701.htm.
65. Evelyn Goh, "East Asia as Regional International Society: The Problem of Great Power Management," in *Contesting International Society in East Asia*, eds., Barry Buzan and Yongjin Zhang (Cambridge: Cambridge University Press, 2014), 184.
66. See Yuen Foong Khong, "Power as prestige in world politics," *International Affairs* 95, no. 1 (2019), 119–42. For a general discussion of status in great power rivalries, see T.V. Paul, Deborah Welch Larson, and William C. Wohlforth, eds., *Status in World Politics* (New York: Cambridge University Press, 2014). Even leadership long-cycle theorists argue that the United States and China are engaged in a competition for the status of the *primus inter pares* (or first among equals) in the economic and technological domains. See William R. Thompson, *American Global Pre-Eminence: The Development and Erosion of Systemic Leadership* (New York: Oxford University Press, 2022).
67. Wertheim, *Tomorrow, the World*, 7.
68. Graham Allison, Robert D. Blackwill, and Ali Wayne, *Lee Kuan Yew: The Grand Master's Insights on China, the United States, and the World* (Cambridge, MA: MIT Press, 2013), Kindle Loc. 244.
69. U.S. Department of Defense, "Quadrennial Defense Review Report," September 30, 2001, 2 (footnote 1).
70. For an important Australian perspective on the Indo-Pacific, see Rory Medcalf, *Contest for the Indo-Pacific: Why China Won't Map the Future* (Carlton: Black Inc., 2020).
71. Evan Braden Montgomery, "Contested Primacy in the Western Pacific: China's Rise and the Future of U.S. Power Projection," *International Security* 38, no. 4 (2014): 1151–49.
72. Eric Heginbotham, Michael Nixon, Forrest E. Morgan, Jacob L. Heim, Jeff Hagen, Sheng Tao Li, Jeffrey Engstrom, Martin C. Libicki, Paul DeLuca, David A. Shlapak, et al., *The U.S.-China Military Scorecard: Forces, Geography, and the Evolving Balance of Power, 1996–2017* (Santa Monica, CA: RAND, 2015).
73. Jack S. Levy and William R. Thompson, "Balancing on Land and at Sea: Do States Ally Against the Leading Global Power?" *International Security* 35, no. 1 (2010): 17.
74. There is a vast literature on America's postwar hub-and-spokes system. See Christopher Hemmer and Peter J. Katzenstein, "Why Is There No NATO in Asia? Collective Identity, Regionalism, and the Origins of Multilateralism," *International Organization* 56, no. 3 (2002): 575–607; Victor D. Cha, "Powerplay: Origins of the U.S. Alliance System in Asia," *International Security* 34, no. 3 (2009/2010): 158–96; Amitav Acharya, "Norm Subsidiarity and Regional Orders: Sovereignty, Regionalism, and Rule-Making in the Third World," *International Studies Quarterly* 55, no. 1 (2011): 95–123; and Yasuhiro Izumikawa, "Network Connections and the Emergence of the Hub-and-Spokes Alliance System in East Asia," *International Security* 45, no. 2 (2020): 7–50.

75. Matteo Dian and Hugo Meijer, "Networking Hegemony: Alliance Dynamics in East Asia," *International Politics* 57, no. 2 (2020): 131–49. This is the lead article on a special issue titled "Networking Hegemony: Alliance Dynamics in East Asia."
76. Evelyn Goh, "In Response: Alliance Dynamics, Variables, and the English School for East Asia," *International Politics* 57, no. 2 (2020): 278–84.
77. Feng Zhang, "China's Curious Nonchalance Towards the Indo-Pacific," *Survival* 61, no. 3 (2019): 200.
78. Li Li, "The New Trend of India's Rising as a Great Power," *Contemporary International Relations* 28, no. 2 (2018): 45.
79. Sumit Ganguly, Manjeet S. Pardesi, and William R. Thompson, *The Sino-Indian Rivalry: Implications for Global Order* (Cambridge: Cambridge University Press, 2023).
80. The White House, "Indo-Pacific Strategy of the United States," February 2022, Washington, 10, https://www.whitehouse.gov/wp-content/uploads/2022/02/U.S.-Indo-Pacific-Strategy.pdf.
81. "Aukus: UK, US and Australia Launch Pact to Counter China," *BBC News*, September 16, 2021, https://www.bbc.com/news/world-58564837.
82. Rory Medcalf, "Grand Stakes: Australia's Future between China and India," in *Strategic Asia 2011–12: Asia Responds to its Rising Powers, China and India*, eds. Ashley J. Tellis, Travis Tanner, and Jessica Keough (Seattle: National Bureau of Asian Research, 2011), 200.
83. Hugh White, "Old Friends in the New Asia: New Zealand, Australia, and the Rise of China," in *New Zealand and the World: Past, Present, and Future*, eds. Robert G. Patman, Iati Iati, and Balazs Kiglics (Singapore: World Scientific, 2018), 193.
84. "Science of Military Strategy (2013)," 18–19 and 309. The full text of this document that was prepared by China's Academy of Military Sciences was translated into English and published under the auspices of Project Everest and the China Aerospace Studies Institute on February 8, 2021, https://www.airuniversity.af.edu/CASI/Display/Article/2485204/plas-science-of-military-strategy-2013/.
85. John W. Garver, "Calculus of a Chinese Decision for Local War with India," in *India and China in Asia: Between Equilibrium and Equations*, ed. Jagannath P. Panda (London: Routledge, 2019), 93.
86. Hu Bo, "China in a Multipolar World," in *Navies in Multipolar Worlds: From the Age of Sail to the Present*, eds. Paul Kennedy and Evan Wilson (New York: Routledge, 2021), 225.
87. Andrea Ghiselli, "The Chinese People's Liberation Army 'Post-modern Navy,'" *The International Spectator* 50, no. 1 (2015): 117–36.
88. Wang Gungwu, "China, ASEAN, and the new Maritime Silk Road," *ThinkChina*, 16 November 2021, https://www.thinkchina.sg/wang-gungwu-china-asean-and-new-maritime-silk-road.
89. David I. Steinberg, "China's Myanmar, Myanmar's China: Myths, Illusions, Interactions," in *The Deer and the Dragon: Southeast Asia and China in the 21st Century*, ed., Donald K. Emmerson (Stanford, CA: Walter H. Shorenstein Asia-Pacific Research Center, 2020), 366.
90. Hailin Ye, "The Strategic Landscape of South Asia and Indian Ocean Region," in *Annual Report on the Development of International Relations in the Indian Ocean Region (2014)*, eds. Rong Wang and Cuiping Zhu (Heidelberg: Springer, 2015), 38.

91. Joseph Chinyong Liow, "The Strategic Rationale of China's Belt and Road Initiative," in *Research Handbook on the Belt and Road Initiative*, eds. Joseph Chinyong Liow, Hong Liu, and Gong Xue (Cheltenham: Edward Elgar, 2021), 103 and 109.
92. Hu Bo (translated by Zhang Yanpei and edited and preface by Geoffrey Till), *Chinese Maritime Power in the 21st Century: Strategic Planning, Policy and Predictions* (New York: Routledge, 2020), 185.
93. Nguyen Khac Giang, "China Is Making Mekong Friends," *East Asia Forum*, May 19, 2018, https://www.eastasiaforum.org/2018/05/19/china-is-making-mekong-friends/.
94. Edward Wong, "China and Neighbors Begin Joint Mekong River Patrols," *New York Times*, December 10, 2011, https://www.nytimes.com/2011/12/11/world/asia/china-and-neighbors-begin-joint-mekong-river-patrols.html.
95. Martin Stuart-Fox, *A History of China and Southeast Asia: Tribute, Trade, and Influence* (Crows Nest: Allen & Unwin, 2003), 241.
96. Amitav Acharya, *Constructing a Security Community in Southeast Asia: ASEAN and the Problem of Regional Order*, 3rd ed. (London: Routledge, 2014), 43–79.
97. Amitav Acharya, "Norm Subsidiarity and Regional Orders: Sovereignty, Regionalism, and Rule-Making in the Third World," *International Studies Quarterly* 55, no. 1 (2011): 95–123.
98. Acharya, *Whose Ideas Matter?*, 145.
99. See Seng Tan, "Consigned to Hedge: South-east Asia and America's 'Free and Open Indo-Pacific' Strategy," *International Affairs* 96, no. 1 (2020): 131.
100. Joseph Chinyong Liow, *Ambivalent Engagement: The United States and Regional Security in Southeast Asia after the Cold War* (Washington, DC: Brookings, 2017), 16–17.
101. David Shambaugh, *Where Great Powers Meet: America & China in Southeast Asia* (New York: Oxford University Press, 2021), 61.
102. Goh, "In Response," 280.
103. Amitav Acharya, "Why ASEAN's Indo-Pacific Outlook Matters?," *East Asia Forum*, August 11, 2019, https://www.eastasiaforum.org/2019/08/11/why-aseans-indo-pacific-outlook-matters/.
104. Acharya, *ASEAN and Regional Order*, 76–77.
105. Ang Cheng Guan, *Southeast Asia after the Cold War: A Contemporary History* (Singapore: NUS Press, 2019), 191.
106. ASEAN, "ASEAN Outlook on the Indo-Pacific," June 23, 2019, https://asean.org/speechandstatement/asean-outlook-on-the-indo-pacific/.
107. Ian Storey, "Southeast Asia's Minilateral Counter-Piracy/Sea-Robbery Initiatives," in *Maritime Cooperation and Security in the Indo-Pacific Region: Essays in Honor of Sam Bateman*, eds. John E. Bradford, Jane Chan, Stuart Kaye, Clive Schofield, Geoffrey Till (Leiden: Brill, 2023), 309.
108. John Garofano and Andrea J. Dew, "Conclusion: Access and Security in the Indian Ocean," in *Deep Currents and Rising Tides: The Indian Ocean and International Security*, eds. John Garofano and Andrea J. Dew (Washington, DC: Georgetown University Press, 2013), 302.
109. Storey, "Southeast Asia's Minilateral," 308.
110. Prashanth Parameswaran, "India, Myanmar Ink New Naval Patrol Pact," *The Diplomat*, February 23, 2016, https://thediplomat.com/2016/02/india-myanmar-ink-new-naval-pact-on-coordinated-patrols/.

111. Dinakar Peri, "India and Vietnam Sign Mutual Logistics Agreement," *The Hindu*, June 8, 2022, https://www.thehindu.com/news/national/india-vietnam-ink-military-logistics-support-pact-vision-document-to-expand-defence-ties/article65506502.ece.
112. Koh Swee Lean Collin, "China-India Rivalry at Sea: Capabilities, Trends and Challenges," *Asian Security* 15, no. 1 (2019): 5–24. There is some debate on whether India can play a strategic role to the east of the Strait of Malacca. See Rahul Roy-Chaudhury and Kate Sullivan de Estrada, "India, the Indo-Pacific and the Quad," *Survival* 60, no. 3 (2018): 181–94.
113. Thompson, *American Global Pre-Eminence*, https://doi.org/10.1093/oso/9780197534663.003.0009; and Tunsjø, *The Return of Bipolarity in World Politics*.
114. Amitav Acharya and Manjeet S. Pardesi, *Divergent Worlds: What the Ancient Mediterranean and Indian Ocean Can Tell Us About the Future of International Order* (New Haven, CT: Yale University Press, *forthcoming*).

CHAPTER 3

Norms in Great Power Competition: Peaceful Change in a Spheres of Influence World[1]

Anders Wivel

The—potentially existential—crisis of the so-called liberal world order has caused considerable concern among scholars and policymakers in North America and Europe. According to observers, a globalized order embedded in shared norms and institutions is "in trouble,"[2] "in crisis,"[3] or even giving way to the transactional and power-based self-help politics of the past.[4]

One important aspect of this crisis is the re-articulation of "spheres of influence" as a central tenet of great power politics,[5] exemplified by Russia's brutal invasion of Ukraine in February 2022 and Russian President Vladimir Putin's explanation of the war as a response to NATO expansion violating Russia's rights to exercise its privileged interests in the post-Soviet space.

Spheres of influence were an integral part of the history of international relations even before the creation of the modern states system, and they continue to be central to the organization of international relations. Thus, while the concept of the sphere of influence has been rearticulated in political discourse in recent years, it never left political practice. There have been spheres of influence as long as human beings have organized themselves in geographically bounded political communities and been aware of other communities. Thucydides military history of Peloponnesian War (431–404 BC) is at least partly a story about conflicts driven by concern for spheres of influence, and the European competition for overseas colonies from the fifteenth century created an extensive pattern of spheres of influence. The conclusion of the Congress of Vienna in 1815 and the ensuing Concert of Europe bestowed a set of special rights and obligations on the great powers and effectively divided the world into spheres of influence—that is, geopolitical regions dominated by one great power and implicitly or explicitly giving this great power certain rights and obligations within the region.

In the Western hemisphere, the United States' Monroe Doctrine from 1823 was a prominent example of sphere of influence policy. Named after President James Monroe, who first articulated the central principles of the doctrine, it argued that the "New World" and the "Old World" were distinct spheres of influence that must be kept separate and saw any political or military intervention in the Americas by foreign powers as a threat to US security. This sphere of influence way of organizing the international realm subsequently served as a basis for US foreign policy after the two world wars. After the First World War and in the early stages of the Second World War, the United States was reluctant to engage in international politics in Europe, outside its traditional sphere of influence. After the Second World War, the United States expanded its sphere of influence to Western Europe, but generally respected the sphere of influence of its main competitor, the Soviet Union. US thinking about the postwar order was from the outset embedded in a spheres of influence understanding of the world as expressed in President Roosevelt's vision of four policemen (great powers) running the world, a concept that evolved into the United Nations Security Council and served as a point of departure for a clear distinction between great powers and small states in US postwar security policy.[6] Thus, as noted by Fried, the "U.S. was not willing to risk war against the Soviet Union when Moscow put down the Hungarian Revolution in 1956 and the Prague Spring in 1968, or when it pushed Poland's government into imposing martial law in 1981."[7]

The US vision for a "new world order" introduced by US president George H.W. Bush in his 1991 State of the Union speech in the immediate aftermath of the Cold War challenged the sphere of influence organization of the international system by presenting a vision for one globalized, seamless, liberal international order promising sovereign equality and territorial integrity for all states.[8] This view was mirrored by UN secretary general Boutros Boutros-Ghali in his 1992 report *An Agenda for Peace*, which argued that the "time of absolute and exclusive sovereignty" had "passed."[9] The ensuing post–Cold War liberal international order—what G. John Ikenberry has termed "Liberal Internationalism 3.0"—was universal in scope, increasingly intrusive of state sovereignty, and held together by a rule-based governing system coupled with network based types of cooperation,[10] although in practice it remained a "partial order"[11] largely excluding major powers (China, Russia) and most parts of some regions (the Middle East, Africa). Today, increasing great power rivalry is challenging the liberal international order's claim to universality in an international order once again increasingly organized into spheres of influence.

This chapter uses spheres of influence as an analytical lens to assess the prospects for peaceful change in an international system increasingly characterized by great power rivalry. The main argument is that the prospects for peaceful change depend on the compatibility of states' expectations of what spheres of influence are and ought to be, and their willingness to negotiate and compromise on these expectations. I argue that spheres of influence entail repertoires of expectations regarding appropriate behavior, relative influence and gains, and contributions to the maintenance and development of the sphere. In doing so they create challenges and opportunities for dominance, resistance, and peaceful change. Spheres of influence are negotiated hegemonies reflecting different compromises on what international affairs is and ought to be. For this reason, they are sites of contestation and negotiation: horizontally between great powers agreeing and disagreeing on common rules for all spheres in the international system and how much action space to allow hegemons in their respective spheres of influence, and vertically between the sphere's hegemon and small states and middle powers located inside the sphere.

The argument proceeds in three sections followed by a conclusion. The first section asks, "What is a sphere of influence?" and identifies three characteristics. The second section asks, "What are the prospects for peaceful change in a sphere of influence world?" It discusses liberal and realist takes on the sphere of influence and introduces an alternative way of understanding spheres of influence as repertoires of expectations. The third section asks, "What are the implications of US Chinese rivalry in a spheres of influence world for regional and global peace and order?" Building on the previous sections, it discusses the characteristics of US and Chinese spheres of influence, the compatibility of the spheres, and the chances of finding a modus vivendi allowing for peaceful change in the coming years. Finally, I conclude the paper.

WHAT IS A SPHERE OF INFLUENCE?

A sphere of influence is a key ordering device for international relations. It contrasts with the idea that the global political space is organized into one order with shared norms, rules, and institutions. It divides the world into spheres characterized by (1) the ability of a great power or a regional power to dominate and exercise control over a space of several formally sovereign entities,[12] (2) the willingness of other great powers to recognize the legitimacy of this dominance,[13] and (3) the acceptance of some degree of dominance and control by small states and middle powers within the sphere. Consequently, a sphere of influence has two dimensions: a horizontal dimension between great powers and a vertical dimension between the dominant great power of the sphere and small states and middle powers within the sphere.

The sphere of influence remains an undertheorized and understudied concept in international relations. It is largely ignored as a theoretical concept, although occasionally the subject of case studies.[14] Most research focuses on the great power hegemons rather than the states populating the spheres of influence and it tells us little about the prospects for peaceful change within or between spheres of influence.[15] There is no consensus on what constitutes a sphere of influence. The concept is used as an analytical notion and in political discourse, in the latter case typically in a pejorative sense.[16] The concept is used in at least three potentially overlapping ways:[17] (1) as an analytical concept allowing us to understand what goes on international relations, (2) as an idea or doctrine guiding foreign policy decision-making, and (3) as a defining tenet of international relations, a fundamental institution of international society.[18]

We can crystallize three characteristics of the sphere of influence, no matter if we think of it as an analytical concept, a foreign policy doctrine, or an international institution. First, the sphere of influence is a spatial concept. It denotes a way of organizing the international system (into "spheres") and a geographical area of interest to individual states. Viewed from the system, the sphere of influence is a key ordering device for international relations. It divides the international system into spheres with different logics of consequence and appropriate action based on the great powers' "observance of mutual respect for each other's spheres of local preponderance."[19] Viewed from the perspective of the individual state, a sphere of influence often equals the geopolitical neighborhood of the state itself, because power and incentive wane with distance from their home base.[20] The geopolitical neighborhood is at the same time the area where the state is best able to project its own power and where it has the greatest interest in preventing other states from projecting their power.[21] It serves as a useful buffer between the state and its potential enemies. In this way the sphere of influence is linked to the location of the state and the defense of the realm. However, we cannot deduce spheres of influence from looking at a map. Spheres of influence are not a function of geographic proximity, but the product of the perceived security interests of the state—that is, a combination of historical experience, strategic culture, and power. Thus, during the Cold War, Cuba was in the Soviet sphere of influence, while Japan, the Philippines, and Western Europe were in the US sphere of influence even though they were not in the geopolitical vicinity of the two superpowers.

Second, spheres of influence make little sense without awareness of an international realm beyond the sphere. It is by definition a subset of something bigger. For the foreign-policy maker, the sphere of influence is privileged, more important, than other spheres. Thus, it is both an acknowledgment of a wider world and a prioritization, a hierarchy, of spheres within this wider world. This was the case in the old Cold War, when US- and Soviet-dominated spheres of influence served a geopolitical anchoring and basis for great power rivalry, and it is increasingly the case in what might develop into a new cold war between China and the United States.

Finally, spheres of influence institutionalize inequality among states. Spheres of influence are "international formations that contain one nation (the influencer) that commands superior power over others."[22] A sphere of influence is the expression of "hegemonic control."[23] However, it should not be conflated with an imperial order, which is based on ongoing and direct control of the colonies, whereas the hegemon typically relies on intermittent and indirect means to control its sphere of influence. Thus, it does not formally challenge principles of sovereign equality and nonintervention, although it might do so in practice.

WHAT ARE THE PROSPECTS FOR PEACEFUL CHANGE IN A SPHERE OF INFLUENCE WORLD?

In scholarly and public debates, spheres of influence are most often viewed as archaic and dangerous. Liberal scholars and policymakers identify three reasons why spheres of influence should be viewed as detrimental to peaceful change. First, spheres of influence are seen as creating lacunas in international society outside the usual norms and rules giving great powers a large action space to do as they please. Critics have associated spheres of influence with a return of international relations to the dynamics of the nineteenth and twentieth centuries, seeing Russia, in particular, as the exponent of this type of politics, because of the Russian wars in Ukraine (2022) and Georgia (2008) and Russian actions in Syria.[24] In this view, autocratic great powers deal "in spheres of interest and reciprocity in interstate relations" and view international relations primarily as "a struggle for power and security among states striving to maximize their interests in international anarchy—with military means if necessary."[25] The concept is viewed as a threat to efforts of a United States–led West to avoid "a world divided into competing empires, blocs, and spheres of influence controlled by hostile great powers."[26] They are associated with an international order resembling colonial and racist pre–World War II international relations, when a few privileged powers managed to dominate the world.

Second, spheres of influence are viewed as an expression of neomercantilism and consequently as an obstacle to creating a more interdependent world. China's Belt and Road Initiative is sometimes mentioned as an example because of its explicit ambition to create "a new global geo-political map," promising "a mega geoeconomic agenda to deepen regional economic cooperation" at the same time as it "sets up a great power strategy to advance China's geopolitical and geostrategic interests in Eurasia and beyond."[27] Likewise, the energy policies of China and Russia in Central Asia have been characterized as neomercantilist, building on the more general argument that "illiberal states such as Russia and China that selectively accept elements of capitalism and the market economy, operate in illiberal environments (Central Asia), and compete for vital commodities (oil and gas), will adopt neomercantilism as opposed to policies based on liberal assumptions and expectations."[28] Spheres of influence produce "contestation of the open global commons that are the basis for the unprecedented prosperity produced by the liberal international economic order."[29] To liberals, a sphere of influence world is the antithesis to a liberal order, a "'Beijing model' [...] organized around exclusive blocs, spheres of influence, and mercantilist networks [which would allow] a few states opportunistically exploit an open system of markets. But if everyone does, it is no longer an open system but a fragmented, mercantilist, and protectionist complex—and everyone suffers."[30]

Finally, spheres of influence are viewed as delaying or stopping the spread of democracy.[31] The political discourse may vary considerably between spheres of influence. Even if hegemony is negotiated and contested, democratization may not be the outcome of the negotiations, if none of the negotiators are democrats. Since the collapse of the Soviet Union, the post-Soviet republics have followed "a pattern of cycling or oscillation as regimes waver back and forth between the autocratic and democratic ends of the political-rights spectrum."[32] With no pull factors inside the sphere of influence and outside powers reluctant to intervene, there might be no real prospects of changing this situation. In sum, liberals tend to associate spheres of influence with "the dark forces of world politics" and along with "illiberalism, autocracy, nationalism, protectionism [and] territorial revisionism,"[33] they constitute one of the main dangers to peace and prosperity in today's world. Spheres of influence are to be avoided and reacted against.

Whereas the emergence of a sphere of influence world is a call to action for liberals, realists tend either to ignore spheres of influence or to take a more mechanistic view of spheres of influences and their consequences for peaceful change. Despite the strong link between geopolitics and realist strategic studies and the prominence of scholars such as Halford J. Mackinder and Nicholas Spykman for early and mid-twentieth century realist thought,[34] the dominance of structural realism for more than three decades after the publication of Kenneth Waltz's *Theory of International Politics* in 1979[35] left little room for the exploration of sub-systemic dynamics. The more recent wave of neoclassical realist work has mostly taken the form of a "logical" extension of structural realism filling out its blanks or discussing its shortcomings in explaining international relations and foreign policy.[36] To the extent that realists are concerned with spheres of influence, they tend to take a mechanistic view with little acknowledgment of other states than great powers. If one great power violates the sphere of influence of another great power, this is likely to lead to conflict and ultimately interstate war.[37] However, from a realist perspective, the balance of power is a useful mechanism for keeping rival great powers in check and, inside spheres of influence, a dominant state can be a source of hegemonic stability, although unequal growth rates are likely to undermine this stability over time and lead to war.[38] Consequently, the analytical tools of realism to understand spheres of influence remain surprisingly blunt.[39] Whereas the liberal perspective on spheres of influence tend to emphasize the illiberal nature of spheres of influence and call for their (unlikely) eradication, realists risk depoliticizing and naturalizing spheres of influence with little other prospect than to accept the atrocities following from great power politics. For both perspectives, spheres of influence are a source of violent change: either because spheres of influence undermine liberal sources of peaceful change (liberal norms, interdependence, and democracy) or as an extension of great power politics in an anarchic international system.

Building on recent theoretical developments linking classical realist and English school thinking to the literature on social norms and practices,[40] I take a different route for understanding spheres of influence. Beginning from an acknowledgment that spheres of influence are constructed through the interaction of normative and materialist factors, rather than one or the other, I operationalize a sphere of influence as a repertoire of expectations regarding appropriate behavior, relative influence and gains, and contributions toward the maintenance and development of the sphere. Spheres of influence are constructs of inter-subjective interaction: neither given nor permanent but constantly shaped and reshaped by interaction processes and discourses creating expectations and rules of engagement.[41] In essence, "the ideas, theories and conceptualizations of spheres of influence should not be seen as mere explanations of world politics, but as constitutive of the practices of international relations. References to a sphere of influence enable certain political imaginations while limiting others."[42]

Repertoires of expectations have both a horizontal and a vertical dimension. Horizontally, spheres of influence can be understood as parallel mini systems. The hegemon of each sphere, or mini system, has a repertoire of expectations on the role of the hegemon vis-à-vis the hegemons of other spheres, its action space within its own sphere, and what rules of the game should be the same for all spheres—that is, the international system. To the extent that these repertoires of expectations are compatible—or at least negotiable—peaceful change is possible. If they are incompatible and nonnegotiable, peaceful change is unlikely and "cold war" or violent conflict will be the result.

Vertically, spheres of influence are negotiated hegemonies between the influencer and the influenced debating, contesting, and compromising on the rules of engagement.[43] A sphere of influence is the expression of "hegemonic control."[44] However, hegemonic control is rarely exercised through the direct use of violence or threats of violence. It is typically exercised by "softer" means through a repertoire of expectations regarding appropriate behavior, relative influence and gains, and contribution to the maintenance and development of the sphere. Thus, control tends to be "intermediary: lower than that of an occupying or colonizing nation, but higher than that of a coalition leader."[45] Historically, sphere of influence–based orders bore stronger resemblance to semi-suzerain orders than to imperial orders.[46] Today, we may view spheres of influence as asymmetrically structured regions understood as "security spaces and as spheres where power relations between states are negotiated."[47] The nature of this negotiation varies from responding to direct threats and attempts at coercion over material incentives to genuine persuasion and agreement on common goals between the hegemon and weaker states within the sphere of influence.

The horizontal and vertical dimensions are rooted in realism insofar as great powers act as systemic competitors and regional agenda-setters. However, cooperation and conflict between and inside spheres of influence are decided not by power itself but repertoires of expectations on what power can and should do. Consequently, the risk of war and the prospects for peaceful change within and between spheres hinges on the compatibility of repertoires and the willingness of state actors to negotiate to find common ground on what international society is and what it ought to be.

GREAT POWER RIVALRY BETWEEN THE UNITED STATES AND CHINA IN A SPHERE OF INFLUENCE WORLD

Looking through the sphere of influence prism, the New Cold War between the United States and China differs in important respects from the old Cold War between the United States and the Soviet Union. In the old Cold War, two universalistic ideologies served as sources of repertoires of expectations. Each superpower saw itself locked in an ideological conflict between good and evil (although with contrasting views on who was good and who was evil). Soviet foreign policy took its point of departure in Marxist-Leninism. Even if there was "no automatically 'correct translation', no one-to-one correspondence, between any segment of ideology and any particular act," Marxism-Leninism was interpreted by Soviet policymakers as a "combative ideology" viewing international relations in the context of an enduring class struggle that cannot be confined to domestic politics.[48] Soviet policymakers saw capitalism as an "internationally expansive system" leading to "an inevitable international struggle with capitalist states."[49]

The foreign policy repertoire following from this starting point had three characteristics. First, the accumulation of military power and capabilities became absolutely central to Soviet foreign policy. Military power was seen as essential for winning the struggle against capitalist imperialism and informed by their Marxist-Leninist ideology, decision-makers did not consider Soviet armament as an impetus for balancing or security spirals, since the expansion of the West was viewed to be domestically driven by Liberal-Capitalist ideology and not a response to Soviet armament.[50] Second, the support and creation—Sovietization—of regimes in Eastern Europe and the Global South were seen as essential tools in the ideological struggle against the United States and its allies.[51] Finally, while these policies succeeded in establishing a Soviet sphere of influence, the Soviet expectation was that the struggle was by definition systemic and ongoing, and therefore the whole system was, in principle, subject to the creation and re-creation, expansion and deterioration of spheres of influence. This understanding had a strong feedback to the two former characteristics: an ongoing systemic struggle called for even stronger military capabilities and intensified Sovietization.

In contrast, US policymakers viewed Marxist-Leninist communism as expansive and tended to agree with "Abraham Lincoln's confident assertion that this country is 'the last best hope of earth.'"[52] Consequently, Americans would "think of other nations' internal practices and institutions as either 'good' or 'bad', depending on their conformity to individualistic pluralism" and view the promotion of "liberal values abroad [...] as a principal U.S. value."[53]

As noted by Adam Quinn and Michael Cox, "The foundation of the United States was itself the embodiment of liberal principles triumphant," although liberalism only became "a defining feature of American foreign policy thinking" from the early twentieth century, and the Woodrow Wilson presidency, in particular, and only led to a foreign policy repertoire focused on "the need for independent capability and action on the part of the United States" in the Cold War.[54]

The foreign policy repertoire following from liberal ideology had stronger internal tensions than in the Soviet case. Liberalism may serve as the basis for both a liberalism of imposition actively intervening to secure the necessary conditions for individual freedom and a liberalism restraint respecting self-determination and freedom from outside intervention.[55] US Cold War foreign policy oscillated between the two, often pursuing them in parallel in different regions and toward different states in the same region,[56] and they are better understood as two ends in a continuum than two dichotomous categories. Thus, US Cold War foreign policy included widespread support for coup d'états and military interventions and peacetime deployment of US troops as well as a sustained effort to portray the United States as a "city on a hill," a model for the rest of the world. While liberalism in itself did not produce clear expectations about foreign policy, the context of a struggle with an anti-liberal expansionist ideology had a strong pull effect in the direction of a liberalism of imposition safeguarding against or preempting Soviet expansion.

In sum, the two hegemons' repertoires of expectation were incompatible and nonnegotiable. The United States and the Soviet Union saw themselves as part of a systemwide conflict with "no peripheries," each superpower being the "obsessing danger" of the other.[57] Each tolerated the sphere of influence of the other but viewed it as illegitimate and subject to change in an ongoing struggle between two expansive and universalistic ideologies over which norms were to dominate the international system.

In contrast, the universal struggle between repertoires of expectations in the new Cold War is more particularistic and less expansive. China has since the early 1990s played a central role in a group of non-liberal states, which have often offered a critical perspective on the actions and initiatives of the United States–led liberal West. However, so far Chinese policymakers have not conceptualized this critique in terms of a universalistic alternative to the United States. In contrast, the Chinese leadership continues to portray their country's path as "socialism with Chinese characteristics," while emphasizing the right of states to choose their own model for societal development and refraining from promoting the so-called Beijing

Consensus as a universalistic alternative to the liberal international order.[58] Despite the Biden administration's high-profile "Summit for Democracy" (and against China), liberal internationalism today plays a much less prominent role in US foreign policy than in the past. The summit has been criticized for including several countries with problematic human rights and democracy records—for example, Angola, Pakistan, and the Philippines—and the administration has continued the Trump administration's focus on a foreign policy for the middle class.[59] These characteristics of the New Cold War have important implications for the current struggle over the constitution and limitations of spheres of influence in the present international order.

Horizontal Repertoires of Expectations

How do the United States and China view their roles as hegemons vis-à-vis the hegemons of other spheres and the rules of the game for the international system?

China and the United States agree on a set of fundamental norms and practices for the international system. These norms and practices correspond to what English school theorists call "pluralist international society": a Westphalian order composed of "constitutionally insular" states viewing the territorial and political independence and survival of their own state as the most fundamental foreign policy raison d'être, and typically valuing the maintenance of international order above advances toward a more just international society. From this point of departure, the United States and China agree that great powers have special responsibilities (to maintain international order) and privileges (they need a larger room for manoeuver than small states and middle powers) to take care of these responsibilities.

While China has consistently pursued this course, it represents a change, if not transformation, in US foreign policy since the early post–Cold War period, when US policymakers pursued wars of regime change and actively supported international society's responsibility to protect civilians against their government. From President Obama's "leading from behind" policy over President Trump's "America First" to President Biden's "Foreign Policy for the middle class" and decision to leave Afghanistan after twenty years of warfare, the United States has retrenched from its post–Cold War policy of actively—and with military means if necessary—seeking to deepen and widen the membership of the liberal international order. During the Trump administration, the United States acknowledged not only the unavoidability but also the desirability of dividing the world into "one of grand spheres of influence apportioned to the United States, China and Russia."[60] Foreign secretary Rex Tillerson characterized the Monroe Doctrine as a "success" as he warned against Chinese influence in Latin America.[61] The Biden administration was different but seemed to follow a course of "organized hypocrisy": rejecting the notion of spheres of influence in principle but pursuing a sphere of influence policy in practice—for example, Europe and the Indo-Pacific.

This agreement on a pluralist Westphalian order has resulted in cooperation and agreement on a number of issues such as climate policy (including a joint announcement at the COP26 climate summit in 2021), counterterrorism (sharing information and intelligence), and even renewed efforts to enhance trade talks—all beginning from the shared starting point in a repertoire of expectations based on a pluralist Westphalian understanding of international society.

The Westphalian repertoire is both good and bad news for the prospects of peaceful change in a spheres of influence world. One positive effect is that pluralism is a better starting point for "agreeing to disagree" than a relationship locked in by expansive ideologies. This lowers the risk of great power war. The old Cold War was characterized by two rival repertoires of expectation based on incompatible ideologies. The new Cold War is based on a shared repertoire of expectations of autonomy and order as fundamentals of the international system. However, this does not preclude rivalry and conflict. Spheres of influence may take the form of "bounded orders"[62] rather than ideologically based "empires,"[63] but this creates new security challenges, most importantly how to identify and agree on the borders between these orders, and what room for maneouver to accept for each great power within its sphere of influence.

The nature and form of security challenges vary with the levels of contestation and sedimentation of the sphere of influence. The Indo-Pacific is the most prominent example of a contested sphere of influence, and for this reason it has become the epicenter for US-China rivalry. The region is politically, societally, and geographically diverse: a combination of landlocked states and island states, some of them geographically isolated, political regimes spanning the continuum from liberal democracy to various forms of autocratic regimes, and economic and societal development varying from small island developing states such as Tuvalu, Timor-Leste, and the Solomon Islands to globalized high-income countries such as Singapore, Taiwan, South Korea, and Australia. This diversity is mirrored in the region's institutional landscape with rivaling and relatively weak international organizations, and a number of states willing to change or diversify their allegiances as illustrated by the Solomon Islands' "switch" from recognizing Taiwan to cooperation with China in 2019. One country, India, has a claim to future great power status, and US-China disagreement over Taiwan makes the Indo-Pacific the most likely subject of a direct military confrontation between the two great powers. The boundaries of the Indo-Pacific as well as spheres of influence within the region remain disputed and are subject to constant negotiation and renegotiation and instability following from unequal growth rates and armaments and countries moving from one camp to the other or seeking to hedge between the two. For this reason, security challenges in the contested sphere of influence resemble the dynamics in a multipolar international system identified by Kenneth Waltz: multiple actors with shifting patterns of allegiance and alliance creates a risk of miscalculation that may lead to war even if this was not the intention of any of the states.

In contrast to the Indo-Pacific, the Euro-Atlantic is a highly sedimented sphere of influence dominated by the United States. China has no chance of challenging US hegemony, and US power is projected both bi- and multilaterally, the latter primarily through NATO. The area is populated by middle- to high-income liberal democratic states, most of them landlocked small states and middle powers embedded in NATO and the European Union, a close partner of the United States and unlikely to be a challenger in the foreseeable future, because of its security dependency on the United States. The sedimented nature of the Euro-Atlantic sphere of influence means that US-China rivalry takes place in the margins of the Euro-Atlantic in an ongoing negotiation on the outer boundaries of the sphere, mainly in Eastern Europe and the Arctic. Whereas hedging and non-alliance makes sense for small states and middle powers in the contested Indo-Pacific sphere of influence, they flock to Euro-Atlantic institutions not to be left in the contested margins, most recently exemplified by Sweden's and Finland's NATO membership. In the sedimented Euro-Atlantic sphere of influence, security challenges resemble those identified by Kenneth Waltz for a bipolar system: overreaction. The Chinese expectation that the Euro-Atlantic, including its institutional infrastructures, serves as a the most important basis for US power projection and the US expectation that China will seek to challenge and undermine this position results in both great powers focusing on the challenges and potential threat of the other.

However, the security dynamics inside and on the margins of the Euro-Atlantic also point to the importance of actors other than China and the United States for the emerging spheres of influence world. The European Union and Russia both play important roles for how the US-China rivalry will play out. The next section looks inside the spheres of influence and discusses the relationship between great powers and other states and how this relationship is shaped by competing repertoires of expectation.

Vertical Repertoires of Expectations

The emerging spheres of influence order will not only be decided by China's and the United States' repertoires of expectation and their ability to back these expectations with capabilities and competence. The internal constitution of spheres of influence depends on how the United States and China view their roles as hegemons within their spheres of influence and to what extent this is compatible with the expectations of the middle powers and small states within the sphere. Different means of governance within spheres will be based on different logics of consequence and appropriate action. There are likely to be tensions between great power supply of order and small state and middle power demand. Small states and middle powers mainly demand security and stability, allowing them to pursue their own agendas, whereas great powers tend to supply more elaborate orders, requiring other states to buy into their normative agendas. Variation in these normative agendas is likely to create significant differences between spheres of influence, both in terms of governance instruments and room for negotiation and, consequently, very different orders with different prospects for peaceful change. Again, the Indo-Pacific and the Euro-Atlantic illustrate the differences.

In the Indo-Pacific, small and middle power expectations to great power governance are diverse, reflecting the complexity of the states and their security challenges. Some small island development states without their own armed forces seek mainly aid for societal development as well as regime protection against outside dominance and domestic civil unrest. Some states, as exemplified by the Solomon Islands, may still be reluctant to trade autonomy for security to one great power and seek instead to hedge between the two. Other states like Vietnam seek to play a role akin to the one traditionally played by small states in the Euro-Atlantic: supporting multilateralism (in the case of Vietnam: the United Nations, UN, and the Association of Southeast Asian Nations, ASEAN) and seeking to act as bridgebuilder in the region and internationally.[64] Still other states might seek to pick and choose from the regional and international orders offered by the great powers. One example is Thailand, a country likely to continue to seek security shelter from the United States and to support economic liberalism while refusing to embrace liberal democracy.[65] Some countries, like the Philippines, have strong economic ties with China and security ties to the United States and may be subject to strengthening ties to either as repertoires of expectation vary with public opinion and leadership.[66] Countries with more capabilities and a history of independent foreign policymaking, most notably India and Australia, are likely to have their own take on what the Indo-Pacific is and should be.

In sum, repertoires of expectation in the Indo-Pacific vary widely, but where they converge is in the expectation of most states that a selective engagement in any order offered by the United States or China is both desirable and feasible. Consequently, neither the United States nor China is likely to dominate the region, and boundaries between US and Chinese orders in the Indo-Pacific are likely to remain subject to negotiation (and even blackmail as some smaller states may threaten to leave one great power for the other) in the foreseeable future. This is not necessarily bad for peaceful change in the region as it leaves a space for continued negotiation over what the Indo-Pacific is and should be, with a role for small states and middle powers to carve out their own space and act as bridgebuilders.

In the Euro-Atlantic, repertoires of expectation are converging around the two major institutions, NATO and the European Union. Most small states and middle powers in the region view the two organizations as suppliers of shelter against threats and risks and platforms for status seeking, voice opportunities, and, potentially, influence on the future regional order. While this has occasionally resulted in "capabilities-expectation" gaps[67]—that is, expectation for successful action exceeding the actual problem-solving capacity of the organization—no rival organization has emerged and both organizations remain pivotal for the Euro-Atlantic order. They are resilient and have proven their ability to adapt even to fundamental changes such as the end of the Cold War and the wars in former Yugoslavia and Ukraine. In contrast to the Indo-Pacific, small states and middle powers in the Euro-Atlantic on some issues seem to demand more order than the United States is willing to supply, as exemplified by the long-running attempt by US policymakers to make Europeans take more responsibility for their own security and order and downscale US engagement. However, on other issues, most notably when it comes to negotiations of a global order and linkages between the Euro-Atlantic order and the global order, European small states and middle powers vary in their support as well as in their expectations of the EU to take the role as a "third way" between rival great powers: a "normative power" based on liberal values rather than military power.[68]

Since the early 2010s, this set of expectations from European small and middle powers has been challenged by two developments. First, a large share of European electorates has votes for anti-liberal parties on the left and (in particular) the right. Second, some Central and Eastern European countries, most notably Hungary and Poland, have challenged parts of political liberalism, and the extent to which international organizations, the EU in particular, should uphold these values. This does not necessarily challenge US leadership as this challenge to political liberalism seems to mirror similar developments in the United States. However, as witnessed by the rapprochement between parts of the European right and Russia before the Russian invasion of Ukraine, the development shows that at least in part of Europe there is a demand for a less liberal order. This may leave a window of opportunity for China in future negotiations over the Euro-Atlantic order with a less prominent role for the United States. In particular, China may challenge the US Euro-Atlantic sphere of influence at the margins taking advantage of European dynamics of power and national interest, which continue to coexist with rationalist agendas of a shared interest in Euro-Atlantic cooperation and normative visions of a civil league of nations exercising normative power inside and outside the region.[69]

CONCLUSIONS

The sphere of influence is a key ordering device for international relations. With waning US power and willingness to bear the costs of international hegemony, spheres of influence are key for future regional and international orders. The constitution, maintenance, and impact of spheres of influence depend on the repertoires of expectations of the great powers, the compatibility of great power repertoires of expectation and the match between the great powers' repertoires, and the expectations of small states and middle powers.

The United States' and China's repertoires of expectation are converging around a view of the international system as an arena for power politics and contestation and with an—explicit or tacit—acknowledgment of the sphere of influence as a key ordering device for international affairs. While this is not surprising for China, it constitutes an important change of US expectations and a departure from the post–Cold War vision of a globalized liberal international order. This will not necessarily lead to a great power war. In contrast to the Cold War, the two dominant great powers' repertoires of expectations converge around a shared understanding of a pluralist international society with special roles and privileges for great powers, but at the same time more pragmatic and less ideologically driven than great power politics in the Cold War. In the Indo-Pacific, a contested sphere of influence, this is likely to result in an ongoing negotiation and renegotiation of spheres of influence and their boundaries as small states and middle powers hedge, bridge, and shift sides. In the Euro-Atlantic, a sedimented sphere of influence, a Chinese challenge to the United States is likely to take place in the margins, potentially taking advantage of skepticism toward liberal agendas in NATO and the EU.

Overall, a convergence around a norm of ordering by spheres of influence may increase stability in the international system, but it is also likely to reduce the potential for maximalist peaceful change—that is, "transformational change that takes place non-violently at the global, regional, interstate, and societal levels due to various material, normative and institutional factors, leading to deep peace among states, higher levels of prosperity and justice for all irrespective of nationality, race or gender."[70] At the same time, the risk of great power conflict will remain, where the borderlines between US and Chinese spheres of influence are contested—for example, Ukraine and Taiwan. For small states and middle powers, there are additional challenges. When the sphere of influence is a key ordering device of international affairs, sovereign equality is challenged, making small states and middle powers more vulnerable. Second, the increasing importance of spheres of influence creates more variation among small states and middle powers. Small states' strategic options are likely to be very different in the Euro-Atlantic and the Indo-Pacific, and whereas nonalignment becomes potentially more costly in the borderlands between spheres of influence, it is having a comeback in other parts of the international system.

NOTES

1. A first draft of this paper benefited from comments at the workshop "Resurging Great Power Conflicts and Changing Regional Orders" at McGill University, March 14, 2023. I would like to thank T.V. Paul, Alexandra Zeitz, Andrej Krickovic, Deborah Welch Larson, Amitav Acharya, Xiayou Pu, and Thierry Balzacq for comments. I thank Dwight Wilfred Robinson for research assistance.
2. Markus Kornprobst and T.V. Paul, "Globalization, Deglobalization and the Liberal International Order," *International Affairs* 97, no. 5 (September 2021): 1305.
3. G. John Ikenberry, "The End of Liberal International Order?," *International Affairs* 94, no. 1 (2018): 7–23.
4. John J. Mearsheimer, "Bound to Fail: The Rise and Fall of the Liberal International Order," *International Security* 43, no. 4 (April 2019): 7–50; Stewart M. Patrick, "Trump and World Order: The Return of Self-Help," *Foreign Affairs* 96, no. 2 (March 2017): 52–57.

5. Andrew Hurrell, "Kissinger and World Order," *Millennium: Journal of International Studies* 44, no. 1 (July 2015): 168.
6. Jeremy Shapiro, "Defending the Defensible: The Value of Spheres of Influence in U.S. Foreign Policy," Brookings, March 11, 2015, https://www.brookings.edu/articles/defending-the-defensible-the-value-of-spheres-of-influence-in-u-s-foreign-policy/.
7. Daniel Fried, "Two Alternatives to Trump's Global Vision," *The Atlantic*, October 11, 2018. This does not mean that the two superpowers always agreed on the boundaries of the spheres of influence. Much of the Global South was disputed and even in the 1948–49 Berlin blockade and throughout the Cold War, the United States refused to recognize the incorporation of the three Baltic states into the Soviet Union.
8. George H. W. Bush, "State of the Union Address," January 29, 1991.
9. Boutros Boutros-Ghali, "An Agenda for Peace: Preventive Diplomacy, Peacemaking and Peace-Keeping: Report of the Secretary-General pursuant to the Statement Adopted by the Summit Meeting of the Security Council on 31 January 1992" (New York: United Nations, January 31, 1992), https://digitallibrary.un.org/record/145749.
10. G. John Ikenberry, "Liberal Internationalism 3.0: America and the Dilemmas of Liberal World Order," *Perspectives on Politics* 7, no.1 (February 12, 2009): 71–87.
11. Charles L. Glaser, "A Flawed Framework: Why the Liberal International Order Concept Is Misguided," *International Security* 43, no. 4 (April 2019): 53.
12. Hal Brands and Charles Edel, "The Disharmony of the Spheres," *Commentary*, January 2018.
13. Colin Dueck, *Reluctant Crusaders Power, Culture, & Change in American Grand Strategy* (Princeton, NJ: Princeton University Press, 2008), 87; Evan N. Resnick, "Interests, Ideologies, and Great Power Spheres of Influence," *European Journal of International Relations* 28, no. 3 (June 7, 2022): 556.
14. Resnick, "Interests, Ideologies, and Great Power Spheres of Influence"; Amitai Etzioni, "Spheres of Influence: A Reconceptualization," *The Fletcher Forum of World Affairs* 39, no. 2 (Summer, 2015): 117.
15. For example, Graham Allison, "The New Spheres of Influence: Sharing the Globe with Other Great Powers," *Foreign Affairs* 99, no. 2 (March/April 2020): 30–40; Marcin Kaczmarski, "Non-Western Visions of Regionalism: China's New Silk Road and Russia's Eurasian Economic Union," *International Affairs* 93, no. 6 (September 23, 2017): 1357–76; Evan R. Sankey, "Reconsidering Spheres of Influence," *Survival* 62, no. 2 (March 3, 2020): 37–47; Benjamin Zala, "Interpreting Great Power Rights in International Society: Debating China's Right to a Sphere of Influence," *Journal of International Political Theory* 16, no. 2 (February 17, 2020): 210–30.
16. Susanna Hast, *Beyond the Pejorative: Sphere of Influence in International Theory Volume 239 of Acta Universitatis Lapponiensis* (Rovaniemi: Lapland University Press, 2011).
17. This understanding takes inspiration from Barry Buzan's discussion of international society. For the original argument on international society as a set of ideas in minds of foreign policymakers, a set of ideas in the minds of academics and a set of concepts defining the material and social structures of the international system, see Barry Buzan, *From International to World Society? English School Theory and the Social Structure of Globalisation* (Cambridge: Cambridge University Press, 2004), 12–14.

18. This third understanding is implicit in many policy discussions of spheres of influence but typically not included in English school understandings of primary or fundamental institutions, which include sovereignty, diplomacy, great power management, international law, and the balance of power as well as trade and environmental stewardship in more recent accounts. However, Hedley Bull views the sphere of influence as a tool for great power management. Hedley Bull, *The Anarchical Society* (London: Palgrave, 1977). For a discussion of the English school understanding of fundamental institutions, see Tonny Brems Knudsen, "The Institutions of International Society," *Oxford Research Encyclopedia of International Studies*, April 26, 2021, https://doi.org/10.1093/acrefore/9780190846626.013.547.
19. Stanley Hoffmann, "Hedley Bull and His Contribution to International Relations," *International Affairs* 62, no. 2 (1986): 193; Bull, *The Anarchical Society*.
20. Kenneth Ewart Boulding, *Conflict and Defence: A General Theory* (New York: Harper & Brothers, 1962), Chapter 12.
21. Etzioni, "Spheres of Influence: A Reconceptualization," 119.
22. Etzioni, "Spheres of Influence: A Reconceptualization," 117.
23. Nicholas Onuf, "A Constructivist Manifesto," in *Constituting International Political Economy (Vol. 10)*, eds. Kurt Burch and Robert Allen Denemark (Boulder, CO: Lynne Rienner Publishers, 1997), 108.
24. See for example, Angela Merkel, "Policy Statement by Federal Chancellor Angela Merkel on the Situation in Ukraine," https://www.bundesregierung.de/breg-en/service/archive/archive/policy-statement-by-federal-chancellor-angela-merkel-on-the-situation-in-ukraine-443796; Jeffrey Goldberg, "THE OBAMA DOCTRINE: The U.S. President Talks Through His Hardest Decisions about America's Role in the World," *The Atlantic*, April 2016, https://www.theatlantic.com/magazine/archive/2016/04/the-obama-doctrine/471525/; Hal Brands, "US Can't Let Russia Create a Sphere of Influence," *Bloomburg Opinion*, February 18, 2022, https://www.aei.org/op-eds/us-cant-let-russia-create-a-sphere-of-influence/.
25. Anders Wivel, "Living on the Edge: Georgian Foreign Policy between the West and the Rest," *Third World Thematics: A TWQ Journal* 1, no. 1 (January 2, 2016), 96. For the original argument on modern states and how they compare with postcolonial and postmodern states, see Georg Sørensen, *Changes in Statehood* (Houndmills: Palgrave, 2001).
26. G. John Ikenberry, "The Plot against American Foreign Policy: Can the Liberal Order Survive," *Foreign Affairs* 94, no. 1 (2017): 1–7.
27. Weifeng Zhou and Mario Esteban, "Beyond Balancing: China's Approach towards the Belt and Road Initiative," *Journal of Contemporary China* 27, no. 112 (2018): 487–501.
28. Charles E. Ziegler and Rajan Menon, "Neomercantilism and Great-Power Energy Competition in Central Asia and the Caspian," *Strategic Studies Quarterly* 8, no. 2 (Summer 2014): 17.
29. Daniel Twining, "Abandoning the Liberal International Order for a Spheres-of-Influence World Is a Trap for America and Its Allies | German Marshall Fund of the United States," German Marshall Fund of the United States, 2017, https://www.gmfus.org/news/abandoning-liberal-international-order-spheres-influence-world-trap-america-and-its-allies-0.
30. G. John Ikenberry, "The Future of the Liberal World Order: Internationalism after America," *Foreign Affairs* 96, no. 3 (2011): 56–68.

31. John G. Ikenberry, "Liberalism and Empire: Logics of Order in the American Unipolar Age," *Review of International Studies* 30, no. 4, (2004): 609–30.
32. Henry E. Hale, "25 Years after the USSR: What's Gone Wrong?," *Journal of Democracy* 27, no. 3 (2016): 27.
33. Daniel Deudney and G. John Ikenberry, "Liberal World: The Resilient Order," *Foreign Affairs* 97 (2018): 16.
34. Lucian M. Ashworth, "Realism and the Spirit of 1919: Halford Mackinder, Geopolitics and the Reality of the League of Nations," *European Journal of International Relations* 17, no. 2 (2011): 279–301.
35. Kenneth Waltz, *Theory of International Politics* (Boston: McGraw-Hill).
36. Brian Rathbun, "A Rose by Any Other Name: Neoclassical Realism as the Logical and Necessary Extension of Structural Realism," *Security Studies* 17, no. 2 (May 22, 2008): 294–321; Anders Wivel, "Realism in Foreign Policy Analysis," in *Oxford Research Encyclopedia on Politics*, 2017, 1–27.
37. John J. Mearsheimer, "The Causes and Consequences of the Ukraine War," *The National Interest*, June 23, 2022, https://leiterreports.typepad.com/files/causes-and-consequences-of-the-ukraine-crisis.national-interest.pdf.
38. See the discussion in Robert Gilpin, *War and Change in World Politics* (Princeton, NJ: Princeton University Press, 1981).
39. However, there seems to be some potential for developing neoclassical realism based on neoclassical realist attempts at theorizing what is between systemic structure (anarchy and polarity) and units (states), and how structural effects may vary with different conditions and contexts. A major contribution to the research program, Norrin M. Ripsman, Jeffrey W. Taliaferro, and Steven E. Lobell, *Neoclassical Realist Theory of International Politics* (Oxford: Oxford University Press, 2016) emphasizes the importance of the strategic environment. Hans Mouritzen and Anders Wivel, *Explaining Foreign Policy: International Diplomacy and the Russo-Georgian War* (Boulder, CO: Lynne Rienner Publishers, 2012) finds that factors at the "interstate level" (i.e., geopolitics) are most important for explaining foreign policy. A number of authors the importance of great power politics for regional security and policy, see, for example, Elias Götz, "Enemy at the Gates: A Neoclassical Realist Explanation of Russia's Baltic Policy," *Foreign Policy Analysis* 15, no. 1 (2019), 99–117.
40. See for example, J. Samuel Barkin and Patricia A. Weitsman, "Realist Institutionalism and the Institutional Mechanisms of Power Politics," in *International Institutions and Power Politics: Bridging the Divide*, eds. Anders Wivel and T.V. Paul (Washington, DC: Georgetown University Press, 2019), 23–40; Susanna Hast, *Spheres of Influence in International Relations* (London: Routledge, 2016); Cornelia Navari, "The Concept of Practice in the English School," *European Journal of International Relations* 17, no. 4 (2011): 611–30.
41. Onuf, "A Constructivist Manifesto," 13.
42. Hast, *Beyond the Pejorative*, 16.
43. Filippo Costa Buranelli, "Spheres of Influence as Negotiated Hegemony—the Case of Central Asia," *Geopolitics* 23, no. 2 (2018): 378–403.
44. Onuf, "A Constructivist Manifesto," 108.
45. Etzioni, "Spheres of Influence: A Reconceptualization," 17.
46. Geddes W. Rutherford, "Spheres of Influence: An Aspect of Semi-Suzerainty," *American Journal of International Law* 20, no. 2 (1926): 300–325.

47. Brigitte Weiffen, Andrea Gawrich, and Vera Axyonova, "Reorganizing the Neighborhood? Power Shifts and Regional Security Organizations in the Post-Soviet Space and Latin America," *Journal of Global Security Studies* 6, no. 1 (2021): 1.
48. Bertram D. Wolfe, "Communist Ideology and Soviet Foreign Policy," *Foreign Affairs* 41, no. 1 (1962): 157–58, 161–62.
49. Nicholas Ross Smith, *A New Cold War: Assessing the Current US-Russia Relationship* (Cham: Palgrave, 2022), 41.
50. William Curti Wohlforth, *The Elusive Balance: Power and Perceptions during the Cold War* (Ithaca, NY: Cornell University Press, 1993).
51. Nicholas Ross Smith, *A New Cold War: Assessing the Current US-Russia Relationship* (Cham: Palgrave, 2022), 41–42.
52. Tony Smith, "Making the World Safe for Democracy in the American Century," in *The Ambiguous Legacy: U.S. Foreign Relations in the "American Century,"* ed. Michael J. Hogan (Cambridge: Cambridge University Press, 1999), 30.
53. Joseph Lepgold and Timothy McKeown, "Is American Foreign Policy Exceptional? An Empirical Analysis," *Political Science Quarterly* 110, no. 3 (1995): 372.
54. Adam Quinn and Michael Cox, "For Better, for Worse: How America's Foreign Policy Became Wedded to Liberal Universalism," *Global Society* 21, no. 4 (October 2007), 502, 506, 510.
55. Georg Sørensen, "Liberalism of Restraint and Liberalism of Imposition: Liberal Values and World Order in the New Millennium," *International Relations* 20, no. 3 (2006): 251–72.
56. Brendan Rittenhouse Green, "Two Concepts of Liberty: US Cold War Grand Strategies and the Liberal Tradition," *International Security* 37, no. 2 (2012), 9–43.
57. Kenneth N. Waltz, "The Stability of a Bipolar World," *Daedalus* 93, no. 3 (1964), 882.
58. Andreas Bøje Forsby, "The Nexus of Systemic Power and Identity: Structural Variations of the US-China Great Power Rivalry," in *Polarity in International Relations: Past. Present, Future*, eds. Nina Græger, Bertel Heurlin, Ole Wæver, and Anders Wivel (Cham: Palgrave, 2022), 244–45.
59. Andrew Gawthorpe, "Taking US Foreign Policy for the Middle Class Seriously," *The Washington Quarterly* 45, no. 1 (2022): 57–75.
60. Nathan Gardels, "Trump Is Not the Leader of the U.S.—Just of His Base," *The Washington Post*, July 19, 2018.
61. Robbie Gramer and Kieth Johnson, "Tillerson Praises Monroe Doctrine, Warns Latin America of 'Imperial' Chinese Ambitions," *Foreign Policy*, February 2, 2018.
62. Mearsheimer, "Bound to Fail."
63. Geir Lundestad, "'Empire by Invitation' in the American Century," *Diplomatic History* 23, no. 2 (1999): 189–217.
64. Thuy T. Do, "Vietnam's Prudent Pivot to the Rules-Based International Order," *International Affairs* 99, no. 4 (2023): 1557–73.
65. Chanintira na Thalang, "Unpacking Thailand's Conceptions of and Position within the Liberal International Order," *International Affairs* 99, no. 4 (2023): 1519–36.
66. Charmaine Misalucha-Willoughby, "The Philippines and the Liberal Rules-Based International Order," *International Affairs* 99, no. 4 (2023): 1537–55.
67. For the original conceptualization of the capabilities-expectations gap (which focused on the EU), see Christopher Hill, "The Capability-Expectations Gap, or

Conceptualizing Europe's International Role," *JCMS: Journal of Common Market Studies* 31, no. 3 (1993): 305–328.
68. Ian Manners, "Normative Power Europe: A Contradiction in Terms?," *JCMS: Journal of Common Market Studies* 40, no. 2 (2002): 235–58.
69. Anders Wivel, "Peaceful Change in Western Europe: From Balance of Power to Political Community?," In *The Oxford Handbook of Peaceful Change in International Relations*, eds. T.V. Paul, Deborah Welch Larson, Harold A. Trinkunas, Ralf Emmers, and Anders Wivel (Oxford: Oxford University Press, 2021), 569–86.
70. T.V. Paul, "The Study of Peaceful Change in World Politics," *The Oxford Handbook of Peaceful Change in International Relations*, eds. T.V. Paul, Deborah Welch Larson, Harold A. Trinkunas, Ralf Emmers, and Anders Wivel (Oxford: Oxford University Press, 2021), 4.

CHAPTER 4

The Ideological Sources of Great Power Competition in the Regions

Thierry Balzacq and Vera Grantseva

Major power competitions are primarily a contest of ideas.[1] At first sight, this verges on a facile claim. But heated debates over the origins and evolution of the Cold War invite moderation of our judgment. In fact, scholars have spent considerable analysis in establishing whether, for example, the Cold War was determined by material circumstances such as the distribution of capabilities or conditioned by ideological commitments derived from domestic social processes. At the theoretical level, the debate involved realism, which defended a material account, and liberalism, which granted more credit to domestic configurations. Refusing to take sides, constructivism has shown that the either/or approach to the Cold War's logic was limited and limiting.[2] This account is apt, for the Cold War sprang from different ideas about world politics, which underpinned and endowed material structures with meaning. Seen thus, the Cold War expressed a distinctive social order that drew its signature character from the ideas that contestants attached to it. Ergo, the demise of the Cold War was preceded and accompanied by a waning of the socialist ideology that had once provided steam for the Soviet Union's grand strategy.[3] In sum, that the implications of ideological divides *may* be obvious does not make them less epochal. Profound changes in both their content and manifestation in major powers' grand strategies set new problems that beg for scrutiny.

The aim of this chapter is to explore how the commitment to certain ideas shapes the grand strategies of major power contestants and influences the contours and evolution of regional orders today. It is true that the new competition between major powers is different both in terms of the polarity of the system and the tone of ideological constructs that underpin it. Yet, the enduring reality is that ideological constituents of great powers' grand strategies are the basic wiring of regional orders. Also crucial, but less frequently remarked on and therefore meriting more attention, is that despite the importance of the ideational underpinning of great power competition, our tools for explaining how ideologies produce the imputed effects remain vestigial. In grand strategy, a neglected approach is to emphasize policies that states pick in order to transform the outside world. As Paul Kennedy puts it, the "crux of grand strategy lies . . . in *policy*."[4] Major states have their own preferences about the policies they privilege in responding to others' challenges. We can nonetheless categorize the policies according to the degree of agency that major powers allow to their contestants—keep them in check, overthrow or capture them—balancing, subversion, and usurpation. Of course, these are three ideal policies (in the abstract) through which the major power contest is played out. More often than not, indeed, major powers combine these policies in a variety of ways. Further, it is possible to identify other policies that serve as the vehicle of great power competition. In our view, these three seem the most frequent.

This essay's main contribution is the identification of policies that reveal how ideology affects major powers' approach to ordering the world, at the regional and international levels. Its outline is as follows. The first section examines the concept of ideology, with an eye toward understanding its external manifestations. The second section explores what this conceptualization implies, regarding the creation and implementation of grand strategy. In the third section, the essay excavates the policies through which regional competition takes shape. Three policies are discussed, one relatively well understood in International Relations (IR), another whose study is rising, and a third that is less common: balancing, subversion, and usurpation. The fourth section investigates how great powers employ ideology in order to cultivate a regional order that provides a congenial environment for their grand strategies. The fourth section evaluates the relative empirical merit of our policies. Because it is difficult to study the various interactions between a broad range of major powers' grand strategies across several countries, we chose instead to examine how ideological contests between China, Russia, and the United States influence Central Asia, focusing on Kazakhstan. In this light, Kazakhstan is an exemplar of great power competition in the region. This offers us better access to the relational nature of grand strategies as much as it allows us to tap into the inner workings of the three policies.

IDEOLOGY AND GRAND STRATEGY

The word grand strategy is used differently in reference to state's relation to the rest of the world.[5] Here it is defined as a meaningful articulation of relevant resources to realize an actor's highest political priorities of what a state cares about in the medium to long term. States can calculate how to best align means and ends in order to create an environment that is conducive to what they care about. But such efforts occur "against a backdrop of certain entrenched national ideas about what behavior is appropriate."[6] Ideas and ideologies are the glue that hold together constitutive components of a grand strategy. Ideology, simply put, refers to an interrelated set of actionable ideas about the state's identity and place in the world; its goals, values, and interests; and the foundations of its relations to others. Ideology forges an image of the world and shapes how actors perceive and engage with it. In pluralist societies, ideologies compete for prominence. Subnational groups that participate in the development of grand strategy are mostly divided along ideological lines.[7] Once an ideology achieves dominance, it exerts influence on grand strategic choices by providing meaning and direction to a state's overall foreign policy action.

Grand strategy is a thought-practice. Unless one examines how the ideas a grand strategy embodies play out in the world, it is difficult to ascertain whether such ideas exist. A. I. Richards puts it in the following way: "An idea or a notion, like the physicists' ultimate particles and rays, is only known by what it does. Apart from its dress or other signs it is not identifiable."[8] We can trace the influence of ideology on regional order by assessing how it affects state's strategic agendas. Of course, it is easy to counter that states often justify their action by calling on a specific ideology. As such, scholars should be wary not to accord too much weight to what states claim; states, so the argument goes, do not mean what they say. We disagree with this view. In a constructivist vein, we take discourse seriously, but we do not do so unreflexively. Beginning with a working definition of ideology, this section continues with the discussion of how ideology achieves its effects, including naming and argumentation. However, we do not just explore their inner workings but crucially rely on these ideological pathways to indicate how ideology connects thinking and practical aspects of grand strategy.

Conceptualizing Ideology

We start with a simple assumption: Ideologies are mainly belief systems that are common to a cluster of people.[9] Two semantic dimensions underlie this assumption. First, ideologies are a kind of mental representation. Second, such mental representations are not individuals' properties but are shared across a given community. Political ideology, writes Michael Freeden, refers to: "A set of ideas, beliefs, opinions, and values that (1) exhibit a recurring pattern, (2) are held by significant groups, (3) compete over providing and controlling plans for public policy, [and] (4) do so with the aim of justifying, contesting or changing the social and political arrangements and processes of a political community."[10] It is in this very specific sense that ideologies are said to be a form of social cognition—that is, a "socially shared beliefs system."[11] These two semantic dimensions are interdependent. Taken together, however, they risk validating the view that ideologies are only a set of mental propositions. We, therefore, direct attention to external manifestations of ideology—that is to say, enter into the ways in and through which ideologies contribute to policy functions. According to Wendt, an externalist approach means three things. "The first is that thoughts are constituted at least in part by external context rather than solely in the heads of individuals, since how thoughts get carved up or 'individuated' depends on what 'conceptual grid' is used. (. . .) Thinking depends *logically* on social relations, *not just* causally," asserts Wendt.[12] Second, "truth conditions are 'owned' by the community, not by individuals."[13] Third, "meanings depend on the practices, skills, and tests that connect the community to the objects represented in discourse."[14]

In grand strategy, to narrow our focus, ideology achieves its external impact in two fundamental ways: "naming" and argumentation. According to Ernesto Laclau, naming gives meaning and coherence to a phenomenon.[15] In addition, it is through naming that people come to identify themselves with an account or a policy. Thus, naming is a process through which people "come to see themselves or their interests as expressed by [ideologies]— that is, how they develop sometimes passionate emotional identification with ideological propositions or promises."[16] Such naming takes the form of concepts that aim to supply the grand strategy of the day with an intellectual "framework," an "organizing principle," and an "orienting principle" or a "decisive point."[17] In US grand strategy, for example, such names include "deep engagement," "restraint," "selective engagement," and "primacy."[18] Interestingly, these names usually work one against another, in ways that mirror ideological functions.

The second way through which the external manifestation of ideology can be traced is by means of rhetoric, narrative, and discourse. This is not the place to discuss the content and form of each of these concepts. Nor do we have time and space to adjudicate their relative appropriateness. Instead, what we would like to indicate is that ideologies are both conveyed by and embodied in talk and text.[19] Ideology has a bearing on grand strategy by virtue of its cognitive function and its argumentative leverage. But this leaves the exact magnitude of ideology's impact unspecified. We recognize that such effect is at best indeterminate, but we do not want to support the view that it is an epiphenomenon, as rationalists would encourage us to think. Rather, the most interesting question is: How does ideology produce its effect? We suggest that ideological arrangements provide actors with convenient answers to a variety of circumstances and challenges as much as a way of understanding the world and their place within it. In this sense, ideology, like culture, has a filtering effect on decision-making processes.[20]

The notion of ideology as a "filter" means several things that boil down to two important ideas. On the one hand, ideology is not only a shared mental representation but also an "argumentional resource; it is a playbook as it were, providing ready-made 'cognitive shortcuts' to assist in grasping a situation but also ways of making political claims about it."[21] On the other hand, ideology establishes a normative order—that is, an order of justification that throttles certain options as much as it legitimizes others.[22] Such a palliative purpose enables ideology, among other things, to suppress ambiguity and impose which political alternative prevails. An essential manner in which this justification works is through argumentation and narratives.[23] However, what constitutes an appropriate justifying approach to grand strategy belongs to research that situates ideology within its context, which then allows it to "acquire its significance and at the same time the emotional power to inspire identification."[24]

Ideologies, Policies, and Regional Orders

Major powers can mobilize their ideology in many different ways and react to competing ideological pressures in distinctive fashions. That caution duly acknowledged, ideology can connect states to the world peacefully or through rivalry and war. Ideology integrates, selects, and separates. In *Sailing the Water's Edge*, for example, Helen V. Milner and Dustin Tingley use the variance in the degree of ideological differences to account for preferences among policy instruments.[25] For them, ideology means "beliefs about the dispositions of foreign actors and the appropriate way to deploy government resources to deal with them."[26] Henceforth, different ideological commitments, say between conservatives and liberals, support distinct policy choices and related means to achieve them. The wider the gap between ideologies over a given policy resource, the more difficult it is for the executive to fashion consensus across the dividing lines.

This essay, as we have argued above, emphasizes how ideology allows states to challenge or create a regional order that serves its interests. We are not inquiring into the formation of these ideologies. While useful, such accounts often suggest rather than explain why ideology matters let alone how it affects international order. In contrast, we are more concerned with how ideology is put into circulation—that is, how it becomes active and alive. To do so, we excavate policies that energize given ideologies to produce regional orders, of a specific shape and content. The essay identifies three policies that link ideologies to a set of strategic comportments: balancing, subversion, and usurpation. Whether they are status quo or revisionists, states rely more often than not on a combination of balancing, subversion, and usurpation to hook their ideas to the world. These policies are therefore core explanatory forces yielding ideological effects.

It is fair to ask whether these policies tell us something about the objectives sought and the means selected. They don't. In peace or war, a fundamental subject of discussion is threat identification and the connection of means and ends—that is, resources mobilization and allocation. The role of grand strategy is to help a state ensure its security at costs that it can sustain. Yet, that a material assessment takes precedence over others is highly dependent on the extent to which it is either effectively supported by or integrated with an ideational account. Ideology provides coordinates that lend intellectual significance to the relations between means and ends. Many of the problems of states' grand strategies arise from the fact they treat the relationship between means and ends as a mere technical problem devoid of meaning. This is another way of saying that even when means and ends are poorly reconciled or states seem to overstretch, ideology serves as a justificatory if not legitimation tool, one function of which is to inhibit alternative domestic voices. Below, we move from a policy that is probably most familiar to IR scholars to the ones we are less acquainted with.

The first policy is balancing.[27] A consistent tract of research in social psychology shows that ideological rivalries are zero-sum games. Because actors are pessimists about one another's intentions, they tend to assume that confrontation with the opposite ideology is unavoidable.[28] "Ideological polarization," which is a function of the "degree of ideological differences" between two states, tends to disable cooperation between actors.[29] But cooperation remains possible between nations that entertain different sets of ideological commitments, "when any one of the four major sources of alliance are extremely strong, or when there are a number of these factors in existence [balancing against a shared threat, advancing offensive international goals, countering a domestic threat, advocating and protecting shared ideological principles]."[30]

Be that as it may, the default policy inclination, in the context of ideological polarization, is offensive strategy, particularly in a bipolar situation, wherein ideological aversion erects uphill barriers to ideological alignment.

A typical consequence of ideological polarization is the policy of ideological outreach. Exporting ideology abroad can serve two functions. First, states may want to convert other states or groups within other states to their ideology in order to sap its social cohesion or contain the influence of the rival's sets of values, beliefs, and attitudes. Second, ideological export is suitable for widening the network of allies. Taken together, as they should, these functions indicate that ideological outreach's primary aim is to improve a nation's security, by deterring aggression against it and raising the costs of any attack against its interests. However, the success of such a strategy hinges on the state's ability to translate any deleterious action into ideological terms, which constitute the legitimating principle of the influence it wields.

The competition that used to pit Iran against Saudi Arabia in the Middle East is a typical case of ideological balancing. In the Yemeni conflict, for example, both regimes supported groups that come closer to their ideological line. Thus, Iran sides with the Houthis while the former Yemeni government is aided by Saudi Arabia. However, this ideological balancing rests on the material power that Iran and Saudi Arabia are able to wield in favor of their allies. The ideological balancing that characterizes Iran's and Saudi Arabia's strategic moves in the region helps account for some of the dynamics that affected the Syrian war and the 2017 Lebanese political crisis. Of course, each situation exhibits specificities that ideological balancing alone cannot fully explain or encompass.

The second policy is subversion. It is defined here as the "undermining or detachment of the loyalties of significant political and social groups within the victimized state, and their transference, under ideal conditions, to the symbols and institutions of the aggressor."[31] Subversion allows states to engage in conflictual interactions that remain short of war. Subversion can be direct or indirect.[32] It is direct when a state intervention is unmediated—that is, it does not rely on an identifiable support inside another polity. By contrast, indirect subversion refers to the mobilization of proxy forces within a foreign state, the aim of which is to coerce, blackmail, or undermine the cohesion of the latter. The primary purpose of subversion is to interfere in another state's domestic politics in order to challenge and weaken its authority. During the Cold War, for example, both the United States and the Soviet Union employed different forms of subversion, including covert action and propaganda.[33] Today, the scholarship on subversion focuses on sponsorship of local opposition groups, electoral intrusion, and disinformation.[34] It is in this specific way that subversion intersects with hybrid warfare.[35] Being opaque, subversion can be difficult to pin down. However, it can become visible and overtly spoken about by the state that employs it when it is portrayed as counter-subversion.

The third policy is usurpation, which we conceptualize as the creation of a new discursive order that builds on but reorients the normative commitments constitutive of postcolonial politics in a way that facilitates domination.[36] Some states that present themselves as subaltern subjects in world politics, due either to past colonization or a perceived exclusion from centers of institutional power, often claim to speak on behalf of the oppressed.[37] That is, usurpation draws upon a broad sentiment of victimization to support its case. However, authoritarian regimes deny the oppressed, who are

Table 4.1: A Typology of Policies in Grand Strategy Competition

Policies	Logics	Examples
Balancing	Ideologies are zero-sum alternatives; states react to the rise of a competing ideology by promoting their own or aligning with a rival ideology that fits the core goals they pursue; this maintains a degree of ideological polarity within the region/system.	China-US in the Gulf region
Subversion	A state tries to alter the ideological appeal of another state or group of states by undermining their authority either directly or indirectly; if successful, this erodes the ideological edge of the competing state or at least exposes ideological cleavages within the targeted country, which a third country can exploit to its foreign policy advantage.	Russia in the Donbass region to counter Kiev leaning toward a liberal EU
Usurpation	To fight a rival ideology that enjoys primacy in a third country, states resort to discourses of anti-domination to justify their intervention; paradoxically, this negates the agency of the third country. Sometimes, an authoritarian state justifies its alignment with a state of a similar political regime against a liberal country, which it portrays as a colonial power. It denies its own people what it claims the colonial power took from it: representation. Thus, subversion relies upon silencing and denial of representation. It is an appropriation of local domination to fight international domination.	Russia in Central African Republic, Burkina Faso, and Mali

the target of their policies, an autonomous voice in world politics.[38] Usurpation occurs often, but not only, in postcolonial settings. Indeed, former colonies are more sensitive and receptive to anti-domination discourses.[39] Be that as it may, a state usurps other states' voices when they evoke anticolonialism/anti-domination of adversaries to conceal their own policies of control.[40] Usurpation is less about domination against anti-domination. Rather, it involves both terms but redraws the boundaries and the relation between the two in order to assert a moral authority, which ultimately reproduces structures of domination at the regional or local levels.[41] Table 4.1 summarizes these three ideal types.

IDEOLOGIES AND GRAND STRATEGIES' COMPETITION IN CENTRAL ASIA

Grand strategizing is conducted at three levels: designing, mobilization, and implementation. While it is possible to demarcate the implementation stage from the other two, at least in theory, designing and mobilization rarely occur in separate sequences. Be that as it may, ideology does not change meaning and form to fit each level's processes and objectives. Rather, features associated with ideology are expressed in distinct ways by each level of grand strategizing. For example, at the design level, ideology manifests a community's political thinking. In this sense, ideology illuminates political principles and goals around which a nation organizes its relations with the rest of the world. According to John Gerring, "By organizing and interpreting the world an ideology helps the subject to act within that world."[42] But the characterization of the world opposes different domestic groups that hold competing ideas about what constitutes a threatening development. The ability to set threat priorities yields political benefits, both in terms of material power position and symbolic authority, hence the struggle between domestic blocs both over threat identification and the most appropriate remedies. In Robert Jervis's words, "The way people perceive data is influenced not only by their cognitive structure and theories about other actors but also by what they are concerned with at the time they perceive the information."[43] That is, ideology participates in threat assessment, along with material concerns. According to Haas: "Power and ideologies ... frequently work in tandem to generate threat perceptions. Power variables determine the universe of groups that possess the capacity to harm others."[44] True, but core ideological beliefs influence what a group considers threatening, and domestic politics involves groups whose singularity is in large part ideologically based. That is, ideology is an action-inspiring shared beliefs system. In other words, "the significance of ideology in mobilization is not that it 'causes one to do' but that it 'gives one cause for doing.'"[45] Below, we examine the ideological competition between Russia, the United States, and China in Kazakhstan, focusing on the policy preferences of their respective grand strategies.

With the dissolution of the Soviet Union, Central Asia has gone through a sustained transformation. United under the Russian Tsarist control and consequently by the Communist state in the past, five Central Asian countries (Kazakhstan, Kyrgyzstan, Tajikistan, Turkmenistan, and Uzbekistan) found themselves, at the end of the twentieth century, apparently free to formulate their political and economic trajectories. Gradually, however, this promise melted away and most of the Central Asian countries turned out to be torn between various great powers' ambitions in the region.[46] Specifically, the competition for primacy in Central Asia mainly involves Russia, China, and the United States. Each of these great powers has its own history of relations with the Central Asian region. Russia has a long colonizer's past, China had imperial projects for the region, and the United States appeared as a new and (presumably) different type of contender. We discuss each major power's strategy below. But we insist on the interactive nature of a regional order in the making. That is, these apparent separate strategies only acquire their meaning in their relationships with others.

Russia's strategy toward Kazakhstan is intertwined with its vision of the post-Soviet area. Accordingly, for the past thirty years, the Russian government has striven to create a new regional order in the post-Soviet zone. The shared past within the Soviet empire underlines paradoxical relationships. It creates profound dependencies between the former metropole and its colonies and at the same time burdens the relationship with painful and sometimes contested memories. Be that as it may, throughout the 1990s, Russia pursued an integrationist policy, the aim of which was to reunite the fifteen former Soviet republics—Commonwealth of Independent States (CIS). However, this project lacked concrete economic and political strategies. Eventually, only eleven former republics became members of the CIS—three Baltic republics and Turkmenistan refrained from joining it. Indeed, many participants acknowledge that this initiative was less an original project than a form of civilized divorce. Thus, in early 2000, Moscow rebranded the scheme and moved toward a Eurasian concept of "cooperation" in the post-Soviet space.

The New Eurasian project was initially designed as a purely economic endeavor, the core elements of which were custom rules and trade. By 2015, this project took a concrete shape. An agreement between five former Soviet republics—Russia, Belarus, Kazakhstan, Kyrgyzstan, and Armenia—was signed, with an open door to all other former members of the USSR. Among them, however, only Moldova (in 2017) and Uzbekistan (in 2020) made a step toward a closer cooperation with the Eurasian Economic Union (hereinafter EAEU) by signing an agreement to strengthen economic transactions. But the Eurasian project was promoted by Russia even beyond the former USSR zone: Vietnam, Singapore, Serbia, Iran, and China signed a free trade agreement with EAEU. Yet, none of them agreed to become a full member of a Russian-led economic union. Moscow nonetheless tried to draw in its orbit Tajikistan, through cooperation arrangements in the security sector. This proved a little bit more successful, due to the fact that Tajikistan has remained significantly dependent on Russia's army for the protection of its borders with Afghanistan. In sum, over three decades, Russia made significant effort to bind its neighbors through and within economic and security projects. Figure 4.1 provides an overview.

In addition to economic and security goals, Russia sought to provide an ideological underpinning to its regional order.[47] Although never articulated explicitly in a state strategy, an ideological connotation has accompanied Russian regional projects since the early 2000s. By 2014, the contours of the emerging Russia's ideology took a sharper relief, though it remained an eclectic form of conservatism.[48] This ideology consists of three main features: the revival of the religion,[49] statism,[50] and a strong opposition to gender self-identifications.[51] Moscow's ideas remained very unclear about the concrete details of its understanding of the modern state, society, and family and hasn't transformed into a full-fledged and coherent ideology. But labeled as "traditional values," this

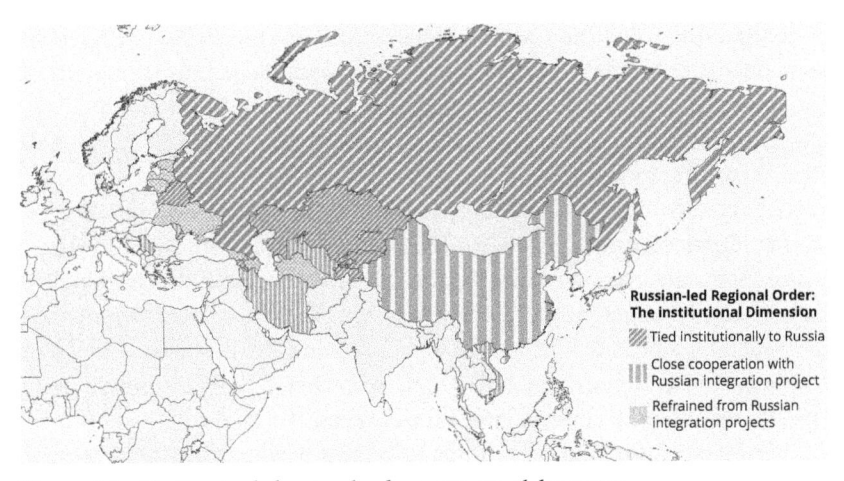

Figure 4.1. The Russian-led regional order: institutional dimension

ideology's core ideas attract countries whose governments oppose the universal liberal values promoted by the West, in particular the United States and the EU. The influence of this ideology ripples across not only neighboring countries but also Africa, Latin America, and the Middle East.[52]

In Kazakhstan, Russian ideological balancing targets Western influence as much as it signals an alternative to European and American values. As the Russian government secured its control over mass media in Kazakhstan, it invested in promoting a conservatist agenda and keeping back Western ideas, in order to protect "traditional values," which are considered as important constituents of national identity and a pillar of political stability. This narrative is often recalled by the Russian strategic elite in meetings and conferences with Kazakh leaders.

Subversion is a crucial mechanism in Russia's attempts to control Kazakhstan. It is not a freestanding mechanism, however. Russia uses subversion, in this context, both as a complementary approach to outperform Western adversaries and as a backup instrument, should balancing fail. To that effect, Russia has developed an extensive network of Russian-speaking populations across various regions in Kazakhstan (mostly in the north and in the east). These very diverse groups are seen as "naturally" aligned with the Russian agenda and ready to defend their national identity and traditional values, including against their home state, Kazakhstan.[53] Russia employs two main forms of leverage to convince these populations that their authentic character is Russian, namely propaganda and financial support (e.g., the phenomenon of "professional compatriots"). Further, given the Kazakhstani vulnerability in the oil pipelines network, subversion strategy sometimes takes the form of energy blackmailing.[54] Thus, in spring 2022, the Russian government blocked the Caspian pipeline, which exports 90% of Kazakhstani oil, when Astana refused to express open and unconditional support of the war and the annexation of Ukrainian territories.

As the Russian government used oppressive methods in domestic politics, it exported these techniques to Central Asia's societies, which it perceived as its "natural" zone of influence. In Kazakhstan, for example, it tried on numerous occasions to silence Kazakhstani opposition, which rejected Kazakhstani involvement in EAEU, on the grounds that it was both politically counterproductive and detrimental to its economy. The Russian state TV routinely attacked officials in Astana for being feeble and too indulgent toward domestic opposition voices that, in its view, have been undermining the strategic alliance between the two countries.

However, usurpation turned out to be less productive and sometimes destructive when it came to the promotion of its ideology. Kazakhstan's resistance toward Russian conservatism lie in the postcolonial nature of the relations between the two states. Although Moscow has never acknowledged the colonial type of the Soviet rule during seventy years, Kazakhstani society perceived its relations with Russia from the colonial perspective: without dealing openly with it, Russian ongoing neocolonialism remained a major impediment to Kazakhstan ideological alignment.[55]

The postcolonial prism, which frames the interactions between Russia and Kazakhstan, matters in understanding the relationships between the latter and China, on the one hand, and the United States, on the other. Thus, the Kazakhstani civil society accused China of neocolonialism while the political elites benefiting from Chinese financial support remained silent. The civil society reacts to what it fears is a Chinese expansionist policy. The strategic engagement between the two states started as an essentially economic cooperation, foreshadowing mutual Kazakhstani-Chinese benefits. But it gradually morphed into a wide-ranging political project under China's aegis.

Although the Chinese government has never openly articulated the ideological components of its foreign policy, a set of assumptions has been implicitly included in Chinese offers to Central Asian countries. Since the reforms of Deng Xiaoping in 1980s and the collapse of the communist project in Russia at the end of the twentieth century, Beijing has been adjusting its socialist ideology to the capitalist market rules embodied by the United States and the West.[56] For three decades, Chinese leadership successfully combined these elements and pursued the "peaceful rise" strategy, which emphasized economic growth, poverty alleviation, and political stability.[57]

Behind the proclaimed political neutrality of China's grand strategy lies an ideological hesitancy: China has abandoned the idea of the socialist expansion and worldwide revolution after Mao Zedong and at the same time opposed the Western liberal project.[58] By 2013, when Xi Jinping came to power and initiated regional ambitious projects such as One Belt, One Road, it became apparent that ideology uncertainty has been weakening Chinese grand strategy and undermining its status in the great power competition both at a regional and international level. As a consequence, Chinese officials started to talk publicly about the Chinese ideological project of "common destiny for mankind," which now stitches together the different segments of its grand strategy.[59] Yet, the lack of specification impaired the general appeal of this ideological mantra. Nevertheless, China continued to exert a certain ideological influence on its counterparts in order to balance Western influence. As Temur Umarov observes, Beijing officials started to be more assertive and pushier regarding political and ideological conditions that they included in their economic cooperation with Central Asian countries.[60] But compared to the Western political conditions, which are articulated openly in the beginning of the negotiations, the Chinese ideological claims were introduced at later stages of the project. Beijing made a lot of effort to present its cooperation projects to Kazakhstani elites and society in exclusively economic terms with "no strings attached." In contrast, Western cooperation arrangements involved stringent political conditions (transparency, anti-corruption, rule of law, and so on). China knew that any such criteria were regarded by the Kazakhstani as humiliating aspersions.[61]

The US approach to cooperation is based on conditionality, while China relies more on entrapment. It requires ideational commitments from its partners when the project's implementation is well underway—that is, when the stakes for their counterparts have become high and the fears of losing economically beneficial projects with China are strong.[62] China's ideational entrapment demands the respect of the territorial integrity (more precisely, positioning toward Taiwan issue) and noninterference with domestic political affairs (i.e., neither reproof of human rights violation nor condemnation of Uyghurs' persecution). The two principles were subsequently embedded in joint projects with China. It is worth noting, however, that silencing the Uyghurs' problem—and more broadly persecution of the Muslim community in China where ethnic Kazakhs are present, too (about 1.5 million persons)—was imposed by Beijing and accepted by Astana despite discontent and pressure from Kazakhstani civil society. China was able to use such implicit subversions to control Kazakhstani elites due to the increasing significance of the trade with China and its investments, which have increasingly rendered Kazakhstan dependent on and vulnerable to China's influence.

Since 2016, however, China's presence in the country has taken heat. There have been, for example, massive protests against the implantation of additional Chinese factories in Kazakhstan. It appears that China has faced a significant challenge in usurpation of ideological narratives in Kazakhstan as local society perceived its Eastern neighbor as a neocolonial power intending to subjugate and control smaller actors in the region. Thus, the attempts to discredit Western (more precisely American) projects as neocolonial and exploitative have been mostly limited to the blog of the Chinese ambassador on Facebook.[63] In other words, the complete ignorance of the civil society level—that is, the absence of dialogue both about economic plans and political problems in Xinjiang—has created serious limitations of Chinese ideological balancing in the region as its moral legitimacy has been loudly questioned and contested in Kazakhstan.

Finally, over the past thirty years, the US ideological presence has been an important geopolitical factor in Central Asia. Besides numerous business projects, the US government has invested considerable resources in constructing an alternative (to Russia) political project with Central Asian countries.[64] Security is a crucial part of American strategy toward Central Asia. During the US operation in Afghanistan, local security infrastructures were nodal transit points for logistics and technical support. In 2001–2014, the United States rented a military base in Kyrgyzstan, but cooperation was frozen, and subsequently American officials started to explore opportunities for military cooperation with Uzbekistan and Tajikistan.[65] However, following the withdrawal of the US troops from Afghanistan in 2021, the topic's urgency waned.

Evidence suggests that, since the 1990s, the United States has been trying to give more flesh to a liberal regional order. For instance, organizations such as GUAM—the Organization for Democracy and Economic Development—was founded in 1997 with US support.[66] The members gathered were Georgia, Ukraine, Azerbaijan, and Moldova. In 1999, it expanded to Central Asia to included Uzbekistan. But Uzbek membership didn't last long, and after the Andijan massacre in 2005, it withdrew from GUAM. The next attempt to unite Central Asian countries under US leadership was made in 2015 when American diplomats launched the "C5 + 1" initiative that brought together the Central Asian countries—that is, Kazakhstan, Kyrgyzstan, Tajikistan, Turkmenistan, and Uzbekistan. This format implied regular meetings between foreign affairs ministers from the Central Asian countries and the United States. In this framework, summits have been held twice a year (one on the ground in one of the Central Asian countries and another one in the United States). The most visible result of these discussions is the Central Asia Investment Partnership.[67]

The liberal ideas that support US grand strategy in Central Asia are: individual freedom, democracy, and human rights. These sets of ideas have accompanied US political, economic, cultural, and humanitarian actions in Kazakhstan since the 1990s. Further, liberal ideas have tightened their grips on the region through the conditions imposed by the IMF loans and funding. In addition, a large number of American organizations and NGOs (e.g., USAID, NED, and the Soros foundation) are actively promoting liberal forms of interactions and institutions in the region.[68] According to Kazakhstani officials, up to 70 percent of the NGO external funding in Kazakhstan comes from the United States.[69] In the higher education sector, US universities are very popular among the most promising Kazakhstani students, and local universities launched joint educational programs and exchanges with American universities.

For the United States, economic engagement and NGO funding is constitutive of ideological balancing aimed at countering vestiges of Russian influence and emerging Chinese presence. Balancing is reinforced by indirect usurpation of the colonial discourse. However, in the US grand strategy, critics about the former colonizer (Russia) and the neo-colonial power (China) remain subtle and disguised by more general attacks on authoritarianism, lack of transparency, and oppression of the people's voice. In fact, to push this point to perhaps an extreme, this approach seems to empower a new generation of Kazakhstani politicians who promote more Western liberal values (such as Dossym Satpaev). In contrast, there is no evidence of US direct subversion actions against the state of Kazakhstan. Perhaps, US history of subversion in Latin America deters US leaders from attempting to replicate a similar approach in Central Asia. But it might also be that subversion presents a greater risk for the United States than for China and Russia. It runs counter to liberal values of emancipation through democracy. In Kazakhstan, data from polls conducted by Open Democracy show that the support for American leadership in the world dropped from 37 percent in 2013 to 8 percent in 2015, but then raised to 24 percent in 2017. The main reasons for this decrease, the report concludes, are "American aggressive foreign policy, especially towards the Muslim world," the promotion of "immoral" values such as LGBT rights, and cultural imperialism.[70] In other words, the considerable efforts by the United States to establish liberal values as a credible alternative to the Chinese and Russian models remains fragile.

CONCLUSION

This chapter's principal aim was to show that the existence of ideological asymmetries between opposing countries helps explain why major powers lock horns. Breaking this down, first, ideology affects how states perceive of and react to one another. Second, ideology influences the security of the states who hold it, either from the inside out (e.g., when a state intervenes to promote its ideology in a foreign polity) or from the outside in (such as when a state has to think about remedies to respond to a recognized threatening ideology from without). Third, ideology influences the state's appraisal of the resources available and, more importantly, prescribes the adequate degree of integration between means and ends. We do not mean to imply that inquiries that fail to focus on ideas are in any way unworthy. Rather, we only wish to stress that we stand to lose something important to understanding great power competition if we fail to look beyond material factors.

While we do not claim that ideological cleavages determine the distribution of power, we have shown that it influences power rivalries, the outcome of which is a distinctive configuration of power relations in world politics. The link between ideology and power distribution is therefore indirect and indeterminate. Fourth, because ideology clothes strategic problems with the language of inevitability, it blurs the distinction between what a state *is* with what it *does*.[71]

However, limiting our study of ideology to its inner workings risks missing how ideologies actually shape major powers' interactions. Thus, we have spelled out three policies that major powers employ in attempting to leverage the effectiveness of their grand strategy: balancing, subversion, and usurpation. The analysis of the Kazakhstan case developed in this chapter has revealed that the extent to which major powers pool these policies together in a certain way is relational. That is, it depends, mostly, on the choices made by others. It may well be that no ecumenical understanding of relationism can be found, but it is evident from our case study that, to cultivate a renewed approach to great power competition, relations between actors must become the focal point of reflection.

NOTES

1. See, for example, Jeffrey W. Legro, *Rethinking the World: Great Power Strategies and International Order* (Ithaca, NY: Cornell University Press, 2005); John Mueller, "The Impact of Ideas on Grand Strategy," in *The Domestic Bases of Grand Strategy*, eds., Richard Rosecrance and Arthur A. Stein (Ithaca, NY: Cornell University Press, 1993), 48–64.
2. See Mark L. Haas, *The Ideological Origins of Great Power Politics, 1789–1989* (Ithaca, NY: Cornell University Press, 2005).
3. Francis Fukuyama, "Patterns of Soviet Third World Policy," *Problems of Communism*, no. 36 (September–October 1987): 12.
4. Paul Kennedy, "Grand Strategy in War and Peace: Toward a Broader Definition," in *Grand Strategy in War and Peace*, ed., Paul Kennedy (New Haven, CT: Yale University Press, 1991), 5. Emphasis in the original.
5. For a review of the literature on grand strategy, see Thierry Balzacq and Mark Corcoral, "Modern Grand Strategic Studies: Research Advances and Controversies," *Oxford Research Encyclopedia in International Studies*, accessed December 2022, https://doi.org/10.1093/acrefore/9780190846626.013.498. For recent extensive discussions about the concept of grand strategy, see, for example, Nina Silove, "Beyond the Buzzword: The Three Meanings of 'Grand Strategy,'" *Security Studies* 27, no. 1 (2018): 27–57; Rebecca F. Lissner, "What Is Grand Strategy? Sweeping a Conceptual Minefield," *Texas National Security Review* 2, no. 1 (2018): 52–73.
6. Jeffrey W. Legro, *Rethinking the World*, 8.

7. See Richard C. Snyder, H. W. Bruck, and Burton Sapin, *Decision-Making as an Approach to the Study of International Politics* (Princeton, NJ: Princeton University Press, 1954).
8. A. I. Richards, *The Philosophy of Rhetoric*. The Mary Flexner Lectures on the Humanities 3 (Oxford: Oxford University Press, 1936), 5.
9. This section dwells in part on previous research, Thierry Balzacq and Pablo Barnier-Khawam, "Ideas and Ideology in Grand Strategy," in *The Oxford Handbook of Grand Strategy*, eds. Thierry Balzacq and Ronald R. Krebs (Oxford: Oxford University Press, 2021), 159–72.
10. Michael Freeden, *Ideology: A Very Short Introduction* (Oxford: Oxford University Press, 2003), 32.
11. Teun A. Van Dijk, "Ideology and Discourse," in *The Oxford Handbook of Political Ideologies*, eds. Michael Freeden, Lyman Tower Sargent, and Marc Stears (Oxford: Oxford University Press 2013), 177.
12. Emphasis added. Alexander E. Wendt, *Social Theory of International Politics* (Cambridge: Cambridge University Press, 1999), 175.
13. Ibid., 175.
14. Ibid., 176.
15. See Ernesto Laclau, *On Populist Reason* (London: Verso, 2005).
16. Alan Finlayson, "Ideology and Political Rhetoric," in *The Oxford Handbook of Political Ideologies*, eds. Michael Freeden, Lyman Tower Sargent, and Marc Stears (Oxford: Oxford University Press, 2013), 199.
17. William C. Martel, *Grand Strategy in Theory and Practice: The Need for an Effective American Foreign Policy* (Cambridge: Cambridge University Press, 2015); "An Orienting Principle for Foreign Policy: The Deficiencies of 'Grand Strategy,'" *Policy Review*, no. 163 (October), https://www.hoover.org/research/orienting-principle-foreign-policy.
18. Robert J. Art, *A Grand Strategy for America* (Ithaca, NY: Cornell University Press, 2003); Stephen G. Brooks and William C. Wohlforth, *America Abroad: The United States' Global Role in the 21st Century* (Oxford: Oxford University Press, 2016); Barry R. Posen, *Restraint: A New Foundation for U.S. Grand Strategy* (Ithaca, NY: Cornell University Press, 2014); Barry R. Posen and Andrew Ross, "Competing Visions for U.S. Grand Strategy," *International Security* 21, no. 3 (1996): 5–53.
19. Ronald R. Krebs, "Pluralism, Populism, and the Impossibility of Grand Strategy," in *The Oxford Handbook of Grand Strategy*, eds. Thierry Balzacq and Ronald R. Krebs (Oxford: Oxford University Press, 2021), 673–89; Markus Kornprobst and Corina-Iona Traistaru, "Language and Grand Strategy," in *The Oxford Handbook of Grand Strategy*, eds. Thierry Balzacq and Ronald R. Krebs (Oxford: Oxford University Press, 2021), 173–89.
20. See David M. McCourt, "Culture and Identity in Grand Strategy," in *The Oxford Handbook of Grand Strategy*, eds. Thierry Balzacq and Ronald R. Krebs (Oxford: Oxford University Press, 2021), 303–21.
21. Finlayson, "Ideology and Political Rhetoric," 199.
22. Aaron L. Friedberg, *In the Shadow of the Garrison State: America's Anti-Statism and Its Cold War Grand Strategy* (Princeton, NJ: Princeton University Press, 2000), 22.
23. Stacie E. Goddard and Ronald R. Krebs, "Rhetoric, Legitimation, and Grand Strategy," *Security Studies* 24, no. 1, 5–36.; Stacie E. Goddard in *The Oxford Handbook of Grand Strategy*, eds. Thierry Balzacq and Ronald R. Krebs (Oxford: Oxford University Press, 2021), 322–37.

24. Rainer Forst, *Normativity and Power: Analyzing Social Orders of Justification* (Oxford: Oxford University Press, 2017), 55; Peter Hay Gries, *The Politics of American Foreign Policy: How Ideology Divides Liberals and Conservatives over Foreign Affairs* (Stanford, CA: Stanford University Press, 2014).
25. Helen Milner and Dustin V. Tingley, *Sailing the Water's Edge: The Domestic Politics of American Foreign Policy* (Princeton, NJ: Princeton University Press, 2015), 57–58.
26. Milner and Tingley, *Sailing the Water's Edge*, 57.
27. On balancing, see, for example, William C. Wohlforth, Stuart J. Kaufman, and Richard Little, eds., *The Balance of Power in World History* (New York: Palgrave Macmillan, 2007); Jack S. Levy, "What Do Great Powers Balance against and When?," in *Balance of Power: Theory and Practice in the 21st Century*, eds. T.V. Paul, James J. Wirtz, and Michael Fortmann (Stanford, CA: Stanford University Press, 2004), 29–51.
28. John Jost, C. M. Federico, and Jaime L. Napier, "Political Ideologies and Their Social Psychological Functions," in *The Oxford Handbook of Political Ideologies*, eds. Michael Freeden, Lyman Tower Sargent, and Marc Stears (Oxford: Oxford University Press, 2013), 232–350.
29. John M. Owen, *The Clash of Ideas in World Politics: Transnational Networks, States, and Regime Change, 1510–2010* (Princeton, NJ: Princeton University Press, 2010), 40.
30. Mark L. Haas, *The Clash of Ideologies: Middle Eastern Politics and American Security* (New York: Oxford University Press, 2012), 27.
31. Paul W. Blackstock, *The Strategy of Subversion: Manipulating the Politics of Other Nations* (Chicago: Quadrangle Books, 1964), 56.
32. See William C. Wohlforth, "Realism and Great Power Subversion," *International Relations* 34, no. 4, (2020): 461–63; Austin Carson, *Secret Wars: Covert Conflict in International Politics* (Princeton, NJ: Princeton University Press, 2018; Melissa Lee, *Crippling Leviathan: How Foreign Subversion Weakens the State* (Ithaca, NY: Cornell University Press, 2020).
33. For a good study on the US approach, see Lindsey A. O'Rourke, *Secrecy and Security: U.S.-Orchestrated Regime Change during the Cold War* (Ithaca, NY: Cornell University Press, 2021). See also Richard Cottam, *Competitive Interventions and 20th Century Diplomacy* (Pittsburgh, PA: University of Pittsburgh Press, 1967).
34. See, for example, Dov H. Levin, "Partisan Electoral Interventions by the Great Powers: Introducing the PEIG Dataset," *Conflict Management and Peace Science* 36, no. 1, (2019): 88–106; John M. Owen, "The Foreign Imposition of Domestic Institutions," *International Organization* 56, no. 2, (2002): 375–409; Melissa Willard-Foster, *Toppling Foreign Governments: The Logic of Regime Change* (Philadelphia, PA: University of Pennsylvania Press, 2018); Lori Fisler Damrosch, "Politics across Borders: Nonintervention and Nonforcible Influence over Domestic Affairs," *American Journal of International Law* 83, no. 1, (1989): 1–50.
35. See, for example, Frank G. Hoffman, *Conflict in the 21st Century: The Rise of Hybrid Wars* (Arlington, VA: Potomac Institute for Policy Studies, 2007); Alex Deep, "Hybrid War: Old Concept, New Techniques," *Small Wars Journal*, 2015, https://smallwarsjournal.com/jrnl/art/hybrid-war-old-concept-new-techniques.
36. Viatcheslav Morozov, "Subaltern Empire? Toward a Postcolonial Approach to Russian Policy," *Problems of Post-Communism* 60, no. 6 (2013): 16–28.
37. See Fiona Hill and Omer Taspinar, "Turkey and Russia: Axis of the Excluded?," *Survival* 48, no. 1, (2006): 81–92; Viatcheslav Morozov and Bahar Rumelili, "The

External Constitution of European Identity: Russia and Turkey as Europe-Makers," *Cooperation and Conflict* 47, no. 1, (2012): 28–48.
38. See Gayatri Chakravorty Spivak, "Can the Subaltern Speak?," in *Marxism and the Interpretation of Culture*, eds. Cary Nelson and Lawrence Grossberg (Basingstoke, UK: Palgrave, 1988), 271–313.
39. See Achille Mbembe, *On the Postcolony* (Berkeley: University of California Press, 2001).
40. See Gayatri Chakravorty Spivak, *A Critique of Postcolonial Reason: Toward a History of the Vanishing Present* (Cambridge, MA: Harvard University Press, 1999).
41. See Alexander Edkind, *Internal Colonization: Russia's Imperial Experience* (Cambridge, UK: Polity, 2011).
42. Gerring, "Ideology: A Definitional Analysis," 972.
43. Robert Jervis, "Hypotheses on Misperception," *World Politics* 20, no. 3, (1968): 472.
44. Haas, *The Clash of Ideologies*, 49.
45. Willard A. Mullins, "On the Concept of Ideology in Political Science," *American Political Science Review* 66, no. 2, 509.
46. Apart from Turkmenistan, which with the onset of independence has pursued an isolationist strategy.
47. Mikhail Suslov, "'Russian World' Concept: Post-Soviet Geopolitical Ideology and the Logic of 'Spheres of Influence,'" *Geopolitics* 23, no. 2, (2018): 330–53.
48. Vera Ageeva, "The Rise and Fall of Russia's Soft Power. Results of the Past Twenty Years," *Russia in Global Affairs* 19, no.1, (2021): 118–45.
49. Aleksandr Verkhovsky, "The Role of the Russian Orthodox Church in Nationalist, Xenophobic and Antiwestern Tendencies in Russia Today: Not Nationalism, but Fundamentalism," *Religion, State and Society* 30, no. 4 (2002): 333–45.
50. Andrey Tsygankov and Pavel Tsygankov, "National Ideology and IR Theory: Three Incarnations of the 'Russian Idea,'" *European Journal of International Relations* 16, no. 4, (2010): 663–86; Fabian Linde, "State Civilisation: The Statist Core of Vladimir Putin's Civilisational Discourse and Its Implications for Russian Foreign Policy," *Politics in Central Europe* 12, no. 1, (2016): 21–35; Ivan Fomin, "Sixty Shades of Statism: Mapping the Ideological Divergences in Russian Elite Discourse," *Demokratizatsiya: The Journal of Post-Soviet Democratization*, 2022. Project MUSE, muse.jhu.edu/article/850765.
51. Baunov Alexander, "Seksual'nyj suverenitet rodiny kak novaja vneshnjaja politika Rossii" [Sexual sovereignty of the motherland as a new Russia foreign policy] (Republic, August 21, 2013, https://republic.ru/posts/33413 21.08.2013); E. Edenborg, "Homophobia as Geopolitics: 'Traditional Values' and the Negotiation of Russia's Place in the World," in *Gendering Nationalism*, eds. J. Mulholland, N. Montagna, and E. Sanders-McDonagh (Basingstoke, UK: Palgrave Macmillan, 2018); Nikita Sleptcov, "Political Homophobia as a State Strategy in Russia," *Journal of Global Initiatives: Policy, Pedagogy, Perspective* 12, no. 1 (2018), https://digitalcommons.kennesaw.edu/jgi/vol12/iss1/9.
52. Andrey Tsygankov, ed., *Routledge Handbook of Russian Foreign Policy*, 1st ed. (London: Routledge, 2018).
53. Igor Zevelev, *Russia and Its New Diasporas* (Washington, DC: United States Institute of Peace Press, 2001).

54. Similar to the Kremlin's energy strategy in the Baltic states, see Irina Zeleneva and Vera Ageeva, "Russia's Soft Power in the Baltics: Media, Education and Russian World Narrative," *Mediaobrazovanie*, no. 4 (2017): 181–88.
55. Viatcheslav Morozov, "Kazakhstan and the 'Russian World' is a New Intervention on the Horizon?," *PONARS Eurasia Policy Memo*, no. 364, June 2015.
56. Chun Lin, *China and Global Capitalism. Reflections on Marxism, History, and Contemporary Politics* (Basingstoke, UK: Springer, 2013).
57. Ivan Krastev and Stephen Holmes, *The Light That Failed: Why the West Is Losing the Fight for Democracy* (New York: Pegasus Books, 2020).
58. Krastev and Holmes, *The Light That Failed*.
59. D. Zhang, "The Concept of 'Community of Common Destiny' in China's Diplomacy: Meaning, Motives and Implications," *Asia & the Pacific Policy Studies*, no. 5 (2018): 196–207.
60. Temur Umarov, "What's behind Protests against China in Kazakhstan?," *Moscow, Carnegie Foundation*, 2019. https://carnegiemoscow.org/commentary/80229.
61. Umarov, "What's behind Protests."
62. Umarov, "What's behind Protests."
63. See the Chinese Ambassador to Kazakhstan's Facebook page, https://www.facebook.com/ChinaAmbassadorKazakh.
64. A. Diener and D. Artman, "US Soft Power in Central Asia," in *Soft Power in Central Asia: The Politics of Influence and Seduction*, eds. K. Nourzhanov and S. Peyrouse (New York: Rowman and Littlefield, 2021).
65. Temur Umarov, "Is There a Place for a U.S. Military Base in Central Asia? Relaunching U.S.-Russia Dialogue," *Moscow Carnegie Endowment*, 2021, https://carnegiemoscow.org/commentary/84685.
66. G. Paul, "The United States and GUAM: From Tactic to Partnership," *Central Asia and the Caucasus* 3–4, no. 51–52 (2008): 156–60.
67. US Embassy and Consulate in Kazakhstan, "Joint Statement on the Announcement of the Central Asia Investment Partnership," January 7, 2021, https://kz.usembassy.gov/joint-statement-on-the-announcement-of-the-central-asia-investment-partnership/.
68. See for example, National Endowment for Democracy in Kazakhstan, https://www.ned.org/region/eurasia/kazakhstan-2021/.
69. Madina Mamyrkhanova, "V Kazahstane ezhegodnoe inostrannoe finansirovanie NPO sostavlyaet poryadka 5 mlrd tenge" [In Kazakhstan, annual foreign funding for NGOs is about 5 billion tenge]—Kursiv, November 27, 2018, https://kz.kursiv.media/2018-11-27/v-kazakhstane-ezhegodnoe-inostrannoe-finansirovanie-npo-sostavlyaet-poryadka-5/.
70. "Kazakhs are wary of neighbors bearing gifts," Open Democracy report, April 30, 2020, https://www.opendemocracy.net/en/odr/kazakhs-are-wary-neighbours-bearing-gifts/.
71. Jack Holland, "Foreign Policy and Political Possibility," *European Journal of International Relations* 19, no. 1 (2011): 55.

CHAPTER 5

Great Power Competition and Regional Orders
A Neoclassical Realist Interpretation

Mark Brawley and Jonathan Paquin

The United States and its allies are increasingly concerned about the prospect of war with China and Russia.[1] China's rapid economic growth has fueled the expansion of its influence as it asserts itself more forcefully on the global stage. Under President Xi Jinping, China has bolstered its military presence in the South China Sea, increased patrols around the contested Senkaku/Diaoyu Islands, cracked down on Hong Kong's autonomy, and openly acknowledged its intention to regain control of Taiwan by force if necessary.[2] Meanwhile, Russia took advantage of its oil and gas reserves to finance its expansionist and revisionist aims in the Caucasus and Eastern Europe. Moscow has attempted to increase its sphere of influence and rejected Europe's current security order.[3] In recent years, President Putin annexed Crimea, fomented a war in the Donbass region, invaded Ukraine, and even threatened NATO members with nuclear weapons. These dangerous developments contrast with the dynamics of the 1990s and 2000s, where America's hegemonic power globally remained unchallenged and international ties were shaped by economic globalization. The current situation, often referred to as the New Cold War, mirrors some aspects of the past but will surely differ as well.

Our contribution to this volume explores how fluctuations in great power competition shape sub-systemic regional dynamics. Specifically, we investigate how fluctuations in great power engagement in a region shape the strategies pursued by second-tier (or local) powers. To address this issue, we apply a neoclassical realist (NCR) framework. NCR is well suited to this task for three main reasons. First, it explains systemic outcomes by modeling the interaction of strategic choices. In a given region, states select policies intended to attain their preferred outcomes, under the combined pressure of systemic and domestic constraints. Great power engagement in a region—or lack thereof—can be easily captured in this framework. Second, NCR is a middle-range approach that can efficiently (and parsimoniously) depict competition within a region. Outcomes will be determined by a handful of countries' choices. Third, the traits of neoclassical realism allow us to apply it across numerous settings.

The chapter proceeds in three sections. It first presents the NCR framework and explains how states select a strategy, then demonstrates how strategies interact to determine regional outcomes. It spells out the conditions driving regional orders to either remain peaceful or tilt toward conflict. Second, to demonstrate its utility, the framework is applied to three historical cases that capture variations in great power involvement: the USSR's greater involvement in the Middle East in the 1950s, the reduction in US engagement in East Asia under President Nixon's Guam doctrine, and then the collapse of the USSR in 1991. Third, the chapter moves to a foresight exercise by looking at two important contemporary regional settings: East Asia and Eastern Europe. The last section summarizes our empirical and theoretical findings and draws some policy implications.

A TWO-STEP NEOCLASSICAL REALIST FRAMEWORK

We begin by assuming that, in each region, states can be broadly categorized as either status quo oriented or revisionist. We claim that status quo–oriented states benefit from the existing international system and therefore have a stake in upholding and defending it.[4] These states happily participate in the Liberal International Order (LIO)[5] and support international law, a free-market economy, and the respect of international borders. The LIO's features provide the basis for status quo states' cooperation. Among the great powers, we assume that the United States and the European Union are status quo oriented. In her 2022 state of the Union address, president of the European Commission Ursula von der Leyen stated, "Since the end of World War 2, we have pursued the promise of democracy and the rule of law. And the nations of the world have built together an international system promoting peace and security, justice and economic progress. Today this is the very target of Russian missiles."[6] The level of American and European involvement in a region will shape the strategic choices of local powers in that area. In contrast, revisionist states are often run by authoritarian regimes that either feel that they are denied the benefits of the liberal international order or simply reject some of its key principles and values. Depending on their situation, these states may seek to challenge or undermine the LIO by flouting international law, undermining free markets, or expanding their territorial claims. As David Lake, Lisa Martin, and Thomas Risse point out, "While Russia is not actively promoting an alternative to the LIO, it resembles China in its support for a strictly 'Westphalian' order that removes the 'liberal' from the existing international order."[7]

As revisionist great powers, Russia and China not only try to change regional power configurations by violating international borders (the former in Eastern Europe and the Caucasus, the latter in the South China Sea), but they also act in ways undermining or challenging the broader LIO. In an interview with the *Financial Times* in 2019, President Putin said that the liberal international order had become "obsolete" and that liberalism had "outlived its purpose."[8] Meanwhile, his foreign minister Sergei Lavrov stated that the United States must accept a new multipolar order and stop dictating policies to the rest of the world.[9] China is usually less macropolitical in its criticisms of the liberal order, selectively contesting aspects of the United States–led security order. For instance, Beijing defends its maritime claims in the South China Sea, rejecting the 2016 ruling of the Permanent Court of Arbitration, which rebuffed its claims of historic rights over several islands, reefs, shoals, and waters of the region. At the same time, President Xi Jinping promised "incomparable glory" to the Chinese people and pledged to make China a global power by 2049.[10] This could hardly be done without significant transformations of the current international order.

Before we proceed further, two clarifications are in order. First, recent scholarship has criticized the usefulness of the status quo/revisionist classifications claiming their lack of objectivity and bias in favor of the most powerful and privileged states.[11] We agree that rising powers may not necessarily be revisionist and that status quo states may sometimes take destabilizing actions to bolster their dominance or prevent their decline. President Bush's 2003 invasion of Iraq and President Trump's America first policy were not status quo driven. Similarly, President Xi's 2017 Davos speech, in which he defended globalization, did not reflect revisionist aims. However, by focusing on the content of the international order (i.e., its liberal traits), we contend that the status quo/revisionist categories are useful and offer a fair representation of observed historical trends. Furthermore, by defining these categories clearly as we did above, we argue that they provide a useful conceptualization for our analysis.

Second, neoclassical realism does not offer much insight into whether a state has revisionist aims or is satisfied with the LIO. Rather, NCR informs our understanding of the means employed to challenge or defend that order. States' preferences are better determined by an analytical form of liberalism, which uses domestic interests to explain state preferences.[12] To categorize states in the later empirical section, we rely on their stated preferences. We turn to NCR because we believe that states change their strategies more frequently than their goals. In other words, if liberal theories provided a better explanation for the variation in second-tier states' strategies, we would expect to see states frequently switching categories from revisionist to status quo, or vice versa. Since states change their strategies more often than their ends, we assume that their preferences remain stable, while the means they employ shift according to other factors.

We also wish to point out that the existing literature on great power rivalry tends to neglect the role played by second-tier states in the protection or transformation of regional order. Scholars often portray local states as mere pawns of great powers on the geopolitical chessboard.[13] Our framework transcends this assumption by paying attention to their motivations, behaviors, resources, and partners. As will be demonstrated in our cases, the actions of second-tier states remain pivotal for determining regional outcomes. Their choices, however, are conditioned by decisions great powers make.

Step 1: Second-Tier States' Strategies

Neoclassical realism assumes that all states prioritize security over other goals—that is, they first seek to maintain their existing position in the system.[14] Other aims may matter, but these do not supersede the need for security. Status quo–oriented states wish to maintain the LIO as well as retain their position in the system. The foreign policy executive (FPE) represents that element of the state responsible for identifying external threats, and then formulating a response.[15] Like structural realism, NCR grants primacy to systemic factors for understanding states' foreign policy options.[16] However, NCR accepts that the international structure can be indeterminate. This assumption rests on the notion that the international environment may not always be objectively assessed by FPEs; moreover, states often have more than one policy option available. As a result, NCR assumes that states do not mechanically respond to systemic changes.[17]

Once the FPE identifies a threat, the state must develop a counter to that danger. This choice reflects both systemic and domestic constraints. The

FPE evaluates potential allies, especially seeking any others who confront the same threat. The FPE also assesses its ability to mobilize the internal resources needed to pursue its foreign policy goals.[18] We do not need to consider domestic forces shaping states' preferences, since we have assumed that preferences are relatively static; nor do we anticipate domestic changes lifting a minor state to the level of a great power. Instead, when we speak of domestic constraints, we refer to a state's ability to amass resources from its own economy. Mobilized resources fluctuate depending on the country's overall economic performance, as well as any changes in the state's ability to extract a portion of the country's assets.[19] A state with a weakening economy faces rising limitations on its resources and is thus more likely to turn to strategic partners to attain its goals; conversely, one ruling over a growing economy has a wider array of strategies open to it. Likewise, a state with declining social and political cohesion will have difficulty tapping domestic resources and will therefore be more likely to turn to available strategic partners to attain its goals, but a state enjoying a strengthening of its social and political cohesion will be able to draw more from its existing economy, offering it more strategic options. Both external and internal constraints and opportunities can alter the FPE's strategic calculations.[20]

We assume that status quo–oriented states share a preference ranking of strategies, all else being equal. States would prefer to buck-pass first. Buck-passing, a strategy in which a state counts on another powerful actor to bear the cost of deterring or defeating a common threat, is cheap.[21] However, local states may find it difficult to pass the buck to another local state,[22] and while some might be able to pass the buck to a great power, the great power is more likely to demand that the local state participate in an alliance. Pure buck-passing by a second-tier state may therefore be uncommon. Status quo–oriented states' second-preferred strategy would be to balance against the threat with the assistance of others. Aligning with a great power that shares a preference regarding the LIO is clearly attractive, since that great power is likely to bear a disproportionate share of any burdens. External balancing by allying with other local status quo–oriented states should be cheaper than going it alone through internal balancing, which is the third option. The fourth-ranked strategy is security hedging, where a state makes counterbalancing security/defense decisions to avoid exclusive defense alignment.[23] This option carries significant risks, as it creates ambiguity about one's intentions. Note that this strategy is unlikely to be chosen if a state has already made a formal alliance commitment, as breaking prior arrangements would result in a loss of trust and the disruption of established benefits. Finally, bandwagoning is the least-preferred choice as it carries the greatest risk.

Bandwagoning implies an alignment with a threatening revisionist power.[24] It occurs when a state believes that the costs of opposing a threatening power exceed the anticipated benefits of supporting it. By bandwagoning, a state essentially concedes its international preferences to avoid defeat.

We now turn our attention to second-tier revisionist states. The framework continues to focus on how the FPE reads its systemic and domestic environments, not in terms of defending the LIO but in terms of the opportunities and barriers that shape its capacity to challenge that order. The FPE assesses the systemic setting to establish the level of power it must attain to succeed. This includes finding any potential partners who share complementary or overlapping goals. When evaluating the domestic environment, the FPE identifies resources that the state can use to achieve its international objectives. Holding other things constant, we assume that centralized authoritarian regimes will more easily mobilize and harness their nations' power than liberal democracies, since they exert more control over their constituents. However, a state can only pursue internal balancing if it has the material resources, as well as the required social and political cohesion, to harness those assets.

Despite their opposing preferences, we argue that revisionist states rank their strategies in the same order as status quo states. To determine which strategy is ultimately selected, we make the following logical claims: First, if the buck cannot be passed to another state, then buck-passing is not possible. The presence or absence of other states in the region (potential allies or the receiver in buck-passing) can be easily observed, underscoring the parsimony of this approach. Second, if there are no potential allies, then external balancing and security hedging are not viable options. Third, if a state's domestic economy performs poorly or lacks domestic cohesion, then internal balancing is not feasible. For instance, if a status quo–oriented great power is maintaining or increasing its presence in a region, local status quo–oriented states can either buck-pass to this great power or at least align with it to counter a threat. Revisionist states may similarly align with a revisionist great power to overturn local circumstances. If a great power starts withdrawing from a region, it alters local states' options. The combination of arguments presented above produces the simplified table shown in table 5.1.

Note that there are situations with more than one potential outcome. Buck-passing rarely exists in its ideal form; more often, a local state will align with a great power that shares its preferences and concerns regarding the LIO but then rely on that great power to carry a disproportionate share of security burdens. In the scenario combining weak domestic constraints and the availability of local allies but with the great power withdrawing from a

Table 5.1: Second-Tier States' Strategic Selection

	Great power increasing its presence	Great power withdrawing, but local allies available	No allies available
Weak domestic constraints	External balancing with great power	External balancing with other local states only	Internal balancing
Strong domestic constraints	Buck-passing	External balancing/ security hedging	Bandwagoning

region, the prediction should be clearer: the local states share a preference for external balancing, and thus they should ally together. In the scenario combining strong domestic constraints with the availability of local allies but no possible support from a great power, the state can either pursue external balancing, or it can hedge by diversifying its security partnerships (security hedging should therefore occur rarely). It is also worth noting that if a second-tier state is forced to pursue internal balancing and finds itself alone against a great power or a coalition led by a great power, it has a strong incentive to attain weapons of mass destruction.

Step 2: Strategic Interaction—Determining Regional Outcomes

To describe and predict outcomes for a region, neoclassical realism models the interaction of strategic choices. Table 5.2 depicts the possible results of strategic interaction. We argue that any situation where both sides are balancing against each other will result in a local arms race, which could escalate into open conflict. The status quo is clearly maintained when the revisionist state chooses to hedge or bandwagon in response to the balancing of status quo states. Conversely, if the revisionist state pursues balancing, but the local status quo power is forced to hedge or bandwagon, then local revision may occur. Only in situations where both sides feel compelled to hedge or bandwagon, (i.e., where states on both sides face considerable domestic constraints) is a compromise probable.

Our two-step neoclassical realist framework is rather straightforward. By opening the "black box" of the state, step one aims to capture how and when domestic constraints interact with external factors to produce the strategies of status quo and revisionist states within a region. Then, by aggregating these strategic choices in the second step, our framework can be used to explain and predict the likelihood of conflict or peace in a region. Unfortunately, this

Table 5.2: Second-Tier States' Strategic Interaction and Regional Outcomes

		Revisionist states			
		Buck-passing to revisionist great power	Great power withdrawing; Local powers coalesce in revisionist effort	Local power isolated with weak domestic constraints; internal balancing	Local power isolated with strong domestic constraint; security hedging or bandwagoning
Status Quo States	Buck-passing to status quo great power	Great powers compete in the region (mutual deterrence)	Race against status quo great power and its allies	Status quo defended	Status quo defended (or SQ great power exerts will on revisionist state)
	Great power withdrawing; Local powers coalesce to defend status quo	Local SQ powers race against revisionist great power	Local alliances race	Local powers defend status quo	Local powers defend status quo
	Local power isolated with weak domestic constraints; Internal balancing	Local SQ power races against Revisionist great power (conflict is possible)	Revision possible (conflict likely)	One-on-one local arms race	Status quo defended
	Local power isolated with strong domestic constraints; Security hedging or bandwagoning	Revision	Revision very likely	Revision likely	Compromise

second stage produces a wider variety of outcomes than we can test in this chapter. To partly overcome this problem, we will focus on several historical examples illustrating past episodes when great powers chose to increase or reduce their engagement in a region. Three episodes are of interest: when a status quo–oriented great power reduced its commitments, when a revisionist great power increased its engagement, and when a revisionist great power withdrew.

EMPIRICAL SECTION

We provide three historical episodes to illustrate the utility of our framework. First, we explore the Middle East in the 1950s–1960s to understand what happens when a revisionist power, the USSR, increased its role in a region. This intensified regional competition but ultimately produced mutual deterrence. Second, during the Nixon Administration, the United States reduced its engagement in several regions. Our attention centers on East Asia, particularly the responses of South Korea and Japan. When the status quo–oriented great power reduced its commitments to the region, the local status quo–oriented states responded in ways captured by the framework. Finally, we examine the period following the collapse of the Soviet Union to understand what happens when a revisionist power reduced its engagement in a region, again returning to East Asia, but this time focusing on North Korea.

HISTORICAL CASES

The Soviet Involvement in the Middle East

The USSR chose to invest resources in the Middle East starting in the mid-1950s, engaging in a competition with the United States and European powers. The Soviets offered increased aid, as well as weapons sales, to revisionist states in the region including, importantly, Egypt. More specifically, local revisionist states such as Egypt, Syria, and Iraq coalesced around a shared objective of eliminating Israel. While these states had already been cooperating, the Soviet Union's decision to increase its presence in the region empowered the local revisionists. Referring to table 5.2, this move was expected to result in mutual deterrence since Israel could draw on its status quo great power, the United States, for support.

After Gamal Abdel Nasser took power, Egypt's relations with Israel deteriorated. Nasser's government initially pursued weaponry from the United States and Europe but faced rejection. As border skirmishes escalated, Nasser turned to the Soviet Union. The Soviets, seeking to enhance their influence in the region, seized this opportunity.[25] Soviet economic assistance began in mid-1954 and progressively expanded. American reluctance to fund the construction of the Aswan Dam prompted Nasser to seek alternative revenue streams by taking control of the Suez Canal. This prompted a brief and sharp conflict involving Egypt on the one hand and Britain, France, and Israel on the other. The Soviets threatened their own military intervention, leading the United States to use diplomatic pressure to resolve the crisis. The Soviets quickly made up the equipment losses Egypt had suffered. Over the subsequent decade, the Soviets sold military equipment to Egypt at discounted rates and dispatched advisors to restructure and train the Egyptian armed forces.

In 1963, Egypt joined Syria and Iraq in an alliance against Israel. The existence of a revisionist alliance in the region prompted the Soviets to enhance the weaponry they offered; Egypt could now purchase frontline military equipment. These shipments emboldened Egyptian rhetoric, but the equipment was largely lost in the 1967 Six-Day War. Once again, the Soviets compensated for the losses through additional arms sales. The scope and caliber of the offered weaponry expanded, alongside an increase in the number of Soviet advisors. The Egyptian military's desire to reestablish its reputation led to the "war of attrition"; Soviet backing sustained this low-level conflict while simultaneously curbing Egypt from initiating a new war. Egypt's opportunity arose in the 1973 Yom Kippur War, but this could only happen after Anwar Sadat ordered the withdrawal of Soviet forces from the country, leaving Egypt well-equipped but eliminating Moscow's veto power.

This sequence of events underscores how a revisionist great power can alter the situation in a region by increasing its engagement with local revisionist states. Although the USSR did not share a specific objective with Egypt—given Nasser's anti-Communist stance as a nationalist—their interests complemented each other. By repeatedly supporting Egypt, the USSR created greater tensions in the region. The arms race between Egypt and its allies on one side, and Israel on the other, triggered several brief intense clashes. However, the involvement of both the status quo–oriented great power (the United States) and the revisionist great power (the USSR) prevented these clashes from escalating, which is consistent with our NCR framework.

East Asia and Nixon's Guam doctrine

The Nixon Administration took several steps to reduce American commitments to bring those into alignment with its finite resources. It notably delegated ground combat responsibilities in Vietnam to others. In a speech delivered in Guam on July 25, 1969, President Nixon defined this as a broader approach toward regional allies. He announced that the United States might not provide defense for allies unwilling to assume greater responsibility for their own security. The Guam (or Nixon) Doctrine signaled that the United States would be reducing its role in several regions, including East Asia. Nixon underscored that while the United States had "no intention of withdrawing from the world," it aimed to offer assistance and intervene in situations "where it ma[de] a real difference and [was] considered in its interest."[26] This doctrine caught East Asian allies off guard, intensifying abandonment concerns in countries like Japan, South Korea, and Australia, among others. Despite the Cold War dynamics favoring enduring alliances, the apprehension of being left behind became a factor in allies' strategic deliberations.[27] Subsequently, alterations in American trade and monetary policies, along with the rapprochement with China in 1971, further unsettled US allies.

The two East Asian status quo–oriented states we focus on, Japan and South Korea, started off in roughly similar positions. Both were allied with the United States, though the United States had encouraged Japan to lean toward buck-passing,[28] whereas South Korea was compelled to commit greater resources to its own defense (as well as participate in the Vietnam War). Referring to table 5.1, both Japan and South Korea were expected to seek collaboration with other local status quo states to counterbalance external threats (namely the USSR and North Korea). Contrary to this expectation, both countries opted for increased internal balancing strategies.

Japanese policymakers expressed concerns that the Nixon Doctrine might trigger further withdrawals of American presence from the region. In response, Prime Minister Yasuhiro Nakasone was assigned the task of formulating plans to enhance defense spending. The United States endorsed these measures, concurrently aiming to sustain its alliance with Japan and thereby maintain American influence over Japan's foreign policy.[29] However, Nakasone's proposals encountered a lack of domestic support. While Japan had the financial capacity to increase spending, the public resisted substantial alterations.[30] Nevertheless, Japan's defense expenditure rose from 0.77 percent of its GDP in 1970 to 0.91 percent in 1975, and this level persisted for the remainder of the Cold War.[31] During negotiations in 1972, Japan urged the United States to retain troops in South Korea, arguing that this was pivotal not only for South Korea's security but also for Japan's own security.[32] However, Japan did not engage in more comprehensive collaboration with South Korea's defense efforts.

For South Korea, the Nixon Doctrine triggered the withdrawal of approximately twenty thousand US military personnel between 1969 and 1971, accounting for roughly a third of the stationed forces. In response, the South

Koreans began exploring the possibility of developing their own nuclear weapons, though American officials soon nixed the idea.[33] To enhance the government's capacity to garner more resources from its populace, President Park Chung Hee implemented the Yushin reforms. These reforms entailed the suspension of the National Assembly, suppression of opposition groups, and the reinstatement of martial law. Capitalizing on South Korea's economic success during this period, the expanded governmental authority allowed the state to allocate more resources to defense. The proportion of South Korea's GDP dedicated to security escalated from 4.4 percent in 1970 to 5.9 percent in 1976, and this level was maintained until the mid-1980s.[34]

Although both status quo local powers responded as anticipated (namely through balancing), they did not seek greater military cooperation with each other during this period. One could even argue that alliances between local status quo states deteriorated during this time. This was due to Japan's tacit support for Taiwan, which came into question as Japan established diplomatic ties with the People's Republic of China, mirroring Nixon's approach. Additionally, South Korea initiated the withdrawal of its forces from South Vietnam to replace American troops withdrawing from its own territory. Although the general expectations derived from the model find support, the intricate nature of regional interactions indicates that the framework might be incomplete.

East Asia and the Collapse of the Soviet Union

The dissolution of the USSR reduced tensions in several regions of the world, and this was potentially true for East Asia. South Korea, for instance, reduced defense spending from 6.4 percent of GDP in 1980 to 4 percent in 1990, further declining to 2.74 percent in 1996.[35] The South Korean government reallocated funds toward economic development and the welfare of its citizens.[36] Concurrently, US defense spending decreased from 5.61 percent of GDP in 1990 to 3.56 percent in 1996,[37] although the presence of American forces on the Korean peninsula experienced only marginal reduction during the post–Cold War period. However, the deteriorating Soviet economy in the 1980s had stirred concerns in North Korea about potential abandonment, and the collapse of the USSR in 1991 dramatically transformed North Korea's circumstances. Without other local revisionist states available, North Korea resorted to internal balancing, facilitated by its ability to continue extracting resources from its domestic economy, albeit at a severe cost to its citizens. Moreover, to establish a credible deterrent, North Korea intensified its pursuit of nuclear weapons.

Estimates of North Korea's defense budget remain contested, but experts claim the country spent a greater percentage of its output on defense than any other in the world in the 1990s. This partly compensated for the country's tiny economic base; to reach a significant amount, it must take a greater percentage of its small production. This could only be achieved by isolating the population and ruling in a brutal fashion. This strategic approach persisted throughout the post–Cold War era. During the 1990s, North Korea channeled additional resources into its nuclear weapons development. While this program was initiated much earlier, it had primarily focused on generating weapons-grade material. However, following the collapse of the Soviet Union, North Korea redirected its efforts toward constructing delivery systems, with a specific emphasis on developing missiles capable of reaching the United States. This highlights North Korea's intent to deter potential American aggression.[38]

This episode aligns effectively with our NCR framework, yet it also raises a significant question and underscores an important observation. As a revisionist second-tier state, North Korea was abandoned by its revisionist great power patron when the Soviet Union collapsed. North Korea subsequently resorted to internal balancing, highlighting the necessity of incorporating the decisions made by second-tier states into a model aimed at explaining regional outcomes. However, a pertinent question emerges: How could we predict North Korea's sustained ability to uphold internal balancing, given the considerable toll it exacts on its own society? Here follows the observation: one might expect the withdrawal of a revisionist great power from a region to produce greater stability, but the result depends on how local revisionist states respond. Despite the preservation of the status quo, the potential threat of a costly conflict in East Asia endures.

A FORESIGHT EXERCISE

The three historical outcomes discussed above demonstrate how the framework we developed can effectively capture important sub-systemic dynamics, as great powers adjust their engagement in regions. We now turn our attention to contemporary outcomes in Eastern Europe and East Asia.

Eastern Europe

This empirical section focuses on Poland, which is an important status quo power in Eastern Europe, and Belarus, which is closely allied with Russia and supports Moscow in its war in Ukraine. In contrast to East Asia, we are currently witnessing a war in Eastern Europe in which the main revisionist great power, Russia, is directly involved and the American power is fighting a proxy war. So, let's look at past events to see if our NCR framework accurately predicted the war in Ukraine.

Poland's primary security concern is Russia, and as a NATO member, it relies on external balancing as its default strategic posture. Following the 2008 Russo-Georgian War, Vladimir Putin's ambitions to enhance Russia's position in the global order became clearer.[39] Subsequently, Russia and Belarus conducted extensive military exercises on Belarusian territory and in the Kaliningrad Oblast, including simulated scenarios like a nuclear attack on Poland and the suppression of a Polish minority uprising in Belarus.[40] These events, coupled with Russia's significant military activities along Poland's border, prompted Warsaw to admit underestimating the threats posed by Russia.[41]

While the Bush administration's robust commitment to defending Poland after the Russia-Georgia war helped ease concerns, subsequent events under the Obama and Trump administrations shook Poland's confidence in America's engagement. President Obama's "reset" policy with Russia, including the abandonment of a missile defense system in Europe,[42] and his administration's pivot to Asia caused apprehensions in Poland. Then, President Trump's transactional approach and his praising of Putin further fueled Poland's unease,[43] as did his comments on NATO's cost and relevance. Consequently, Poland sought reassurance from the United States but questioned its availability and commitment to defending Polish territory.

Simultaneously, Poland viewed the European Union as an inadequate alternative to address the Russian threat.[44] The disparity in focus between Poland's military security concerns and western European countries' emphasis on nonmilitary security issues intensified this perception.[45] Additionally, the idea of greater European strategic autonomy, promoted by French president Macron, raised red flags in Poland, potentially weakening US military engagement in Europe and jeopardizing Poland's security.[46]

In response, Poland adopted the "Komorowski Doctrine," prioritizing internal defense capabilities to counter Russian threats. This involved redirecting the nature of its armed forces, increasing defense expenditures, and modernizing equipment. Consequently, Poland's defense budget surged from US$8.9 billion in 2014 to US$12.8 billion in 2020, with a significant portion allocated for modernization.[47] The "Komorowski Doctrine" mandated that no less than 2 percent of the GDP annually be dedicated to defense, with at least 20 percent of that for modernization.[48] This approach resulted in Poland having the third-highest defense spending as a share of its GDP among NATO members in 2022, rising to an unprecedented 4 percent of GDP in 2023 due to the Russian invasion of Ukraine.[49]

Poland also pursued an enlarged US military presence on NATO's eastern flank, seeking to bolster deterrence against Russia. This entailed agreements at the 2016 Warsaw Summit for increased NATO military presence in Eastern Europe, including Poland, where a rotational force of three thousand soldiers would be stationed as well as one United States–led NATO-enhanced Forward Presence Battlegroup.[50] By beefing up its internal defense capabilities with American equipment, Warsaw sought to demonstrate its credibility as a reliable ally and strained to enlarge the US military footprint in Poland. Polish president Andrzej Duda also submitted a request to the Trump administration for a permanent US presence in Poland to bolster deterrence against Russia. President Duda even went so far as to cater to Donald Trump's narcissism by referring to the proposed military base as "Fort Trump."[51] Although the Polish government offered to contribute up to US$2 billion for its construction, the project was eventually shelved. Warsaw nevertheless convinced Washington to dispatch additional troops to its territory, showcasing its deepened alignment with Washington. In sum, Poland increased its alignment with Washington and substantially invested in national defense capabilities to bolster its attractiveness and reliability rather than to aim at defense self-sufficiency.

Belarus has limited strategic maneuverability due to its deep-seated ties with Russia. In the 2010s, Minsk tried to distance itself from Moscow by seeking Western partnerships.[52] However, despite its attempts to establish a distinct identity beyond being a mere Russian satellite, Belarus has not executed any substantial shifts in its international stance.[53] Belarus could not afford to balance against Russia, but it does not want to bandwagon either. Then came the social unrest following the 2020 presidential election, for which President Alexander Lukashenko falsified the results.[54] This reckless behavior from his part isolated Belarus from the international community. Moreover, it led to weeks-long mass demonstrations that rocked the country. These demonstrations threatened Lukashenko's regime and forced him to fly to Sochi in urgent need of help from Russia. In response, Putin extended support by offering a $1.5 billion loan to prop up Lukashenko's regime, consequently driving Belarus even closer to Russia.[55] This solidified the alignment between Lukashenko and Putin, resulting in an upsurge of joint military exercises between Moscow and Minsk. Belarus subsequently escalated its militarization efforts and integrated its military with that of Russia.[56] Lukashenko declared, "We effectively have a single army, with the

Belarusian military forming its backbone in the western direction. If, God forbid, a war starts, the Belarusian army will be the first to engage in the fight."[57] By rigging the election, concentrating his power, and getting Putin's support, Lukashenko faced weak domestic constraints, enabling him to enhance external balancing with Russia against Western influences.

Based on the previous analysis and by referring to table 5.2, the strategic configuration in Eastern Europe should logically have led to a localized arms race rather than a full-scale war in Ukraine. To comprehensively understand this war, it is imperative to delve into Vladimir Putin's perception of the strategic dynamics and his assessment of Washington's commitment to Ukraine. Both Putin and Lukashenko presumed that NATO's unity had been compromised by the tumultuous withdrawal from Afghanistan, and, furthermore, they doubted Washington's willingness to intervene in support of Ukraine (essentially, that the United States was scaling down its regional involvement). Consequently, Putin believed that status quo–oriented states would yield concessions when faced with such a robust display of Russia-Belarus external balancing. Yet, his assessment was flawed, and the anticipated territorial revisions he aspired to achieve might ultimately prove unsuccessful.

East Asia

This second section centers on two key states: Japan, which is an important status quo power, and North Korea, the quintessential revisionist state in East Asia. Japan faces two main security threats: North Korea with its nuclear program and China's revisionist policies in the South and East China Seas. It could hardly defend itself against China, or against North Korea's missile strikes, without Washington's protection. Japan has benefited from a bilateral security treaty signed with the United States in 1951. It is part of a formal alliance with Washington. As a result, buck-passing is not an option as Japan's default position is external balancing.

Facing China and North Korea's threats, Tokyo has bolstered its alignment with the United States over the past decade. This effort has entailed a significant enhancement in interoperability and procurement of American military equipment. Simultaneously, during the Obama administration and even more so under Trump, Prime Minister Shinzo Abe's government grew increasingly apprehensive about the United States potentially diminishing its commitment in the future.[58] During the 2016 presidential campaign, Trump criticized the US-Japan defense treaty as being one-sided and too expensive, a critique he reiterated while in office, including at the 2019 G20 summit in Osaka.[59] Indications of waning US involvement spurred Tokyo to prepare for the possibility of internal balancing if required.

Despite contending with demographic challenges impacting its economy, Japan retains the world's third-largest economy, enabling substantial bolstering of its defensive autonomy. Moreover, despite constitutional limitations on its military, the Japanese government benefits from a broad consensus on the fact that China and North Korea pose threats. Hence, there are no significant socio-political constraints that could prevent it from bolstering its domestic defense. Recent years have witnessed Japan strengthening its naval prowess, enhancing projection capabilities, acquiring 105 F-35s (the second-largest foreign procurement of US-made military equipment), investing in space domain capabilities,[60] and developing hypersonic weaponry.[61] Plans are also underway to replace the Mitsubishi F-2s with a new homegrown fighter jet capable of challenging Chinese and Russian fifth-generation fighters.[62]

Moreover, Prime Minister Abe embarked on two major reforms. In April 2014, Japan revised its 1976 arms export ban to expand the range and nature of international arms transfers.[63] Abe was also resolute in pursuing a more assertive defense policy, leading to a breach of the 1954 ban on exercising collective self-defense. Despite the Japanese constitution allowing only for self-defense forces, the Legislation for Peace and Security endorsed by the Diet in 2015 redefined "self-defense" to permit the Japanese military to engage abroad in the name of collective self-defense alongside allies without geographical constraints.[64]

Concurrently, Japan's Legislation for Peace and Security, championed by the Abe government and enacted in 2015, expanded the realm for Japan to foster multiple defense partnerships. This legislation formally authorized Tokyo's strategic diversification, which had been in progress since the early 2010s. Japan forged strategic partnerships with Australia, India, New Zealand, and the Philippines, while intensifying security cooperation with Malaysia and Singapore. For example, the Japanese Ministry of Defense negotiated an access agreement with Australia to facilitate joint military exercises involving Australian and Japanese forces.[65] Abe also collaborated with India to enhance their military interoperability.[66] Furthermore, Abe played a pivotal role in establishing the Quadrilateral Security Dialogue, encompassing Australia, India, and the United States. Japan's strategic diversification transcended the Indo-Pacific sphere as it deepened security ties with France and the United Kingdom.

Tokyo's diversification of security partnerships extends to like-minded democracies, which incidentally are also American allies. This strategy operates within the confines of America's alliance networks. Through this approach, Japan concurrently pursues three objectives: external balancing with both the United States and regional partners, as well as internal balancing. The perceived erosion of US influence in the region, coupled with the implementation of Donald Trump's "America First" strategy, reinforced Japan's conviction that strategic diversification was a prudent course of action. This diversification laid the groundwork for a more autonomous Japanese policy, which could potentially broaden Tokyo's strategic alternatives and counter reliance on the United States, or even mitigate the risk of strategic isolation in the event of US abandonment.[67] As noted by Atanassova-Cornelis and Sato, "Tokyo's objective is to reinforce the US-led security system in the short term, while pursuing strategic diversification and preparation for US abandonment in the long term."[68]

North Korea remains a revisionist power. It claims the entirety of the Korean peninsula, does not obey international law, and is seen as an international pariah. North Korea has been a champion blackmailer in the post–Cold War era. Through its active nuclear weapons program, it was able to obtain—or to extort—economic concessions from the United States.[69] The presence of the United States in the region, allied with South Korea and Japan, has posed a significant threat to Pyongyang and more specifically to the Kim regime. President Bush's war on terror and his "axis of evil" speech at his 2002 State of the Union address led Pyongyang to withdraw from the 1968 Nuclear Nonproliferation Treaty in 2003 and to become a nuclear power by 2006. Over the last years, it conducted short-range missile tests near South Korea and long-range ballistic missile tests over Japan.[70] In the case of a confrontation between the United States and China, there is little doubt that Pyongyang would prefer to pass the buck to Beijing and free ride to better concentrate on the preservation of its regime. But in a more practical way, Pyongyang has cultivated friendly relations with Beijing for economic purposes but also to balance against external threats. That said, there is no alliance between North Korea and China.[71] It seeks to maintain enough ties with China but not too much as to jeopardize the leader's authority.

Meanwhile, it invested in internal balancing by building a nuclear weapon program that deters the US status quo power as well as regional status quo states. This was a game changer for North Korea since, prior to that, it had found itself unable to balance internally against regional threats, leaving external balancing or bandwagoning as the only two options available. Nuclear deterrence is now at the core of its strategic positioning. However, neither China nor Russia necessarily has complementary or overlapping aims with Pyongyang. Russia has territorial disputes with Japan over the southern Kuril Islands; China eyes both conquest of Taiwan as well as controlling the South China Sea. The question then is, how long can North Korea continue to pursue internal balancing? How much longer will it be able to do so?

Based on this strategic configuration, the region appears locked in a local arms race, as captured by table 5.2. This section, however, only deals with Japan, North Korea, and the two main great powers, China and the United States. To attain a more comprehensive perspective of the East Asian landscape, other pertinent issues demand attention, including Taiwan and the East China Sea. Similar to the historical case examined earlier, the multitude of actors in the region amplifies the intricacy of potential interactions.

EMPIRICAL FINDINGS AND PREDICTIONS

The NCR framework we developed offers a simplified view of how great power competition shapes the behavior of second-tier states, whose interactions in turn determine regional outcomes. It should help us understand which regions are more at risk of erupting into conflict compared to those more likely to remain peaceful. Our empirical analysis found our framework to be informative and capable of capturing most of the significant strategic behavior of both status quo and revisionist states. It demonstrates one way of using historical experiences to understand what may happen in the New Cold War. It is important to note that theoretical frameworks are not designed to elucidate every intricate detail of states' strategic actions; rather, they illuminate overarching trends that are observed. In this aspect, our framework holds valuable utility.

Looking at the contemporary cases, the two status quo states—Japan and Poland—were both formal US allies, either through NATO or bilateral treaties. Hence, while buck-passing might have been their preferred option in a perfect world, external balancing was actually their default position. In the two regional settings studied, the US status quo power was involved through security guarantees. However, with America's relative decline and talks of withdrawal from world affairs, especially under the Trump Administration, status quo states feared that Washington would reduce its great power regional involvement. As a result, Tokyo and Warsaw combined internal balancing and external balancing by increasing significantly their defense budget and military purchases. This is where the similarity in the comparison ends, as the other aspects of their strategic behavior were significantly different. Poland did not trust the EU as an alternative status quo great power to assure its security. As a result, Warsaw was forced to double down on external balancing with the United States. Japan, however, relied on strategic alternatives. Japan moved closer to like-minded states that are part of the US alliance network in the Indo-Pacific.

Our initial thoughts on this subject were shaped by a sense that the United States was destined to reduce its role in several regions in the near future. The Obama Administration, hamstrung by the consequences of the 2008 financial crisis, cut defense obligations where it could. Sensing the competition from China, Obama pivoted to Asia whereby US resources were withdrawn from some areas to be concentrated in East Asia. This was done due to resource constraints; the subsequent Trump administration, on the other hand, demonstrated a desire to reduce American commitments in several regions. President Biden and his advisors have attempted to reverse Trump's actions, but it is safe to assume that the United States will continue to have to prioritize among its commitments, emphasizing some regions over others. Further withdrawals are therefore likely. Meanwhile, China remains assertive in East Asia but is also seeking to enhance its position elsewhere, such as the Middle East. China's future actions depend on whether it can maintain its economic momentum—and here it faces several challenges. The government is still learning how to manage a market-based system; more importantly, a major demographic crisis looms in China's future. We were also concerned about the impact an emboldened and empowered Russia would have on several regions. Russia's fate as a revisionist great power depends greatly on the outcome of its war against Ukraine. The cost of that conflict will surely reduce its capacities for some time.

A New Cold War appears to have begun. As in the past, great powers' capabilities will wax and wane during this coming competition. Their attention will shift from one region to another as well. We therefore need the tools to predict how such changes will play out. We also need to include the decisions of second-tier states in our calculations to ensure the accuracy of our predictions. Our framework is a first step in this direction.

NOTES

1. Matthieu Kroenig, *The Return of Great Power Rivalry: Democracy versus Autocracy from the Ancient World to the U.S. and China* (Oxford: Oxford University Press, 2020); Graham Allison, *Destined for War: Can America and China Escape Thucydides's Trap?* (New York: Houghton Mifflin Harcourt, 2017).
2. Jun Mai, Wendy Wu, and Guo Rui, "'Incomparable Glory' Awaits China on World Stage, Xi Jinping Tells Party Congress," *South China Morning Post* (October 17, 2022),

https://www.scmp.com/news/china/politics/article/3196167/incomparable-glory-awaits-china-world-stage-xi-jinping-tells.
3. Michael E. Becker, Matthew S. Cohen, Sidita Kushi, and Ian P. McManus, "Revisiting the Russian Empire: The Crimean Intervention Through a Neoclassical Realist Lens," *European Security* 25, no. 1 (2015): 112–33.
4. Steve Chan, "Can't Get No Satisfaction? The Recognition of Revisionist States," *International Relations of the Asia-Pacific* 4, no. 2 (2004): 207–238.
5. David A. Lake, Lisa Martin, and Thomas Risse, "Challenges to the Liberal Order: Reflections on International Organization," *International Organization* 75, no. 2 (2021): 225–57.
6. Ursula Von der Layen, "State of the Union Address," *The European Commission* (September 14, 2022), https://ec.europa.eu/commission/presscorner/detail/en/speech_22_5493.
7. Lake, Martin, and Risse, "Challenges to the Liberal Order," 243.
8. Lionel Barber and Henry Foy, "Vladimir Putin Says Liberalism Has 'Become Obsolete,'" *Financial Times* (June 27, 2019), https://www.ft.com/content/670039ec-98f3-11e9-9573-ee5cbb98ed36.
9. Sabra Ayres, "U.S. Must Accept a New, Multipolar World Order, Russian Foreign Minister Says," *Los Angeles Times* (January 15, 2018), https://www.latimes.com/world/la-fg-russia-lavrov-20180115-story.html.
10. Mai, Wu, and Rui, "'Incomparable Glory.'"
11. Andrej Krickovic, "Revisionism Revisited: Developing a Typology for Classifying Russia and Other Revisionist Powers," *International Politics* 59, no. 3 (2021): 616–39; Steve Chan, "Challenging the Liberal Order: The US Hegemon as a Revisionist Power," *International Affairs* 97, no. 5 (2021): 1335–52; Andrey A. Sushentsov and William C. Wohlforth, "The Tragedy of US-Russian Relations: NATO Centrality and the Revisionists' Spiral," *International Politics* 57, no. 3 (2020): 427–50; Steve Chan, Weixing Hu, and Kai He. "Discerning States' Revisionist and Status-Quo Orientations: Comparing China and the US," *European Journal of International Relations* 25, no. 2 (2019): 613–40.
12. Andrew Moravcsik, "Taking Preferences Seriously: A Liberal Theory of International Politics," *International Organization* 51, no. 4 (1997): 513–53.
13. Evelyn Goh, "In Response: Alliance Dynamics, Variables, and the English School for East Asia," *International Politics* 57, no. 2 (2020): 278–84; Mark Beeson and Alan Bloomfield, "The Trump Effect Downunder: U.S. Allies, Australian Strategic Culture, and the Politics of Path Dependence," *Contemporary Security Policy* 40, no. 3 (July 2019): 335–61; Jaeyoung Kim, "The Agency of Secondary States in Order Transition in the Indo-Pacific," *The Pacific Review* (online, 2022): 1–29.
14. Kenneth Neal Waltz, *Theory of International Politics* (Menlo Park, CA: Addison-Wesley 1979), 129; Gideon Rose, "Neoclassical Realism and Theories of Foreign Policy," *World Politics* 51, no. 1 (1998): 150–54; Jeffrey Taliaferro, "Security Seeking under Anarchy," *International Security* 25, no. 3 (2000): 128–61.
15. Foreign policy executives refer to small groups of Cabinet members in a government. Norrin Ripsman, "Neoclassical Realism," in *The International Studies Compendium Project*, eds. Robert Denemark et al. (Oxford: Wiley-Blackwell, 2011).

16. Norrin M. Ripsman, Jeffrey W. Taliaferro, and Steven E. Lobell, *Neoclassical Realist Theory of International Politics* (New York: Oxford University Press, 2016); Rose, "Neoclassical Realism and Theories of Foreign Policy."
17. Gustav Meibauer, "Interests, Ideas, and the Study of State Behaviour in Neoclassical Realism," *Review of International Studies* 46, no.1 (2020): 20–36; Nicholas Kitchen, "Ideas of Power and the Power of Ideas: Systematising Neoclassical Realist Theory," in *Neoclassical Realism in European Politics: Bringing Power Back In*, eds. Asle Toje and Barbara Kunz (Manchester: Manchester University Press, 2012), 79–95.
18. Elias Götz, "Neoclassical Realist Theories, Intervening Variables, and Paradigmatic Boundaries," *Foreign Policy Analysis* 17, no. 2 (2021): 4–5; Brian Rathbun, "A Rose by Any Other Name: Neoclassical Realism as the Logical and Necessary Extension of Structural Realism," *Security Studies* 17, no. 2 (2008): 294–321; Fareed Zakaria, *From Wealth to Power* (Princeton, NJ: Princeton University Press, 1998), 38–40.
19. Gideon Rose, "Neoclassical Realism and Theories of Foreign Policy," *World Politics* 51, no. 1 (1998); Mark R. Brawley, "Britain's Trade Liberalization in the 1840s: A Defensive Neoclassical Realist Explanation," *Foreign Policy Analysis* 18, no. 4 (2022).
20. If threats are not present, NCR is not particularly informative.
21. Thomas J. Christensen and Jack Snyder, "Chain Gangs and Passed Bucks: Predicting Alliance Patterns in Multipolarity," *International Organization* 44, no. 2 (1990).
22. Buck-passing is usually contingent on the geographic location of the threat. By focusing on interstate competition within regions, we assume the states we are examining are all in close proximity to one another.
23. Darren J. Lim and Zack Cooper, "Reassessing Hedging: The Logic of Alignment in East Asia," *Security Studies* 24, no. 4 (2015): 696–727.
24. Denny Roy, "Southeast Asia and China: Balancing or Bandwagoning?" *Contemporary Southeast Asia* 27, no. 2 (2005): 305–22; John J. Mearsheimer, *The Tragedy of Great Power Politics* (New York: W. W. Norton & Company, 2014); Robert G. Kaufman, "To Balance or To Bandwagon? Alignment Decisions in 1930s Europe," *Security Studies* 1, no. 3 (March 1, 1992): 417–47; Stephen Walt, *The Origins of Alliances* (Ithaca, NY: Cornell University Press, 1987).
25. Karel Holbik and Edward Drachman, "Egypt as Recipient of Soviet Aid, 1955–1970," *Zeitschrift für die gesamte Staatswissenschaft / Journal of Institutional and Theoretical Economics* 127, no. 1 (1971), 137–65.
26. Richard Nixon, "U.S. Foreign Policy for the 1970s: A New Strategy for Peace, *A Report to the Congress by Richard Nixon, President of the United States, February 18, 1970*" in *Foreign Relations of the United States, 1969–1976*, Foundations of Foreign Policy (1969–1972): (Office of the Historian), https://history.state.gov/historicaldocuments/frus1969-76v01/d60.
27. Lindsey Ford and Zack Cooper, "America's Alliances after Trump: Lessons from the Summer of '69," *Texas National Security Review* 4, no. 2 (2021): 100–116.
28. Jennifer Lind, "Pacificism or Passing the Buck? Testing Theories of Japanese Security Policy," *International Security* 29, no. 1 (2004), 91–121.
29. Yukinori Komine, "Whither a "Resurgent Japan": The Nixon Doctrine and Japan's Defense Buikdup, 1969–1976," *Journal of Cold War Studies* 16, no. 3 (2014): 88–128.
30. Peter J. Katzenstein, *Cultural Norms and National Security* (Ithaca, NY: Cornell University Press, 1996), 328.

31. Macrotrends, "Japan Military Spending/Defense Budget 1960–2023," 2023, https://www.macrotrends.net/countries/JPN/japan/military-spending-defense-budget#:~:text=Japan%20military%20spending%2Fdefense%20budget%20for%202021%20was%20%2454.12B,a%205.02%25%20increase%20from%202018.
32. Kyungwon Choi, "Japan's Foreign Policy toward Korean Peninsula in the Détente Era," *Wilson Center* NKIDP Working Paper, no. 6 (2017), https://www.wilsoncenter.org/publication/japans-foreign-policy-toward-korean-peninsula-the-detente-era-attempt-multilayered.
33. Leon Whyte, "Evolution of the U.S.-ROK Alliance: Abandonment Fears," *The Diplomat*, 2015, https://thediplomat.com/2015/06/evolution-of-the-u-s-rok-alliance-abandonment-fears/.
34. Macrotrends, "South Korea Military Spending/Defense Budget 1960-2023" 2023, https://www.macrotrends.net/countries/KOR/south-korea/military-spending-defense-budget#:~:text=South%20Korea%20military%20spending%2Fdefense%20budget%20for%202021%20was%20%2450.23,a%201.91%25%20increase%20from%202018.
35. Macrotrends, "South Korea Military Spending/Defense Budget 1960-2023," 2023.
36. Chung-in Moon and Sangkeun Lee, "Military Spending and the Arms Race on the Korean Peninsula," *Asian Perspective* 33, no. 4 (January 2009): 69–99.
37. Macrotrends, "U.S. Military Spending/Defense Budget 1960-2023," 2023, https://www.macrotrends.net/countries/USA/united-states/military-spending-defense-budget#:~:text=U.S.%20military%20spending%2Fdefense%20budget%20for%202020%20was%20%24778.40B,a%205.53%25%20increase%20from%202017.
38. Victor D. Cha and David C. Kang, *"Nuclear North Korea: A Debate on Engagement" Strategies* (New York: Columbia University Press, 2003).
39. Ministry of National Defence. "The Defence Concept of the Republic of Poland," *Republic of Poland* (Warsaw, May 2017), https://www.gov.pl/web/national-defence/defenceconcept-publication.
40. Anna Dunin, "Intel Brief: Poland on Edge over Russian Drills," *ISN Security Watch*, (November 18, 2009), https://css.ethz.ch/en/services/digital-library/articles/article.html/109702#:~:text=Russia's%20largest%20ever%20post%2D%E2%80%8B,writes%20for%20ISN%20Security%20Watch.
41. Ministry of National Defence. "The Defence Concept of the Republic of Poland," 6.
42. Luke Harding and Ian Traynor, "Obama Abandons Missile Defence Shield in Europe." *The Guardian* (September 17, 2009), https://www.theguardian.com/world/2009/sep/17/missile-defence-shield-barack-obama#:~:text=Barack%20Obama%20has%20abandoned%20the,long%20soured%20relations%20with%20Russia.
43. Alexander Lanoszka, "Poland in a Time of Geopolitical Flux," *Contemporary Politics* 26, no. 4 (August 2020): 458–74.
44. Lanoszka, "Poland in a Time of Geopolitical Flux."
45. Justyna Zajac, *Poland's Security Policy. The West, Russia, and the Changing International Order* (London: Palgrave Macmillan, 2016), 138.
46. ThefirstNews, "Polish PM Voices a Clear Stance on EU Strategic Autonomy at EU Summit," *ThefirstNews* (February 28, 2021), https://www.thefirstnews.com/article/polish-pm-voices-a-clear-stance-on-eu-strategic-autonomy-at-eu-summit-20174.
47. Military expenditures in constant (2019) US dollars. SIPRI, SIPRI Arms Transfers Database. (March 15, 2021). https://www.sipri.org/databases/armstransfers.
48. Zajac, *Poland's Security Policy.*

49. Alexandra Fouché, "Poland Boosts Defence Spending over War in Ukraine," *BBC News* (January 30, 2023). https://www.bbc.com/news/world-europe-64457401.
50. Lanoszka, "Poland in a Time of Geopolitical Flux," 464.
51. W. J. Hennigan, "Fort Trump? The Pentagon Takes a Step Toward Establishing Base in Poland," *Time*, March 13, 2019, https://time.com/5551061/poland-military-base-fort-trump/#:~:text=Polish%20President%20Andrzej%20Duda%20floated,be%20named%20%E2%80%9CFort%20Trump.%E2%80%9D.
52. Olena Lennon and Aemin Becker, "Belarus at the United Nations: An Analysis of Belarus's Global Policy Alignment Following the Maidan Revolution in Ukraine," *Demokratizatsiya: The Journal of Post-Soviet Democratization* 27, no. 3 (2019): 319–47.
53. Yauheni Preiherman, "Belarus's Asymmetric Relations with Russia: The Case of Strategic Hedging?," Working Paper, no. 4 (2017).
54. Janek Lasocki, "Repression and Isolation: Four Ways a Stolen Election Had Changed Belarus," *The Royal United Services Institute (RUSI)*, September 1, 2021, https://www.rusi.org/explore-our-research/publications/commentary/repression-and-isolation-four-ways-stolen-election-has-changed-belarus.
55. Vladimir Soldatkin, "Putin Throws $1.5 Billion Lifeline to Embattled Belarus Leader," *Reuters*, September 15, 2020, https://www.reuters.com/article/belarus-election-russia-int-idUSKBN26521Z.
56. Brian Whitmore, "Russian-Belarusian Military Merger Accelerates on NATO's Eastern Flank," *Atlantic Council*, September 15, 2021. https://www.atlanticcouncil.org/blogs/belarusalert/russian-belarusian-military-merger-accelerates-on-natos-eastern-flank/.
57. Brian Whitmore, "Russian-Belarusian Military Merger Accelerates on NATO's Eastern Flank."
58. Andrew Oros, *Japan's Security Renaissance: New Policies and Politics for the Twenty-First Century* (New York: Columbia University Press, 2017), https://doi.org/10.7312/oros17260.
59. Linda Sieg, "Trump's Criticism of U.S.-Japan Security Pact Could Be Headache for Abe," *Reuters*, (July 1, 2010). https://www.reuters.com/article/us-japan-usa-security-analysis-idUSKCN1TW1XH.
60. Mari Yamaguchi, "Japan Reveals Plan for Space Defense Unit," *Defense News*, January 21, 2020, https://www.defensenews.com/space/2020/01/21/japan-reveals-plan-for-space-defense-unit/#:~:text=The%20space%20unit%20will%20be,than%20being%20on%20the%20ground.
61. Mike Yeo, "Japan Unveils Its Hypersonic Weapons Plans," *DefenseNews*, March 13, 2020, https://www.defensenews.com/industry/techwatch/2020/03/13/japan-unveils-its-hypersonic-weapons-plans/#:~:text=Japan's%20road%20map%20also%20revealed,service%20in%20the%20early%202030s.
62. Nikkei Asia, "Lockheed to Back Mitsubishi Heavy-Led Japan Fighter Project," *Nikkei Asia*, December 11, 2020, https://asia.nikkei.com/Business/Aerospace-Defense-Industries/Lockheed-to-back-Mitsubishi-Heavy-led-Japan-fighter-project.
63. Ministry of Foreign Affairs of Japan, "The Three Principles on Transfer of Defense Equipment and Technology," *Press Releases*, April 1, 2014, https://www.mofa.go.jp/fp/nsp/page1we_000083.html. Chris W. Hughes, "Japan's Emerging Arms Transfer Strategy: Diversifying to Re-centre on the US–Japan Alliance," *The Pacific Review* 31, no. 4 (2018).

64. Christopher W. Hughes, *Japan's Foreign and Security Policy under the 'Abe Doctrine': New Dynamism or New Dead End?* (New York: Palgrave Pivot, 2015), 114.
65. Lauren Richardson, "The Autonomy-Alignment Trade-Off: Japan's Evolving Defense Posture," *Asian Politics & Policy* 12, no. 1 (2020): 27–39.
66. Richardson, "Autonomy-Alignment Trade-Off."
67. Paul Midford, "New Directions in Japan's Security: Non-US Centric Evolution," *Pacific Review* 31, no. 4 (2018): 407–23.
68. Elena Atanassova-Cornelis and Yoichiro Sato, "The US-Japan Alliance Dilemma in the Asia-Pacific: Changing Rationales and Scope," *International Spectator* 54, no. 4 (2019): 86.
69. Tristan Volpe, "The Unraveling of North Korea's Proliferation Blackmail Strategy," *Carnegie Endowment for International Peace*, April 10, 2017, https://carnegieendowment.org/2017/04/10/unraveling-of-north-korea-s-proliferation-blackmail-strategy-pub-68622; Victor Gilinsky, "Nuclear Blackmail: The 1994 U.S.-Democratic People's Republic of Korea Agreed Framework on North Korea's Nuclear Program," *Hoover Institution* 1997, https://www.hoover.org/research/nuclear-blackmail-1994-us-democratic-peoples-republic-korea-agreed-framework-north-koreas.
70. Hyung-Jin Kim and Kim Tong-Hyung, "North Korea Fires 2 Missiles in Tests Condemned by Neighbors," *AP News*, February 20, 2023, https://apnews.com/article/north-korea-south-5568ed671ba7983dee7f07693a44b3ba; Hyonhee Shin, Josh Smith, and Kantaro Komiya, "North Korea Conducts Longest-Range Missile Test Yet over Japan," *Reuters*, October 4, 2022, https://www.reuters.com/world/asia-pacific/nkorea-fires-missile-towards-east-skorea-military-2022-10-03/#:~:text=It%20was%20the%20first%20North,avoid%20flying%20over%20neighbouring%20countries.
71. Weiqi Zhang and Dmitry Zinoviev, "How North Korea Views China: Quantitative Analysis of Korean Central News Agency Reports," *The Korean Journal of Defense Analysis* 30, no. 3 (September 2018): 377–96.

CHAPTER 6

Status Competition in the Regions
Past, Present, and Future

Xiaoyu Pu

Great power competition returns to the front and center of international politics in the twenty-first century. Scholars and practitioners are actively debating how today's great power competition might be different from the US-Soviet rivalry in the Cold War era.[1] Status competition is viewed as a source of international conflict. In some circumstances, states are willing to fight for status.[2] The Ukraine war was driven by Russia's desire to regain its former status as the dominant power in the post-Soviet space. US-China tension is shaped by status competition as well. As China implements a more assertive and active foreign policy, the United States is concerned about China's potential to challenge its global position. The China experts such as Michael Pillsbury and Rush Doshi believe that China has a coherent grand strategy to replace the United States as the leading global power.[3] The international relations scholar Graham Allison warns that the United States and China are likely headed toward confrontation due to the "Thucydides' Trap."[4]

Despite this alarmist perspective in the field of international relations, the struggle for status is more complex than it may seem. Status politics is often competitive, but it is not always a zero-sum game. The emerging multiplex world is more complex than the previous multipolar world, with diverse actors and modernities coexisting in various regions.[5] The struggle for great power status can take various formats, and the choices made by these great powers have the potential to significantly influence peace and war within a regional order. The nuanced aspect of status politics deserves further examination. The first section will draw a comparison between the emerging New

Cold War and the old Cold War. The second section will explore the enduring relevance of status competition in international politics. It will shed light on how status competition among nations plays a crucial role in shaping international relations. The third section will analyze the dynamic changes in status competition, encompassing various formats observed in the past, present, and potential future scenarios. The fourth and fifth sections will compare divergent regional outcomes, specifically the Ukraine conflict in Eurasia and the state of cold peace in East Asia. In contrast to the earlier prediction that Asia is ripe for great power conflict,[6] East Asia has enjoyed several decades of relative peace while Europe is once again at war.[7] We will examine the Russia-Ukraine conflict as an illustration of a full-fledged New Cold War scenario between Russia and the West. Additionally, we will investigate how China's rise and the responses from other countries create a cold peace situation in East Asia. Facing numerous security challenges, East Asia has not yet plunged into a full-fledged New Cold War. The conclusion will discuss implications for international relations and regional order in particular.

STATUS POLITICS AND THE NEW COLD WAR

Scholars and strategists are currently actively debating whether the resurgence of great power competition signals the emergence of a New Cold War.[8] Understanding the role of status competition in great power politics becomes pivotal in framing this discussion appropriately.

The Cold War was a period characterized by geopolitical tension and ideological rivalry between the United States and the Soviet Union. It comprised several key features. Firstly, in the security domain, the international system was split into two opposing military alliances: the Western bloc, led by the United States and its allies of the North Atlantic Treaty Organization (NATO), and the Eastern bloc, dominated by the Soviet Union and its Warsaw Pact allies. While the Soviet Union engaged in intense security competition with the United States, the mutually assured destruction (MAD) doctrine prevented direct military confrontations between the superpowers. However, the Cold War did not mean that there were no military conflicts, as proxy wars occurred in various locations such as Korea, Vietnam, and Africa, with the superpowers supporting opposing regimes and factions. Secondly, the world economy was divided into two distinct systems, one led by the United States and the other by the Soviet Union. The two economic systems had minimal ties with each other. Thirdly, the Cold War era was marked by fervent ideological competition, with the United States and the Soviet

Union representing opposing ideologies. Both superpowers vigorously competed for power and influence in Europe and the Global South, each believing their systems were superior to the other.

Some analysts contend that a New Cold War is unfolding in the twenty-first century, primarily involving the United States, China, and Russia. Nonetheless, debates persist on whether we should indeed characterize the current great power politics as a New Cold War.[9] To gain clarity on this matter, it is crucial to examine both the similarities and differences between the New Cold War and its predecessor. Certain trends in the contemporary era bear resemblances to the Cold War era. For instance, there exists a profound strategic rivalry and a sense of mistrust among major powers. Additionally, the presence of nuclear weapons poses a considerable risk of escalation and conflict, constituting a challenge to world peace.

However, unlike the old Cold War, the New Cold War exhibits several distinct features. Firstly, while there are rising tensions between the United States and China, there are no rigid opposing military alliances akin to those seen in the Cold War era. Although China and Russia maintain a strategic partnership with a military component, the Sino-Russia relationship should be more appropriately understood as a strategic partnership rather than a military alliance as there are significant limitations in this relationship.[10] Similarly, India and the United States have strengthened their military cooperation to counterbalance China, but India does not have an immediate plan to establish a military alliance with the United States.[11] Furthermore, instead of building formal alliances, China, Russia, and India are striving to maintain their strategic autonomy in the contemporary era. Secondly, great power competition in the new era occurs within the context of deep economic globalization. In contrast, during the Cold War era, the United States and the Soviet Union had extremely limited economic ties with each other. The contemporary era presents a paradox where extensive economic interdependence coexists with growing political tensions and security competition. While the United States and its allies need to build their economic resilience in the era of great power competition, decoupling with China will disrupt the translational production network, causing significant problems for the world.[12] Lastly, unlike the gradual establishment of boundaries and rules of engagement seen during the old Cold War, the new era is characterized by unpredictability and ambiguity. Great powers compete in various domains, and the rules of the game have not been firmly established in certain areas, such as artificial intelligence (AI) and cyberspace.[13]

By recognizing these salient features of the New Cold War, we can better comprehend the complexities of the current global geopolitical landscape.

In this context, the study of status politics can offer new insights into the dynamics of the New Cold War. Great powers engage in competition not only for security reasons but also driven by motivations related to status. Status competition remains an enduring aspect of international politics, though the format and emphasis of such competitions may vary across different contexts. The New Cold War, unlike its predecessor, encompasses a broader range of domains where great powers compete, including trade, finance, cyberspace, outer space, and technology. Thus, great power competition extends beyond the traditional military and security domains. Moreover, in the New Cold War era, it is essential to recognize that great powers vie for influence and followers, and their competitions shape the choices and options available to secondary states in a profoundly globalized world. By understanding the role of status politics and the expansion of competition into various domains, we can better understand the complex interactions and power dynamics that define the New Cold War.

STATUS COMPETITION IN WORLD POLITICS: THE ENDURING RELEVANCE

It is widely documented that states care about international status, which can be defined as "collective beliefs about a given state's ranking on valued attributes (wealth, coercive capabilities, culture, demographic position, socio-political organization, and diplomatic clout)."[14] Status competition refers to a process by which states compete with each other for a higher standing in international society. It is the pursuit of relative respect and prestige among states in the international system. States might compete for status in multiple domains in various ways. They could pursue status through the acquisition of military weapons, through soft power and cultural promotion, and by pursuing policies that generate rapid development and high economic growth, and great powers typically pursue their status in all these together.

Based on social science research, there are several reasons why states compete for status in international relations. First, international competition is often driven by the scarcity of status in the international society. When status is viewed as a positional good, it is a limited resource that cannot be equally shared among all states. Status competition is widely recognized as an important cause of conflict in international politics, and some even see it as a zero-sum game.[15]

Second, international status competition is also driven by the discrepancy of status aspiration and status recognition. Rising powers are often concerned that their desired high status cannot be fully recognized by the established powers. The conflict between an established power and a rising power becomes more probable as the gap in relative power between them narrows and the rising power's grievances with the current international order can no longer be resolved peacefully. This is in line with the power transition theory, which states that conflict is more likely as the power difference between established and rising powers decreases and the rising power's dissatisfaction with the current order increases.[16] For instance, rising powers such as China and India are often driven by psychological insecurity and postcolonial ideologies.[17] These countries are classified as "parvenu powers" by Richard Lebow and are highly sensitive to their status.[18] When global power shifts, the success of this transition rests on the ability of established powers to accommodate the rising powers. However, the status ambition of these rising powers and the denial of their status by established powers can lead to conflict. Situations might become dangerous when material power of rising powers increases while their statuses do not follow. The lack of recognition of their statuses by established powers can drive rising powers to pursue revisionist behaviors, even though the status quo might benefit these rising powers.[19]

Finally, status competition is not just a motivation for state behavior but also influences domestic contests over foreign policy.[20] The denial of status to Japan by the Western powers was one of the key events that eventually led to the attack on Pearl Harbor in 1941.[21]

While recognizing the enduring relevance of status competition, we should be aware that status conflict could be exaggerated in several respects.

Status competition is not always a zero-sum game. Status competition is a zero-sum game if the status is only considered as a positional good in an absolute sense. However, the concept of a club good adds some nuances to this perspective. A club refers to a group that shares certain benefits and resources among its members.[22] Although clubs can be crowded, they do not necessarily operate as a zero-sum game. Adding new members to an elite club may dilute some privileges of the existing members, but it will not erase them entirely. Furthermore, adding new members can actually benefit the club and its members as a whole.

The idea that status is a limited resource is sometimes overstated. While both individuals and nations place importance on their status, they are not always solely focused on increasing their status. As achieving higher status often comes at a cost, people may weigh the trade-offs between their desire for status and other goals, and may not always prioritize increasing their status. In particular, leaders may not always take an aggressive approach in enhancing their nation's status due to various trade-offs with other objectives.[23] It is also important to note that while status and power may be related, they are not the same. Status is more connected to social and cultural factors, and nations and individuals may strive for status in different ways and through various means. This versatility could provide more opportunities for nations to coexist and reconcile their differing status aspirations.

Status competition should be differentiated from a situation of status dilemma, which is a situation where two states with largely compatible status aspirations are driven into a vicious circle of conflict due to uncertainty about and misperception of status signals.[24] In a status dilemma situation, conflict is driven by misunderstandings and misperceptions of status challenges, not by the zero-sum nature of the status competition. The status dilemma is also different from the security dilemma, which is when a country's efforts to increase its military capability can lead to a vicious cycle of an arms race, reducing security for all involved states. The status dilemma is characterized by high stakes and heavy investments that are driven by status concerns, and the process of signaling and recognizing status claims is shaped by uncertainty and complex incentives. Even states with defensive intentions can miscommunicate and misperceive status signals.

STATUS COMPETITION AND WORLD POLITICS: THE CHANGING DYNAMICS

Status competition has played a significant role in shaping world politics, and it has enduring relevance in contemporary international relations. The formats and meanings of status competition have changed over time.

As status is primarily rooted in social interaction, the standards of status are subject to change in different contexts. At the domestic societal level, there are many social spheres with different status criteria. Recognizing the continual formation of new social realms in our society requires us to reconsider certain presumptions made by sociologists about status. The inclination to associate status with the long-standing framework of class disregards the relatively effortless manner in which standards of status can be established and altered. While scholars often conflate status with class or power, status is "more fluid, more easily changed than class or power."[25] In world politics, the perimeters of status competition have changed over time and across societies. Recognizing the possibility that status standards are changeable and flexible, people do not always have to see the status as a scarce resource, and there seems to be a proliferation of prizes in every corner. There are similar situations in world politics. On the global stage, while some international organizations such as the United Nations Security Council (UNSC) are highly privileged status clubs, there is a proliferation of international clubs such as the G20 and BRICS (Brazil, Russia, India, China, and South Africa). Rising powers play important roles in these multilateral platforms, and their status aspirations could be accommodated in a broader context. The social nature of status and the possibility of status abundance give nation-states more flexibility to pursue status accommodation.[26] Admittedly, in the twenty-first century, altering Western domination in international institutions and discursive power is not a straightforward task, primarily due to the Western hegemony's dual nature, encompassing both material and ideational dimensions.[27] Despite China's rise as a global economic power, it is less likely that China can replace the United States as a new hegemonic power, mainly because its illiberal political system is unlikely to garner support from great powers with liberal ideologies.[28]

In the past, status competition in world politics was largely a contest between empires and great powers for the sphere of influence and territorial dominance, with military power being a key factor in determining the competition outcome. Military power was considered crucial not only for controlling territory but also as a key mechanism for settling uncertainty and dispute over hegemonic struggle. The hegemonic war was traditionally regarded as a primary mechanism for deciding who should have the authority to rule in an international system.[29] The international order was fundamentally broken in the two world wars in the first half of the twentieth century. During the Cold War era, the United States and the Soviet Union did not fight a hot war against each other. But the two superpowers competed for influence in various regions, and this resulted in proxy wars, such as the Vietnam War and the Soviet-Afghan War.[30]

The current geopolitical landscape is fraught with uncertainty, and the future trajectory remains unclear. Various scenarios are possible, such as a bipolar system led by the United States and China[31] or the emergence of a "multiplex world order."[32] While military power continues to be a crucial tool in statecraft, it is no longer the sole determining factor in shaping international outcomes. In the contemporary world, international competition resembles a complex interplay of multiple-dimensional chess games, unfolding across various domains, including military, economic, technological, and diplomatic areas. The standards of status are changing, and different actors might view different things as status symbols. Since the end of the World War II, Germany and Japan have achieved high status through their economic and technological success.[33] In its Reform and Opening era, China has enhanced its national power and international status primarily through high economic growth, and Chinese leaders have promoted the idea of "peaceful rise."[34] However, this does not mean that contemporary Chinese leaders would ignore hard power. Chinese elites often emphasize that their country should develop its comprehensive national power, including both military and nonmilitary dimensions.[35] The rise of globalization and interdependence has created new avenues for competition, with great powers seeking to project their power and influence through technological, economic, and diplomatic means. From Hollywood movies to international aid programs, states are seeking to enhance their status and image on the world stage. The end of the Cold War marked a new era in international relations. With the collapse of the Soviet Union, the United States emerged as the sole superpower, and the rest of the world struggled to find its position in this new world order. It is unclear if and when the current distribution of power will be further shifted in the coming years. In recent years, the United States remains the only superpower, but it is not as dominant as it was before. Non-Western powers have played a more active role.[36]

Looking ahead, status competition in world politics will continue to evolve, with new dynamics and new norms shaping the competition. Great powers might promote new norms and a new culture of status symbols in the international system. Traditionally, military power has been a major source of status in international politics, but other factors such as ideological appeal, economic growth, popular culture, and technological innovation can play an increasingly important role. It is important to examine whether great powers still see military capability as a key tool for gaining power and status in the twenty-first century. The increasing importance of technology has created new opportunities for competition, with states vying for dominance in fields such as cybersecurity and artificial intelligence.[37]

International leadership through the provision of public goods will become even more crucial in the future. In domestic society, individuals often desire to belong to a group or community, and status hierarchies can form through cooperative social interactions to achieve a common goal.[38] Similarly, in international relations, great powers can signal their status through the provision of public goods. According to Gilpin, there are three main sources of legitimacy for great powers in international politics: military victory, the provision of public goods, and a widely accepted ideology.[39] In the contemporary era, can great powers effectively provide the necessary public goods to address global issues? The provision of public goods is a crucial aspect of statecraft that can elevate a nation's international status and image. When a great power assumes the responsibility of providing public goods, it may be driven by its ambition to play a more significant role in international affairs. However, it is essential to acknowledge that international leadership is often a rare occurrence, as great powers tend to prioritize their domestic political considerations and national interests. With the numerous international challenges ranging from financial crises to climate change, the world often faces a deficit in global leadership. When both the dominant hegemonic power and the rising power fail to shoulder responsibilities in providing public goods during international crises, the lack of international leadership can lead to turmoil. This problem has been referred to as the "Kindleberger Trap" by Joseph Nye Jr.[40] While international leadership may not always be forthcoming, great powers sometimes engage in public goods provision as a means of enhancing their status and image on the world stage. One such example was vaccine diplomacy during the Covid crisis, where major powers engaged in the conspicuous giving of vaccines to project a positive international image.[41] For instance, India's vaccine diplomacy was partly motivated by signaling its regional leadership and countering China's growing influence in South Asia.[42] During the Trump presidency, the United States prioritized domestic vaccine supply. But the Biden administration sought to restore US global leadership through its own vaccine diplomacy. Samantha Power highlighted in *Foreign Affairs* that "the Biden administration can spearhead global vaccine distribution in a way that reminds the world of what the United States can uniquely do."[43]

In the post–Cold War era, the international order has undergone significant changes, and the competition for status among nations has become increasingly intense. The strategies adopted by great powers to achieve status have shaped the post–Cold War era and have had a profound impact on regional order. Regional order can be defined as "a pattern of regularized interactions among states and between states and key non-state actors in a regional domain characterized by conflict, cooperation, peace, or mixed patterns."[44] In particular, Russia and China have taken different approaches to status competition, with Russia relying on military means and China focusing on both military and nonmilitary means.

The following two sections will shed light on various features of the emerging New Cold War. Russia's invasion of Ukraine and the response from NATO illustrate key features of the New Cold War. China's rise generates concerns about the New Cold War but also highlights important differences between the current situation and the old Cold War in Asia.

THE RUSSIA-UKRAINE CONFLICT AND THE NEW COLD WAR

The end of the Cold War marked a significant shift in the global power dynamic. The West emerged as the dominant player on the world stage. However, Russia, once a superpower in its own right, was discontented with its diminished status and sought to reassert itself as a great power.[45]

Russia's invasion of Ukraine and the response from the West vividly illustrate some key features of the New Cold War in Eurasia. First of all, although Russia is fighting a war with Ukraine, which is supported by NATO countries, both the United States and Russia have been cautious about engaging in direct military confrontation with each other. This situation bears a resemblance to the proxy wars seen during the Cold War era. Second, great powers compete in a context of deep economic globalization. Since the end of the Cold War, Russia has tried to integrate into the West-led global economic system. In response to Russia's aggressive behaviors, the United States has mobilized its allies to punish Russia through extreme sanctions. This has led Russia to become more reliant on China in economic and trade domains.[46] Finally, there is a limited ideological component in the New Cold War scenario. American leaders criticize Russia's invasion as a violation of international law, and they often frame the competition as a battle between democracy and autocracy.[47]

Status competition can help explain why countries engage in actions that may not be in their strategic or economic interests but may be motivated by their status concerns. While the Ukraine conflict is driven by multiple motives, it is clearly fueled by Russia's desire to assert its dominant status in the former Soviet republics. Once a superpower in its own right, Russia is seeking to establish itself as a great power and the protector of Russian speakers, both within and outside its borders. Russia sees Ukraine as an important part of its historical and cultural identity, and the conflict has been fueled by Russia's desire to maintain its influence in the region.

Russia views its military strength as a means of projecting power and sending a message to the West that it is still a force to be reckoned with. Russia's military modernization efforts, including the development of new weapons systems and the strengthening of its armed forces, have contributed to its efforts to reestablish its status as a great power. Russia's invasion of Ukraine in 2022 was a clear demonstration of Russia's willingness to use military force to assert its political and territorial claims. Russia took a bold act outside of international law and norms in order to achieve its objectives. Before taking military action against Ukraine in 2022, Russia already conducted military actions in various contexts, including the Russo-Georgian war in 2008 and the Russian military involvement in the Syrian conflict in 2015.

States may choose different strategies for enhancing their international status, and their choice is constrained and shaped by their resources and national capabilities. Russia and China have taken different approaches toward the current international order. Russia is a relatively declining power, and it has taken a confrontational approach to reasserting its great power status on the world stage. China, as a cautious rising power that has benefited from the existing international order, has largely taken a more moderate approach to shape the incremental change of the existing order.[48] Russia has fallen back on coercion and military power largely because it cannot effectively use a nonmilitary approach. In contrast, China has the economic resources and comprehensive national capabilities to seek international status in a more peaceful manner.[49] Russia previously tried to integrate Ukraine through nonmilitary means such as economic inducement and soft power promotion, but its efforts largely failed as Ukraine chose to move closer to the European Union.[50] In response, Russia chose to employ more coercive means, and Putin made the fateful decision to attack Ukraine militarily in 2022.

In sum, Russia's reliance on military means to assert its status as a great power has profoundly impacted regional order. The Russia-Ukraine conflict illustrates some key features of the New Cold War. The conflict is similar to proxy wars in the Cold War era. While there is a direct military confrontation between Russia and Ukraine, the United States and its NATO allies do not engage in direct military fighting with Russia. The conflict occurs in the context of deep globalization. The West is weaponizing interdependence to punish Russia, while Russia is eager to seek an alternative system of economic and political support. Russia's invasion of Ukraine has challenged the post–Cold War order and demonstrated Russia's willingness to use military force to assert its great power status and political influence.

THE RISE OF CHINA AND THE COLD PEACE IN EAST ASIA

The rise of China has altered the balance of power in East Asia. It has led to a situation of cold peace where the United States and China competition has intensified but not yet escalated into direct military conflict. The Sino-US competition is not only about strategic and economic interests but also about status, which has important implications for the future of the region.

The term "cold peace" does not imply a state of enduring peace without security problems. In East Asia, China's development of comprehensive capabilities, including military and economic coercive power, poses potential threats to neighboring states. China's expansion of influence and the United States' active efforts to counterbalance it have contributed to heightened tensions in the region, raising concerns about the possibility of a New Cold War or even the risk of a hot war.[51] However, it is essential to acknowledge that multiple regional factors have had stabilizing effects.[52] These factors have thus far prevented East Asia from plunging into a full-fledged New Cold War scenario.

Admittedly there are worrying trends in Asia as China's rise generates complicated reactions from the United States and regional states. First of all, China's military moderation and US competitive strategy against China have intensified in recent years. Taiwan is still an unresolved issue that could potentially drag China and the United States into direct military confrontation. China's actions in the South China Sea have led to tensions with neighboring countries such as Vietnam and the Philippines. These countries view China's assertiveness as a threat to their territorial claims and sovereignty. Similarly, China's expanding military capabilities and growing economic power have led to concerns among countries such as South Korea, Japan, India, and Australia, who fear that China may seek to use its power to coerce them. China still has unresolved territorial disputes with India and maritime disputes with Japan, the Philippines, and Vietnam. These countries have all strengthened security cooperation with the United States.

Second, the rising political tensions and security competitions have negative implications for the broad economic and social ties between the United States and China. While complete decoupling is still unlikely, China and the United States have taken actions to selectively reduce economic dependency on each other. Third, while ideological elements in the United States-China competition are still limited, there is growing ideological competition between the two countries. Some American leaders such as President Joe Biden claim that the United States does not seek a New Cold War with China.[53] However, American leaders and officials typically frame their competition with China and Russia as "the battle between democracy and autocracy."[54] Finally, while most regional states have rational incentives to avoid choosing sides between the United States and China, it is debatable how sustainable the hedging strategy of regional states could be in the long term. Some analysts suggest that it is increasingly difficult for regional states and developing countries to maintain neutrality in Sino-US competition.[55]

While there are security tensions, China's status competition with the United States has not yet led to military conflict in East Asia. China's regional aspiration is both ambitious and limited. China does want to play a leading role in East Asia, and China has resentment against US primacy in East Asia. However, it is debatable if China has intentions and means to exclude the United States out of Asia. Even with resentment against US military presence in Asia, Beijing has not yet offered a viable alternative vision of how the Asian security order should be organized.[56] In recent years, the Chinese government proposed various ideas such as the Global Security Initiative, and Chinese officials often criticize US alliances as examples of Cold War mentality.[57] China's criticism of US hegemony (including American military presence in Asia) should be largely interpreted as a delegitimating narrative.[58] Beijng's narrative has not yet transformed into its official action against the US alliance in Asia. Across the Indo-Pacific region, many countries still rely on the United States to provide security even though they have broad economic ties with China.

Unlike Russia, which is a military superpower and a declining economic power, China is an economic superpower and a regional military power. China has leveraged its economic power and technological innovations to enhance its status and expand its influence in the world. By focusing on economic growth, China has built strong economic ties with most of its neighboring countries. China, as a rising global power, has taken its advantage in infrastructure building to enhance its status and influence in the international arena. Great powers in the past emphasized territorial expansion as the symbol of great power status. Admittedly China still takes a strong position to defend its territorial and maritime claims in various disputes with its neighboring countries. Beijing has settled most of its border disputes with neighboring countries through considerable concessions.[59] The Chinese leaders in the Reform and Opening era have emphasized economic growth as the crucial factor in shaping China's international competitiveness. Instead of focusing on traditional military balancing, Beijing has also developed various nonmilitary tools, including institutional balancing, to advance its power and status in the region.[60] One of the most prominent examples of China's subtle approach is its Belt and Road Initiative (BRI). This infrastructure development project aims to connect countries across Asia, Europe, and Africa through trade and investment.[61] Furthermore, China has not only actively participated in regional institutions, but it has actively built new institutions through a variety of platforms, such as Asian Infrastructure Investment Bank and Shanghai Cooperation Organization.

As China's economic power has grown, it has developed and implemented various coercive tools regionally and globally.[62] Given China's strength in economic power, nonmilitary tools are still prioritized in China's regional diplomacy. China's economic power has enabled it to engage in economic coercion, which has also led to concerns among other countries in the region. For example, China has used its economic power to punish South Korea for their deployment of the THAAD missile defense system and has also used economic coercion to pressure other countries to conform to its political agenda.[63] Facing backlash and rising political tensions, Chinese leaders are rethinking economic interdependence.[64] Previously they might have emphasized the positive effects of economic globalization and interdependence. Now they increasingly see the vulnerability and problems interdependence might bring to China. China's strategy is to reduce its own economic dependency on other countries while selectively using other countries' dependence on China as a coercive tool.

Since Russia's invasion of Ukraine in early 2022, Western policymakers and media have often highlighted the danger of military conflict over Taiwan. While the danger of military confrontation is real, it is crucial not to ignore the political nature of the problem. "The current tensions in the Taiwan Strait are a product of a strategic dilemma with a military component and not a military dilemma with a military solution. If war arrives in the Taiwan Strait and involves PRC, Taiwan, and U.S. forces, it is difficult to imagine a scenario whereby any party could prevail and come out strengthened by conflict."[65] Thus, Beijing, Taipei, and Washington still have rational incentives to avoid military confrontation. Even for Beijing, military confrontation is not a preferred approach to solving the dispute. Beyond military coercion, Beijing has developed and implemented comprehensive nonmilitary tools, including economic, diplomatic, and political means to restrain pro-independence forces in Taiwan and to promote eventual unification. Unlike Putin who has boldly used force to attack Ukraine, the use of force is Xi Jinping's last resort in dealing with Taiwan. As long as Taipei is not permanently moving toward de jure independence, peace and stability across the Taiwan Strait can still be maintained. For the United States, the best strategy is still to deter Beijing from using military force while politically reassuring the Chinese leaders that a long-term peaceful solution is still possible.[66]

Although East Asia has faced growing security challenges, a New Cold War has not yet occurred in the region. While Russia has sought to reestablish its status as a great power through military means, China has pursued a more comprehensive approach, using its economic power and technological innovations to project its influence and status both regionally and globally. Even if China's rising power has generated concerns, its overall strategy is less militaristic than that of Russia. Numerous regional states have maintained robust economic relations with China while also fostering security cooperation with the United States, indicating their reluctance to take sides between the two major powers.

CONCLUSION

As there is a resurgence of great power competition, scholars and strategists are debating whether this tension amounts to a New Cold War. While some suggest that a New Cold War is underway, others remain uncertain about this characterization. It is important to examine both the similarities and differences between the current situation and the original Cold War. Similarities between the two eras include profound strategic rivalry among major powers, as well as the presence of nuclear weapons posing a threat to world peace. However, unlike in the old Cold War era, there are no rigid opposing military alliances. In addition, great powers compete in the context of economic globalization, creating a paradox of extensive economic interdependence alongside escalating political tensions and security competition.

Understanding these features of the new era is essential to comprehend the complexities of the current global geopolitical landscape. Status politics plays a significant role in the New Cold War era, with great powers vying for influence and followers across domains beyond military domain, including trade, finance, technology, and space. The actions of major powers have far-reaching implications for the international order, shaping the choices made by other nations.

While status competition is often seen as an important source of conflict and tension between states in international relations, status politics is not always a zero-sum game, and the choices of great powers can shape peace and war in regional order in fundamental ways. There are various formats of status competition in international relations. Great powers may engage in status competition through military, economic, and cultural means. While status competition has enduring relevance in world politics, its formats and meanings have changed over time and across different contexts. In the past, great powers competed for power and sphere of influence with military power as the decisive factor. In the contemporary era, great powers find more diverse sources to enhance their power and status, and military power is not always a prioritized tool. Going forward, the standards of status will continue to change. Economic growth and technological innovation might be even more important in shaping international status competition.

Status competition plays a significant role in shaping regional order, with the choice of great power strategy being crucial. Russia and China have adopted different approaches to advance their power and status. Pursuing a military-centric strategy, Russia has used force to assert influence in former Soviet republics. In contrast, China has employed a combination of military and nonmilitary means to enhance its power and status. This difference in approach has had profound implications for regional order. The Russia-Ukraine conflict and the response from the West exemplify key features of the New Cold War. The conflict bears similarities to proxy wars seen during the Cold War era. Additionally, the conflict unfolds amid deep globalization, with the West weaponizing interdependence to punish Russia. Despite growing security problems, East Asia has not yet experienced a full-fledged New Cold War. China leverages its economic power to enhance its status and project influence. Although China's assertive foreign policy has generated international concerns, its overall strategy is less militaristic compared to Russia's. Many regional states in East Asia maintain strong economic ties with China while fostering close security cooperation with the United States, indicating their reluctance to take sides between the two major powers.

While the Sino-US relationship is generally more peaceful than the relationship between Russia and the West, there is still a sense of uncertainty. China has been displaying a growing assertiveness in its foreign policy. At the same time, the US policy toward China has become more hardened. Russia's pursuit of status has proven to be excessively costly and self-destructive. The questions arise: Will China fall into the same trap as Putin's Russia? Can the United States and China mutually accommodate each other in the region as well as globally? The dominant view in the United States is that China has both intentions and capabilities to challenge the US global leadership.[67] However, the Chinese leadership has often complained that the US has misperceived and miscalculated China's strategic intention.[68] Is there a situation of the status dilemma between the United States and China that is partially driven by misperception and miscommunication? To mitigate potential conflicts in East Asia, both China and the United States must handle their status game prudently. This requires careful diplomatic actions as well as maintaining open channels of communication to avoid misunderstandings and miscalculations.

NOTES

1. Hal Brands and John Lewis Gaddis, "The New Cold War," *Foreign Affairs* 100, no. 6 (November/December 2021): 10–20; Peter Harris and Iren Marinova, "American Primacy and US–China Relations: The Cold War Analogy Reversed," *Chinese Journal of International Politics* 15, no. 4 (2022): 335–51.
2. Jonathan Renshon, *Fighting for Status: Hierarchy and Conflict in World Politics* (Princeton, NJ: Princeton University Press, 2017).
3. Michael Pillsbury, *The Hundred-Year Marathon: China's Secret Strategy to Replace America as the Global Superpower* (New York: Henry Holt and Company, 2015); Rush Doshi, *The Long Game: China's Grand Strategy to Displace American Order* (New York: Oxford University Press, 2021).
4. Graham Allison, *Destined for War: Can America and China Escape Thucydides's Trap?* (Boston: Houghton Mifflin Harcourt, 2017).
5. Amitav Acharya, "After Liberal Hegemony: The Advent of a Multiplex World Order," *Ethics & International Affairs* 31, no. 3 (2017): 271–85; Manjeet S. Pardesi and Amitav Acharya, "Regional Orders and Great Power Rivalry in a Multiplex World," chapter 2.
6. Aaron L. Friedberg, "Ripe for Rivalry: Prospects for Peace in a Multipolar Asia," *International Security* 18, no. 3 (1993): 5–33.
7. Kishore Mahbubani, "Asia's Third Way," *Foreign Affairs* 102, no. 2 (March/April 2023): 130–41.
8. Brands and Gaddis, "The New Cold War"; Odd Arne Westad, "The Sources of Chinese Conduct: Are Washington and Beijing Fighting a New Cold War?," *Foreign Affairs* 98, no. 5 (September/October 2019): 86–95; Minghao Zhao, "Is a New Cold War Inevitable? Chinese Perspectives on US–China Strategic Competition," *Chinese Journal of International Politics* 12, no. 3 (September 2019): 371–94; Thomas J. Christensen, "There Will Not Be a New Cold War," *Foreign Affairs*, March 24, 2021, https://www.foreignaffairs.com/articles/united-states/2021-03-24/there-will-not-be-new-cold-war.
9. For instance, Brands and Gaddis, "The New Cold War"; Christensen, "There Will Not Be a New Cold War."
10. Igor Denisov, "'No Limits'? Understanding China's Engagement with Russia on Ukraine," Diplomat, 2022, https://thediplomat.com/2022/03/no-limits-understanding-chinas-engagement-with-russia-on-ukraine/; Patricia M. Kim, "The Limits of the No-Limits Partnership," *Foreign Affairs* 102, no. 2 (March/April 2023): 94–105.
11. Ashley J. Tellis, "America's Bad Bet on India," *Foreign Affairs*, May 1, 2023, https://www.foreignaffairs.com/india/americas-bad-bet-india-modi.
12. Thomas J. Christensen, "Mutually Assured Disruption," *World Politics* 75, no. 5 (2023): 1–18.
13. Joseph S. Nye Jr., "Deterrence and Dissuasion in Cyberspace," *International Security* 41, no. 3 (Winter 2016/2017): 44–71; Michael C. Horowitz and Lauren Kahn, "Leading in Artificial Intelligence through Confidence Building Measures," *Washington Quarterly* 44, no. 4 (November 2021): 91–106.
14. Deborah W. Larson, T.V. Paul, and William C. Wohlforth, "Status and World Order," in *Status in World Politics*, eds. T.V. Paul, Deborah W. Larson, and William C. Wohlforth (New York: Cambridge University Press, 2014), 7.

15. Allan Dafoe, Jonathan Renshon, and Paul Huth, "Reputation and Status as Motives for War," *Annual Review of Political Science* 17 (June 2014): 371–93; Deborah Welch Larson and Alexei Shevchenko, "Status Seekers: Chinese and Russian Responses to U.S. Primacy," *International Security* 34, no. 4 (April 2011): 63–95; Paul K. MacDonald and Joseph M. Parent, "The Status of Status in World Politics," *World Politics* 73, no. 2 (April 15, 2021): 358–91; Renshon, *Fighting for Status*; Steven Ward, *Status and the Challenge of Rising Powers* (Cambridge: Cambridge University Press, 2017).
16. Stephen Brooks, "Power Transitions, Then and Now: Five New Structural Barriers That Will Constrain China's Rise," *China International Strategy Review* 1, no. 1 (June 1, 2019): 65–83.
17. Yong Deng, *China's Struggle for Status: The Realignment of International Relations* (Cambridge: Cambridge University Press, 2008); Manjari Chatterjee Miller, "Re-Collecting Empire: 'Victimhood' and the 1962 Sino-Indian War," *Asian Security* 5, no. 3 (September 2009): 216–41.
18. Richard Lebow, *A Cultural Theory of International Relations* (Cambridge: Cambridge University Press, 2008).
19. Rohan Mukherjee, *Ascending Order: Rising Powers and the Politics of Status in International Institutions* (Cambridge: Cambridge University Press, 2022).
20. Steven Ward, "Decline and Disintegration: National Status Loss and Domestic Conflict in Post-Disaster Spain," *International Security* 46, no. 4 (April 1, 2022): 91–129.
21. Steven Ward, "Race, Status, and Japanese Revisionism in the Early 1930s," *Security Studies* 22, no. 4 (October 2013): 607–39.
22. Richard Cornes and Todd Sandler, *The Theory of Externalities, Public Goods, and Club Goods*, 2nd ed. (Cambridge: Cambridge University Press, 1996), 370–93.
23. Xiaoyu Pu, *Rebranding China: Contested Status Signaling in the Changing Global Order* (Stanford, CA: Stanford University Press, 2019); Ziyuan Wang, "Political Logic of Status Competition: Leaders, Status Tradeoffs, and Beijing's Vietnam Policy, 1949–1965," *Chinese Journal of International Politics* 14, no. 4 (2021): 554–86.
24. William C. Wohlforth, "Status Dilemmas and Inter-State Conflict," in *Status in World Politics* (New York: Cambridge University Press, 2014), 115–40; Xiaoyu Pu, "Status Dilemma in World Politics: An Anatomy of the China–India Asymmetrical Rivalry," *Chinese Journal of International Politics* 15, no. 3 (September 2022): 227–45.
25. Joel Best, *Everyone's a Winner: Life in Our Congratulatory Culture*, 1st ed. (Berkeley: University of California Press, 2011), 11.
26. Larson and Shevchenko, "Status Seekers."
27. G. John Ikenberry and Daniel H. Nexon, "Hegemony Studies 3.0: The Dynamics of Hegemonic Orders," *Security Studies* 28, no. 3 (July 2019): 395–421.
28. Bentley B. Allan, Srdjan Vucetic, and Ted Hopf, "The Distribution of Identity and the Future of International Order: China's Hegemonic Prospects," *International Organization* 72, no. 4 (January 2018): 839–69.
29. Robert Gilpin, *War and Change in World Politics* (Cambridge: Cambridge University Press, 1981).
30. Richard Ned Lebow and Janice Gross Stein, *We All Lost the Cold War*, rev. ed. (Princeton, NJ: Princeton University Press, 1995).
31. Øystein Tunsjø, *The Return of Bipolarity in World Politics: China, the United States, and Geostructural Realism* (Columbia University Press, 2018).

32. Amitav Acharya, "After Liberal Hegemony: The Advent of a Multiplex World Order."
33. Thomas U. Berger, *Cultures of Antimilitarism: National Security in Germany and Japan* (Baltimore: Johns Hopkins University Press, 1998). It should be noted that Germany and Japan are rethinking the role of military power in the context of the Ukraine war.
34. Kai He, "China's Rise, Institutional Balancing, and (Possible) Peaceful Order Transition in the Asia Pacific," *The Pacific Review* 35, no. 6 (November 2, 2022): 1105–34.
35. Qi Haixia, "Disputing Chinese Views on Power," *Chinese Journal of International Politics* 10, no. 2 (2017): 211–39.
36. Amitav Acharya, *The End of American World Order* (Malden, MA: Polity, 2014); Oliver Stuenkel, *Post-Western World: How Emerging Powers Are Remaking Global Order* (Malden, MA: Polity, 2016).
37. Yan Xuetong, "Bipolar Rivalry in the Early Digital Age," *Chinese Journal of International Politics* 13, no. 3 (September 2020): 313–41.
38. Amihai Glazer and Kai A. Konrad, "A Signaling Explanation for Charity," *The American Economic Review* 86, no. 4 (1996): 1019–28.
39. Gilpin, *War and Change in World Politics*.
40. Joseph S. Jr. Nye, "The Kindleberger Trap by Joseph S. Nye, Jr.," Project Syndicate, January 9, 2017, https://www.project-syndicate.org/commentary/trump-china-kindleberger-trap-by-joseph-s--nye-2017-01.
41. Xiaoyu Pu, "Status Signalling in the Indo-Pacific: Strategic Spinning, Military Posturing, and Vaccine Diplomacy," *British Journal of Politics and International Relations*, 2024, https://doi.org/10.1177/13691481241230862.
42. Bawa Singh et al., "India's Neighbourhood Vaccine Diplomacy During COVID-19 Pandemic: Humanitarian and Geopolitical Perspectives," *Journal of Asian & African Studies*, February 17, 2022, https://doi.org/10.1177/00219096221079310.
43. Samantha Power, "The Can-Do Power," *Foreign Affairs* 100, no. 1 (January/February 2021): 17.
44. T.V. Paul and Markus Kornprobst, introduction to this volume.
45. Nye, "The Kindleberger Trap."
46. Alexander Gabuev, "What's Really Going on Between Russia and China," *Foreign Affairs*, April 12, 2023, https://www.foreignaffairs.com/united-states/whats-really-going-between-russia-and-china.
47. The White House, "Remarks of President Joe Biden—State of the Union Address," The White House, March 2, 2022, https://www.whitehouse.gov/briefing-room/speeches-remarks/2022/03/01/remarks-of-president-joe-biden-state-of-the-union-address-as-delivered/.
48. Andrej Krickovic, "The Symbiotic China-Russia Partnership: Cautious Riser and Desperate Challenger," *Chinese Journal of International Politics* 10, no. 3 (September 2017): 299–329.
49. Andrej Krickovic and Zhang Chang, "Fears of Falling Short versus Anxieties of Decline: Explaining Russia and China's Approach to Status-Seeking," *Chinese Journal of International Politics* 13, no. 2 (2020): 219–51.
50. G. Gaddy Clifford and Barry Ickes, "Ukraine: A Prize Neither Russia Nor the West Can Afford to Win," Brookings, May 22, 2014, https://www.brookings.edu/articles/ukraine-a-prize-neither-russia-nor-the-west-can-afford-to-win/.

51. Christopher Layne, "Preventing the China-U.S. Cold War from Turning Hot," *Chinese Journal of International Politics* 13, no. 3 (September 2020): 343–85.
52. David C. Kang, "Still Getting Asia Wrong: No 'Contain China' Coalition Exists," *Washington Quarterly* 45, no. 4 (November 2022): 79–98.
53. MFA-PRC, "President Xi Jinping Speaks with U.S. President Joe Biden on the Phone," April 2, 2024, https://www.fmprc.gov.cn/eng/zxxx_662805/202404/t20240403_11275451.html.
54. The White House, "Remarks of President Joe Biden—State of the Union Address."
55. Richard Fontaine, "The Myth of Neutrality," *Foreign Affairs*, July 12, 2023, https://www.foreignaffairs.com/china/myth-of-neutrality-choose-between-america-china.
56. Adam P. Liff, "China and the US Alliance System," *The China Quarterly* 233 (March 2018): 137–65, https://doi.org/10.1017/S0305741017000601.
57. Sheena Chestnut Greitens, "Xi Jinping's Quest for Order: Security at Home, Influence Abroad," *Foreign Affairs*, October 3, 2022, https://www.foreignaffairs.com/china/xi-jinping-quest-order.
58. Randall L. Schweller and Xiaoyu Pu, "After Unipolarity: China's Visions of International Order in an Era of US Decline," *International Security* 36, no. 1 (2011): 41–72.
59. M. Taylor Fravel, "International Relations Theory and China's Rise: Assessing China's Potential for Territorial Expansion," *International Studies Review* 12, no. 4 (December 2010): 505–32.
60. He, "China's Rise."
61. Yong Deng, "How China Builds the Credibility of the Belt and Road Initiative," *Journal of Contemporary China* 30, no. 131 (September 2021): 734–50; Selina Ho, "Infrastructure and Chinese Power," *International Affairs* 96, no. 6 (November 2020): 1461–85.
62. Ketian Zhang, *China's Gambit: The Calculus of Coercion* (Cambridge: Cambridge University Press, 2023).
63. See-won Byun, "Interdependence, Identity, and China-South Korea Political Relations: Asia's Paradox," *Asian Survey* 61, no. 3 (June 5, 2021): 473–99.
64. Julian Gewirtz, "The Chinese Reassessment of Interdependence," *China Leadership Monitor* 64 (2020): 1–16.
65. Ryan Hass, "An American Perspective on the Role of Taiwan in US-China Relations," Brookings, July 2022, https://www.brookings.edu/articles/an-american-perspective-on-the-role-of-taiwan-in-us-china-relations/.
66. Jude Blanchette and Ryan Hass, "The Taiwan Long Game: Why the Best Solution Is No Solution," *Foreign Affairs* 102, no. 1 (February 1, 2023): 102–14; Bonnie S. Glaser, Jessica Chen Weiss, and Thomas J. Christensen, "Taiwan and the True Sources of Deterrence: Why America Must Reassure, Not Just Threaten, China," *Foreign Affairs* 103 (January/February 2024): 88–100.
67. The White House, "National Security Strategy, 2022," October 2022, https://www.whitehouse.gov/wp-content/uploads/2022/10/Biden-Harris-Administrations-National-Security-Strategy-10.2022.pdf.
68. MFA-PRC, "President Xi Jinping Speaks."

CHAPTER 7

New Institutional Economic Statecraft beyond the Border
Technology Competition in the Asia-Pacific[1]

Vinod K. Aggarwal and Andrew W. Reddie

"With the TPP, we can rewrite the rules of trade to benefit America's middle class. Because if we don't, competitors who don't share our values, like China, will step in to fill that void."

—President Barack Obama

In the 2000s and 2010s, the United States proposed and led multiple rounds of negotiations on two key mega free trade agreements (FTAs)—the Trans-Pacific Partnership (TPP) and Transatlantic Trade and Investment Partnership (TTIP). Its goal was to reshape its influence in both Europe and East Asia. Both of these endeavors collapsed as politicians on both the left and the right of the US political spectrum abandoned the pro–free trade consensus that had marked US global economic policy for six decades. The abandonment of these mega FTAs marked an underappreciated shift in US institutional economic statecraft—and one that continues to shape economic outcomes in a world where "decoupling," "derisking," and "strategic competition" have entered the lexicon.

Abhorring a vacuum, other states—and most significantly China—stepped into the gap provided to them by Washington, with downstream consequences for the contours of the global economy that we grapple with today. Indeed, as we outline below, China plays a growing role as a regulatory standard-maker, rather than a regulatory standard-taker. It successfully promoted the conclusion of the Regional Comprehensive Economic Partnership (RCEP) with fourteen countries in 2022 after India chose not to sign the accord. In addition, it has been active in promoting the 2014 New

Development Bank, the 2013 Belt and Road Initiative, and the 2016 Asian Infrastructure Investment Bank. For its part, Japan, not traditionally a global institution-builder, helped to lead the creation of the 2018 Comprehensive and Progressive Agreement for Trans-Pacific Partnership (CPTPP), the successor agreement to the failed Trans-Pacific Partnership from which President Trump withdrew. Meanwhile, the United States has shifted its focus to the far less ambitious Indo-Pacific Economic Framework (IPEF), without provisions for any serious market opening given the lack of political consensus on using free trade as a key instrument of US policy.

This chapter focuses on the Indo-Pacific context as a geography in which US and Chinese visions for the regional order are at greatest odds—with both states seeking to shape regional (or more accurately, transregional) institutions that serve their respective preferences. We now see a "noodle bowl" of arrangements between the TPP's successor, CPTPP, the China-led RCEP, United States–led IPEF, and APEC—each with varying and overlapping membership with downstream consequences for their respective agendas, voting rights, and impact on global regulatory standard setting (as regional preferences trickle up to global institutions)—from the World Trade Organization (WTO) to the International Telecommunications Union (ITU). In our empirical discussion, we pay particular attention to attempts by Washington to reshape economic relations in the region via first the failed TPP (and successor CPTPP); we then turn to its major competitor, RCEP, before concluding with newest arrangement, Biden's IPEF initiative.

Section 2 begins by categorizing types of state intervention from an analytical standpoint that include behind-, at-, and beyond-the-border measures; it briefly outlines our theorized drivers of new economic statecraft to explain these measures, focusing in particular on the possible institutional characteristics of transregional arrangements. Section 3 examines theoretical approaches to understand beyond-the-border institutional strategies. In sections 4, 5, and 6, we turn to our focus in this chapter to the types of institutional economic statecraft that we have seen the United States and China pursuing in the Asia-Pacific. Finally, section 7 examines how the return to an era of great power competition is likely to continue the trend of states turning to economic statecraft to shape their regional markets and, by extension, the global economy.

NEW ECONOMIC STATECRAFT

"Economic statecraft" emerged as a concept from theories of structural power, with Baldwin[2] arguing that states use economic tools as a means to further their security objectives.[3] More contemporary scholarship concerning economic statecraft examines the implications of economic development in a globalized economy where security, technology, and innovation are highly interdependent.[4] Although the traditional economic statecraft literature focuses on linking economic tools like sanctions with security objectives, new research extends this concept to security externalities arising from an interconnected economy characterized by rapid technological development.[5] Our formulation of economic statecraft, or what we term "new economic statecraft" draws on the literature on the economics of innovation but expands its scope by discussing the security of the state through the framework of national innovation systems.[6]

In our approach, we focus on two key aspects to define new economic statecraft.[7] First, we seek to characterize state intervention in technology markets by looking at behind-, at-, and beyond-the-border measures. Second, we theorize about the driving forces of these intervention measures, developing a five-factor model that identifies different types of variables that influence policy choices across countries. Since our focus in this chapter is primarily on beyond-the-border institutional measures, we elaborate on how we might conceptualize institutional arrangements and discuss the rationale behind national choices with respect to institutional design.

State Intervention in Markets

Scholars have pointed to various types of state intervention in national markets that have effects on the global economy including economic sanctions, tariffs, quotas, subsidies, and industrial policies.[8] Rather than treat each of these measures individually, this chapter, building on our previous work, outlines three types of trade and investment policies—at the border, behind the border, and beyond the border—that encapsulate interventions that are both collectively exhaustive and mutually exclusive.[9]

Trade Policy

Trade policies *at the border* "discriminate against foreign goods, companies, workers and investors."[10] These interventions can take a variety of forms including import-taxing tariffs, which make domestic goods more competitive than their foreign counterparts. Governments may also tax exports if they want to keep specific types of goods inside the country. Quotas operate similarly in that they limit goods arriving in, or exported from, the country.

Customs regulations represent an additional border measure that adds friction to the trade process—with attendant consequences for the competitiveness of imports and advantages for local firms.

In addition to these policies at the border, there are several *behind-the-border* measures that affect trade patterns. Often, these are described as measures used to drive "backdoor" or "murky" protectionism.[11] The most obvious behind-the-border trade measure is a regulatory environment manipulated to discriminate against a foreign good or service. Regulatory standards, whether binding or voluntary, have an impact on market access and include measures that ostensibly promote goals such as security, health, the environment, or safety, for example.

In addition, product-content requirements, also known as localization rules, are often used to limit foreign-market access by mandating the minimum percentage of a product that needs to be built inside the country. As countries attempt to re-shore manufacturing in sectors deemed strategically important, these types of rules are back in vogue. Relatedly, the government is also a customer and can influence trade patterns through procurement rules that are discriminatory to foreign firms. Domestic-market trade subsidies are designed to make goods from the targeted industry cheaper than their foreign counterparts.[12] This has the dual effect of making imports less attractive and goods for export cheaper.

States also act to shape trade policy *beyond their border*—via institutional arrangements at the regional or global level. These organizations subsequently shape the rules governing various types of intervention—with some institutions being more or less restrictive in terms of what policies member states are expected to adopt and which actions they are expected to avoid.

Investment Policy

Investment policy offers a second vehicle for states to intervene in their domestic markets. The most obvious intervention *at the border* are rules concerning foreign direct investment. Governments might limit shareholding of a publicly held firm at a specific percentage or review foreign acquisitions of domestic firms based on national security considerations. For example, in the United States, the Foreign Investment Risk Review Modernization Act (FIRRMA) of 2018 expanded the jurisdiction of the Committee on Foreign Investment in the United States (CFIUS) to address mandatory filing requirements for investments involving foreign governments, as well as foreign investment in firms deemed to represent critical infrastructure.[13]

Governments also influence direct and indirect investment *behind the border*. Traditionally, this type of state behavior has been captured in the context of industrial policy.[14] In terms of direct investment, governments often involve themselves directly in specific sectors of the economy or create state-owned vehicles that operate on their behalf. As with trade rules designed to protect foreign firms, direct and indirect investment provides domestic firms with an advantage within the domestic market and in preparation of their goods and services for export. Governments may also identify specific firms in which to invest and regulate both within the home country and abroad. This practice is particularly common in the defense sector in the United States and Europe as firms are often limited in terms of the goods and services that they can provide abroad, narrowing their ability to achieve economies of scale.

Governments also pursue indirect investment in strategic industries through human capital development programs. Indirect or horizontal government interventions do not target a specific firm but rather identify a strategic need and subsidize the cost of creating knowledge networks necessary for the functioning of a particular industry.

States also act to shape investment policy *beyond their border*. For example, states may play a role in third-party markets by dictating rules for market access for firms beyond their borders. For example, a state might only provide market access to a foreign firm if it creates a local subsidiary or otherwise adds value to local labor markets. In addition, global, transregional, and regional institutions can be used to influence technology policies, as we will see later in this chapter.

New Economic Statecraft: A Five-Factor Model

In our work, we have focused on the conditions under which governments intervene in their respective markets using the tools of economic statecraft described above. Over the past decade, we have argued that state intervention has been more ubiquitous than neoliberal economists let on, even in the United States.[15] Of course, the US model for innovating predominantly via venture capital with indirect contributions via the funding of basic R&D via the National Science Foundation, National Institutes of Health, and National Laboratories looks different from past examples of state-directed R&D support in the likes of Japan and South Korea or the contemporary example of China.

In an attempt to explain this variation, we suggest that domestic politics (e.g., bureaucratic politics), market dynamics (and particularly firm-state

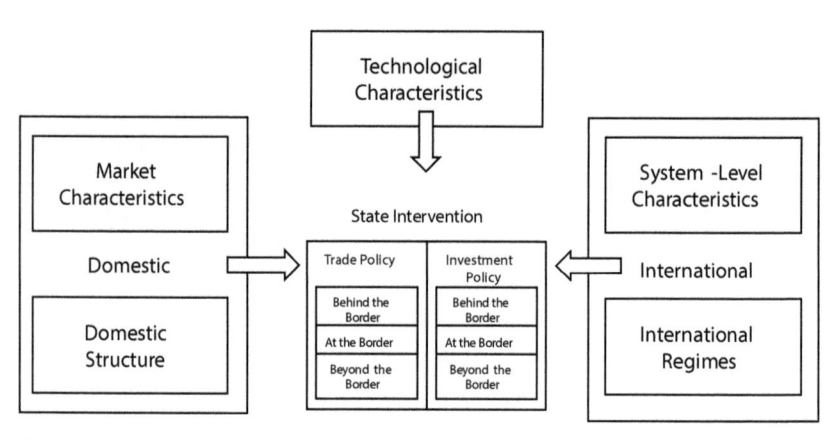

Figure 7.1. The determinants of state intervention

relations), technological characteristics, dynamics of the international system (e.g., polarity), and the contours of international cooperation (via intergovernmental organizations) combine to shape the types of interventions that we see across various domains—from cybersecurity markets to nuclear energy. Figure 7.1 illustrates our conceptual framework. Below we provide a short discussion of these elements.[16]

Market Characteristics

Many factors influence state choices, but we focus here on three: barriers to entry, the number of competitors in the market, and the vulnerability of the supply chain. If barriers to entry are very low, then governments have little to worry about since firms either on their own or with government encouragement can rapidly ramp up production. What affects such barriers? A key factor is economies of scale. Industries such as aircraft production, auto production, and steel production all have significant economies of scale given the capital requirements for production. Such scale economies are linked to the number of competitors, as high economies of scale are likely to favor industry concentration.

The second variable we consider is the number of competitors in a given industry. For the most part, neoliberal economists criticize state intervention to bolster specific firms or industries on the basis of inefficiency, focusing instead on an array of antitrust tools to ensure that firms do not unfairly secure an oligopolistic or monopolistic position in the market. By contrast with neoliberal countries, a wide variety of states have promoted specific firms in a number of industries, seeking to create economies of scale that would create "national champions" in these countries to compete with large American or other countries' firms. These calls are particularly prevalent where goods and services have claimed national security applications.[17]

A third variable is global security of supply. Efficiency is paramount for neoliberals, but the onset of COVID-19, alongside other global supply chain disturbances, has increased concerns about the diffusion of supply chains and the consequences of relying on distribution networks with little slack to address crises. The clearest empirical example of these concerns follows recent shortages in semiconductors—leading to efforts by multiple states to reshore or friend-shore production (with the assumptions that both efforts would increase the likelihood that a given good or service would be available during a crisis given the tighter control of the supply chain). The Biden administration has reified this support via the Creating Helpful Incentives to Produce Semiconductors and Science Act of 2022 (CHIPS Act) and the 2022 Inflation Reduction Act (IRA) that has marked the return of the United States to full-fledged industrial policy.

Domestic Structure

Another key driver of government's propensity to intervene in industries is the structural relationship between firms and governments. Focusing on domestic structure is also, of course, critical to understanding the likelihood of success in the pursuit of industrial policy in high-tech industries. A key factor is the government's ability to resist regulatory capture by private firms. Academics have long distinguished between strong versus weak states, arguing that the former are better able to resist lobbying efforts because of the nature of their bureaucracies and insulation from political pressures.[18] The same literature also focuses on the extent to which societal groups are well organized.

When analyzing strategic-intervention decisions, a strong state is more likely to succeed in resisting calls for simple industrial-policy protection. At the same time, coordination between well-organized societal groups cooperating with the state should also lead to more realistic intervention for strategic purposes. Examples of such coordination include South Korea and Singapore, both of which feature strong leadership by state bureaucrats in consultation with business groups.

There are a number of more contemporary examples that highlight the importance of bureaucratic structures and firm-state relations related to strategic intervention in domestic markets—from those firms that are very closely tied to government or coerced into meeting government goals (with some suggesting that this is the case in Beijing) to those firms that agitate against the state (where failed efforts to establish binding cybersecurity standards in the United States represents just one example).

Technological Characteristics

The technological characteristics of a particular technology or sector also conditions whether a government intervenes in a technology industry as well as what types of intervention are deemed appropriate. First, is a technology perceived as primarily civilian or military in nature? Some, such as nuclear technology, have been viewed as primarily military and subsequently receive large amounts of direct investment and funding for research, development, and deployment—with an attendant regulatory burden. Empirically, we might expect those technologies that have clear military applications to be subject to fairly significant market interventions.

Second, is the new technology likely to have emergent externalities for other industries or society as a whole? For example, fears regarding the effects of artificial intelligence (AI) on the future of work, provision of credit, and patterns of surveillance have led to calls for government regulation of private firms developing AI technologies at the same time as government funding for basic AI research has been plentiful across a number of countries. All else equal, the emergent externalities associated with specific technologies appear likely to increase the likelihood of state intervention, in general, and of regulatory barriers, in particular.

Third, are the constituent components or precursors associated with a particular technology easily appropriable? Technologies that are simple to reverse engineer represent a challenge for state intervention as the easier they are to appropriate, the higher the chance that they may lead to technology transfer. Software, for example, is notoriously difficult to address using export control mechanisms. At the same time, intervention may be considered less necessary when the technology in question is difficult to appropriate, leading to a hands-off approach.

Systemic Characteristics

A fourth element influencing state intervention in strategic industries is variation in the global political environment, both across countries and time.[19] The distribution of capabilities in the international system—variously described as system polarity—represents a major structural characteristic of the international system worthy of consideration in driving state intervention in their domestic markets. For example, in a bipolar global political environment, each of the pole powers will be in a competitive situation that may lead to a higher likelihood of pressure on state decision-makers to intervene and bolster critical industries. To some extent, recent policy documents in both China and the United States reflect this pressure—with both states viewing technological competition as central to the broader political competition developing between the two.

In contrast to the situation that we find ourselves in today, a unipolar global political environment with a single dominant power might pose the least risk. In this case, due to the strong position of the pole vis-à-vis potential peer competitors, there would be less pressure for state intervention to protect key industries. With that said, states outside of the single dominant power may be more likely to intervene—viewing this intervention as one of the only vehicles to increase their competitiveness.

Finally, we consider the multipolar case. As with a number of variables discussed above, the hypothesized direction of the relationship between the multipolarity and the likelihood of state intervention remains a subject of debate. However, we posit that multipolarity might make mercantilist pressures most acute—driven by self-help behavior on the part of the governments involved.

International Regime Characteristics

The use of international arrangements by states varies significantly. International institutions vary between those with global, overarching responsibilities such as the WTO and those concerned with sectoral or regional/transregional arrangements. Sectoral agreements include the 1996 Information Technology Agreement (expanded in scope in 2015) or the 1997 Basic Telecom Agreement (BTA), both of which have provisions concerning tariffs, competition policy, licensing, regulatory independence, and other policies that influence state intervention. In addition to global arrangements such as the WTO or global sectoral arrangements, we have also seen minilateral agreements that influence policies. Minilateral accords can be quite large such as the relatively new Regional Comprehensive Economic Partnership and Comprehensive and Progressive Trans-Pacific Partnership, which we discuss at length in the next section. Other minilateral accords, including the North American Free Trade Agreement (NAFTA), its successor the US-Mexico-Canada Agreement (USMCA), and the European Union (EU), also contain a host of rules and regulations that influence what states are allowed to do.

UNDERSTANDING NEW INSTITUTIONAL STATECRAFT AS A BEYOND-THE-BORDER STRATEGY

With respect to beyond-the-border measures, in this chapter we focus in particular on efforts to change or create existing institutions.[20] Also, given our interests in examining US and Chinese regional strategies, our primary focus is on three transregional accords that have been developed over the last few years. Specifically, we focus on the Trans-Pacific Partnership (TPP) and its successor, the Comprehensive and Progressive Agreement for Trans-Pacific Partnership (CPTPP); the Regional Comprehensive Economic Partnership (RCEP); and the Indo Pacific Economic Framework (IPEF). Before turning to an empirical analysis of how these institutional arrangements affect high-technology policies, we consider how our adapted framework can shed light on institutional change, both modifications and new institutions.

Figure 7.2 provides a schematic view of how to think about institutional change. If countries are unhappy with existing institutional constraints, or if they believe that some institutional modification might benefit their economic statecraft strategies, then they will make an effort to pursue beyond-the-border institutional change.

Drawing on our categories of key variables described above, we can consider how each one will influence state decisions. Market characteristics will play a key role as we see the interplay between domestic structure and market actors. Firms may engage in nonmarket strategies to influence governments to change institutions and their regulatory elements to gain advantages over their rivals, both domestic and international. For their part, governments will also weigh the pros and cons of working with existing institutions or seeking to modify or create new ones for their political and strategic goals.

A key factor here will be the nature of the international regime in terms of the technology at stake: where governments believe that their firms are highly advanced, they may choose to avoid excessive regulation by other actors by either seeking liberal regimes, or, in the case where a regime might not exist (such as AI or cybersecurity markets), they may attempt to scuttle global regulatory efforts. In this context, the global political structure will play a key role. In a bipolar world, we are likely to see competition over regime design, as well as regime characteristics. In a more multipolar system, we might see coalitions among states as countries vie to alter or create new regimes. Finally, efforts to create new international regimes will be influenced by preexisting regimes: the choice here will be to either nest or create horizontal or simply independent regimes.[21] An example of nesting in trade would be the creation of a regime

```
                  ┌──────────────────┐
                  │  Technological   │
                  │  Characteristics │
                  └────────┬─────────┘
                           ⇩
┌──────────────────┐              ┌──────────────────┐
│      Market      │              │   System-Level   │
│  Characteristics │              │  Characteristics │
└──────────────────┘              └──────────────────┘
┌──────────────────┐   ┌──────────────────┐   ┌──────────────────┐
│     Domestic     │⇨  │ New or modification of │⇦ │   International  │
└──────────────────┘   │ existing international │  └──────────────────┘
┌──────────────────┐   │        regimes         │  ┌──────────────────┐
│     Domestic     │   └──────────────────┘       │     Existing     │
│     Structure    │                              │   International  │
└──────────────────┘                              │     Regimes      │
                                                  └──────────────────┘
```

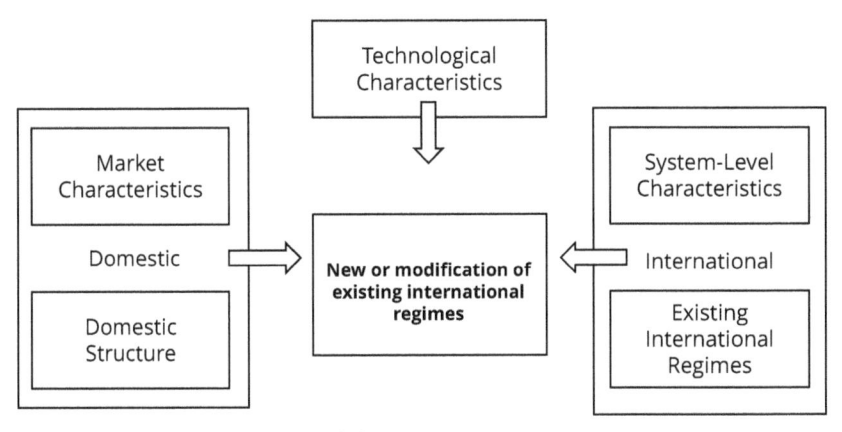

Figure 7.2. Explaining institutional change

consistent with the WTO. A horizontal regime is one that reflects a division of labor, such as the IMF and World Bank in finance. And an independent regime would be the case of trade institutions and security institutions.

We now turn to an empirical examination of transregional regimes in the Asia-Pacific, with an emphasis on their technology provisions. As we shall see, efforts to create such arrangements clearly reflect the differing incentives and interest of the United States and China as they pursue beyond-the-border regional institutional strategies.

FROM TPP TO CPTPP: A US OWN GOAL?

Digital commerce and trade involving advanced technologies have become central to twenty-first-century trade agreements. Whereas in prior eras, trade agreements focused primarily on efforts to reduce tariffs, now they feature a whole host of provisions like intellectual property rights protections that go well beyond basic trade issues, and they also serve to encourage technology transfer.[22]

Given the centrality of digital trade in the global economy today and the fact that prior trade agreements did not typically specify adequate frameworks for handling such trade, it is no surprise that studies find that the inclusion of tech-related provisions in regional trade agreements influences trade volumes between signatories.[23] In particular, regional trade agreements with such provisions—which run the gamut from incentives for innovation and technology dissemination to technical cooperation to intellectual property protection—generating a higher volume of trade, especially in tech-intensive goods, between member countries.[24]

The Trans-Pacific Partnership (TPP) of twelve countries built on the 2006 Trans-Pacific Strategic Economic Partnership (P4) among Brunei, Chile, New Zealand, and Singapore.[25] The TPP was ambitious and wide-ranging from multiple vantage points, including numerous issue areas and types of goods and services covered in its thirty chapters, with attention to tariff and non-tariff, and a large portion of the world economy represented. Among the parties were Japan, Australia, Canada, and Mexico, which are all key US trade allies and among the twenty largest economies in the world. The twelve members of the TPP comprised roughly 38 percent of the world's GDP, or about $28.7 trillion, with a total population of more than eight hundred million.[26] The TPP would have been the largest plurilateral regional trade agreement in history.[27]

The TPP included many digital trade concerns reflecting the centrality of trade in technology to regional and global markets. For example, chapter 14 of the TPP addresses cross-border data flows. Owing to a need to "prevent [the internet's] breakup into multiple, balkanized networks in which data flows are more expensive and more frequently blocked," parties are to commit to ensuring that individuals and firms can freely move data across borders without being burdened by excessive or unnecessary restrictions (or at least those restrictions would do not fulfill a necessary public policy purpose).[28] Other articles in chapter 14 prohibit localization requirements for servers and data centers, by which a government would require a company "to use or locate computing facilities in that Party's territory as a condition for conducting business."[29] Although no party of the TPP had data localization requirements, a few countries were reportedly considering them, and there were fears that others would follow.[30] Such requirements would reduce barriers to market access and reduce costs on businesses that would otherwise have to build redundant facilities in each country.[31] Under chapter 14, customs duties on digital products and discriminatory treatment of foreign suppliers would be prohibited.[32]

The TPP took care to make parties commit to consumer protection standards including for privacy and security. Chapter 14 also requires each party to have laws on the books to bar and prevent fraudulent and deceptive activity that targets consumers engaged in e-commerce.[33] Other articles likewise give each party the responsibility to devise rules that afford legal protections to consumers' personal information. Although each country is tasked with writing the rules and enforcing them in their own jurisdictions, the article asks them to cooperate in ensuring the compatibility of their legal and regulatory regimes. Although these provisions lack specificity, they do enjoin governments to abide by "guidelines of relevant international bodies," including the Asia-Pacific Economic Cooperation (APEC) Privacy Framework.[34] Governments are to provide regulatory transparency to firms and to assist small- and medium-sized enterprises (SME) in navigating the challenges of e-commerce.[35] Parties are to cooperate with one another by exchanging information, experiences, and best practices relating to the provisions of the chapter.[36] Intergovernmental collaboration in planning for and responding to cybersecurity incidents is emphasized in article chapter 14.16.

Additional provisions include a requirement that parties commit to a legal framework for electronic transactions, mutual recognition of e-signatures and electronic authentication, and prohibitions against disclosure requirements for sharing software source code. Elsewhere, the TPP prohibits parties from requiring disclosure of proprietary information for products using cryptography—with exceptions for products for government use or access to government-controlled networks.[37]

Exceptions in chapter 14 have to do with government procurement and financial services, and it is to the latter that we now turn. The way in which the TPP dealt with the financial services sector deserves scrutiny. The e-commerce chapter neglects to include financial services, which instead is addressed in chapter 11.[38] (In fact, article 14.1 defines terms to explicitly exclude financial services suppliers, financial institutions, investors therein, and financial instruments from the auspices of chapter 14 on e-commerce.[39] These terms are instead covered in article 11.1.[40]) This choice parallels the disparate treatment financial services receive in the rules laid out in the agreement. Just as was the case for e-commerce, the TPP offers protections for cross-border trade and data flows—in a provision that bears resemblance to a part of the US-Korea Free Trade Agreement (KORUS).[41] However, a notable difference from the TPP's treatment of e-commerce is that there is no restriction on data localization requirements on financial services firms.[42] This is a key point of contention that has attracted criticism from stakeholders in the industry and has attracted worries that it creates inefficiencies that stunt the growth of the industry; it also has cascading effects on other industries that rely on the expeditious flow of financial data across borders.[43]

Telecommunications are covered by chapter 13 of the TPP.[44] Ensuring fair treatment of telecommunications services is crucial because rules in this area have ramifications in other sectors of the digital trade economy, including e-commerce and financial services. Free markets and competition in the American telecommunications sector have played a large role in making the United States the largest information and communications technology market in the world.[45] As a summary of the TPP's telecommunications provisions distributed by the Office of the Trade Representative points out, telecommunications services in the economies of the TPP members other than the United States total $300 billion annually, or approximately 3 percent of their GDP.[46] The telecommunications chapter aims to ensure pro-competitive network access for mobile suppliers, which otherwise may be pushed out of the market due to the influence of a dominant incumbent supplier.[47] Article 13.6 encourages cooperation on international mobile roaming such that rates for these services are transparent and reasonable.[48]

The TPP briefly covers agricultural products made with biotechnological methods like genetic engineering. The parties are to ensure transparency in their legal and regulatory decisions.[49] Furthermore, they are to commit to sharing information especially as it pertains to low-level presence of genetically modified content in food and agricultural products—which can cause trade disruptions and uncertainty.[50] Given the countries' disparate regulations about genetically modified organisms, harmonizing their regulatory regimes for the purposes of international trade seems intractable.[51] To facilitate information sharing and cooperation, article 2.29 creates a working group on agricultural biotechnology.[52] Neither this working group nor any other provision in the TPP would hold countries responsible for altering their domestic policies toward biotechnology.[53] The working group would function as a forum where representatives can improve the compatibility of their regulatory regimes. However, without additional negotiations at a technical level, the working group itself seems unlikely to lead to legal and regulatory harmony.[54]

Unsurprisingly, innovation powerhouses, which are typically developed countries like the United States, were most adamant that intellectual property provisions be included in trade agreements.[55] The TPP's emphasis on strong intellectual property provisions should be understood through the context of American leadership in crafting a favorable agreement for its own industries that safeguards its interests in promoting technological innovation and development.

Despite its thoroughness, or maybe because of it, the TPP was not to be. In his presidential campaign, Donald Trump blasted the TPP and free trade, and upon assuming office, withdrew the United States from the agreement in January 2017.[56] The next year, led by Japan, the remaining eleven countries finalized the Comprehensive and Progressive Trans-Pacific Partnership (CPTPP).[57] The agreement went into force for six countries in December 2018, with the five other countries formally becoming party to the agreement between 2019 and 2023.[58]

The CPTPP shares most of its provisions with the TPP, and the two agreements can be considered nearly identical.[59] Differences do exist, however, and many of the changes were implemented to remove controversial US-backed provisions in the original agreement and to possibly tempt the United States into rejoining.[60] Specifically, the CPTPP suspends twenty-two provisions of the TPP.[61] For example, government procurement and labor rules have been altered.[62] The scope of investor-state dispute settlement was also narrowed.[63] The vast majority of the provisions in the agreement, however, were unchanged, including chapters about e-commerce and provisions about digital trade, including those that promote the free flow of information across borders and prohibit computing facility data localization requirements.[64] The most significant changes to the agreement, including those that implicate technology and digital commerce, concern intellectual property.

The intellectual property rules included in the TPP were largely driven by the United States. With the United States no longer part of the agreement, the remaining parties saw fit to remove many of the more stringent protections. Articles concerning patent term adjustment, undisclosed test data biologics, and seventy-year copyright protection (technological protection measures, rights management information, encryption for satellite and cable signals, and legal remedies and "safe harbors" for internet service providers) were suspended in their entirety, and provisions about patentable subject matter and national treatment were narrowed.[65]

Despite Washington's efforts to offer IPEF as an alternative, as we shall see below, several countries have expressed interest in joining the CPTPP. South Korea is widely seen as a likely applicant to join, and Thailand and Colombia may consider applying as well.[66] So far, China, Costa Rica, Ecuador, Taiwan, Ukraine, and Uruguay have all applied to join CPTPP.[67] China applied to join in September 2021, which was seen as a symbolic slight to the United States, which initially served as an architect of the TPP in part to counter Chinese economic influence in the Asia-Pacific.[68] In the short term, however, it is unlikely that China will be granted membership.[69] The United States has shown little interest in rejoining the agreement that it pioneered.[70] The first new member to successfully join the original CPTPP grouping was the UK, which became a member in July 2023.

RCEP: A CHINA-LED TECHNOLOGICAL ECONOMIC ORDER?

China has sought to create its own mega-regional arrangement that reflect its preferences. The Regional Comprehensive Economic Partnership (RCEP) is a free trade agreement among fifteen countries in the Asia-Pacific region, including ASEAN member states and five other countries—Australia, China, Japan, New Zealand, and South Korea. Despite being involved in negotiations, in the end India chose to withdraw from the RCEP owing mainly to concerns about the competitive threat to its agriculture and manufacturing sector. The agreement creates an integrated market, spanning over 2.3 billion people, with a combined GDP of $26.3 trillion.[71] The RCEP aims to reduce tariffs and quotas between member countries, thereby promoting free trade and investment.[72] The agreement also includes provisions for intellectual property rights, aiming to provide comprehensive and high-standard protections.[73] Moreover, the RCEP includes commitments to facilitate cross-border data flow, which is crucial for e-commerce activities.[74] Future negotiations may include sustainability clauses, addressing issues like climate change and labor rights.[75]

The RCEP pact has clauses that pertain to e-commerce. Recognizing the escalating role of digital tech in boosting international trade and investment, the agreement seeks to encourage the utilization of digital platforms and tools within the region. For instance, Article 13.1 of the RCEP specifies that no customs duties or additional fees should be levied on electronic transmissions, including those for e-commerce. This clause aims to eliminate e-commerce obstacles and foster the expansion of digital commerce in the area.[76]

The RCEP also contains clauses concerning data movement and data localization. In contrast to CPTPP, which is antagonistic toward data localization, RCEP disallows data localization mandates, except under particular conditions. For example, Article 13.8 allows data localization only if it serves a valid public interest, like personal data protection or national security.[77] The limits of this article remain untested, however, with various historical examples of governments claiming spurious national security protections. Indeed, one of the major questions facing regional agreements like the RCEP is what remedial mechanisms ought to exist to remedy disputes and serve as an arbiter of disputes over claims like these.

To enhance digital commerce and online trade in the region, RCEP members have made several commitments across multiple areas. For instance, they have agreed to recognize and accept digital signatures and verification methods from other RCEP countries, provided they meet certain conditions. Additionally, they have pledged to enforce electronic contracts that satisfy specific legal criteria. In the realm of online consumer protection, RCEP members aim to strengthen collaborative efforts, including the sharing of effective strategies and experiences.[78]

Regarding electronic payments and digital currencies, the members have pledged to encourage their use, subject to existing legal and regulatory frameworks. They have also committed to improving digital trade facilitation through automated customs procedures and paperless trading.

Lastly, RCEP members have promised to provide capacity-building assistance to help developing countries in the region improve their capabilities in areas like e-commerce, digital payments, and cybersecurity.[79] These commitments, while not forming a set of technology regulatory standards per se, reflect a shared understanding of the importance of digital trade and a commitment to creating a conducive environment for its growth.[80]

Although these commitments don't establish a full framework of technology regulations, they do signify a shared recognition among RCEP members of the importance of promoting cooperation and coherence in digital commerce and online trade.

Interestingly, many of the provisions included in the TTP have close cousins within RCEP—for example, even intellectual property received a provision (18.3) within RCEP, despite long-held claims that China has been engaged in efforts to undermine the intellectual property of firms and governments in the West (whether via local joint transfer requirements for foreign firms to receive market access or more surreptitious efforts to get access to IP). To some extent, the common language between TPP and RCEP reflects the technocratic basis upon which trade agreements are being negotiated across the globe and the common training received by trade lawyers and the epistemic community represented by the cadre of trade negotiators charged with representing states in both regional and global trade arrangements.

While it would be unfair to characterize RCEP as wholly benefiting China (indeed, all states party to the agreement have to be convinced to sign it), its rules tend to be looser than arrangements that might involve US and European states while also focusing on trade issues of proximate concern to China and India, in particular. While this paper is not concerned with the normative consequences of whether any particular regional trade relationship is "good" or "bad," an underappreciated aspect of the RCEP is the manner in which it might increase the interdependence of Beijing and New Delhi, which might be advantageous to strategic stability in a world in which the two capitals tend toward being increasingly at odds with each other. On the flip side, regional value chains that are entirely outside of more "global" rules become difficult to control via primary and secondary sanctions regimes, as we have seen with attempts to sanction Russia following the invasion of Ukraine and in which Moscow has managed to maintain trade ties with many of the countries that are part of RCEP and its sister arrangements like the Belt and Road Initiative—escaping the most deleterious consequences of US and European sanctions.

THE INDO-PACIFIC ECONOMIC FRAMEWORK FOR PROSPERITY: BIDEN'S RESPONSE

As the United States has started to think more seriously about leveraging economic statecraft, it is embarking on a new strategy to engage with the Asia-Pacific region. The Indo-Pacific Economic Framework for Prosperity (IPEF) represents a multinational economic initiative proposed by President Joe Biden in May of 2022: "IPEF will strengthen our ties in this critical region to define the coming decades for technological innovation and the global economy."[81] Australia, Brunei, Fiji, India, Indonesia, Japan, South Korea, Malaysia, New Zealand, the Philippines, Singapore, Thailand, and Vietnam are IPEF partners. It is important to note that the IPEF does not cover market access, owing to US domestic conflicts over trade liberalization.

The IPEF seeks to challenge China's growing regional dominance and capacity for leadership. In a press briefing, US secretary of commerce Gina Raimondo noted that the IPEF constituted "an important turning point in restoring US economic leadership in the region, and [presented] Indo-Pacific countries an alternative to China's approach to these critical issues."[82] Given the geopolitical importance of the agreement, after the announcement of the IPEF, fifty-two senators wrote a bipartisan letter urging the Biden administration to include Taiwan in the framework. Led by Senator Joe Manchin, the group wrote, "Excluding Taiwan from IPEF would significantly distort the regional and global economic architecture, run counter to U.S. economic interests, and allow the Chinese government to claim that the international community does not in fact support meaningful engagement with Taiwan."[83]

Chinese officials responded to the IPEF by framing it as aggressive and antagonistic. Chinese Foreign Minister Wang Yi commented on the IPEF, stating, "Is the US trying to accelerate the recovery of the world economy, or is it creating economic decoupling, a technological blockade, industrial chain disruption, and aggravating the supply chain crisis?"[84] However, although USTR representative Katherine Tai said that the United States would increase trade ties with Taiwan in May of 2023, Taiwan is not yet a member of the IPEF.[85]

The IPEF framework is shaped around four key pillars: connected economy, resilient economy, clean economy, and fair economy. Partners can choose to opt in or out of individual pillars. Here we focus on the "connected" economy pillar, which refers to creating collaborative frameworks with regard to the digital economy, coordinating standards for data localization, keeping e-commerce competitive, protecting online privacy, and regulating AI.[86]

As of September 2023, the IPEF is still in the process of being negotiated. However, in January 2023, the under secretary of state for economic growth, energy and the environment Jose Fernandez said that the Biden administration is aiming to complete the IPEF by the end of the year.[87] One intuitive issue the IPEF brings up is the overlap between the IPEF and other agreements[88] and the ability to opt out of any particular pillar. This calls into question whether the prospective provisions within the framework will hold water and shape regional norms.

The IPEF's Ministerial Statement describes the digital trade objectives as "building an environment of trust and confidence in the digital economy," "enhancing access to online information and use of the Internet," "facilitating digital trade," "addressing discriminatory practices," and advancing "resilient and secure" digital infrastructure and platforms. In April 2023, the USTR released a summary of the digital trade chapter proposal that included the five following provisions: "Provisions addressing data protection, consumer protection, and artificial intelligence that support inclusive growth by promoting trust in the digital economy"; "provisions that promote access to the Internet and online services"; "provisions designed to avoid unfair trade practices, while recognizing the need for Parties to be able to address legitimate public policy objectives"; "provisions aimed at ensuring an effective legal framework for electronic transactions that is consistent with international best practices"; and "provisions promoting the security of the Internet and ICT infrastructure."[89]

With the IPEF covering approximately 40 percent of global economic output, it does not come as a surprise that industry titans sought to play a role in the connected economy negotiations. During the IPEF's November 2022 negotiations in Australia, Google and IBM hosted a reception for negotiators, catching the attention of activists with some claiming that the influence of tech giants in IPEF provisions will allow them to sustain their anticompetitive behavior. During May negotiations, "34 of the 40 stakeholders who gave presentations in Singapore represented corporations or their groups, most of which had ties to tech."[90]

The involvement of technology companies has also provoked criticism of the ability of the IPEF to promote competitive behavior. In May 2023, Senator Warren released emails that showed that officials with the USTR invited Apple and Google lobbyists to meet with deputy trade representative Sarah Bianchi. Commenting on the release, Google spokesperson Jose Castaneda said Google has "very publicly advocated for the Indo-Pacific Economic Framework to include strong digital trade provisions that ensure digital technologies are widely accessible, and that support privacy, security, and trust in cross-border data flows."[91]

Others predict that technology firms will lobby for digital rules that prevent governments from the regulation and governance of artificial intelligence: "This critical AI oversight authority is precisely what would be undercut by the source code and algorithmic secrecy rules industry interests want included in IPEF and other trade deals. The stakes are very high."[92]

Technology companies are also looking closely at the data provisions of any arrangement in the region. Data localization refers to regulations that require companies to store data within the borders of a specific country or region, rather than allowing it to be stored anywhere in the world. However, data localization laws can increase operational costs, increase regulatory ambiguities, create barriers to market entry, decrease economic efficiency, restrict innovation, and create interoperability issues.[93]

In our view, the IPEF is likely to present an alternative to Europe's data localization paradigm. Similar to the fashion in which the USMCA restricts data localization policies, the IPEF could also impose restrictions for partner countries that reverse the trend of increasing data localization. What could also be replicated from the USMCA are bans on restrictions of cross-border data transfers.[94] With a lack of a regional data localization agreement and with the existing regulatory infrastructure of the USMCA, the United States could maintain its first mover advantage if it can successfully establish a data localization regulatory framework within the connected economy pillar of the IPEF.

If the IPEF fails to produce a comprehensive framework for data flows, it is possible that data flows will continue to develop through bilateral rather than multilateral channels. For example, IPEF partner Singapore has entered separate digital economy agreements (DEAs) with the United States, Australia, and South Korea.[95] However, it may be difficult to compel partners to increase data flows without the incentive of market access. India, the only partner country to refuse to join all four pillars, cited the preference for strong data localization policies as a reason to choose not to join the trade pillar of the IPEF.[96] With concerns for data sovereignty rising as the United States and China continue to compete, it is difficult to imagine a swift path to a consensus on data localization policy under the IPEF.

The IPEF is widely seen as a mechanism for the United States to operationalize its view of the twenty-first century digital trade regime. Despite the benefits of increasing data flows, intellectual property protections, and technology transfer, there are several intersections where partner countries are unable to harmonize perspectives. First, there are broad disagreements over digital trade governance. While countries like the United States and Japan prefer to integrate the market into regulations, countries like Indonesia prefer to maintain sovereign control over digital regulatory policymaking and infrastructure.

Another controversial issue involves setting the standards for intellectual property rights. As Lurong Chen notes,[97] intellectual property exporting countries like the United States and Japan are likely to be at odds with intellectual property importing countries—reflected in markets for digital goods and perhaps most obviously in the market for pharmaceuticals in which countries have provisions for the production of generics at a lower cost than imported products.

As mentioned above, it is difficult to see why countries would be compelled to replicate American digital architecture when market access cannot be used as an incentive. Further compounding this problem is the ability for partners to simply opt out of the connected economy pillar while continuing to engage in the pillars that would, for example, enhance supply chain resiliency. A third problem are claims that US privacy and security are being sacrificed to the benefit of incumbent technology companies.

CONCLUSION: STRATEGIC MISTAKES REDUX

This chapter examines beyond-the-border institutional strategies to further develop our work on what we have termed new economic statecraft—measures to influence high-technology industries through intervention in trade, finance, investment, and industrial policy. In previous work, we have argued that countries have used a combination of measures to influence markets behind the border, at the border, and beyond the border. In addition to bilateral accords or technology or trade promotion, we have seen how countries have also used beyond-the-border institutional measures to influence high-technology industries.

In terms of attempting to explain the use of measures at different levels, we have created a five-factor model focusing on countries' domestic structure, market structure, the nature of technology, international arrangements, and the global structure. In other work, we have examined variation in countries' strategies based on this framework, particularly in the nuclear sector, cybersecurity, and AI. To understand institutional strategies in the competition between the United States and China, we drew upon work on institutional design and adapted our framework to go beyond looking at international regimes from a static perspective that influence policies. Specifically, we showed how different factors can influence institutional strategies to modify or create new institutions.

The empirical goal of this chapter has been to identify the various measures that countries have used in key Asia-Pacific economic arrangements rather than to causally explain variation in strategies. These include the evolution of TPP into the Japanese-led CPTPP, the RCEP led by China, and now the new US initiative known as the IPEF in an effort to restore US institutional participation in the Asia-Pacific. As we have seen, all of these accords contain a host of provisions on the digital economy, intellectual property, and a host of provisions that are likely to influence the evolution of key high-technology industries in the future.

Much ink has been spilled, particularly in the United States, on debates about suitable industrial policies to promote high-technology industries. As we have seen, countries are increasingly competing to bolster their semiconductor, AI, quantum, biotechnology, and other cutting-edge industries.[98] Lost in the debate about government intervention, however, has been the role of a beyond-the-border institutional strategy to successfully compete in the global economy.

From an American perspective, the Trump administration's rejection of TPP and TTIP and the domestic focus of the Biden administration has undercut the clear institutional strategy pursued by the Obama administration to set global rules through creating institutional arrangements with Asia-Pacific countries and the EU. The IPEF effort, while an example of an institutional strategy, provides only a weak effort and little in the way of using market opening to attract cooperation among like-minded countries. By contrast, China appears to have learned the lesson of the importance of setting technology standards, and CPTPP, without the United States, is also moving forward. We view this lack of vision as a failure of economic policy that will end up hurting the American goal of setting global technological standards to bolster its high-technology industries.

NOTES

1. An earlier version of this chapter was presented at the Resurging Great Power Conflicts and Changing Regional Orders Workshop, March 14, 2023, McGill University, Montreal. For research assistance, we are grateful to Shantanu Kamat, Satyam Sharma, Ellen Wu, and Luca Zislin. Both of us are grateful for the support of the UC National Laboratory Fees Research Program.
2. David A. Baldwin, *Economic Statecraft* (Princeton, NJ: Princeton University Press, 1985).
3. The grand strategy literature also acknowledges the economic aspects of national policymaking, even if much of the literature remains focused on military capabilities and objectives. Avery Goldstein, in *Rising to the Challenge: China's Grand Strategy and International Security. Studies in Asian Security* (Palo Alto, CA: Stanford University Press, 2005), for example, describes grand strategy as "the distinctive combination of military, political, and *economic* means by which a state seeks to ensure its national interests." p. 17.
4. Henry Farrell and Abraham L. Newman, 2019, "Weaponized Interdependence: How Global Economic Networks Shape State Coercion," *International Security* 44, no. 1 (2019): 42–79.
5. David C. Mowery, "National Security and National Innovation Systems." *The Journal of Technology Transfer* 34, no. 5 (2008): 455.
6. Clayton M. Christensen, *The Innovator's Dilemma: When New Technologies Cause Great Firms to Fail* (Cambridge, MA: Harvard Business Review Press, 2013).
7. Vinod K. Aggarwal and Andrew W. Reddie, "Security of Supply: The Determinants of State Intervention in Emerging Technology Sectors," *AsiaGlobal Papers*, no. 3 (October 2020), https://www.asiaglobalinstitute.hku.hk/researchpaper/security-supply-determinants-state-intervention-emerging-technology-sectors-asiaglobal-papers-no-3; Vinod K. Aggarwal and Andrew W. Reddie, "Economic Statecraft in the 21st Century: Implications for the Future of the Global Trade Regime," *World Trade Review* 20, special issue 2 (May 2021): 137–51.
8. Peter Nolan, *China and the Global Economy: National Champions, Industrial Policy and the Big Business Revolution* (New York: Springer, 2001); Ken Warwick, "Beyond Industrial Policy: Emerging Issues and New Trends," *OECD Science, Technology and Industry Policy Papers*, no. 2 (2003): 1–57, http://dx.doi.org/10.1787/5k4869clw0xp-en; Gary Gereffi and Timothy Sturgeon, "Global Value Chain-Oriented Industrial Policy: The Role of Emerging Economies," in *Global Value Chains in a Changing World*, eds. Deborah K. Elms and Patrick Low (Geneva: WTO Publications 2013), 329–360, 329; Tai Ming Cheung, *Fortifying China: The Struggle to Build a Modern Defense Economy* (Ithaca, NY: Cornell University Press, 2013); Geoffrey Carliner, "Industrial Policies for Emerging Industries," in *Strategic Trade Policy and the New International Economics*, ed. Paul Krugman (Cambridge, MA: MIT Press, 1995), 21–32.
9. See Aggarwal and Reddie, "Security of Supply" for a discussion of behind- and at-the-border measures. Here we introduce the concept of beyond-the-border measures for analytical completeness. Note that a variety of actors, including firms, local authorities and other types of sub-national entities, have a role in various types of state intervention. This chapter focuses primarily on the determinants of state intervention by national governments as affected by these interests.

10. Richard Baldwin and Simon J. Evenett, "Introduction and Recommendations for the G20," in *The Collapse of Global Trade, Murky Protectionism and the Crisis: Recommendations for the G20*, eds. Richard Baldwin and Simon J. Evenett (Geneva: Center for Economic Policy Research, 2009), 1–9.
11. Cathleen Cimino-Isaacs and Jan Zilinsky, "Local Content Requirement: Backdoor Protectionism Spreading under the Radar," *PIIE Trade and Investment Policy Watch* (blog), July 22, 2016, https://www.piie.com/blogs/trade-and-investment-policy-watch/local-content-requirements-backdoor-protectionism-spreading; Vinod K. Aggarwal and Simon J. Evenett, "The Transatlantic Trade and Investment Partnership: Limits on Negotiating behind the Border Barriers," *Business and Politics* 19, no. 4 (December 2017): 549–72.
12. Baldwin and Evenett, "Introduction and recommendations."
13. Vinod K. Aggarwal and Andrew W. Reddie, "Regulators Join Tech Rivalry with National-Security Blocks on Cross-Border Investment," *Global Asia* 14, no. 1 (2019).
14. Vinod K. Aggarwal and Simon J. Evenett, "Industrial Policy Choice during the Crisis Era," *Oxford Review of Economic Policy* 28, no. 2 (Summer 2012): 261–83.
15. Aggarwal and Reddie, "Economic Statecraft in the 21st Century"; Aggarwal and Reddie, "Security of Supply"; Aggarwal and Reddie, "Regulators Join Tech Rivalry"; Vinod K. Aggarwal and Andrew W. Reddie, "Comparative Industrial Policy and Cybersecurity: The US Case," *Journal of Cyber Policy* 3, no. 3 (2018): 445–66.
16. For a more thorough discussion of these factors, see Aggarwal and Reddie, "Security of Supply."
17. In our view, more work is needed to explore the consequences of these interventions in circumstances where the government represents the singular client and the downstream effects of monopsonies on outcomes.
18. Peter J. Katzenstein, "Conclusion: Domestic Structures and Strategies of Foreign Economic Policy," *International Organization* 31, no. 4 (Autumn 1977): 879–920.
19. Kenneth N. Waltz, "Structural Realism after the Cold War," *International Security* 25, no. 1 (2000): 5–41; Kenneth N. Waltz, *Theory of International Politics* (Reading: Addison-Wesley Publishing, 1979). Given our focus, we discuss international regimes last in this exposition.
20. See Vinod K. Aggarwal, *Institutional Designs for a Complex World: Bargaining, Linkages, and Nesting* (Ithaca, NY: Cornell University Press, 1998).
21. Vinod K. Aggarwal, "The Unraveling of the Multi-Fiber Arrangement, 1981: An Examination of International Regime Change." *International Organization* 37, no. 4 (Autumn 1983): 617–646; and Aggarwal, *Institutional Designs*.
22. Ana Maria Santacreu and Jesse LaBelle, "Technology Transfer and Regional Trade Agreements," Federal Reserve Bank of St. Louis, September 20, 2021, https://doi.org/10.20955/es.2021.23.
23. Inmaculada Martínez-Zarzoso and Santiago Chelala, "Trade Agreements and International Technology Transfer," *Review of World Economics* 157, no. 3 (2021): 631–65.
24. Martínez-Zarzoso and Chelala, "Trade Agreements," 640, 651.
25. See Vinod K. Aggarwal, "Introduction: The Rise of Mega-FTAs in the Asia-Pacific," *Asian Survey* 56, no. 6 (November/December 2016): 1005–1016, on the creation of the TPP and RCEP.
26. Jeffrey J. Schott, "The TPP: Origins and Outcomes," in *Handbook of International Trade Agreements: Country, Regional and Global Approaches*, ed. Robert E. Looney (London: Routledge, 2018), 401–11 (401, 403).

27. Ian F. Fergusson and Brock R. Williams, "The Trans-Pacific Partnership (TPP): Key Provisions and Issues for Congress" (Congressional Research Service, June 14, 2016), 1, https://sgp.fas.org/crs/row/R44489.pdf; Kevin Granville, "What Is TPP? Behind the Trade Deal That Died," *New York Times*, August 20, 2016, sec. Business, https://www.nytimes.com/interactive/2016/business/tpp-explained-what-is-trans-pacific-partnership.html.
28. United States Trade Representative, TPP Chapter Summary: Electronic Commerce, 1–2, https://ustr.gov/sites/default/files/TPP-Chapter-Summary-Electronic-Commerce.pdf.
29. United States Trade Representative, TPP Chapter 14: Electronic Commerce, 7, https://ustr.gov/sites/default/files/TPP-Final-Text-Electronic-Commerce.pdf.
30. Rachel F. Fefer, "TPP: Digital Trade Provisions" (Congressional Research Service, September 7, 2017), 1–2, https://www.everycrsreport.com/files/2017-09-07_IF10390_e35d2190932a3a654cd2db12c4182438b81edf55.pdf.
31. Fefer, "TPP: Digital Trade Provisions," 1; United States Trade Representative, TPP Chapter Summary: Electronic Commerce, 2.
32. United States Trade Representative, TPP Chapter 14: Electronic Commerce, 3.
33. United States Trade Representative, TPP Chapter 14: Electronic Commerce, 4.
34. Fefer, "TPP: Digital Trade Provisions," 2.
35. United States Trade Representative, TPP Chapter 14: Electronic Commerce, 8.
36. United States Trade Representative, TPP Chapter 14: Electronic Commerce, 8–9.
37. Fefer, "TPP: Digital Trade Provisions," 2.
38. Fergusson and Williams, "The Trans-Pacific Partnership," 33; Fefer, "TPP: Digital Trade Provisions," 2; United States Trade Representative, TPP Chapter 11: Financial Services, https://ustr.gov/sites/default/files/TPP-Final-Text-Financial-Services.pdf.
39. United States Trade Representative, TPP Chapter 14: Electronic Commerce, 1.
40. United States Trade Representative, TPP Chapter 11: Financial Services, 1–4.
41. Fergusson and Williams, "The Trans-Pacific Partnership," 2.
42. Fergusson and Williams, "The Trans-Pacific Partnership," 2.
43. Fergusson and Williams, "The Trans-Pacific Partnership," 2.
44. United States Trade Representative, TPP Chapter 13: Telecommunications, https://ustr.gov/sites/default/files/TPP-Final-Text-Telecommunications.pdf.
45. United States Trade Representative, TPP Chapter Summary: Telecommunications, https://ustr.gov/sites/default/files/TPP-Chapter-Summary-Telecommunications.pdf, 4.
46. United States Trade Representative, TPP Chapter Summary: Telecommunications, 4.
47. United States Trade Representative, TPP Chapter Summary: Telecommunications.
48. United States Trade Representative, TPP Chapter 13: Telecommunications, 8–10; Fergusson and Williams, "The Trans-Pacific Partnership," 35.
49. Fergusson and Williams, "The Trans-Pacific Partnership," 42.
50. Fergusson and Williams, "The Trans-Pacific Partnership," 42.
51. Viju, Crina, William A. Kerr, and Stuart Smyth, "Approaches to Set Rules for Trade in the Products of Agricultural Biotechnology. Is Harmonization under Trans-Pacific Partnership Possible?" *Journal of Agricultural & Food Industrial Organization* 15, no. 1 (2017).
52. Fergusson and Williams, "The Trans-Pacific Partnership," 42; Viju et al., "Approaches to Set Rules," 7.

53. Fergusson and Williams, "The Trans-Pacific Partnership," 42.
54. Viju et al., "Approaches to Set Rules for Trade," 7.
55. Ana Maria Santacreu and Jesse LaBelle, "Intellectual Property Rights Have Become a Key Part of Trade Deals," *Federal Reserve Bank of St. Louis* (blog), July 14, 2021, https://www.stlouisfed.org/on-the-economy/2021/june/intellectual-property-rights-become-key-part-trade-deals.
56. Peter Baker, "Trump Abandons Trans-Pacific Partnership, Obama's Signature Trade Deal," *New York Times*, January 23, 2017, sec. U.S., https://www.nytimes.com/2017/01/23/us/politics/tpp-trump-trade-nafta.html.
57. James McBride, Andrew Chatzky, and Anshu Siripurapu, "What's Next for the Trans-Pacific Partnership (TPP)?" Council on Foreign Relations, September 20, 2021, https://www.cfr.org/backgrounder/what-trans-pacific-partnership-tpp; Cathleen D. Cimino-Isaacs, "CPTPP: Overview and Issues for Congress" (Congressional Research Service, June 16, 2023), 1, https://crsreports.congress.gov/product/pdf/IF/IF12078.
58. Cimino-Isaacs, "CPTPP," 1.
59. Cimino-Isaacs, "CPTPP," 1.
60. McBride, et al., "What's Next for the Trans-Pacific Partnership (TPP)?"
61. Matthew P. Goodman, "From TPP to CPTPP," Center for Strategic & International Studies, March 8, 2018, https://www.csis.org/analysis/tpp-cptpp; Cimino-Isaacs, "CPTPP: Overview and Issues for Congress," 1.
62. Cimino-Isaacs, "CPTPP: Overview and Issues for Congress," 2.
63. Cimino-Isaacs, "CPTPP: Overview and Issues for Congress," 2.
64. Goodman, "From TPP to CPTPP"; Cimino-Isaacs, "CPTPP: Overview and Issues for Congress," 2.
65. Australian Government Department of Foreign Affairs and Trade, "Comprehensive and Progressive Agreement for Trans-Pacific Partnership," https://www.dfat.gov.au/sites/default/files/tpp-11-treaty-text.pdf.
66. McBride, et al., "What's Next for the Trans-Pacific Partnership (TPP)?"; Cimino-Isaacs, "CPTPP: Overview and Issues for Congress," 1.
67. Cimino-Isaacs, "CPTPP: Overview and Issues for Congress," 1; Ken Parks, "Mercosur Tensions Rise as Uruguay Seeks Trade Deal outside Bloc," Bloomberg, accessed September 16, 2023, https://www.bloomberg.com/news/articles/2022-12-01/mercosur-tensions-rise-as-uruguay-seaks-trade-deal-outside-bloc; Kantaro Komiya and Lucy Craymer, "Ukraine Asks to Join CPTPP Trade Pact," Reuters, July 6, 2023, https://www.reuters.com/world/ukraine-has-requested-join-cptpp-trade-pact-japan-minister-says-2023-07-07/.
68. McBride, et al., "What's Next for the Trans-Pacific Partnership (TPP)?"
69. McBride, et al., "What's Next for the Trans-Pacific Partnership (TPP)?"; Aidan Arasasingham, Emily Benson, Matthew P. Goodman, and William Alan Reinsch, "The United Kingdom Is Joining the CPTPP. What Comes Next?" March 31, 2023, https://www.csis.org/analysis/united-kingdom-joining-cptpp-what-comes-next.
70. McBride, et al., "What's Next for the Trans-Pacific Partnership (TPP)?"
71. Australian Government Department of Foreign Affairs and Trade, Regional Comprehensive Economic Partnership, https://www.dfat.gov.au/trade/agreements/in-force/rcep.

72. ASEAN, "The Regional Comprehensive Economic Partnership (RCEP)," https://asean.org/our-communities/economic-community/integration-with-global-economy/the-regional-comprehensive-economic-partnership-rcep/.
73. ASEAN, "The Regional Comprehensive Economic Partnership."
74. ASEAN, "The Regional Comprehensive Economic Partnership."
75. ASEAN, "The Regional Comprehensive Economic Partnership."
76. So Umezaki, "E-Commerce Provisions in the Regional Comprehensive Economic Partnership: A Milestone for a Global Rule?," *Institute of Developing Economies—Japan External Trade Organization*, August 2022, https://www.ide.go.jp/English/ResearchColumns/Columns/2022/so_umezaki.html.
77. Australian Government Department of Foreign Affairs and Trade, Regional Comprehensive Economic Partnership, https://www.dfat.gov.au/trade/agreements/in-force/rcep.
78. So Umezaki, "E-Commerce Provisions in the Regional Comprehensive Economic Partnership: A Milestone for a Global Rule?," *Institute of Developing Economies—Japan External Trade Organization*, August 2022, https://www.ide.go.jp/English/ResearchColumns/Columns/2022/so_umezaki.html.
79. Jane Kelsey, "Chapter 6: Opportunities and Challenges for ASEAN and East Asia from the Regional Comprehensive Economic Partnership on E-Commerce," in *Dynamism of East Asia and RCEP: The Framework for Regional Integration*, eds. Fukunari Kimura, Shujiro Urata, Shandre Thangavelu, and Dionisius Narjoko (Jakarta: Economic Research Institute for ASEAN and East Asia 2022), 119–44, https://www.eria.org/uploads/media/Books/2022-RCEP-Book2/10_ch.6-RCEP-on-E-Commerce.pdf; Australian Government Department of Foreign Affairs and Trade, Regional Comprehensive Economic Partnership, https://www.dfat.gov.au/trade/agreements/in-force/rcep.
80. Cathleen D. Cimino-Isaacs, Ben Dolven, and Michael D. Sutherland, "Regional Comprehensive Economic Partnership (RCEP)" (Congressional Research Service, October 17, 2022), 2, https://crsreports.congress.gov/product/pdf/IF/IF11891; "The Regional Comprehensive Economic Partnership: A New Paradigm for Asian Cooperation" (Asian Development Bank, May 2022), https://www.adb.org/sites/default/files/publication/792516/rcep-agreement-new-paradigm-asian-cooperation.pdf.
81. The White House, "Fact Sheet: In Asia, President Biden and a Dozen Indo-Pacific Partners Launch the Indo-Pacific Economic Framework for Prosperity," May 23, 2022, https://www.whitehouse.gov/briefing-room/statements-releases/2022/05/23/fact-sheet-in-asia-president-biden-and-a-dozen-indo-pacific-partners-launch-the-indo-pacific-economic-framework-for-prosperity/.
82. The White House, "On-the-Record Press Call on the Launch of the Indo-Pacific Economic Framework," May 23, 2022, https://www.whitehouse.gov/briefing-room/press-briefings/2022/05/23/on-the-record-press-call-on-the-launch-of-the-indo-pacific-economic-framework/.
83. Joe Manchin Newsroom, "Manchin, Capito Lead 52 Bipartisan Senators in Pressing Biden Administration to Include Taiwan in Indo-Pacific Economic Framework," May 18, 2022, https://www.manchin.senate.gov/newsroom/press-releases/manchin-capito-lead-52-bipartisan-senators-in-pressing-biden-administration-to-include-taiwan-in-indo-pacific-economic-framework.

84. Ministry of Foreign Affairs of the People's Republic of China, "Wang Yi: There Should Be a Big Question Mark on the U.S. Indo-Pacific Economic Framework," May 22, 2022, https://www.fmprc.gov.cn/eng/wjb_663304/wjbz_663308/activities_663312/202205/t20220523_10691134.html.
85. Robert Delaney, "US-Taiwan Trade Negotiations Should Be Updated 'Soon', White House Official Says," *South China Morning Post*, May 4, 2023, sec. China / Diplomacy. https://www.scmp.com/news/china/diplomacy/article/3219313/washington-taipei-trade-negotiations-should-be-updated-soon-us-official-says.
86. The White House, "Fact Sheet."
87. World Trade Online, "Fernandez: Administration Looking to Complete IPEF, APEP This Year," Inside Washington Publishers, January 24, 2023, https://insidetrade.com/daily-news/fernandez-administration-looking-complete-ipef-apep-year.
88. Matthew Goodman, "'Variable Geometry' Diagram of Indo-Pacific Economic Architecture," Image, *Center for Strategic & International Studies Economics Program*, June 6, 2022, https://twitter.com/MPGoodman88/status/1533961139113140225.
89. Ian Saccomanno, Naoto Saika, and Frank Schweitzer, "The Rise of Artificial Intelligence, Big Data, and the Next Generation of International Rules Governing Cross-Border Data Flows and Digital Trade," *JD Supra*, September 15, 2023, https://www.jdsupra.com/legalnews/the-rise-of-artificial-intelligence-big-4627994/.
90. Emily Birnbaum and Eric Martin, "Critics Slam Big Tech Lobbying in U.S. Indo-Pacific Trade Talks," *Time*, July 10, 2023, https://time.com/6293489/tech-firms-us-indo-pacific-trade-talks/.
91. Emily Birnbaum and Leah Nylen, "Google, Amazon Lobbyists Helped U.S. Shape New Indo-Pacific Trade Framework," *Bloomberg*, May 2, 2023, https://www.bloomberg.com/news/articles/2023-05-02/google-amazon-lobbyists-helped-shape-new-trade-framework.
92. Rethink Trade, "Press Release: Tech Firms Seek to Hijack Biden's Indo-Pacific Economic Framework (IPEF) Negotiations to Derail AI Oversight Via "Digital Trade" Rules," July 27, 2023, https://rethinktrade.org/press-releases/press-release-tech-firms-seek-to-hijack-bidens-indo-pacific-economic-framework-ipef-negotiations-to-derail-ai-oversight-via-digital-trade-rules/.
93. Brad Carr, Conan French, and Clay Lowery, "Data Localization: Costs, Tradeoffs, and Impacts across the Economy," Institute of International Finance, December 22, 2020, https://www.iif.com/Publications/ID/4225/Data-Localization-Costs-Tradeoffs-and-Impacts-Across-the-Economy.
94. Inu Manak, "Unpacking the IPEF: Biden's First Big Trade Play," Council on Foreign Relations, June 8, 2022, https://www.cfr.org/article/unpacking-ipef-bidens-first-big-trade-play.
95. Kevin Chen, "The Case for a US Digital Trade Deal in IPEF—and Why It's an Uphill Battle," *The Diplomat*, June 5, 2023, https://thediplomat.com/2023/06/the-case-for-a-us-digital-trade-deal-in-ipef-and-why-its-an-uphill-battle/.
96. Anand Raghuraman, "India's Data Localization Pivot Can Revamp Global Digital Diplomacy," Atlantic Council, December 5, 2022, https://www.atlanticcouncil.org/blogs/southasiasource/indias-data-localization-pivot/.
97. Lurong Chen, "The Indo-Pacific Partnership and Digital Trade Rule Setting: Policy Proposals," Economic Research Institute for ASEAN and East Asia, December 14,

2022, https://www.eria.org/publications/the-indo-pacific-partnership-and-digital-trade-rule-setting-policy-proposals/.
98. Vinod K. Aggarwal and Andrew W. Reddie, "Putting the Biden Administration's "New Economic Statecraft" in Context," August 21, 2023, *Lawfare*, https://www.lawfaremedia.org/article/putting-the-biden-administration-s-new-economic-statecraft-in-context.

CHAPTER 8

The United States and Changing Regional Orders in Europe and Asia

Deborah Welch Larson

After the end of the Cold War, many analysts predicted that the collapse of superpower competition would increase the autonomy of regional orders from the global power balance.[1] But Russia's invasion of Ukraine has dealt a shock to the European order, comparable to that following the breakup of the Soviet Union. At the same time, China's extraordinary rise along with its more assertive recent stance has spurred a boost in regional arms spending and US networking among states in the Indo-Pacific. What is the likely future for US policy toward regional orders in Europe and Asia? What are the implications for international relations theory?

In some respects, the European and Asian regional orders are returning to Cold War dynamics, including use of nuclear threats by Russian president Vladimir Putin and constrained economic interactions between rival powers, due to forces not included in the dominant international relations theories. Realist approaches, such as the canonical balance of power theory, explain wars as the outcome of an aspiring hegemon's drive for regional domination and an imbalance of power conducive to successful aggression.[2] Instead of power aggrandizement and a balance favoring the offense, the war between Russia and Ukraine implicates Russia's desire for great power status and the Ukrainians' national identity. Hegemonic stability theory predicts that a great power willing to provide security and enforce economic openness can maintain peace in a region.[3] But the US preponderance did not prevent Russia from invading Ukraine. Nor did the American-led alliance system in Asia inhibit China from making cumulative gains in the South China through salami tactics, such as creating and militarizing artificial islands in the South China Sea.

For the English school, what matters is not the distribution of power and threats but institutions, norms, and practices. An international society exists when a group of like-minded states "consider themselves to be bound by a common set of rules in their relations with one another and share in the workings of common institutions." These rules include war, the great powers, diplomacy, the balance of power, and international law.[4] Today, however, elements of international society are lacking in both Europe and Asia, as there is a lack of agreement among the United States, China, and Russia on what the rules are or should be.

Liberal hegemony theorists argue that the United States has provided leadership to regional orders, offering security assistance through alliances and economic openness in return for states' observance of rules and norms. According to John Ikenberry, American *strategic restraint* reassured its alliance partners that there was no need for them to balance against the United States or each other by acquiring additional arms because they could rely on the United States for defense and predictable trade relations. Recognizing the self-denying aspect of US power, its partners deferred voluntarily to US leadership and sought security through rules and institutions rather than arms and rivalries.[5] The war in Ukraine, however, has called into question the sufficiency of strategic restraint, at least when dealing with potential adversaries.[6]

While casting doubt on liberal hegemony theory, Russia's invasion of Ukraine has also undermined the liberal argument that trade and interdependence foster peace by providing disincentives for war.[7] Economic interdependence undermined deterrence in the sense that Putin believed—wrongly—that Russia would bear little cost for aggression because Europe was dependent on oil and gas and would therefore do nothing in response to the invasion. Russia's biggest trading partner was the European Union, yet Putin was not deterred by the threat of additional economic sanctions. When the EU criticized the invasion, Putin tried to weaponize Russian fossil fuels by cutting off supplies of natural gas to European countries, expecting that the increased hardship would reduce public support for aiding Ukraine.[8]

What these theoretical perspectives overlook is the renewed importance of competition among great powers for status within Europe and Asia—more muscular efforts by Russia and China to assert their global power status and to establish a multipolar system where each major power would have a regional sphere of influence. In international relations, status refers to collective beliefs about a state's ranking on valued attributes such as wealth, coercive capabilities, culture, population, sociopolitical organization, and diplomatic clout. A state's status is manifested by its membership in elite clubs and its position within those clubs. States defer voluntarily to higher-status states through various means, including supporting their leadership in international fora, seeking their opinions, or making state visits to the capital.[9]

Power transitions underway have increased status contestation in regional orders. In Eastern Europe, Russia would like to establish a regional sphere of influence, whereas the United States and Western Europe believe that states should be allowed to choose their own alliances. China aims to weaken the US alliance system in East Asia and to establish its primacy. Both China and Russia believe that they are entitled by history and culture to be recognized as global great powers, with special interests in neighboring areas. The United States wishes to maintain global primacy to safeguard freedom of the seas and of state alignment.

But the United States does not have sufficient power to maintain a substantial presence in all parts of the world. During the Cold War, as part of the containment strategy, the United States sought to prevent a hostile power from dominating military-industrial centers of power in Europe and East Asia.[10] After an ill-fated preoccupation with the Middle East in the "War on Terror," the United States has returned to the earlier Cold War geopolitical priorities, as indicated by the order of regions in the most recent US National Security Strategy, where the Indo-Pacific is listed first, followed by Europe.[11] This essay will focus on the US role in regional orders in Europe and Asia.

Some might question whether the United States should be categorized as an actor in regional orders in Europe or Asia, given its distant geographical location.[12] On the other hand, scholars have generally agreed that an external power can be regarded as part of a region if its policy affects security-based interactions between states geographically located in the area.[13] External great powers may contest over or even capture a region.[14] Currently, the United States is contesting with both China and Russia over Europe and the Indo-Pacific.

In this essay, I first discuss the how the Ukraine War has strengthened the leadership of the United States and NATO in Europe, an outcome that was neither inevitable nor predictable. I then analyze the rivalry between the United States and China over order in East Asia and the responses of key states to the Ukraine War and Chinese assertiveness in the region.

EUROPE

The Russian invasion of Ukraine has altered the European regional order by enhancing the role of the United States and by reaffirming the importance of

NATO, which seemingly had lost its purpose after the end of the Cold War. The Ukraine crisis has increased pressures for economic closure between rival blocs and deterrence, a return to Cold War patterns.

To understand the Russian invasion of Ukraine, we must go back to negotiations that created institutions following the end of the Cold War when Russia disagreed with the West on the architecture of the European order. Instead of establishing a European-wide institution or enlarging the responsibilities of the Organization for Security and Cooperation in Europe (OSCE), as Russia would have preferred, the George H. W. Bush and Bill Clinton administrations decided to enlarge existing institutions, NATO and the EU, to include states that were formerly part of the Soviet alliance, the Warsaw Pact.[15] Incorporation of these states into NATO conflicted with Russia's claim to a sphere of influence in Eastern Europe and states that were formerly part of the Soviet Union, based on its status as a global great power.[16] The United States and other Western countries, however, adhere to the norm that states should be free to choose their own alliances.[17]

To gain influence over neighboring states, Russia created its own regional organizations, such as the Commonwealth of Independent States (CIS), the Collective Security Treaty Organization (CSTO), and the Eurasian Economic Union (EAEU).[18] When integration efforts did not give Russia the control it sought over neighboring countries, Moscow resorted to coercion, such as raising oil and gas prices, economic embargos, and support for secessionist movements.[19]

President George W. Bush took a more assertive stance toward promoting democracy and independence in the post-Soviet states, supporting "color revolutions" in Georgia, Ukraine, and Kyrgyzstan. At the 2008 NATO summit in Bucharest, Bush pushed through a resolution against French and German opposition that Ukraine and Georgia "will" become members of NATO.[20] Four months later, Russia's invasion of Georgia seemingly ended discussion of membership for Ukraine and Georgia in NATO. Russian President Dmitri Medvedev announced that there were regions in which Russia had "privileged interests."[21]

As part of the "reset policy," aimed at reducing tensions with Russia, President Barack Obama adopted a more hands-off approach toward both Eastern Europe and states in the "near abroad" such as Ukraine, Moldova, and Georgia.[22] During the 2014 Maidan Protests in Ukraine, rather than asserting a US interest in Ukraine's democracy, the United States encouraged the European leaders to mediate the conflict between pro-Russian leader Viktor Yanukovych and the opposition.[23] After Russia annexed Crimea and supported secessionist movements in Luhansk and Donetsk, Obama refused to provide lethal assistance to the Ukrainian regime, because he believed that Russia had more at stake than the United States did.[24]

Some have argued that NATO expansion, and in particular the offer of membership to Ukraine, provoked Putin's 2021 invasion of Ukraine by posing an existential threat to Russian security.[25] But Putin's reaction to Ukraine's prospective membership in NATO has varied over time, whereas it should have been constant if existential Russian security interests were affected.[26] Russia's efforts to subordinate Ukraine date back to Kyiv's separation from the Soviet Union, 1991–1994, before the United States had decided to enlarge NATO, when Moscow pressured Ukraine to join the CIS and repeatedly cut off gas and oil.[27] What concerned Russia about NATO expansion was not any potential threat to Russian security, but political marginalization, its exclusion from the high table where major security decisions were made.[28]

The issue of NATO expansion, however, was the ostensible cause of the diplomatic clash between Russia and the United States, which was the prelude to the Russian invasion on February 24, 2022. On December 17, 2021, with about 190,000 thousand Russian troops on the border with Ukraine, Putin issued a series of demands to both the United States and NATO, including a guarantee that Ukraine would not be admitted and that Russia would have the right to veto where NATO troops and weapons could be stationed in Eastern European countries that had been admitted since 1997.[29] While Western countries were cautiously receptive to giving security guarantees to Russia, they rejected the demand that no additional countries should be admitted to NATO as a violation of sovereignty.[30]

Putin's aims in his invasion were more expansive than obtaining Ukrainian neutrality or security guarantees for Russian borders. He openly declared that his goals were regime change in Ukraine and an end to Ukrainian culture and identity.[31] In his February 21, 2022, speech announcing recognition of the so-called separatist "people's republics" of Donetsk and Luhansk, Putin argued that Ukraine had no right to exist, an assertion that he had made repeatedly since 2008. Ukraine, he said, "is an inalienable part of our own history, culture, and spiritual space."[32] Russia's attempt to annex Ukraine to Russia violated the foundational norms of the United Nations Charter in 1945, that territorial integrity is guaranteed and that borders should not be changed through use of force.[33] Putin's war, therefore, is about more than whether Ukraine should join NATO. It is about the future of the European rule-based order, including the principles of territorial integrity, nonuse of force to change borders, and sovereignty.[34]

Ukraine has long been viewed as a borderland state, neither clearly part of the West nor the East. The western half of the country, much of which had been part of the Habsburg empire, inclined toward Western Europe, while the eastern portion, which had been Cossack territory or colonized by the Russian empire, oriented toward Russia.[35] The 2014 annexation of Crimea and detachment of separatist areas of Luhansk and Donetsk, however, had removed many of the pro-Russian inhabitants of Ukraine.[36] The Ukrainians responded with surprisingly strong, united resistance against the Russian invasion.

The Biden administration's calibrated but firm response to Russia's war and their ability to forge a consensus among the often divided members of NATO has enhanced the relative status of the United States.[37] Convinced by October 2021 that Putin was planning an invasion, the Biden administration lay the groundwork for a collective Western response by sharing secret intelligence on Russian military plans with US allies and discussing possible sanctions.[38] To respond effectively to the Russian invasion and help Ukraine, the United States played an essential role in providing organization, military equipment, logistics, and leadership.

As a result of the Russian invasion, both NATO and the EU have been reinvigorated and strengthened. Despite internal disagreements, Western countries have maintained remarkable unity against Russia's aggression and have contributed substantial military aid and equipment to Ukraine. Finland and Sweden joined the NATO alliance, abandoning their policy of neutrality, pursued since the end of World War II. Their presence will make it much easier to defend the Baltic states.[39]

NATO suddenly took on renewed importance because the Russian invasion had upended the liberal premise that economic interdependence and trade lead to peace. Instead, firm and credible deterrence was needed. German chancellor Olaf Scholz declared that the Russian invasion was a turning point, or *Zeitenwende*, and pledged to increase Germany's defense budget to 2 percent of the country's GDP in line with NATO's declarative policy and to contribute more military efforts to the NATO alliance. Germany abandoned its firm commitment not to export arms or weapons to conflict sites, which would enable it to provide military assistance to Ukraine.[40] Germany along with other Europeans had assumed that through trade with Europe, Russia would accept the rule of law and liberalize politically, or "change through trade," *Wandel durch Handel*. With this comforting rationalization, some European states had become dependent on cheap Russian oil and gas, which increased the risk that Russia would "weaponize" interdependence.[41]

Galvanized by the Russian invasion and the first major land war in Europe since World War II, the EU took on new security responsibilities, including coordinating miliary aid, assimilating Ukrainian refugees, and imposing sanctions on Russia.[42] The EU used its newly created European Peace Facility fund to finance arms to Ukraine and coordinated requests from Ukraine to its member states.[43] To be sure, the military contributions to Ukraine were by individual state members rather than the EU as an institution.[44] But the multilateral organization acted in line with expectations, by coordinating and harmonizing policy and sending a signal of determination to the rest of the world, including Russia.

The Russian war against Ukraine has shifted the status hierarchy within the Western coalition in NATO and the EU, giving more precedence to the eastern members, the Baltic states and Poland, that had been prescient in warning about Russian intentions. France and Germany had pursued engagement with Russia since the end of the Cold War, negotiating with Putin until the last few days before Russia's all-out invasion. Twenty years later, French president Emmanuel Macron implicitly apologized for a 2003 remark by then-French president Jacques Chirac that the Eastern European states who had supported the US war against Iraq had "missed a good opportunity to shut up"[45] by stating at a security conference in Bratislava that while "some said you had missed an opportunity to shut up . . . I think we also lost an opportunity to listen to you."[46] In August 2022, Chancellor Scholz stated, "The center of Europe is moving eastward."[47]

Status depends on what states value, and as long as the war in Ukraine continues, Europeans will accord higher status to those states that contribute more to the common effort to support Ukraine. Poland in particular has provided military aid to Ukraine and accepted refugees in the early part of the war when France and Germany were waffling. Poland's status was strengthened by the 2023 election as prime minister of Donald Tusk, who reaffirmed vigorous support for the EU, NATO, and Ukraine.[48]

When the Ukraine war ends, Russia will be isolated from the European security order; yet, institutions will need to be developed that will include Moscow, once it has ceased its aggression. In many respects, the current regional order in Europe resembles that of the Cold War, with polarization and renewed reliance on deterrence for security. Also reminiscent of the early Cold War is Putin's frequent resort to vague nuclear threats, just as Nikita Khrushchev boasted about the Soviet Union's (inferior) ballistic missile capabilities until after the Cuban Missile Crisis, when the superpowers learned that it was too dangerous to make nuclear threats. Deterrence is needed to create conditions conducive for peaceful change.[49] Not only are free trade and interdependence alone insufficient to maintain peace but they strengthened Putin's war machine. Europe needs both the EU for peace through integration and NATO for peace through strength. The United States continues to play an essential leadership role in NATO as well as providing most of its weapons, military equipment, and logistics.[50]

Perhaps the most serious threat to the European security order is Trumpian revisionism, because a fair number of Republicans have turned against providing aid to Ukraine. If Donald Trump is elected president with Republican control of Congress, the United States is likely to reduce its role in defending Europe and in NATO. Worried about this eventuality, Europeans have pledged to increase their defense spending and are making plans for a security order that is less dependent on US arms and logistics.[51]

US policies toward Europe and Ukraine will not change if Kamala Harris is elected president and if the Democrats are able to take back control of the House of Representatives, although overall US funding for Ukraine aid is likely to decline. Continued Republican control of the House could present obstacles to providing substantial assistance to Ukraine. A Harris administration may have to shift some of the burden of supplying arms to European allies or come up with some sort of "lend-lease" similar to that provided by President Franklin D. Roosevelt to allies in World War II.

EAST ASIA

The war in Ukraine has dealt a major shock to the security order in East Asia as well. There is the possibility that the two orders will be linked, as European allies try to assist the United States, which is in danger of overextension.[52] China expects to attain status as the leading power in East Asia, while the United States is trying to retain its primacy in the region.[53] This competition for status is reflected in rival conceptions of the regional order. China's preferred regional order is hierarchical, whereby rights of states would be based on their relative size and the closeness of their relationship to China. The United States' conception is a rules-based order, according to which all states are entitled to the protection of international law and freedom of the seas, a principle that would help maintain the primacy of the United States, which is geographically distant and needs to project power to defend its allies and free trade.[54]

According to hegemonic stability theorists, the United States has maintained a rule-guided order in East Asia since the Cold War as part of a bargain. The United States provided security to its treaty allies—Japan, South Korea, the Philippines, Australia, and Thailand—and partner states in return for their cooperation. The stability provided by the US defense guarantees made it possible for the region to develop economically without internal rivalry and polarization.[55]

China's stunning economic rise and increased defense spending have undermined the US status as the regional hegemon. Some theorists believe that the East Asian region is already bipolar, divided between the United States and China.[56] A variant of the bipolar thesis is the dual structure model, whereby China is the leading economic power while the United States provides security. China's lack of restraint—exemplified by its confrontations with the Philippines and Vietnam over features in the South China Sea and with Japan over the Senkaku islands—has increased the regional demand for the United States as a security partner.[57] But this dichotomy exaggerates the division of responsibility. While China is the leading trading partner for regional states, the United States and Europe are also deeply involved economically in East Asia, especially in direct foreign investment. The United States, Japan, and Europe are attractive markets for Asian states.[58]

The East Asian order is more complex and less polarized than a bipolar structure would imply. So long as the United States is an active participant in East Asia, China will not be able to dominate the region. But the unsettled security structure of the Indo-Pacific and unclear alignments could lead to greater Sino-American tensions and inadvertent conflict.

In response to China's increased assertiveness in the South and East China Seas, in 2011, the Obama administration announced a "pivot to Asia," although the name was misleading in that it represented a return to traditional US geopolitical priorities. The "pivot" included more US engagement in regional multilateral organizations, strengthening of regional partnerships, and some rotation of US military forces to the region.[59]

Building on the pivot, the Donald J. Trump administration adopted a "free and open Indo-Pacific" (FOIP) strategy, a term borrowed from Japanese prime minister Shinzo Abe, as part of its shift to a policy of great power competition with both Russia and China, with an emphasis on containing China.[60] The FOIP enlarges the geographic sphere of the Asia-Pacific region in order to enlist India to counter China. The Biden administration has retained the FOIP strategy but with more emphasis on enlisting the assistance of allies and security partners in the region.[61]

Despite the Russian invasion of Ukraine, the Biden administration announced in its national security strategy that the United States would "prioritize maintaining an enduring competitive edge over the PRC while constraining a still profoundly dangerous Russia." The PRC was the "only competitor with both the intent to reshape the international order and, increasingly, the economic, diplomatic, military, and technological power to do it."[62]

To do so, Washington is seeking to bolster cooperation with allies and security partners to balance rising Chinese power and maintain its superiority in the Indo-Pacific. Instead of establishing a region-wide alliance like NATO, however, the United States is fostering bilateral, quadrilateral, and minilateral security cooperation among states in the region, in a "lattice"-like pattern.[63] The Biden administration revived the "Quad," a security grouping including Australia, Japan, the United States, and India, by elevating it to the summit level. In September 2021, Washington entered into the Australia, United Kingdom, and United States (AUKUS) defense technology pact with Australia and Britain to help Australia acquire nuclear-powered submarines. Nuclear-powered submarines are faster, quieter, and can travel for longer distances before surfacing. The agreement also includes increased cooperation on emerging technologies, such as artificial intelligence, quantum computing, hypersonics, and cyber security. Australian naval personnel will have to be trained with UK and US crews on the submarines. Eventually, a new AU-UK submarine will be developed using UK design and US defense technology. The deal will embed Great Britain in the Indo-Pacific, an example of linking the security orders in the Euro-Atlantic with the Asia-Pacific.[64]

The United States has strengthened its military ties with its long-standing ally, the Philippines, which had been nearly ruptured under populist leader Rodrigo Duterte, who tilted toward China in hopes of obtaining increased Chinese investment and cooperation in exploiting the resources of the South China Sea. But China did not provide the promised assistance in building infrastructure and providing loans. In addition, China stepped up its harassment of Filipino fishing boats in the Philippines Exclusive Economic Zone (EEZ). President Ferdinand Marcos Jr. is balancing against China by strengthening military ties with the United States. In 2023, Marcos agreed to allow the US military to use four additional bases in the Philippines, including three near Taiwan. The US Navy reinstated its joint patrols with the Philippine navy of the South China Sea. President Marcos's change in policy was largely a response to China's increased activity in the South China Sea.[65]

China's assertiveness has been a major concern for Japan, provoking increased military spending and military cooperation with the United States and other regional allies to balance against China. Similar to Scholz, Kishida regards Russia's invasion of Ukraine as a "turning point," remarking that "Ukraine today could be East Asia tomorrow." But Japan's defensive measures are primarily motivated by China's increasingly confrontational maritime tactics. During China's August 2022 military exercises protesting US speaker of the house Nancy Pelosi's visit to Taiwan, China fired five missiles into Japan's EEZ. In December 2022, Kishida announced a revision of Japan's National Security Strategy in which he pledged to increase Japan's defense spending to 2 percent of GDP, above the customary 1 percent, and to acquire "counterstrike capabilities," in other words, the ability to hit Chinese bases in self-defense. From 2022 to 2027, Japan will increase its defense spending by nearly two-thirds.[66]

Russian aggression against Ukraine has increased concerns in the region about a Chinese invasion of Taiwan.[67] There is also the risk of an inadvertent conflict between US and Chinese air and naval forces. The United States periodically sends warships through the Taiwan Strait and the South China Sea to assert the principle of freedom of navigation, but China's warships and aircraft play a game of chicken, increasing the risk of a military incident that could escalate to a US-Chinese conflict. The dangers are increased by the Chinese practice of breaking off military-to-military contact during crises, a form of brinkmanship.[68]

In contrast to Japan and the Philippines, which have increased their ties to the United States in order to balance against China, India has held back from alignment against either Russia or China. India has reaffirmed its historic ties to Russia and purchases large amounts of discounted Russian oil and gas, thereby powering Russia's war against Ukraine. Russia had supported India with aid and arms during much of the Cold War while the United States was allied to India's enemy Pakistan. In addition, India is reliant on arms supplies from Russia, which it needs to contain China. While India's leader Narendra Modi had tried to achieve a rapprochement with Xi Jinping, China has been making incremental encroachments on Indian territory, resulting in armed conflict between Chinese and Indian troops in the Galwan Valley in 2020, in which twenty Indians were killed, and a more recent clash in December 2022. Modi does not wish to provoke China, the more powerful state, by allying against it. India is an enthusiastic participant in the Quad but prefers for the organization to be viewed as an informal security cooperation club.[69]

India's stance of maintaining good relations with the competing great powers enhances its relative status. Indian Foreign Minister S. Jaishankar argues that the current Western-dominated world order is being replaced by a world of "multi-alignment" where countries will choose their own "particular policies, preferences, and interests."[70]

China's naval buildup and increasing assertiveness over its claims in the East and South China Seas reflect its policy of becoming a "great maritime power," a necessary step toward Xi's signature goal of the "great rejuvenation of the Chinese people." In October 2013, Xi Jinping convened an unprecedented work forum on diplomacy toward neighboring countries, in which he called for the transformation of China's immediate neighborhood into a "community of shared destiny," a goal that he has repeated over a hundred times in speeches. Xi's rhetoric indicated that the community of shared destiny would require reshaping the norms and values of peripheral states. States in the region would be connected to China through networks of trade, investment, and exchanges.[71]

The Belt and Road Initiative, outlined in two speeches by Xi Jinping in 2013, seeks to build "policy, infrastructure, trade, financial, and people-to-people connectivity." Xi's plan included a land belt connecting China's inland provinces with Central Asia and Europe, and a maritime silk road linking China's coastal areas with the South China Sea, Indian Ocean, and the Mediterranean.[72] Also part of the community of shared destiny is China's responsibility for regional security. In 2014, at the Conference on Confidence Building and Interaction in Asia, Xi Jinping argued that "It is for the people of Asia to run the affairs of Asia, solve the problems of Asia and uphold the security of Asia."[73]

Challenges to the security order in Europe are linked to the order in Asia, in that China supports Russia's war in Ukraine, not only by purchasing Russian oil and gas but by exporting products that are under sanctions by the West and supporting Russia's position in UN votes.[74] There are close personal ties between Xi Jinping and Putin, who have visited each other an unprecedented number of times, but China's policy is largely motivated by interests. Xi Jinping needs Russia as a counterweight to the United States and as support for the claim that the world is becoming multipolar.[75] Theirs is a status partnership, of outsiders, in which both states rely on the other for affirmation of their status against the liberal West.[76]

Southeast Asian nations have continued their traditional policy of hedging, unwilling to choose between China and the United States. Through hedging, the Southeast Asian states try to play the competing powers off against each other to maximize their benefits while avoiding taking sides.[77] While China is their leading trading partner, many states in Southeast Asia rely on the United States for security, not just defense guarantees, but military training and assistance.[78]

A major component of order in Southeast Asia is the multilateral organization ASEAN (Association of Southeast Asian Nations). But China's subordination of Laos and Cambodia has prevented the organization from developing a coherent response to China's assertiveness in the South China

Sea. Reflecting divisions among the members, ASEAN has declined to take a position on the Russian invasion or even to call it an "invasion."[79]

Trumpism poses less risk of a return to US isolationism in Asia than in Europe, because there is bipartisan support for containing China in the US Congress, and if elected president, Trump is likely to appoint China hawks to key national security positions. States that feel threatened by China's assertiveness are likely to respond with increased balancing, in cooperation with the United States or in partnerships in the region. President Marcos has hedged against the return of Trump and a decline in US support for regional alliances by seeking cooperative agreements with Vietnam, Australia, and Germany.[80]

The United States and China have heightened their competition over status and influence in the Asian region, with ripple effects on the foreign policies of smaller and medium states, which are under increasing pressure to take sides. The United States advocates alliances and informal security partnerships to enhance liberal values and preserve the rule-guided order, whereas China emphasizes economic development and sovereignty. Nevertheless, globalization gives these smaller states more leeway in their foreign policies. Major states in the region—Japan, Australia, and South Korea—provide Southeast Asian states with alternatives to economic dependence on China.[81] While the war in Ukraine and Chinese assertiveness has led to increased balancing by long-standing US allies Japan, Australia, and the Philippines, the rest of the Asian order is up for grabs between China and the United States.

CONCLUSION

Russian and Chinese actions are creating severe challenges for the prospect of peaceful change. Regional orders are likely to be more fluid and shifting, with middle and small states hedging and engaging different sides. Russia is outside the European security architecture because of the war in Ukraine. Because Putin has demonstrated that he cannot be trusted to observe agreements, Europe and the United States will have to offer iron-clad security guarantees to Ukraine, a country that was largely outside NATO and EU structures.

In Asia, however, there is not the degree of polarization between blocs that is so striking in Europe. Asian countries are reacting to China's efforts to assert its status forcefully in the context of what it regards as US gradual decline. Although some balancing is occurring, as Japan, Australia, and the

Philippines react to China's increasing use of coercion in the Taiwan Strait and South China Seas by increasing security cooperation with the United States, it would be overly simplistic to regard this as simple balancing because all intend to maintain economic relations with China. Status competition is more intense and unpredictable than balance of power dynamics because it is subjective and based on perception. The desire for increased status is a psychological need, which can override material concerns such as economic prosperity and security, as indicated by the intensity of competition among Russia, China, and the United States.

NOTES

1. David A. Lake and Patrick M. Morgan, eds., *Regional Orders: Building Security in a New World* (University Park: Pennsylvania State University Press, 1997); Barry Buzan and Ole Waever, *Regions and Powers: The Structure of International Security* (Cambridge: Cambridge University Press, 2003); Peter J. Katzenstein, *A World of Regions: Asia and Europe in the American Imperium* (Ithaca, NY: Cornell University Press, 2005); Amitav Acharya, *Constructing a Security Community in East Asia in South East Asia: ASEAN and the Problem of Regional Order* (London: Routledge, 2001); Benjamin Miller, *States, Nations and the Great Powers: The Sources of Regional War and Peace* (Cambridge: Cambridge University Press, 2007); T.V. Paul, ed., *International Relations Theory and Regional Transformation* (Cambridge: Cambridge University Press, 2014).
2. Kenneth N. Waltz, *Theory of International Politics* (Reading, MA: Addison-Wesley, 1979); T.V. Paul, James Wirtz, and Michel Fortmann, eds., *Balance of Power Theory and Practice in the 21st Century* (Stanford, CA: Stanford University Press, 2004).
3. Robert Gilpin, *War and Change in World Politics* (Cambridge: Cambridge University Press, 1981).
4. Hedley Bull, *The Anarchical Society: A Study of Order in World Politics* (New York: Columbia University Press, 1977), 13.
5. G. John Ikenberry, *After Victory: Institutions, Strategic Restraint, and the Rebuilding of Order After Major Wars* (Princeton, NJ: Princeton University Press, 2001).
6. William Mulligan, "Erosions, Ruptures, and the Ending of International Orders: Putin's Invasion of Ukraine in Historical Perspective," *Society* 59 (2022): 261.
7. For a prediction that trade made war between states obsolete, see Daniel Deudney and G. John Ikenberry, "The Myth of the Autocratic Revival," *Foreign Affairs* 88, no. 1 (January/February 2009): 88–89.
8. Patricia Cohen, "Economic Ties among Nations Spur Peace. Or Do They?," *New York Times*, March 4, 2022, https://www.nytimes.com.
9. Deborah Welch Larson, T.V. Paul, and William C. Wohlforth, "Status and World Order," in *Status in World Politics*, eds. T.V. Paul, Deborah Welch Larson, and William C. Wohlforth (Cambridge: Cambridge University Press, 2014), 7, 10.
10. John Lewis Gaddis, "Was the Truman Doctrine a Real Turning Point?," *Foreign Affairs* 52, no. 2 (1974): 386–402; John Lewis Gaddis, *Strategies of Containment*, rev. and exp. (New York: Oxford University Press, 2005), 29–30; Peter J. Katzenstein, *A World of*

Regions: Asia and Europe in the American Imperium (Ithaca, NY: Cornell University Press, 2005).

11. White House, National Security Strategy, October 2022, https://www.whitehouse.gov/wp-content/uploads/2022/10/Biden-Harris-Administrations-National-Security-Strategy-10.2022.pdf.
12. Buzan and Waever, *Regions and Powers*, 80; Paul, *International Relations Theory and Regional Transformation*, 5.
13. Buzan and Waever, *Regions and Powers*, 46–47, 61–63; T.V. Paul, "Realism, Liberalism and Regional Order in East Asia: Toward a Hybrid Approach," *Pacific Review* 35, no. 6 (2022): 1029–30.
14. Gil Merom, "Realist Hypotheses on Regional Peace," *Journal of Strategic Studies* 26, no. 1 (2003): 112.
15. Mary E. Sarotte, *Not One Inch: America, Russia, and the Making of the Post-Cold War Stalemate* (New Haven, CT: Yale University Press, 2021); Kristina Spohr, *Post Wall, Post Square: Rebuilding the World after 1989* (London: William Collins, 2019).
16. William Hill, *No Place for Russia: European Security Institutions Since 1989* (New York: Columbia University Press, 2018), 9–10, 384–85; Mark Bassin and Konstantin E. Aksenov, "Mackinder and the Heartland Theory in Post-Soviet Geopolitical Discourse," *Geopolitics* 11, no. 1 (2011): 100–101; Elias Gotz and Jorgen Staun, "Why Russia Attacked Ukraine: Strategic Culture and Radicalized Narratives," *Contemporary Security Policy* 43, no. 3 (2002), 485, 490–91.
17. Hill, *No Place for Russia*, 160.
18. Andrej Krickovic and Igor Pellicciari, "From 'Greater Europe' to 'Greater Eurasia': Status Concerns and the evolution of Russia's Approach to Alignment and Regional Integration," *Journal of Eurasian Studies* 12, no. 1 (2021): 86–99; Tatiana Romanova, "Russia's Neorevisionist Challenge to the Liberal International Order," *International Spectator* 53, no. 1 (2018): 79–80; Bobo Lo, *Russia and the New World Disorder* (Washington, DC: Brookings Institution Press, 2015), 43–44, 80–81.
19. Stephen Blank, "The Intellectual Origins of the Eurasian Union Project," in *Putin's Grand Strategy: The Eurasian Union and Its Discontents*, eds. S. Frederick Starr and Svante E. Cornell (Central Asia-Caucasus Institute & Silk Road Studies Program, 2019), 18–19; James Sherr, *Hard Diplomacy and Soft Coercion: Russia's Influence Abroad* (London: Chatham House, 2013), 61–62; Lo, *Russia and the New World Disorder*, 41–42, 96.
20. Hill, *No Place for Russia*, 262–63; Angela E. Stent, *The Limits of Partnership: U.S.-Russian Relations in the Twenty-First Century* (Princeton: Princeton University Press, 2014), 163–68.
21. Hill, *No Place for Russia*, 267–68, 271–72; President Dmitri Medvedev interview given to television channel One, Rossia, NTV, August 31, 3008, https://en.kremlin.ru/events/president/transcripts/48301.
22. Hill, *No Place for Russia*, 285–87.
23. Deborah Welch Larson, "Outsourced Diplomacy: The Obama Administration and the Ukraine Crisis," in *Triangular Diplomacy among the United States, the European Union, and the Russian Federation*, eds. Vicki L. Birchfield and Alasdair R. Young (Cham, Switzerland: Palgrave Macmillan), 55–76.
24. Derek Chollet, *The Long Game* (New York: PublicAffairs, 2016), 174–76.
25. John J. Mearsheimer, "Why the Ukraine Crisis Is the West's Fault: The Liberal Delusions That Provoked Putin," *Foreign Affairs* 93 (September–October 2014): 77–89;

"John Mearsheimer on Why the West Is Principally Responsible for the Ukrainian Crisis," *The Economist*, March 19, 2022, www.economist.com.
26. Samuel Ramani, *Putin's War on Ukraine: Russia's Campaign for Global Counter-Revolution* (London: Hurst & Company, 2023), 5–6.
27. Paul D'Anieri, *Ukraine and Russia: From Civilized Divorce to Uncivil War*, 2nd ed. (Cambridge: Cambridge University Press, 2023), 21–22, 42–44, 55.
28. Kimberly Marten, "Reconsidering NATO Expansion: A Counterfactual Analysis of Russia and the West in the 1990s," *European Journal of International Security* 3, part 2 (2017): 153, 160; Deborah Welch Larson and Alexei Shevchenko, *Quest for Status: Chinese and Russian Foreign Policy* (New Haven: Yale University Press, 2019), 183–84, 227; Kimberly Marten, "NATO Enlargement: Evaluating Its Consequences in Russia," *International Politics* 57 (2020): 401–26; Hill, *No Place for Russia*, 168–69.
29. Andrew E. Kramer and Steven Erlanger, "Putin Moves to Push NATO Out of Former Soviet Republics," *New York Times*, December 18, 2021; Henry Foy, Polina Ivanova, and James Politi, "Moscow Calls the Shots Ahead of US Talks," *Financial Times*, January 8/9, 2022.
30. David E. Sanger, "Cold War-Like Behavior Echoed in Negotiations between U.S. and Russia," *New York Times*, January 11, 2022; Ben Hall and Max Seddon, "Lines Drawn Ahead of US-Russia Talks," *Financial Times*, January 10, 2022; Kristin Eichensehr, "Contemporary Practice of the United States Relating to International Law," *American Journal of International Law*, 116 (2022).
31. Ramani, *Putin's War on Ukraine*, 121–28.
32. Address by the president of the Russian Federation, February 21, 2022, https://en.kremlin.ru/events/president/news/67868.
33. Ingrid (Wuerth) Brunk and Monica Hakimi, "Russia, Ukraine, and the Future World Order," *American Journal of International Law* 116, no. 4 (October 2022): 687–97.
34. Angela Stent, "The Putin Doctrine," January 27, 2022, *Foreign Affairs.com*; Max Fisher, "Putin's Case for War, Annotated," *New York Times*, February 24, 2022.
35. Serhii Plokhy, *The Gates of Europe: A History of Ukraine*, rev. ed (New York: Basic Books, 2021), 362–63.
36. D'Anieri, *Ukraine and Russia*, 255–57.
37. Janan Ganesh, "The US Will Be the Ultimate Winner of the War in Ukraine," *Financial Times*, April 6, 2022.
38. Mark Landler, Katrin Bennhold, and Matina Stevis-Gridnett, "After Zelensky's Plea, the West Raced to Form a United Front," *New York Times*, March 6, 2022.
39. Roger Cohen, "Two Countries Turn to NATO in Face of War," *New York Times*, May 16, 2022; Roger Cohen, "Year of Conflict Has Left Europe Forever Changed," *New York Times*, February 26, 2023; Steven Erlanger, "The NATO Welcoming Sweden is Larger and More Determined," February 26, 2024, https://www.nytimes.com.
40. Melissa Eddy, "In Turnaround, Germany Vows Military Boost," *New York Times*, February 28, 2022.
41. Bernhard Blumenau, "Breaking with Convention? *Zeitenwende* and the Traditional Pillars of German Foreign Policy," *International Affairs* 98, no. 6 (2022): 1895–1913; Henry Farrell and Abraham L. Newman, "Weaponized Interdependence: How Global Economic Networks Shape State Coercion," *International Security* 43, no. 1 (2019): 42–79.
42. Cohen, "Year of Conflict."

43. Henry Foy, "How War Forced the EU to Rewrite Its Defense Policy," *Financial Times*, February 28, 2023.
44. Oriol Costa and Esther Barbé, "A Moving Target: EU Actorness and the Russian Invasion of Ukraine," *Journal of European Integration* 45, no. 3 (2023): 431–46.
45. Andrew Higgins, "Having Been Proved Right on Russia, Poland Savors Its New Influence in NATO," *New York Times*, February 23, 2023.
46. Leila Abboud, "Macron Seeks to Woo Eastern Europe with 'Strategic Humility,'" *Financial Times*, June 3–4, 2023.
47. Steven Erlanger, "In Europe, War Accelerates the Shift of Power toward the East," *New York Times*, January 27, 2023; Mitchell A. Orenstein, "The European Union's Transformation after Russia's Attack on Ukraine," *Journal of European Integration* 45, no. 3 (2023): 337–38.
48. "Tilting East," *Economist*, March 4, 2023, 43–44; Andrew Higgins, "Tusk Begins to Return Poland to E.U.'s Center," *New York Times*, December 14, 2023.
49. RM Staff, "In the Thick of It: A Blog on the U.S.-Russia Relationship, In Nuclear Messaging to West and Ukraine, Putin Plays Bad and Good Cop," Russia Matters, https://www.russiamatters.org/blog/nuclear-messaging-west-and-ukraine-putin-plays-bad-and-good-cop.
50. Orenstein, "European Union's Transformation."
51. "European Security," *Economist*, February 24, 2024, 14–17; Martin Wolf, "Trumps Betrayal of Ukraine," *Financial Times*, March 20, 2024; Sylvie Kauffmann, "Europe Is at Last Adjusting to the New Reality in Ukraine," *Financial Times*, March 8, 2024.
52. James Crabtree and Euan Graham, "War in Ukraine and the Asia-Pacific Balance of Power," in International Institute for Strategic Studies, *Asia-Pacific Regional Security Assessment 2023* (London: International Institute for Strategic Studies, 2023), 22–40.
53. Feng Liu, "The Recalibration of Chinese Assertiveness: China's Responses to the Indo-Pacific Challenge," *International Affairs* 96, no. 1 (2023): 9–27.
54. Hoang Thi Han, "Understanding China's Proposal for an ASEAN-China Community of Common Destiny and ASEAN's Ambivalent Response," *Contemporary Southeast Asia: A Journal of International and Strategic Affairs* 41, no. 2 (2019): 223–54; Willian A. Callahan, "China's 'Asia Dream': The Belt and Road Initiative and the New Regional Order," *Asian Journal of Comparative Politics* 1, no. 3 (2016): 226–43; Demetri Sevastopulo and Kathrin Hille, "The US Build-up in China's Backyard," *Financial Times*, June 2, 2023.
55. G. John Ikenberry, "American Hegemony and East Asian Order," *Australian Journal of International Affairs* 58, no. 3 (2004): 353–67.
56. Yan Xuetong, "The Age of Uneasy Peace: Chinese Power in a Divided World," *Foreign Affairs* 98, no. 1 (2019): 40–46; Oystein Tunsjo, *The Return of Bipolarity in World Politics: China, the United States, and Geostructural Realism* (New York: Columbia University Press, 2018).
57. Evan A. Feigenbaum and Robert A. Manning, "A Tale of Two Asias," *Foreign Policy*, December 4, 2012, https://foreignpolicy.com/2012/10/31/a-tale-of-two-asias/; G. John Ikenberry, "Between the Eagle and the Dragon: America, China, and Middle State Strategies in East Asia," *Political Science Quarterly* 131, no. 1 (2016): 9–43.
58. Liu, "Recalibration of Chinese Assertiveness," 10–11; Feng Liu and Ruonan Liu, "China, the United States, and Order Transition in East Asia: An Economy-Security Nexus Approach," *Pacific Review* 32, no. 6 (2019): 972–95.

59. Hillary Clinton, "America's Pacific Century," *Foreign Policy* no. 189 (2011): 46–63; Michael J. Green, *By More than Providence: Grand Strategy and American Power in the Asia Pacific Since 1783* (New York: Columbia University Press, 2017), 520–21; David Shambaugh, "Assessing the US 'Pivot' to Asia," *Strategic Studies Quarterly* 7, no. 2 (2013): 10–19.
60. Michael D. Swaine, "Creating an Unstable Asia: The U.S. 'Free and Open Indo-Pacific' Strategy," March 2, 2018, Carnegie Endowment for International Peace, https://carnegieendowment.org/2018/03/02/creating-unstable-asia-u.s.-free-and-open-indo-pacific-strategy-pub-75720; see Seng Tan, "Consigned to Hedge: South-East Asia and America's 'Free and Open Indo-Pacific' Strategy," *International Affairs* 96, no. 1 (2020): 136.
61. White House, "Indo-Pacific Strategy of the United States," February 2022, https://www.whitehouse.gov/wp-content/uploads/2022/02/U.S.-Indo-Pacific-Strategy.pdf.
62. White House, National Security Strategy, October 2022, https://www.whitehouse.gov/wp-content/uploads/2022/10/Biden-Harris-Administrations-National-Security-Strategy-10.2022.pdf.
63. "The Chain," *Economist*, June 17, 2023, 19.
64. "The Strategic Reverberations of the AUKUS Deal Will Be Big and Lasting," *The Economist*, September 19, 2021, https://www.economist.com; Nick Childs, Euan Graham, and Ben Schreer, "The AUKUS Plan: A Grand Bargain with Significant Risks," International Institute for Strategic Studies, https://www.iiss.org/online-analysis/online-analysis/2023/03/the-aukus-plan-a-grand-bargain-with-significant-risks/; Michael D. Shear and Edward Wong, "Biden Unveils Landmark Submarine Deal with Australia and Britain," https://www.nytimes.com/2023/3/13/us/politics/nuclear-submarine-deal-australia-britain.html; Demetri Sevastopulo and Kathrin Hille, "The US Build-up in China's Backyard," *Financial Times*, June 2, 2023.
65. Edward Wong and Eric Schmitt, "Eyeing China, U.S. Turns to Manila to Flex Muscles," *New York Times*, February 3, 2023; Sui-Lee Wee and Camille Elemia, "Beijing Flexes and Philippines Turns to the US," *New York Times*, February 21, 2023; "The Indispensable Archipelago," *Economist*, February 25, 2023, 39–40; Kathrin Hille, Demetri Sevastopulo, and Kana Inagaki, "Philippines Grants US Access to More Bases," *Financial Times*, February 3, 2023; Gideon Rachman, "Manila Attempts to Plot Path between US and China," *Financial Times*, January 20, 2023; Sui-Lee Wee, "Deal Gives U.S. Military Access to Four More Locations in the Philippines," *New York Times*, February 3, 2023; Damien Cave, "Beijing Uses Coast Guard Like a Navy," *New York Times*, June 12, 2023.
66. Ben Dooley and Hisako Ueno, "Japan Moves to Double Its Military Spending," *New York Times*, December 17, 2022; Adam P. Liff, "Kishida the Accelerator: Japan's Defense Evolution after Abe," *Washington Quarterly* 46, no. 1 (2023): 63–83.
67. Tiffany May and Mike Ives, "A Drumbeat of Pressure on Taiwan Explained," *New York Times*, August 9, 2022; "Danger Ahead," *Economist*, August 13, 2022, 33–35; Demetri Sevastopulo, "Biden Reiterates Willingness to Defend Taiwan," *Financial Times*, September 20, 2022.
68. "Just Passing By: American Warships Go through the Taiwan Strait," *Economist*, September 1, 2022, https://www.economist.com; Paul Haenle, "Why the US and Chinese Militaries Aren't Talking Much Anymore," Carnegie Endowment for International Peace, August 11, 2022, https://carnegieendowment.org/2021/08/11/why-u.s.-and-chinese-militaries-aren-t-talking-much-anymore-pub-85123; Helene Cooper, "Phone Call on Balloon Is Rebuffed by Beijing," *New York Times*, February 8, 2023.

69. Roger Cohen, "India Presses Own Ideas about the World Order," *New York Times*, January 5, 2023; Lauren Frayer, "A Year into the Ukraine War, the World's Biggest Democracy Still Won't Condemn Russia," February 20, 2023, https://www.npr.org; Emma Chanlett-Avery, K. Alan Kronstadt, and Bruce Vaughn, "The 'Quad': Cooperation among the United States, Japan, India, and Australia," Congressional Research Service, January 30, 2023, https://crsreports.congress.gov; Nirupama Rao, "The Upside of Rivalry: India's Great-Power Opportunity," *Foreign Affairs* 102, no. 3 (May/June 2023): 17–23.
70. Cohen, "India Presses Own Ideas" (quotation); Shreya Upadhyay, "BRICS, Quad, and India's Multi-Alignment Strategy," July 12, 2022, Stimson Center, https://www.stimson.org.
71. Liza Tobin, "Underway—Beijing's Strategy to Build China into a Maritime Great Power," *Naval War College Review* 72, no. 2 (2018), 17–32. Daniel Tobin, "How Xi Jinping's 'New Era' Should Have Ended U.S. Debate on Beijing's Ambitions," Center for Strategic and International Studies, May 2020, 4–5, https://www.csi.org, 15–16, 19; Doshi, *Long Game*, 211–12; Callahan, "China's 'Asia Dream,'" 231; Yao Song, Guangyu Qiao-Franco, and Tianyang Liu, "Becoming a Normative Power? China's Mekong Agenda in the Era of Xi Jinping," *International Affairs* 97, no. 6 (2021): 1710
72. Tobin, "Xi Jinping's 'New Era,'" 19.
73. Doshi, *Long Game*, 230–31; "China's Vision for Global Security," *Economist*, May 7, 2022, 38.
74. "China Will Not Ditch Russia, For Now," *Economist*, September 17, 2022, 40; Sheena Chestnut Greitens, "China's Response to War in Ukraine," *Asian Survey* 62, no. 5–6 (2022): 756, 758–60; Max Seddon, "Visit to Moscow by China Envoy Fuels Concerns of Stronger Ties," *Financial Times*, February 21, 2023.
75. Chris Buckley, "The US Is 'Not Qualified' to Issue Orders on Arms for Russia, China Says," *New York Times*, February 21, 2023.
76. Deborah Welch Larson, "An Equal Partnership of Unequals: China's and Russia's New Status Relationship," *International Politics* 57, no. 5 (2020): 790–808.
77. On hedging in the region, see Cheng-Chwee Kuik, "How Do Weaker States Hedge? Unpacking ASEAN States' Alignment Behavior towards China," *Journal of Contemporary China* 25 (2016): 500–514; Evelyn Goh, "South-East Asian Strategies toward the Great Powers: Still Hedging after All These Years," *Asan Forum* 4, no. 1 (2016): 18–37; John D. Ciorciari, *The Limits of Alignment: South-east Asia and the Great Powers since 1975* (Washington, DC: Georgetown University Press, 2010); Darren J. Lim and Zack Cooper, "Reassessing Hedging: The Logic of Alignment in East Asia," *Journal of Strategic Studies* 24, no. 4 (2015): 696–727.
78. David Martin Jones and Nicole Jenne, "Hedging and Grand Strategy in Southeast Asian Foreign Policy," *International Relations of the Asia-Pacific* 22, no. 2 (2022): 205–35.
79. Ja Ian Chong, "Mixed Motivations, Muddle Messages: What Responses to Russia's Invasion of Ukraine Tell Us about ASEAN," in *Regional Reflections on the War in Ukraine: Diplomacy, Conflict and the Future of Southeast Asia*, ed. Kristie Barrow (Australian Institute of International Affairs, February 2023).
80. Gideon Rachman, "The Squawkus about Aukus Is Getting Louder," *Financial Times*, February 26, 2024, https://www.ft.com; Sui-Lee Wee and Camille Elemia, "Manila Shores Up Ties as Deterrent to China," *New York Times*, March 17, 2024.
81. David Shambaugh, *Where Great Powers Meet: America & China in Southeast Asia* (New York: Oxford University Press, 2021).

CHAPTER 9

China and the Changing Regional Order in East Asia

Selina Ho

East Asia is conventionally regarded as China's historical backyard. Chinese influence is strongest in this region not only because it is the resident hegemon but also because of its historical, economic, cultural, and ethnic ties with countries in the region as well as the large power asymmetry between them. How has China's regional role evolved from the Cold War to the post–Cold War period? What kind of regional order does it want, and what are the strategies it had used to reshape regional order? What are the implications for peaceful change? This chapter follows T.V. Paul's and Markus Kornprobst's definition of regional order as a "pattern of regularized interactions among states and between states and key non-state actors in a regional domain characterized by conflict, cooperation, peace or mixed patterns."[1]

China sees itself as the regional leader and prefers to minimize intervention from other major powers.[2] It seeks to replace the United States as the hegemon in East Asia.[3] While it probably realizes it would not be able to compel the United States to completely withdraw from the region, it nonetheless wants to blunt and limit US influence and ensure that regional countries take its interests and preferences into account when making foreign policy decisions.[4] It relies mainly on four strategies for shaping the regional order: coercion, diplomacy, institutional-building, and normative foundations.[5] Coercion is mainly used in territorial disputes and to apply economic sanctions, while diplomacy is used to attract and induce regional countries and elites. China also uses institutions to set the agenda in regional forums. In addition, narratives and discourses are used to promote Chinese norms and ideas. Through these "regularized interactions," China aims to establish a sphere of influence in East Asia that is characterized by *hierarchical order, control and exclusivity,* and a *collective identity* that is separate from the West's.

The consequences of Chinese efforts to build a sphere of influence in East Asia are mixed. While it has brought alternatives and economic benefits to the region, its contestation with the United States for regional hegemony is destabilizing for the region. China seeks dominance in the region to ensure that it could assert influence on the policies of its smaller neighbors in such a manner that the region does not do US bidding at the expense of Chinese interest. At the same time, the United States, particularly under President Joe Biden, has strengthened its alliance system with Japan, South Korea, and the Philippines, while pressuring its friends and partners in the region to align with its policies. China's quest for a regional sphere of influence and the United States' refusal to accept Chinese aims and actions as legitimate put regional countries in the middle of a tug-of-war between them. The potential for armed conflict in the East and South China Seas and the Taiwan Strait has increased. The unity and centrality of the Association of Southeast Asian Nations (ASEAN), which is a core component of the current regional order, has also come under threat, as both China and the United States create new multilateral institutions to draw regional countries closer to themselves.

However, while there are growing signs of countries taking China's preferences and interests into account, these are by no means indications that the region is in China's pocket.[6] Spheres of influence, as Anders Wivel's chapter in this volume argues, are "negotiated hegemonies." The dominance of the hegemonic state within a sphere is never absolute but is negotiated horizontally between the great powers as well as vertically between the hegemon and the small and middle powers in its sphere. East Asia thus cannot be considered an exclusive Chinese sphere of influence. The United States continues to dominate in the security sphere with its strengthened alliances, the Quadrilateral Security Dialogue (Quad), the trilateral security partnership between Australia, the United Kingdom, and the United States (AUKUS), and the Indo-Pacific strategy. China's economic rise has indeed rapidly expanded Chinese influence over the region's economic architecture. Chinese aid and investment are however not exclusive. Although Chinese investments in Southeast Asia grew by twentyfold during 2005–2019, the European Union, Japan, and the United States remained the largest sources of foreign direct investment for Southeast Asia between 2005 and 2018.[7] Japan remains the region's top aid provider. In addition, Chinese culture and civilization are not widely accepted in the region, with ideas such as *"tianxia"* and a "community of common destiny" gaining little traction.[8]

There is resistance toward Chinese dominance in the region, from US allies and from the smaller Southeast Asian states.[9] As one Chinese scholar puts it, "China is thus a rising but lonely great power."[10]

This chapter proceeds as follows. I first examine the regional order and how China's role in it has transformed since the end of World War II. While it was an outsider in the regional order during most of the Cold War period, it began to occupy a central position from the 1990s onward; not only did it become a significant stakeholder in the region but it also eventually acquired the wherewithal to impact the regional order. I then examine China's vision of regional order and analyze how it uses coercion, diplomacy, institutions, and norms to establish a Sino-centric hierarchical order and collective identity, and to exert control and exclusivity over its neighbors. I conclude by assessing the prospects for peace and stability in the region.

CHINA AND THE REGIONAL ORDER: FROM OUTSIDER TO INSIDER

The transformation of China's role from outsider to insider in the East Asian regional order parallels the transformation of its role on the global stage. During the first two decades of its existence, the People's Republic of China (PRC) was an outsider to the United States–led international and regional orders. The East Asian regional order at that time was established by the United States, as the preeminent power at the end of World War II. Its main feature was a United States–centered security alliance system, consisting of a series of bilateral defense agreements between the United States and Japan, South Korea, the Republic of China, Thailand, and the Philippines. This hub-and-spokes system undergirded the security architecture of the region. The aim was to contain the spread of communism. Economically, the United States provided aid and market access to countries in the region, thus ensuring economic development and stability in the region.

China was not part of the United States–led security and economic architecture in the region. With the outbreak of the Korean War in 1950 and the subsequent insertion of the US Seventh Fleet in the Taiwan Strait, Mao Zedong declared that the PRC will "lean to one side," that is, the side of the Soviet Union. Sino-Soviet relations were consolidated by the Sino-Soviet Treaty signed in 1950, placing China as part of the alternative order led by the Soviet Union. It was heavily dependent on Soviet miliary and economic assistance. Apart from relations with the Soviet bloc, countries of the nonalignment movement, and some familial and cultural ties with overseas Chinese in Southeast Asia, the PRC was internationally isolated; in 1954, the PRC was recognized by only twenty-four countries.[11] Regional countries considered it a threat, as Mao's attempts to export revolution threatened the sovereignty, internal cohesion, security, and nation-building efforts of the newly independent Southeast Asian states.

For the PRC, the United States' containment policy meant that relations with the Soviet Union and the Soviet bloc were an important lifeline that shaped the direction of its foreign policy. Therefore, the consequences of its deteriorating relations with the Soviet Union from the late 1950s culminating in the border clashes at the Ussuri River in 1969 were catastrophic for the PRC. Meanwhile, the United States had begun to escalate its war in Vietnam in the mid-1960s. In response, the Soviet Union ramped up its forces on its borders with China and Mongolia. China became increasingly isolated, facing military threats on two fronts—the Soviet Union in the north and the United States in the south.

As China's external environment rapidly deteriorated and as domestic politics became radicalized with the launch of the Cultural Revolution, Mao began to reconsider China's relations with the superpowers. He assessed the Soviet Union as the greater threat compared to the United States because the latter was embroiled in the Vietnam War. At the same time, US president Richard Nixon saw a strategic opportunity to bring China back into the international system and shift the balance of power as the Sino-Soviet split became apparent. A confluence of interests between the United States and China thus led to rapprochement between them. The strategic alignment between them became a watershed event during the Cold War and a significant consequence was the integration of China into the United States–led international and regional order.

In East Asia, China's new position as an insider in the international and regional orders led to a revolution in its foreign relations. Deng Xiaoping, who became China's paramount leader in 1979, ended Mao's campaign to export revolution to Asian countries and instituted a hands-off policy toward overseas Chinese residing in Southeast Asian countries. As China's opening and reform from 1978 brought tremendous economic opportunities to Southeast Asian countries, Southeast Asian governments began to establish formal diplomatic ties with Beijing, which in turn facilitated its rapid integration into the regional production network. Trade between China and Northeast and Southeast Asia soared. China has been ASEAN's largest trading partner since 2009. Trade between the two received a boost in 2010, when the China-ASEAN Free Trade Area (CAFTA) came into effect.

The demise of the Soviet Union in 1991 and the emergence of American unipolarity introduced a fresh dilemma for the PRC in the 1990s. As it became increasingly economically interdependent with the United States, ironically, the strategic dimensions of their collaboration collapsed with the disappearance of a common threat. With the end of the Soviet Union, differences over human rights, bilateral trade, and Taiwan among others rose to the forefront of their relations and became domestic political fodder. With China's rapid economic growth, Americans began to see an emerging "China threat."

Within the region, there are growing signs of unease over what China's rapid rise portends for the region. From the 1990s, China became a security challenge as territorial disputes over the East and South China Seas intensify. As worries over the implications of China's rapid development increase, regional states view the United States as a benign and stabilizing force that could keep Chinese ambitions as well as potential Japanese military resurgence in check. Evelyn Goh described regional order in the post–Cold War period as a "layered hierarchy" with the United States at the top, followed by China and Japan, and then South Korea and the ASEAN states.[12] Regional countries were "complicit" in keeping the United States engaged in the region to deal with threats from China and a potentially resurgent Japan.[13]

Despite growing concerns over China's meteoric rise, regional states welcomed the economic benefits China brings to the region. They saw China as a resident power that they would need to live with and sought to "socialize" China into the ASEAN way.[14] The aim is to enmesh China into a web of relationships that would encourage it to abide by the rules and norms of the region and to solve problems and disputes in a peaceful nonaggressive manner. To a large extent, regional states succeeded in smoothing China's reemergence. Initially suspicious of multilateral forums, China became an active member of several ASEAN-initiated multilateral forums.

The turning point in China's relations with the West came in 2008 when the Global Financial Crisis revealed the weaknesses of the United States and European countries.[15] China no longer saw itself as a student to the West. Instead, it saw the superiority of its own political and economic model. The narrative of American and Western decline gained ground as domestic developments in the West revealed the problems of democracy and the fractures in Western politics and society. This perception that China's time has come began under President Hu Jintao but gained speed when President Xi Jinping came into power in 2012; in 2011, Hu declared that China "irreversibly start its historic march for development, growth, and great rejuvenation."[16] China has proposed "Chinese solutions for global governance, to seek representativeness and a voice for China and other emerging states, and also to play a greater role in international rule-making."[17] It rejects the United States' renaming of the region as the "Indo-Pacific" and insists on "Asia-Pacific" instead. Its foreign policy also has become increasingly assertive and coercive with respect to territorial disputes and Taiwan. At the same time, it seeks to cultivate and win over states in the region with its economic largesse and promises of aid and investments. It also exercises leadership in the region by setting up institutions and introducing a set of ideas and norms to construct an Asian identity. Taken together, these are indicative of Chinese efforts at reshaping a regional order that reflects its preferences and interests.

CHINESE VISION OF REGIONAL ORDER: BUILDING A SPHERE OF INFLUENCE

China's rise has led to a proliferation of work on China's vision of world/international order. Scholars are divided over China's intentions. The main arguments fall under two categories: China seeks to replace the current international order,[18] and China seeks to revise some aspects of the United States–led liberal international order but does not seek to replace it.[19] Fewer scholars have debated the Chinese vision of the East Asian regional order. Among this group, there is, by and large, agreement that the region is still very much US dominated, although the underlying consensus seems to be that China intends to replace the United States' role in the region.[20] Some argue that China is building a sphere of influence in Southeast Asia.[21] These studies, however, do not explicate what a sphere of influence is and how China goes about building one in East Asia. In this section, I identify the traits of a sphere of influence and systematically examine Chinese moves to construct one in East Asia.

Studies have shown that it is difficult to decipher state intentions. However, patterns of state behavior, whether in discourse or practice, do indicate the trajectory and inclinations of states. Chinese discourses and behavior reflect its intention to replace the United States as the region's hegemon and to establish a sphere of influence. Chinese actions are typical of what great powers do in their own backyard; great powers aspire to dominate the region in which they are located.[22] They do so in search of security; they build their material capabilities and attempt to expel rival great powers, using institutions, culture, norms, and ideas to entrench their dominance in the region.[23] As great powers fear that neighboring countries will allow rival great powers to gain a military foothold in their own backyard, they are also likely to engage in coercion and interfere in the domestic affairs of their neighbors.[24]

China has demonstrated these behavioral traits as it seeks to establish a sphere of influence—that is, a hierarchical order that it dominates and exercises control and exclusivity over, and that has a Sino-centric collective identity. In its basic form, hierarchy is ranked ordering of units,[25] but there is another layer to hierarchy and hegemony—that is, the authority of the hegemon must be viewed as legitimate and socially acceptable. China's utilization of material primacy to coerce and induce is thus not sufficient for it to build regional order. It also needs to provide institutions and norms to gain acceptance and followership. The rest of this section explores how China uses these strategies and tools to build a sphere of influence.

Establishing a Sino-Centric Hierarchical Order

The Chinese hierarchical view of regional order was most clearly demonstrated at the ASEAN Regional Forum meeting in July 2010. Then Chinese foreign minister Yang Jiechi bluntly told Singapore's foreign minister at that time, George Yeo, that "China is a big country and other countries are small countries and that is just a fact."[26] Yang's statement suggests a worldview that is based on hierarchy and hegemony undergirded by brute material primacy. Chinese leaders and government officials also have time and again reminded their regional counterparts that the region should "advance with the times" (*yushi qujing*) in recognizing that China is the future while the United States is the past and hence, regional countries should join China's orbit or risk falling behind as the region marches toward progress and development.[27] Such rhetoric is in line with Chinese views of US decline and that China is set to replace the United States at the top of the region's hierarchical order.

The first step to establishing its status as the preeminent power is to reorder the regional security structure currently dominated by the United States. To this end, President Hu Jintao declared in November 2012 China's intentions to become a maritime power.[28] It has built up its naval capabilities to protect its overseas assets, assert its claims in the East and South China Seas and Taiwan, and mark its status as a great power. Its acquisition of port facilities across the Indo-Pacific has considerably strengthened its power projection capabilities. It aims to achieve military parity with the United States in East Asia and has used its improved military and economic capabilities to compel regional states to accommodate Chinese interests on territorial disputes and security cooperation with the United States.[29] Since 2009, Beijing has increased deployment of its maritime assets and fighter aircraft patrols in and around the waters and features that are disputed with Japan. There are also conflicts between PRC-flagged fishing vessels and South Korean Coast Guards in the waters off western Korea.[30] These culminated in Beijing's unilateral declaration of an Air Defense Identification Zone (ADIZ) over the East China Sea that demands reporting standards that exceed common practice.[31] The aim of the ADIZ is to establish a security buffer in the maritime sphere by developing its anti-access and anti-denial capabilities. Beijing uses military and paramilitary assets to press other vessels to leave contested areas, and since 2016, it has used military aircraft and vessels to circumnavigate Taiwan.[32] China has also militarized the East and South China Seas, seeking to dominate these disputed areas by building military and civilian installations.

China also uses its economic prowess to establish a hierarchy with it at the top. The Belt and Road Initiative (BRI), launched in Kazakhstan and Indonesia, in September and October 2013, respectively, aims to connect Asia to Europe via a land route (the Silk Road Economic Belt) and a maritime route spanning the South China Sea through the Indian Ocean and the Red Sea to the Mediterranean (the Maritime Silk Road). Projects include ports, power plants, electricity grids, railroads, highways, industrial parks, commercial and financial centers, telecommunication facilities, residential housing, and with the COVID-19 pandemic, the "health silkroad" and the "digital silkroad." These projects dovetail with the demands of the Southeast Asian region; Chinese funding and technical skills help plug a big gap in infrastructure development in the region. Beijing created the Silk Road Fund and the Asian Infrastructure Investment Bank (AIIB) to serve as sources of funding for these projects.

The BRI ties the Southeast Asian region in a web of relations with Beijing as the economic, political, and strategic hub. Beijing allocates infrastructure projects to countries in such a manner that strengthens its influence over the latter's domestic and external affairs. It tends to invest in projects that are priorities of local elites whom they seek to cultivate.[33] Beijing also trains local labor—in managing the high-speed railroad in Laos for instance—the aim being to enable Lao people to run and operate their own train line eventually. Belt and Road Initiative scholarships are also being handed out by Beijing, provincial governments, and Chinese state-owned enterprises, which in time will likely bind a younger generation of Southeast Asians closer to China. Such social impact and relational structuring of China-Southeast Asian relations are likely to gradually transform the regional order in Southeast Asia to one that is Sino-centric, with greater dependence and reliance on China as the economic and political hub.

China has also devoted time and resources to building institutions in the region. These initiatives are aimed at establishing China's position at the center of multilateral activities and top of the hierarchical order. Two key institutions are particularly noteworthy: the Lancang-Mekong Cooperation (LMC) and the Xiangshan Forum.

China's establishment of the LMC in 2015 gives it the opportunity to set norms and rules, promote ideas and concepts, and enhance its leadership and influence in the region. In fact, China's institution-building efforts in the Mekong are changing the regional architecture; a Thai academic remarked that "the LMC now looks and feels like the only game in the Mekong town. China won't play by the other rules and frameworks set up in an earlier generation."[34] Since its establishment, the LMC has formed annual foreign ministers' meetings, numerous senior government meetings and training, a secretariat, a Lancang-Mekong Water Resources Cooperation Center based in Beijing, and a Global Center for Mekong Studies linking think tanks across the region.[35]

Through the LMC, Chinese influence in agenda-setting is set to expand. China is using its leadership role to decide which issues should be prioritized.[36] The Lancang-Mekong Water Resources Cooperation has organized a number of activities to improve communication, capacity-building, and interaction with the lower Mekong countries.[37] These activities and forums enable China to control the agenda and to set environmental standards on its own terms, to reflect its preferences as opposed to those set by the Mekong River Commission (MRC). It is also setting technical standards via its technological and infrastructure capability. The numerous projects in the Mekong Region that come under the BRI give China the opportunity to determine technical standards in the construction of dams, roads, and railways. Furthermore, putting discussion of nontraditional security threats on the table sets the LMC apart from the other multilateral forums in the Mekong, the Greater Mekong Subregion (GMS) and the MRC. By doing so, China is generating a new conversation on security in the region, perhaps to reflect its ideas on collective security encapsulated in its Asian Security Concept and its new Global Security Initiative.

In the security realm, China created the Xiangshan Forum in 2006 to establish its leadership in security institutions. The forum is crafted as a platform for defense and political outreach toward other countries to project China as a global player and as an exceptional power that would always care for the interests of medium and small countries.[38] The aim is to project China as a force for peace in the Asia-Pacific region and as a stabilizer of the current international and regional order, roles that are traditionally associated with a regional hegemon. In an oblique reference to narratives of US decline, at the ninth Xiangshan Forum in 2019, Xi Jinping said that regional countries have the responsibility to "build a security architecture fitting the regional reality."[39]

These efforts reflect China's desire to reshape the economic and security architectures of the region by using a mixture of coercive, inducement, and persuasion strategies. By providing regional public goods and setting the agenda in multilateral forums, Chinese behavior is typical of a hegemon. Cumulatively, these actions and rhetoric reflect Chinese intention to replace the United States at the top of the region's pecking order.

Control and Exclusivity

Great powers seek to exclude rival great powers from their sphere of influence. The above institutional arrangements that China established exclude other major powers and present alternatives to those established by the West. One scholar described China as using the LMC "as a cover to exclude other external players by highlighting identity, selectively setting the agenda and providing regional public goods."[40] It views existing mechanisms in the Mekong area, such as the GMS and MRC, to be dominated by Western and Japanese interests and has been reluctant to engage with them. Similarly, the Xiangshan Forum is purportedly an alternative to the Shangri-La Dialogue, which it views as dominated by the United States and its allies. It has always been wary of the Dialogue's focus on security matters and fears being cornered on territorial disputes in the East and South China Seas and the Taiwan issue. In recent years, however, it has upgraded its representation to defense-minister level on par with the other Dialogue countries. This demonstrates China's increasing comfort and confidence in engaging in regional security matters and also the belief that not having a strong representation disadvantages China's discourse and views on security matters while ceding advantages to the West. Despite this, however, China recognizes that the Shangri-La Dialogue will always remain a Western-dominated initiative and has established the Xiangshan Forum as an alternative.

China has also tried to exercise control over ASEAN and the Asia-Pacific Economic Cooperation (APEC). Direct and indirect pressure from Beijing apparently prevented ASEAN from coming up with joint statements about the South China Sea in 2012, 2015, and 2016. During the 2018 APEC summit, Chinese diplomats reportedly tried to barge into the office of the foreign minister of their Papua New Guinean host to ensure compliance with

Beijing's demands and disrupt a speech by then US vice president Mike Pence.[41]

Apart from exercising control and exclusivity in multilateral institutions, China also seeks to control the foreign policies of regional countries. In 2016, Singapore was severely and publicly criticized by Beijing for insisting on consistency with the rule of law over the South China Sea, culminating in the detention of its armored vehicles transiting in Hong Kong in 2017. China has also used its economic heft to impose costs on other states to coerce them into toeing its line. In 2010, Beijing supposedly disrupted the export of rare earth metals to Japan in response to their dispute over the East China Sea.[42] The PRC limited tourism and imposed de facto sanctions on South Korea in 2017 following Seoul's decision to deploy the United States' anti-ballistic missile defense system, the Terminal High Altitude Area Defense.[43] Beijing also imposed sanctions on Australia in 2021 as relations deteriorated.

Despite its noninterference rhetoric, China has used its economic prowess to intervene in the domestic politics of Southeast Asian countries. Studies have shown that it is effective in using investments and aid to cultivate the political, military, and business elites of countries in East Asia.[44] Belt and Road Initiative projects, for instance, are usually located in places that are the constituencies of political leaders in recipient countries.[45] From 2015 to the end of his term in 2018, Chinese cultivation of then Malaysian prime minister Najib Razak rose to new heights; Chinese state-linked firms stepped in to buy assets from the troubled 1Malaysia Development Berhad (1MDB), a semi-sovereign wealth fund owned entirely by the Malaysian Ministry of Finance, after its high debt levels and the alleged involvement of Najib's family in wide-ranging graft were publicized. Beijing also tries to enhance the standing of local elites by stumping for them during election campaigns.[46] For instance, during Malaysia's general election in May 2018, Chinese ambassador to Malaysia Bai Tian reportedly stumped for the president of the Malaysian Chinese Association (which is part of the ruling coalition) in his constituency in Bentong, Pahang.

By providing support for local elites who are more likely to be friendly to Beijing, Beijing is not only attempting to control the behavior of governments in the region but also to step in spaces where relations between regional countries and the United States are weakest. The aim is to weaken these countries' ties with the United States, blunt US influence, and establish a relationship that excludes the United States. Chinese support for Najib for instance occurred at a time when Najib's relations with the United States were deteriorating, particularly from July 2016, when the US Department of Justice opened an investigation into alleged money laundering at 1MDB, which is linked to Najib and his family. The weakening of ties between Najib and Washington provided an opportunity for China to step up its cultivation of the Malaysian government. Similarly, Beijing has supported Thai prime minister Prayut O-Cha at a time when the military coup in Thailand in 2014 strained relations between the United States and Thailand, a US ally. Sino-Thai relations strengthened when the United States suspended one-third of its military assistance to Thailand and imposed sanctions. In November 2014, Xi Jinping and Prayut met during the APEC summit; one month later Prayut made his first official visit to China. In 2015, the two countries held their first joint air force exercise. In 2017, Thailand bought the first of three submarines from China in a deal worth $393 million. By stepping in spaces that the United States has vacated, temporarily or otherwise, China is attempting to carve out an exclusive sphere of influence in its relations with regional countries.

The PRC has also inserted itself in the societies of Southeast Asian countries. In 2014, Xi Jinping defined the "sons and daughters of China" to mean both the Chinese on the mainland and ethnic Chinese living overseas.[47] This expanded definition signals Beijing's intention to utilize the Chinese overseas to work for China's national interest. Prior to Xi's declaration, Beijing had adopted a nonintervention policy in racial matters in Southeast Asian countries. With Xi's new formulation, Beijing signals its intention to interfere in ethnic politics in Southeast Asian countries overseas. In 2022, the twentieth Communist Party of China Congress Work Report lists a section on United Front work that describes the mobilization of ethnic Chinese and PRC nationals overseas.[48]

Sino-Centric Collective Identity

Chinese concepts advocated by Chinese leaders and scholars, such as "Asia for Asians," "Community of Common Destiny," "peripheral diplomacy," and "tianxia" point to the desire to construct a collective identity that is distinct from the West's. "Peripheral diplomacy" advocates that China pay more attention to consolidating its immediate neighborhood to draw countries along its borders closer to China as the hub. It suggests not only that China should induce countries along its periphery by material power alone but also the need to attract followers through Chinese ideas, culture, and norms. Chinese ideas such as "Asia for Asians" and "community of common destiny" thus suggest a civilizational hierarchy with Chinese culture and civilization as the apex. The concepts of *"tianxia"*[49] and "moral authority" imply a moral and normative hierarchy with China at its center. They represent Chinese IR scholars' (yet to be officially endorsed by the Chinese government) attempt to offer a Chinese brand of IR based on a combination of Chinese history and culture, Confucian ideas and values, and China's historical relations with its neighbors, commonly described as the "Chinese tributary system."[50] They emphasize the centrality of Chinese civilization, and Chinese hegemony and benevolent rule over other states in the region. These concepts exclude the United States and Western powers from the region. Indeed, Beijing often promotes its ideas and norms on sovereign equality and noninterference as alternatives to Western notions of democracy. For authoritarian and semi-authoritarian countries in the region, these ideas are appealing.

Some external observers see Beijing as trying to re-create the practices of the ancient tributary system, which was essentially hierarchical, noncoercive, highly ritualistic, deferential, and filled with symbols of Chinese cultural superiority.[51] It is uncertain whether this is China's true intentions and Chinese leaders should know by now that this is an impossible system to re-create in the present with nationalism, sovereignty, and diversity being values that East Asian and Southeast Asian countries guard jealously. Nonetheless, there are indications that China prefers a system where there is deference to China's interests and preferences and a hierarchical order whereby states recognize the superiority of the Chinese system. Former Singaporean diplomat Bilahari Kausikan said, "China does not merely want consideration of its interests. China expects deference to its interests to be internalized by ASEAN members as a mode of thought; as not just a correct calculation of ASEAN interests vis-à-vis China but 'correct thinking' which leads to 'correct behavior.'"[52]

The creation of a regional identity centered on Chinese civilizational values and norms did not begin with Xi Jinping. His predecessor, Hu Jintao, had sought to present the ideas of a "harmonious world" and "harmonious Asia," which are essentially extensions of the domestically oriented "harmonious society." "Harmonious society" requires an interventionist state that seeks to balance China's economic and social polarization.[53] Although it is unclear whether "harmonious world" entails the global scaling up of this interventionist state, Chinese pundits have called for their country to "harmonize" the world according to its own values. "Harmonizing" would require significant acceptance by other states of Chinese discourses, ideas, beliefs, and values.[54] During the Work Conference on Peripheral Diplomacy in October 2013, Xi underscored the need for China to expand from mutual benefit to "shared beliefs and norms of conduct for the whole region."[55] Xi added, "We should connect China's dreams with the wishes of peripheral countries, such as living a happy life and creating beautiful regional development prospect, thereby rooting the sense of common destiny in peripheral countries."[56] In a 2014 speech, then vice foreign minister Liu Zhenmin suggested that "for China to realize its dream of national rejuvenation, it first needs to acquire identification and support from other Asian countries and to tie the dream of the Chinese people with those of the Asian nations."[57]

A key prong of Chinese strategy in this regard is Beijing's proposal to regional countries to build a "community of common destiny" (CCD) to "weave neighboring countries into a Sino-centric network of economic, political, cultural, and security relations."[58] Embedded within the idea of the CCD is the preeminence of Chinese civilization and the creation of a Sino-centric network of relations. Signing up to the CCD would entail acknowledging China's position at the top of a hierarchical order, a collective identity that is Sino-centric, and an exclusive partnership with China. China has also introduced the concept of a "Lancang-Mekong community of common destiny," at the first Senior Officials' Meeting of the LMC in 2015.[59] All of the Mekong states, Cambodia, Laos, and Myanmar, have signed on to the concept. The concept weaves the region into a Sino-centric world order with its own norms, rules, and culture. Although China portrays the concept as inclusive of different political systems and cultures, it has the effect of excluding other major powers from the region.

In its efforts to promote its norms, China has created extensive cultural and educational programs throughout the region. It has become the world's third most popular destination for foreign study, with more than 440,000 students from over two hundred countries studying in China in 2016.[60] Many of them receive scholarships from the Chinese government at both the central and provincial levels as well as from Chinese companies. Beijing has also established more than five hundred Confucius institutes in 142 countries to promote Chinese language and culture.[61]

CONCLUSION: IMPLICATIONS FOR PEACEFUL CHANGE

The post–Cold War order in East Asia is maintained by a security hierarchy dominated by the United States comprising exclusive security alliances and basing rights, and secondarily by American economic, normative, and cultural dominance. Even as China rises, the United States remains dominant. The United States maintains control and exclusivity in security relationships; none of the countries in the region have a security alliance with China, and the

Chinese navy does not have basing rights in the region (although this might be changing with China funding the development of Cambodia's Ream naval base). In a 2019 Pew Research Center survey, around two-thirds or more of the respondents in Japan (63%), the Philippines (64%), and South Korea (73%) cited the United States as a top ally.[62] The United States continues to be viewed as a benign power whose presence in the region is legitimate, and there are presently no alternative sets of values and norms that could pose a serious challenge to American norms and values. Japan, for instance, has remained firmly in the US sphere despite its economy becoming increasingly intertwined with China's—"Japan has not joined the BRI; Okinawa has not declared independence from Japan; the CCP (Chinese Communist Party) has few allies in the Japanese government; Japan has not weakened its alliance with the United States; and China is as unpopular as a country can be in the eyes of the Japanese public."[63]

Nevertheless, China does exercise enormous influence in Southeast Asia, with Southeast Asian states having swung toward China in recent years.[64] Southeast Asian countries for instance are taking heed of Chinese interest even without China exerting pressure.[65] In particular, Cambodia has been described as "China's proxy"; Cambodian officials have maintained that "without China, Cambodia could not survive."[66] However, China does not exercise exclusive control in the economic, military, civilizational, and normative hierarchies in Southeast Asia. While the United States' engagement of Southeast Asia is multidimensional, China's regional presence is mainly economic. As David Shambaugh puts it, "The cultural, diplomatic, economic, and security footprint of the United States across Southeast Asia remains substantial. In most dimensions it is, in fact, greater than China's."[67]

Since the end of the Cold War, the United States not only has economic and military hegemony but also ideational hegemony. American ideals on democracy, liberalism, and institutions continue to shape the world today even as China mounts a challenge with its alternative developmental model. Chinese attempts to form a common civilizational identity with the narrative of "Asia for Asians" and "community of common destiny" has not gained much traction.[68] Those that signed on the "community of common destiny" do so for economic reasons. China has stepped up military engagement with the region, but these are mostly low-level joint exercises and dialogue; scripted meetings make up most of these interactions.[69] Even in mainland Southeast Asia where Chinese influence is most extensive, there is significant resistance and pushback from countries in the form of canceled infrastructure projects, efforts to seek alternatives to China, and preference for multiple partners.[70] In other words, Chinese relations with these countries are far from exclusive. While China is seen as the leading state in the region, there are nevertheless substantial anti-China and anti-Chinese sentiments in regional countries that suggest Chinese hegemony lacks legitimacy.

Although China has publicly and vehemently denied that it is creating a sphere of influence and has rejected spheres of influence as relics of the Cold War, Chinese rhetoric and initiatives, as discussed above, suggest that it intends to establish a sphere of influence with it as the center of the regional order. Chinese concepts advocated by Chinese leaders and scholars, such as "G2," "Asia for Asians," "community of shared destiny," "peripheral diplomacy," and "tianxia" point to a desire for a sphere of influence. "G2" for instance would divide the world into two spheres of influence, one dominated by the Chinese and the other by the Americans. Chinese normative ideas and institutions exclude the United States and Western powers from the region. It uses its military and economic prowess to establish dominance and control over the preferences and behavior of regional states. It imposes costs on countries that step out of line and act in ways that it considers to be unacceptable, broadly defined as making decisions that contradict Beijing's interests and/or do not take into account its interests.

While China is staking its claims for a sphere of influence, the United States is also enhancing its sphere of influence in East Asia, first with the "pivot" or "rebalance" and then, the Indo-Pacific strategy and the revival of the Quad.[71] In the United States' strategy, India, in addition to its allies, the United Kingdom, Australia, and Japan, plays key role in balancing Chinese influence in the region. The term "Indo-Pacific," which the Trump administration coined, is meant to enhance the role of India in balancing China. The effect of the term is to enlarge the regional space in Asia to include multiple stakeholders and dilute the centrality of China in the term "Asia-Pacific." The broadened regional space, combining the economic and military strengths of the United States, Japan, Australia and India, challenges China's ability to dominate the region.[72]

The United States has also moved into mainland Southeast Asia, specifically the Mekong region, an area traditionally dominated by China. In 2009, the United States established the Lower Mekong Initiative (LMI), comprising Cambodia, Laos, Myanmar, Thailand, and Vietnam, with the aim of advancing sustainable economic growth in the region. The LMI was upgraded in September 2020, becoming the Mekong-U.S. Partnership. The US government pledged at least $153 million to the member countries for a variety of projects, including disaster management, hydrological data-sharing, and fighting cross-border crimes. These efforts are seen as countering Chinese influence in the region, particularly following rising concerns that Chinese dams are causing droughts in the lower Mekong states.[73] This is clear from a statement by then secretary of state Mike Pompeo: "We stand for transparency and respect in the Mekong region, where the CCP (Chinese Community Party) has abetted arms and narcotics trafficking and unilaterally manipulated upstream dams, exacerbating an historic drought."[74]

As China and the United States compete for influence in the region, what are the implications for stability in the region? While we may debate whether the current great power rivalry is a "New Cold War," there are parallels between it and the Cold War of the twentieth century. Critically, the concept of spheres of influence has once again become central to international politics. Lessons can be drawn from how spheres of influence were constructed and managed in the "old" Cold War and even further back in history.

During the Cold War, spheres of influence carved out by the United States and the Soviet Union did bring about a measure of stability between them, and between states within their respective spheres of influence.[75] The superpowers were mostly respectful of each other's spheres because their security needs were satisfied and intervention risked provoking a costly military response and potential nuclear annihilation.[76] Intraregional conflict within each sphere of influence also decreased as tight control by the superpowers had in most cases led to an avoidance of confrontation among member states.[77] Disputes had been muted and did not become problems that spilt into the international arena. Order within each sphere was the result of the influencing power actively policing its sphere as well as passive recognition of the hierarchical relationship on the part of the influenced states.[78]

However, spheres of influence did not always lead to stability. In 1914, competing Russian and Austro-Hungarian spheres of influence in the Balkans sparked a military crisis that led to World War I. Japan's pursuit of a Greater East Asia Co-prosperity Sphere led to clashes with China and the United States and brought World War II to Asia. Spheres of influence thus do not always lead to stability and in fact, could contribute to further conflict and wars. What then are the conditions that determine whether spheres of influence lead to stability or instability?

First, a sphere of influence should not compromise the vital or core interest of the other great power. During the Cold War, Eastern Europe was not vital to American interest and Latin America was not vital to Soviet interest. Hence, it was possible for both sides to maintain their respective spheres of influence without serious conflict. Second, great powers must recognize or at least acquiesce to the other's sphere of influence. There was tacit understanding between the Soviet Union and the United States of each other's spheres of influence.[79] By contrast, Japan's Co-prosperity Sphere ran up against Chinese and American interests, and both China and the United States did not concede to Japan's ambitions. Third, stable spheres of influence should also have clear boundaries. Overlapping or competing boundaries are very likely to lead to conflict. The Monroe Doctrine laid out US claims in Latin America and the Caribbean littoral. Likewise, the Yalta and Potsdam conferences made clear the territorial divisions among the United States and the Soviet Union that constituted their respective postwar spheres of influence. Fourth, the dominant power must have the ability to maintain its sphere of influence. Military capability is essential for deterring third-party interference.[80] However, to keep subordinate states quiescent, the dominant power must also have the ability to lead, provide order, and economic and social goods. Fifth, there must be a level of acceptance among subordinate states of the leading power's dominance. While acceptance may be grudging and resistance from subordinate states may occur from time to time, instability will ensue if a sphere of influence is constantly marked by internal strife.

Given these conditions for peace in a world of spheres of influence, the jostling for spheres of influence between the United States and China is likely to lead to instability. Wivel, in his chapter, pointed out that the Indo-Pacific is the most prominent example of a contested sphere of influence, where the risk of great power conflict remains over the contested borderlines between the United States and China. China regards its immediate neighborhood as core to its security. Likewise, the United States views the region as vital to its interest as the region is home to major shipping routes, and Chinese actions in the South China Sea are regarded as disruptive to freedom of navigation. In 2010, then secretary of state Hillary Clinton described open access and a peaceful resolution of the South China Sea dispute as a US "national interest."[81] Moreover, both countries pursue spheres of influence that are overlapping. Both sides do not acquiesce to the other establishing a sphere of influence, as can be seen by their efforts to establish competing institutions in the Mekong region. China is also expanding its naval power and is no longer just a continental force. While China will not surpass US naval power in the near future, its growing naval capability nevertheless remains a serious challenge for American power in the region, especially with its acquisition of port facilities. Hence, militarily, it is unclear whether one can successfully deter the other from venturing into its sphere. The strategies that Southeast Asian states have pursued to prevent exclusive dominance by one great power, such as shifting allegiances, hedging, and playing one against the other, add to the uncertainties and could be destabilizing for the region. In addition, as Wivel argues, for the small and middle powers of East Asia, spheres of influence as an ordering device in the international system are a challenge to their sovereign equality and, thus, increase their vulnerability.

NOTES

1. Introduction, this volume.
2. Nien-chung Chang-Liao, "China's New Foreign Policy under Xi Jinping," *Asian Security* 12, no. 2 (May 3, 2016): 82–91, https://doi.org/10.1080/14799855.2016.1183195.
3. T.V. Paul, "The Rise of China and the Emerging Order in the Indo-Pacific Region," in *China's Challenges and International Order Transition: Beyond Thucydides's Trap*, eds. Huiyun Feng and Kai He (Ann Arbor: University of Michigan Press 2020), 71.
4. Feng Liu, "Balance of Power, Balance of Alignment, and China's Role in the Regional Order Transition," *Pacific Review* 36, no. 2 (2023): 261–83; Feng Zhang, *Chinese Hegemony: Grand Strategy and International Institutions in East Asian History* (Stanford, CA: Stanford University Press, 2015).
5. The latter two are taken from Kai He and Huiyun Feng, "Rethinking China and International Order: A Conceptual Analysis," in *China's Challenges and International Order Transition: Beyond Thucydides's Trap*, eds. Huiyun Feng and Kai He (Ann Arbor: University of Michigan Press 2020), 12. He and Feng define order as "normative and institutional arrangement among sovereign states."
6. David Shambaugh, "U.S.-China Rivalry in Southeast Asia: Power Shift or Competitive Coexistence?" *International Security* 42, no. 2 (Spring 2018): 85–127.
7. Evelyn Goh and Nan Liu, *Chinese Investment in Southeast Asia, 2005–2019: Patterns and Significance* (Canberra: New Mandala, 2021), 3–4.
8. William Callahan, "Chinese Visions of World Order: Post-hegemonic or a New Hegemony?" *International Studies Review* 10, no. 4 (2008): 749–61; Selina Ho, "Infrastructure and Chinese Power," *International Affairs* 96, no. 6 (2020): 1461–485.
9. David M. Lampton, Selina Ho, and Cheng-Chwee Kuik, *Rivers of Iron: Railroads and Chinese Power in Southeast Asia* (Berkeley: University of California Press, 2020).
10. Feng Liu, "Balance of Power," 15.
11. Alice Lyman Miller and Richard Wich, *Becoming Asia: Change and Continuity in Asian International Relations since World War II* (Stanford, CA: Stanford University Press, 2011), 213.
12. Evelyn Goh, *The Struggle for Order: Hegemony, Hierarchy and Transition in Post-Cold War East Asia* (Oxford: Oxford University Press, 2013), 7 and 212.
13. Goh, *The Struggle for Order*, 5.
14. Alastair Iain Johnston, "Socialization in International Institutions: The ASEAN Way and International Relations Theory," in *International Relations Theory and the Asia-Pacific*, eds. John Ikenberry and Michael Mastanduno (New York: Columbia University Press, 2003), 163–90.
15. Liu, "Balance of Power," 1.
16. Hu Jintao, *Full Text of Hu Jintao's Speech at CPC Anniversary Gathering*, July 1, 2011.
17. Liu, "Balance of Power," 2.
18. William Callahan, "Chinese Visions of World Order: Post-hegemonic or a New Hegemony?" *International Studies Review* 10, no. 4 (2008): 749–61.
19. Alastair Lain Johnston, "China in a World of Orders: Rethinking Compliance and Challenge in Beijing's International Order," *International Security* 44, no. 2 (2019): 9–60; Ruonan Liu and Songpo Yang, "China and the Liberal International Order: A Pragmatic and Dynamic Approach," *International Affairs* 99, no. 4 (July 2023): 1383–400.

20. Shambaugh, "U.S.-China Rivalry"; Paul, "The Rise of China."
21. Graham Allison, "The New Spheres of Influence: Sharing the Globe with Other Great Powers," *Foreign Affairs* (March/April 2020), 30–40; Jeremy Shapiro, "Defending the Defensible: The Value of Spheres of Influence in US Foreign Policy," *Order from Chaos*, March 11, 2015, https://www.brookings.edu/blog/order-fromchaos/2015/03/11/defending-the-defensible-the-value-of-spheres-of-influence-in-u-s-foreign-policy/; "The Administration's Approach to the People's Republic of China," U.S. Department of State, May 26, 2022, https://www.state.gov/the-administrations-approach-to-the-peoples-republic-of-china/.
22. John J. Mearsheimer, *The Tragedy of Great Power Politics*, rev. ed. (New York: W. W. Norton, 2014), 94.
23. Jennifer Lind, "Life in China's Asia: What Regional Hegemony Would Look Like," *Foreign Affairs* (March/April 2018), 2.
24. Lind, "Life in China's Asia," 2.
25. David C. Kang, *East Asia before the West: Five Centuries of Trade and Tribute* (New York: Columbia University Press, 2010), 17.
26. Ja Ian Chong, "Other Countries Are Small Countries, and That's Just a Fact: Singapore's Efforts to Navigate US-China Strategic Rivalry, in *China-US Competition: Impact on Small and Middle Powers' Strategic Choices*, eds. Simona A. Grano and David Wei Feng Huang (Palgrave Macmillan, 2023), 307–38.
27. "只要保持相关连 与时俱进 互信 维文：我国不乏与中国合作领域," *Lianhe Zaobao*, August 30, 2021, https://www.zaobao.com.sg/news/singapore/story20211230-1227728.
28. "China Should Become 'Maritime Power,' Hu Jintao Says," *South China Morning Post*, November 8, 2012, https://www.scmp.com/news/china/article/1077858/china-should-become-maritime-power-hu-jintao-says.
29. Robert S. Ross, "Conclusion: The United States, China, and Europe in an Age of Uncertainty," in *US-China Foreign Relations: Power Transition and Its Implications for Europe and Asia*, eds. Robert S. Ross, Oystein Tunsjo, and Wang Dong (London: Routledge 2021), 206.
30. K.B. Lee, "The Korea Coast Guard's Use of Force against Chinese Fishing Vessels: A Note," *Ocean Development and International Law* 49, no. 3 (July 2018).
31. E.J. Burke and A.S. Cevallos, *In Line or Out of Order? China's Approach to ADIZ in Theory and Practice* (Santa Monica, CA: Rand Corporation, 2017).
32. C. Shepherd, "U.S. to Blame If Any South China Sea Clash: Chinese Researcher," *Reuters*, January 9, 2019, https://www.reuters.com/article/us-china-usa-military/us-to-blame-if-any-south-china-sea-clash-chinese-researcher-idUSKCN1P31CK; Phil Stewart, "U.S. Eyes Taiwan Risk as China's Military Capabilities Grow," *Reuters*, January 16, 2019, https://www.reuters.com/article/us-usa-china-military/us-eyes-taiwan-risk-as-chinas-military-capabilities-grow-idUSKCN1P92TP.
33. Samantha Custer, Brooke Russell, Matthew DiLorenzo, Mengfan Cheng, Siddhartha Ghose, Harsh Desai, Jacob Sims, and Jennifer Turner, *Ties That Bind: Quantifying China's Public Diplomacy and Its "Good Neighbor" Effect* (AidData, CSIS, and Asia Society Policy Institute, June 2018).
34. Cited in Murray Hiebert, *Under Beijing's Shadow: Southeast Asia's China Challenge* (London: Rowman & Littlefield, 2020), 318.

35. Xue Gong, "Lancang-Mekong Cooperation," in *Multilateralism in the Indo-Pacific*, eds. Bhubhindar Singh and Sarah Teo (London: Routledge, May 2020), 65.
36. Gong, "Lancang-Mekong Cooperation," 65.
37. Gong, "Lancang-Mekong Cooperation," 65.
38. P. S. Suryanarayana, "Xiangshan Forum: China's Question for Stability: Images and Realities," *RSIS Commentary*, no. 299, November 12, 2019.
39. Cited in Suraynarayna, "Xiangshan Forum," 2.
40. Gong, "Lancang-Mekong Cooperation," 58.
41. J. Rogin, "Inside China's 'Tantrum Diplomacy' at APEC," *Washington Post*, November 20, 2018, https://www.washingtonpost.com/news/josh-rogin/wp/2018/11/20/inside-chinas-tantrum-diplomacy-at-apec/?utm_term=.3cdf6c02e938.
42. C. Hurst, *"Japan's Approach to China's Control of Rare Earth Elements,"* China Brief, April 22, 2011, https://jamestown.org/program/japans-approach-to-chinas-control-of-rare-earth-elements/.
43. E. Kim and V. Cha, "Between a Rock and a Hard Place: South Korea's Strategic Dilemmas with China and the United States," *Asia Policy* 21 (2016): 101–22, https://www.jstor.org/stable/24905094.
44. Custer et al., *Ties That Bind: Quantifying China's Public Diplomacy and Its "Good Neighbor" Effect*, 14.
45. Custer et al., *Ties That Bind*, 14.
46. Lampton et al., *Rivers of Iron*, 124.
47. Leo Suryadinata, *The Rise of China and the Chinese Overseas: A Study of Beijing's Changing Policy in Southeast Asia and Beyond* (Singapore: Institute of Southeast Asian Studies Publishing, 2017), 33.
48. Chinese Communist Party, "20th Party Congress Work Report" (China, October 26, 2022), http://www.news.cn/politics/cpc20/2022-10/25/c_1129079429.htm.
49. Zhao Tingyang, *All under Heaven: The Tianxia System for a Possible World Order*, translated by Joseph E. Harroff (Berkeley: University of California Press, 2021).
50. Kang, *East Asia*.
51. Shambaugh, "US-China Rivalry," 114. Kang, *East Asia*.
52. Bilahari Kausikan, "Dealing with an Ambiguous World Lecture III: ASEAN and US-China Competition in Southeast Asia," IPS Nathan Lectures, March 30, 2016, https://lkyspp.nus.edu.sg/docs/default-source/ips/mr-bilahari-kausikan-s-speech7d7b0a7b46bc6210a3aaff0100138661.pdf?sfvrsn=cec7680a_0
53. William Callahan, "China's 'Asia Dream': the Belt and Road Initiative and the New Regional Order," *Asian Journal of Comparative Politics* 1, no. 3 (2016): 226–43 at p. 235, https://journals.sagepub.com/doi/10.1177/2057891116647806.
54. Ho, "Infrastructure and Chinese Power."
55. Cited in Callahan, "Asia Dream," 231.
56. China Council for International Cooperation on Environment and Development, "Important Speech of Xi Jinping at Peripheral Diplomatic Work Conference," October 30, 2013, http://www.cciced.net/cciceden/NEWSCENTER/LatestEnvironmentalandDevelopmentNews/201310/t20131030_82626.html.
57. Liu Zhenmin, "Insisting on Win-Win Cooperation and Forging the Asian Community of Common Destiny Together," *China International Studies* (March/April 2014),

14. https://www.ciis.org.cn/english/COMMENTARIES/202007/t20200715_2811.html.
58. Callahan, "China's Asia Dream," 226–43.
59. "China Proposes Lancang-Mekong Community of Common Destiny," *China Daily*, April 7, 2015, https://www.chinadaily.com.cn/china/2015-04/07/content_20016571.htm.
60. Lind, "Life in China's Asia," 13 and 17.
61. Lind, "Life in China's Asia."
62. Laura Silver, Kat Devlin, and Christine Huang, *China's Economic Growth Mostly Welcomed in Emerging Markets, but Neighbors Wary of Its Influence* (Pew Research Center Survey, December 2019), 8.
63. Devin Steward, *China's Influence in Japan: Everywhere Yet Nowhere in Particular* (Washington, DC: Center for Strategic and International Studies Southeast Asia Program July 2020), 45.
64. David Shambaugh, *Where Great Powers Meet: America and China in Southeast Asia* (New York: Oxford University Press, 2021), 247.
65. Huong Le Thu, "China's Dual Strategy of Coercion and Inducement toward ASEAN," *Pacific Review* 32, no. 1 (2019); 20–36 at 22–23, https://doi.org/10.1080/09512748.2017.1417325.
66. Hiebert, *Under Beijing's Shadow*, 142.
67. Shambaugh, "US-China Rivalry," 98.
68. Ho, "Infrastructure and Chinese Power," 1483–84.
69. Hiebert, *Under Beijing's Shadow*, 62.
70. Lampton et al., *Rivers of Iron*.
71. Joel Wuthnow, "China's Shifting Attitude on the Indo-Pacific Quad," *War on the Rocks*, April 7, 2021, https://warontherocks.com/2021/04/chinas-shifting-attitude-on-the-indo-pacific-quad/.
72. Paul, "The Rise of China," 73.
73. Sebastian Strangio, "How Meaningful Is the New US-Mekong Partnership?" *Diplomat*, September 14, 2020, https://thediplomat.com/2020/09/how-meaningful-is-the-new-us-mekong-partnership/.
74. Mike Pompeo, "The Enduring U.S. Commitment to ASEAN," U.S. Mission to ASEAN, September 11, 2020, https://asean.usmission.gov/the-enduring-u-s-commitment-to-asean/.
75. Paul Keal, *Unspoken Rules and Superpower Dominance* (London: Palgrave Macmillan, 1983), 199.
76. Evan R. Sankey, "Reconsidering Spheres of Influence," *Survival* 62, no. 2 (March 2020), https://doi.org/10.1080/00396338.2020.1739947.
77. Edy Kaufman, *The Superpowers and Their Spheres of Influence: The United States and the Soviet Union in Eastern Europe and Latin America* (Croom Helm, 1976), 196.
78. Keal, *Unspoken Rules*, 200.
79. Keal, *Unspoken Rules*.
80. Sankey, "Reconsidering Spheres of Influence."
81. Hilary Rodham Clinton, "The South China Sea," U.S. Department of State, July 22, 2011, https://2009-2017.state.gov/secretary/20092013clinton/rm/2011/07/168989.htm.

CHAPTER 10

Russia and the Shaping of the Regional Order in Eurasia

Seçkin Köstem

Regional hegemony has been a long-lasting goal of Russian foreign policy under Vladimir Putin. Taking its roots from the idea of multipolarity, Russian foreign policy elites have imagined a Eurasia that is Russia's sphere of influence, or "privileged interests" in the words of Dmitri Medvedev.[1] That means that great powers are destined to be order-makers in their regions, which must be free from other great powers' attempts at order-creation. Russian foreign policy elites have seen Eurasia as a fundamental region of geopolitical, geo-economic and normative contestation between the West—the United States and Europe—in the age of renewed great power competition and the New Cold War.

Russia has aimed to accomplish two fundamental goals in Eurasia in the twenty-first century. First, it has strived to create a regional order that guarantees the continuation of Russian regional hegemony. This goal includes the establishment of new regional institutions and the strengthening of existing ones. The former has resulted in the creation of the Eurasian Economic Union (EAEU), and the latter has come in the form of consolidating the Collective Security Treaty Organization (CSTO). Second, the Kremlin has sought to prevent the growing Western appeal for regional states. In the economic sphere, this has included closer integration of potential followers of Russian hegemony with the European Union (EU). In the geopolitical sphere, conversely, Russia has sought to prevent the expansion of North Atlantic Treaty Organization (NATO) in the territory of the former Soviet Union beyond the three Baltic States (Estonia, Latvia, and Lithuania). In the ideational and normative sphere, the Kremlin has benefited from the continuity of autocratic regimes in the region and seen democratization as a genuine threat to the sustainability of its regional hegemony.

This chapter argues that Russia's strategy of regional hegemony has created a regional dis-order that is self-defeating. Instead, Russia's perceived partners are moving toward closer cooperation with alternative major powers and deny bandwagoning with Russia in regional geopolitical crises. Moreover, the chapter demonstrates that peaceful change in the Eurasian region has dim prospects due to Russia's persistent coercion that ultimately resulted in its full-scale invasion of Ukraine in February 2022. The chapter will primarily focus on Russia's efforts of regional order creation and the failure to do so in the post-Soviet space after its annexation of Crimea in 2014. The annexation of Crimea was a critical juncture for many regional developments to come and constituted the first step toward the full-scale invasion of Ukraine in 2022. Therefore, the chapter assesses Russia's war on Ukraine as the outcome and part of its desire and failure to create a regional order that privileged Russia as the regional hegemon.

The chapter is organized as follows. The second section after this introduction offers a brief account of the meaning of Eurasia or the post-Soviet space for the Russian ruling elite. The chapter then examines Russia's attempts at order-creation at economic, security and normative dimensions. Then, it evaluates how Russia's invasion of Ukraine has shaped the dynamics of the regional order. The chapter then briefly assesses the influence of China, the EU, and the United States in Eurasia. The concluding section elaborates on the argument's implications for Russia and the regional order in Eurasia in the age of the New Cold War.

WHAT IS EURASIA TO RUSSIA?

Regional order-making has been a fundamental practice for the Russian foreign policy–making circles since at least the mid-1990s. The prevalent identity conception in the Kremlin, great power nationalism, has seen Russia as destined to rule Eurasia or the post-Soviet space through military and economic means. According to this worldview, the appeal of democratic governance of the West for regional states has constituted a national security threat to Russia's own identity. Still, the Kremlin has mimicked Western institutions such as NATO and the EU in creating the Russia-led institutions such as the CSTO and the EAEU. Through its military and economic might, ideological appeal, and regional institutions, Russia has strived to be recognized as a great power just like the United States and China.[2] Therefore, in the renewed age of great power competition, which this volume explores in detail, the regional order in Eurasia has constituted a special place for the Kremlin's geopolitical priorities. Since the mid-1990s, the great power nationalist worldview has been the glue that holds the Russian foreign policy and security elite together.[3]

Great power nationalists often refer to history to legitimize Russia's coercive behavior in Eurasia. Under Putin's rule, the Kremlin has conceptualized Eurasia as a "pole," in which Russia has historically been the sole dominant power. Putin and his allies have attributed a historically superior role for Russia in the region, which has been under Russia's political, economic, and cultural influence for centuries. In this search for a multipolar world order with Russia as the uncontested central power in Eurasia, Russian political elites have increasingly relied on "Eurasian" or "Russian" political values. Putin has often stressed the need to rally around a new national idea. In an article he wrote for the Russian daily *Nezavisimaya Gazeta* on December 31, 1999—the day Yeltsin announced he was resigning as president of the Russian Federation—Putin argued that Russia needed a new national idea to help overcome the destruction of the 1990s.[4] Traditional values of the Russian society, according to Putin, would come to the rescue: patriotism, great powerness (*derzhavnost'*), statism, and social solidarity. Putin argued that Russia had always been and would remain a great power. "Inherent characteristics of Russia's geopolitical, economic and cultural existence," Putin stated, had "determined Russian people's mentality as well as state policies throughout Russian history."[5]

Great power nationalists have a particular understanding of what the world order should look like. A multipolar order, according to the Russian foreign policy elite, resembles a concert-like distribution of power and responsibilities between major powers, much like in the nineteenth-century Concert of Europe that was created after the Napoleonic Wars.[6] This self-conception helps explain why the Russian ruling elites have perceived the colored revolutions, NATO enlargement, the EU's Eastern Partnership program, the Euromaidan, and pro-EU governments in Ukraine and Georgia as efforts to curb Russia's historical leadership role in Eurasia. For example, according to Sergei Lavrov, NATO's expansion toward the post-Soviet territory was a "violation of previous assurances given to Moscow" and a clear example of "containing Russia."[7] More importantly, Putin argued in his Crimea speech of March 2014 that containment policies of the eighteenth, nineteenth, and twentieth centuries were continuing today.[8] According to Libman and Obydenkova, Russia's deliberate support for authoritarian leaders in Belarus (Lukashenko) and Ukraine (Yanukovich) could only be explained by the attractive power of the EU vis-à-vis the EAEU.[9]

Clunan argues that Putin has stressed Russia's greatness to "assert Russia's distinctiveness from other, lesser, European countries."[10] In this worldview, Russia is also distinct from other, lesser post-Soviet states in its near abroad. For Russia's ruling elites, an uncontested leadership role in Eurasia is an inseparable part of its *velikaya derzhava*—great power—identity. As argued by Putin in an article he authored in 2021, the Russian political elites believe in the "historical unity of Russians and Ukrainians," which practically means Russia is the only real country with the right to sovereignty in the region.[11] Accordingly, any resistance to Russia's hegemonic project should be countered with coercion. The Russian political elites have interpreted the decline of the liberal international order and the New Cold War as an opportunity for the rise of "Greater Eurasia" in global politics. Sergei Karaganov, an influential Russian scholar of international relations and advisor to the Kremlin, argued that the non-Western world was not only rising but also consolidating as an alternative power center. Karaganov saw the New Cold War as a "confrontation between the West and the non-West that is taking shape within the framework of Greater Eurasia, the 'Belt and Road' Initiative, and BRICS."[12]

Cooley argues that Moscow has been successful in reversing the prevalence of the norms of the liberal international order and the outreach of Western organizations in the post-Soviet space increasingly since the mid-2000s.[13] Similarly, Bettiza and Lewis contend that Russia has taken the lead in consolidating policymaking based on traditional values and authoritarianism.[14] However, countering Western influence in post-Soviet Eurasia has been only one dimension of Russian foreign policy goals. In addition, and more importantly, the Kremlin has aspired to be the sole major power in the region with order-providing capabilities. That aspiration has worked hand in hand with bandwagoning expectations from potential followers. In a recent article, Tsygankov articulates the meaning of the annexation of Crimea for Russia. He argues that Crimea has "consolidated Russia's reorientation away from Europe as a great power and a culturally distinct civilization."[15] At the same time, Tsygankov recognizes that the annexation of Crimea has made regional integration even harder as regional states have increasingly become wary of Moscow's regional intentions. The deteriorating economic situation in Russia amid Western sanctions also make Russian-led regional order-building harder.[16] In other words, Russia's coercive regional integration strategy has prevented it from issuing credible commitments for follower states in the region.[17] The empirical analysis below serves to demonstrate Russia's post-Crimea region building efforts and how they have further undermined Russia's vision of Eurasia.

PILLARS OF RUSSIA'S REGIONAL ORDER-CREATION IN EURASIA

Regional Economic Order

The Eurasian Economic Union has been central to Russia's economic order-building in the post-Soviet space. Eurasian integration was Putin's poster child for the 2012 presidential elections. The Russian political elite presented Eurasian regionalism and the EAEU as the region's collective response to globalization and the global financial crisis.[18] The official statements as well as elite discourse presented Eurasian integration as a liberalizing and unifying force in the post-Soviet space, which would ultimately allow regional states to be stronger vis-à-vis alternative power centers, most importantly the EU.

The EAEU emerged from the Euromaidan as a regional organization that was weaker than Russia had initially expected. Armenia and Kyrgyzstan joined the organization in 2015. However, given the small GDPs of both countries, they were unable to replace Ukraine's economic and geopolitical weight. In fact, the EAEU has included internal contradictions from day one. While it mimicked the EU as a supranational organization, in essence, it has been a regional institution of authoritarian cooperation that has aimed to boost sovereignty.[19] Over the years, the EAEU has failed to deliver many of its promises to member states. According to Dragnewa and Hartwell, weak common institutions, weak constraints on unilateral action (especially by Russia), and the lack of institutional capacity to deepen integration amid crises have significantly narrowed the EAEU's relevance.[20]

As Libman argues "the building blocks" used by the Russian elite in constructing regionalism in Eurasia have been perceived to be threats to sovereignty by post-Soviet states.[21] Contrary to Russia's expectations, Moscow's attempts at region-building through integration mechanisms have made potential follower states in Eastern Europe, the Caucasus, and Central Asia even more cautious to join those organizations. Libman also shows that political elites of post-Soviet countries are aware that Russian attempts at regionalism and regional integration primarily aim to restore Russia's influence in the region.[22] The "imperialist" discourse used by Russian politicians from various backgrounds has exacerbated the fear of regional states and only served to distance them from deeper Eurasian regionalism.[23]

In 2019, Moscow demonstrated interest in admitting Uzbekistan as a member to the EAEU. Uzbekistan's new president Shavkat Mirziyoyev was also interested in applying for an observer status instead of full membership. Eventually, Russia lost its hopes of Uzbek membership in the EAEU, which could have served the role of a trigger for a renewed purpose for the organization and Eurasian regionalism. Instead of a full membership, Uzbekistan gained an observer status in 2021.

Moscow has attached symbolic importance to the EAEU's external economic relations. To increase the relevance of the organization for regional trade, Russia has pushed for the signing of free trade agreements with Serbia, Singapore, Vietnam, and Iran. However, contrary to Moscow's narrative before the establishment of the EAEU, since 2015, the organization has not served to enhance the member states' foreign trade. As Russia lost Ukraine for its grand Eurasian project, China also started to make inroads into Eurasia with the Belt and Road Initiative (BRI). In the post-Soviet space, especially Central Asia emerged as a significant region for Chinese infrastructure investments as part of the Silk Road Economic Belt. The Kremlin and the Russian political elite have perceived China's BRI as a sign of the move toward multipolarity and the shift in the geopolitical and geo-economic orders. Instead of seeing China as a rival in Eurasia, Russia has strived to be a vital component of China's growing economic clout in the region.[24]

As the United States and EU imposed sanctions on Russia after the annexation of Crimea, the Kremlin devised a new plan to increase the appeal of its Eurasian integration project. The new plan that the Kremlin announced was the Greater Eurasian Partnership (GEP), which aimed to connect the EAEU with China's BRI and the Asia-Pacific region. Once again, the Kremlin presented the Greater Eurasian Partnership as a great modernizing force for regional states. Russian experts argued that the BRI and the EAEU would together address the problem of connectivity for the landlocked economies of Central Asia. They were also expected to complement and reinforce each other.[25] Unlike China's BRI, Russia's GEP has mostly remained as a discursive tool rather than a substantive geo-economic instrument. Russia's invasion of Ukraine in 2022 further challenged its own regional integration efforts in Eurasia due to two reasons. First, just like the Crimea sanctions, members of the EAUE have hesitated to openly violate the joint US-EU sanctions implemented on the Russian economy. Second, they have consolidated their earlier efforts to diversify foreign policy options and resist Moscow's imperialist claims. Having been increasingly isolated by the West, Russia has strived to divert its geo-economic ties toward China, India, Turkey, and Central Asia.

Regional Security Order

In the security sphere, Russia's regional hegemony rests upon its uncontested military might in the post-Soviet space. After the disintegration of the Soviet Union, Russia has maintained military bases throughout the region and especially benefited from the "frozen conflicts" in Moldova, Georgia, and Nagorno-Karabakh to maintain its role as an arbiter between rivaling states and entities. In addition to its military bases and personnel deployed in the region, Russia has strived to keep the CSTO as a relevant military alliance system. In addition to bilateral deals with post-Soviet states, Russia has offered military aid to CSTO members and coordinated counterterrorism and intelligence-sharing activities.[26] After the annexation of Crimea in 2014, the CSTO emerged as a useful tool for Russia's influence in three instances.

The first concerns the protests and CSTO's response to social protests and government change in Kazakhstan. In January 2022 Kazakhstan went through the biggest protests since its independence in 1991. As a result of a chain of events that witnessed clashes between protestors and security forces, more than two hundred people were killed. After the protests, Kazakhstan's president Tokayev consolidated his power by effectively sidelining the former president Nazarbayev. To restore order, Tokayev officially asked for help from the CSTO on January 5. As government forces cracked down on protestors, CSTO deployed a 2,500-strong force in the largest cities of Kazakhstan. The deployment of CSTO forces to suppress the protests was met by skepticism, especially in the Western media and scholarly circles due to fears of a Russian invasion.[27] The use of CSTO during the bloodiest events in the history of independent Kazakhstan has once again demonstrated the appeal and the effectiveness of Russia-led regional institutions for authoritarian leaders of the region.

The second development that has brought CSTO to the forefront for regional security is the border dispute between Kyrgyzstan and Tajikistan, two members of the Russia-led alliance. In April 2021, the armed forces of the two parties entered a three-day armed conflict in Kyrgyzstan's Batken region that resulted in sixty casualties on both sides. Kyrgyz and Tajik governments were able to come to terms rather quickly as they agreed on a ceasefire on April 30, 2021. However, tensions arose again between the two in September 2022. Armed clashes came to an end when the two governments signed a peace deal at the summit of the Shanghai Cooperation Organization (SCO) in Tashkent in September 2022. Since then, both parties have accused each other of violating the terms of the ceasefire. The Kyrgyz defense minister Bekbolotov also stated that the Krygyz government has asked the CSTO to deploy peacekeeping forces at the Kyrgyz-Tajik border.[28] Both countries continue to host Russian military bases, which makes Russia the only country with the capability to prevent the continuation of hostilities between the two CSTO members.[29]

The third development that has highlighted the relevance as well as the paradoxical situation of the CSTO for the security order in Eurasia was the Second Karabakh War that took place between Armenia, a member of the alliance, and Azerbaijan from September to November 2020. With the war, the Azerbaijani military was able to retake most of its internationally recognized territories from Armenian forces.[30] Turkey's direct military support was vital for the successful conduct of the Azerbaijani offensive against Armenian forces.[31] Contrary to Erevan's expectations, Russia only intervened in the war right before Azerbaijan was about to capture Stepanakert, the de facto capital of Nagorno-Karabakh, from Armenian forces. That was a qualitative shift from Russia's earlier position as the official ally and defender of Armenia in the South Caucasus. With Moscow's intervention, Erevan and Baku signed an agreement on November 12, 2020, that ended the war. Russia has increased its military footprint in its near abroad with the insertion of a 2,000-strong "peacekeeping force" in Nagorno-Karabakh. However, this has also exacerbated the Armenian government's skepticism toward Russia's role as an ally of and security provider to Armenia. Moscow signed an alliance agreement with Baku in February 2022, which led to further questioning in Erevan of the CSTO as well as Russia's role as the traditional guarantor of Armenia's national security after the disintegration of the Soviet Union.

Much to Armenia's chagrin, Putin and Aliyev signed the Moscow Declaration in February 2022 during Aliyev's visit to Russia. The forty-three-point document lifts the bilateral relations between Russia and Azerbaijan to the level of alliance.[32] Azerbaijan had already signed an alliance agreement with Turkey, Russia's traditional rival in the South Caucasus, in June 2021. Tensions arose once again in 2022, which led to border clashes between Armenia and Azerbaijan. In September 2022, Armenia initiated Article 4 of the CSTO treaty after renewed fighting on the border with Azerbaijan. Unlike the protests in Kazakhstan, CSTO did not positively respond to Armenia's request to defend its territory from Azerbaijan. Amid growing frustration with Russia's position in Nagorno-Karabakh, Armenia's prime minister Nikol Pashinyan refused to sign the joint declaration of the CSTO during the organization's summit in November 2022. In January 2023, Armenia refused to participate in CSTO's joint military drills.[33] In December 2022, Azerbaijan started to gradually block the Lachin corridor that connects Nagorno-Karabakh to Armenia. By June 2023, passage was under total control of the Azerbaijani army, which has once again put Russia in a paradoxical situation. Armenia has called for help from the international community, arguing that the Armenian population in Nagorno-Karabakh was going through a humanitarian crisis due to Azerbaijan's blockade. In turn, Russia has officially moved closer to Azerbaijan's position, which has claimed that the Lachin corridor was used to transfer arms from Armenia to Nagorno-Karabakh. By September 2023, almost the entire ethnic Armenian population of Nagorno-Karabakh had left the region.

The gradual loss of trust between the Armenian and Russian governments resulted in the former's suspension of its participation in the CSTO in February 2024. In April 2024, Russian peacekeeping forces in Nagorno-Karabakh completed their mission and left the region to total control by the Azerbaijani armed forces. Consequently, the second Karabakh War of 2020 and the following developments have demonstrated Russia's shifting allegiances in a region rife with ethnic conflict and geopolitical rivalry. It has also resulted in a loss of CSTO's credibility in the eyes of Erevan. More recently, the EU has emerged as a more attractive mediator for negotiations between Azerbaijan and Armenia.[34]

Regional Normative Order

In terms of the normative dimension, the sustainability of authoritarian rule in post-Soviet Eurasia has been the Russian government's primary purpose. Authoritarianism has also served the role of a glue that holds Russia and regional states together. As Cooley aptly demonstrates, Moscow has used the instruments of the liberal international order—regional organizations, NGOs, and liberal democracy—in Eurasia as a tool to attract authoritarian leaders of the region to stick together with Russia-led regional organizations.[35] The "color revolutions" of the early twenty-first century were a turning point for Russia and autocratic leaders of the region. Under Putin's rule, Moscow has consistently aimed to undermine the activities of Western-backed NGOs and promoted "traditional values" in Russia and the post-Soviet space.[36] The SCO has similarly played an important role in sustaining a regional order based on authoritarian survival and respect for sovereignty. In fact, Beijing has always held the upper hand in shaping the priorities and key mechanisms of inter-governmental cooperation within the SCO. At the same time, as Cooley demonstrates, through the SCO, China has accommodated Russia's long-standing goal of countering Western norms and policies as well as US presence in Central Asia.[37]

The Kremlin has systematically referred to Euromaidan, the establishment of a pro-European government in Ukraine after 2014, and popular protests taking place in other countries of the region as Western efforts to contain Russia and erode Russia's own sovereignty. In other words, democratization in the region has threatened the ontological security of the Russian foreign policy elites, who have presented authoritarian stability as a blessing for regional order in Russia and Eurasia. Russian political elites even constructed the concept of "the Russian world"—*Russkiy Mir*—to propose a civilizational identity for the societies of Russia, Ukraine, and other post-Soviet countries. The imagined "Russian world" was based on the common "glorious past" of the states and societies in the region, the common denominators of which included "Russian language, Orthodox Christianity and Russian culture," as well as the shared Soviet legacy.[38]

The most recent official Russian foreign policy concept argues that Russia is a "a unique country-civilization and a vast Eurasian and Euro-Pacific power that brings together the Russian people and other peoples belonging to the cultural and civilizational community of the Russian world."[39] The Greater Eurasian Partnership, which this chapter explored above, has not merely been a geo-economic project for the Kremlin. The idea of Greater Eurasia—*Bol'shaya Evraziya*—has also been instrumental for Russia's civilizational perspective on the Eurasian regional order. The Russian foreign policy expert community attributed a civilizational meaning to the idea of Greater Eurasia. In this worldview, the Greater Eurasian Partnership would bolster the civilizational identity of Eurasian states amid challenges from the West.[40] Greater Eurasia would become a "third-way alternative" for illiberal regional states as well as other states in Asia in the age of the decline of the liberal international order.[41] This civilizational perspective on global norms consolidate Russia's self-perception as a historical great power at the expense of views that see Russia as a peripheral state in Europe.[42]

Russia's Invasion of Ukraine and the Regional Order in Eurasia

Despite the growing importance of the CSTO in the regional security architecture and Russia's efforts to revitalize Eurasian economic integration in the last few years, Russia's invasion of Ukraine in 2022 has once again served to push regional states away from Russia. While regional states have not openly pursued an anti-Russia stance, they have demonstrated their unease with the invasion in multiple occasions. Officials of Central Asian states have openly highlighted their support for Ukraine's territorial integrity and sovereignty. For example, in March 2022, Kyrgyz president Japarov stated that the Kyrgyz Republic had the power to influence the outcome of the war but would choose neutrality. Similarly, in March 2022, Uzbek minister of foreign affairs Kamilov stated that Uzbekistan respected the territorial integrity of Ukraine, and would not recognize the Luhansk and Donetsk People's Republics. At the St. Petersburg Economic Forum in June 2022, Kazakh president Tokayev announced that Kazakhstan would recognize neither the self-proclaimed Donetsk and Luhansk People's Republics nor Abkhazia and South Ossetia. Despite expectations that Tokayev's leadership would push Kazakhstan closer to Russia's orbit after the January 2022 events, Astana has since then diversified its foreign relations not only with old partners such as China and Turkey but also with the EU.[43] Both Nazarbayev and Tokayev have repeatedly emphasized Kazakhstan's insistence on committing to the EAEA so long as it does not violate Kazakhstan's sovereignty.[44] While officially supporting Ukraine's territorial integrity and sovereignty, members of the EAEU and CSTO have also pursued a delicate balancing act that has aimed to calm down a potential Russian aggression toward their own territory.

The outcome of several votes that took place under the United Nations (UN) demonstrate that regional states have chosen not to bandwagon with Russia. From March to December 2022, the UN General Assembly voted for six resolutions on the situation concerning Russia's invasion of Ukraine. Georgia and Moldova voted in favor of all resolutions condemning Russia, including the resolution on Russia's suspension from the UN Human Rights Council on April 7, 2022.[45] As expected, Russia's loyal ally Belarus voted against all the resolutions to demonstrate its firm support for Russia. Armenia, Kazakhstan, Kyrgyzstan, and Tajikistan abstained in the majority of the resolutions, while they voted against Russia's suspension from the UN Human Rights Council. Azerbaijan and Turkmenistan did not participate in the voting in any of the six meetings. Similarly, Armenia and Uzbekistan abstained from all three UN Human Rights Council resolutions on the invasion that took place in 2022. Kazakhstan, on the other hand, abstained from two of them and voted against the resolution on the situation of human rights in the Russian Federation.[46]

Even more importantly, Russia's invasion of Ukraine has consolidated the desire for EU membership among Ukraine, Georgia, and Moldova. Ukraine applied for membership to the EU in February 2022, two weeks after the invasion and was granted a candidate country status by the European Council in June 2022.[47] While the EU similarly granted Moldova a candidate country status in June 2022, it expressed its readiness to extend the same status to Georgia after the country addressed the EU's priorities.[48] The invasion has similarly strengthened Ukraine and Georgia's bid for NATO membership. The Ukrainian president Volodymyr Zelensky was even invited to the NATO Summit that took place in Vilnius, Lithuania, in July 2023. At the Summit, Zelensky clearly wanted assurance for Ukraine's membership in the transatlantic alliance after the war was over. NATO members, however, approached the issue with caution while at the same increasing their financial and military support to Ukraine.[49] On the other hand, amid fears that Russia could use Transnistria to open up a new front for the invasion of Ukraine, the Moldovan government has also intensified its cooperation with NATO.[50] All in all, Russia's long-standing goal of keeping the EU and NATO out of the post-Soviet space, its self-proclaimed sphere of influence, has gradually but firmly dissipated due to Russia's own coercion in the region. Beyond the region, Russia's invasion of Ukraine has reconstituted European identity and given a renewed geopolitical purpose to NATO. Lucan A. Way goes even further to argue that Russia's invasion of Ukraine can strengthen the liberal international order as it serves to undermine autocratic leaders in the West, unite Western countries for a common cause, weaken Russia geopolitically and economically, and create divisions among authoritarian states.[51] It is too early to test Way's argument; however, it is clear that the regional order the Russian political elites have been imagining has not emerged and Russia has created a regional disorder that does not fit its hegemonic aspirations.

The Ukrainian military started a counteroffensive in the summer of 2023, which has so far not been successful in recovering large swathes of territory from Russian occupation. As of early 2024, Russia occupies and controls around 18 percent of Ukraine's territory. As both Kyiv and Moscow are prepared for protracted warfare, the former increasingly depends on Western aid to sustain its war effort.[52]

ALTERNATIVE ORDERS IN EURASIA? THE ROLE OF CHINA, THE EU, AND THE UNITED STATES IN THE POST-SOVIET SPACE

In the post–Cold War period, Russia's hegemonic projects in Eurasia have not met any direct alternative regional order-creation efforts. China has become Central Asia's key economic partner in the twenty-first century, while the EU has had a rather incoherent strategy with its Eastern Partnership (EaP) and the renewed Central Asia strategy. The United States, on the other hand, has failed to develop a comprehensive strategy toward the post-Soviet space.

In the past two decades, China has gradually emerged as Central Asia's top trading partner. China's President Xi Jinping announced the BRI in Kazakhstan in 2013, demonstrating the importance Beijing attaches to Central Asia. China has especially invested in the energy infrastructure in the region through its involvement in both pipeline construction and investments in renewable energy.[53] In 2022, China's total trade with five Central Asian countries reached $70 billion, while Russia's trade stood at $42 billion in the same year. China is the primary market for Uzbek and Turkmen natural gas. The China-Central Asia Natural Gas Pipeline, which was opened in 2009, delivers Turkmen natural gas to China passing through Turkmenistan, Uzbekistan, and Kazakhstan before making it into the Xinjiang Uighur Autonomous Region. China has typically made inroads into Central Asia through flexible and bilateral deals with the authoritarian governments of the region. The SCO was traditionally the main platform that brought together China, Russia, and the regional governments to discuss matters related to stability and security in the region. More recently, Beijing has also started to develop its own institutional instruments for regional cooperation, which has excluded Russia. In May 2023, the first China-Central Asia Summit (C + C5) took place in Xi'an with the participation of Xi Jinping and all five regional leaders. At the summit, Xi emphasized China's willingness to increase foreign direct investment (FDI) in Central Asia, boost trade, enhance development cooperation, and assist regional states in security issues. While the C + C5 does not pose a direct challenge to Russian hegemony in the region, it demonstrates China's commitment to build multilateral platforms with post-Soviet states without Russia's support.

What could be more worrying for Moscow is Beijing's potential interest in acting as a security-provider in the region. China's military presence is most visible in Tajikistan, which is also host to Russia's largest military base outside its borders. There have been various reports since 2016 about the activities of the People's Armed Police Force in Tajikistan, which is particularly important for China due to the country's border with Afghanistan.[54] Beyond Tajikistan, China has been engaging in joint military drills with Central Asian states on counterterrorism, some of which have taken place within the SCO format.[55] While it is too early for China to fully emerge as a military power in Central Asia or the post-Soviet space, it would not be far-fetched to argue that China will seek to increase its geopolitical influence in the near future through mechanisms of security cooperation that bypass Russia.

Putin and Xi have consolidated a Russian-Chinese strategic partnership after the annexation of Crimea amid Western sanctions on the Russian economy. The main pillars of the strategic partnership have been widening energy cooperation, maintaining stability in the neighboring regions, and assuring noninterference from the United States in Central Asia.[56] Larson explains the intensifying ties as well as the lack of an open rivalry between the two with social identity theory; Russia and China cooperate to build a "common identity" in reaction to their exclusion by the West.[57] Despite the seeming convergence in Moscow's and Beijing's strategic agendas, China holds the upper hand in the bilateral relationship due mainly to a growing asymmetry in economic ties. With its growing isolation from the United States–led liberal international order after its invasion of Ukraine, good relations with China have become even more crucial for the Kremlin. China has neither directly supported nor condemned Russia's war on Ukraine. While it has been careful in not violating the US-EU sanctions on the Russian economy, it has offered a fresh lifeline to Russia by importing greater amounts of Russian oil and natural gas. Amid restrictions on Russia's use of the US dollar in foreign transactions, the Chinese yuan has become an alternative foreign currency for Russian trade as well as Central Bank reserves. China has also exported the much-needed high technology products to Russia after the sanctions.[58] In February 2023, China has also revealed a twelve-point peace plan for the Ukraine war, which has not been met with excitement from the international community.[59] China is also expected to become one of the leading investors in the postwar reconstruction in the Ukrainian economy together with the United States and the EU.

The EU has been the main source of FDI for countries in Central Asia in the twenty-first century. Contrary to Moscow's persistent fears, the EU has been a reluctant geopolitical player in the post-Soviet space. Its main instrument for Eastern Europe and the Caucasus has been the EaP, launched in 2009. Covering six post-Soviet countries, the EaP has aimed to stabilize the region while at the same time supporting the reform and democratization efforts in these countries.[60] The annexation of Crimea and the war in Ukraine have cast shadow over the effectiveness of the EaP, and the EU has struggled to move the program outside the geopolitical context based on Russian aggression. In 2021, a Comprehensive and Advanced Partnership Agreement (CEPA) between the EU and Armenia entered into force.[61] An important development concerning the EU's geopolitical influence in the post-Soviet space took place in May 2023, as the Armenian and Azerbaijani governments agreed on "a longer-term negotiation plan for a comprehensive peace agreement."[62]

The EU has also announced a new strategy for Central Asia in 2019 and aligned it with the Global Gateway and the European Green Deal. The EU's new regional strategy titled "The EU and Central Asia: New Opportunities for a Stronger Partnership," outlines three priority areas: partnering for resilience, partnering for prosperity, and supporting regional cooperation.[63] The first priority highlights the EU's long-standing goal of promoting democracy, human rights, and the rule of law in the region. The second priority area emphasizes the EU's support for economic reform in the region as well as economic connectivity between Europe and Central Asia. The final priority area calls for a stronger institutional setup to enhance EU-Central Asia cooperation and focuses on the role of civil society and cooperation with local authorities in boosting the relationship. As part of the new strategy, two EU-Central Asia summits have taken place with the presence of Charles Michel, the president of the Council of the EU and the five regional leaders in 2022 in Kazakhstan, and in 2023 in Kyrgyzstan. The EPCA with Kazakhstan, the EU's biggest trade and investment partner in the region, entered into force in 2020. An EPCA with Kyrgyzstan is pending approval, and negotiations are ongoing at various stages with Uzbekistan and Tajikistan. After Russia's invasion of Ukraine, the EU has intensified its focus on the Middle Corridor, with the goal of bypassing Russia and revitalizing connectivity between China and Europe through Central Asia, the Caucasus, and Turkey. However, the Global Gateway is far from achieving BRI-like investment levels in these regions.

The US strategy toward Eastern Europe and the Caucasus has been primarily motivated by containing Russia and strengthening NATO. The war in Ukraine has brought the United States back to the region, but overall, Washington continues to lack a coherent and comprehensive strategy in Eurasia. The American outlook toward Central Asia, on the other hand, has been occupied with the withdrawal of forces from Afghanistan and the following developments.[64] Washington adopted a new Central Asia strategy document in February 2020. The document clearly lays out American priorities in the region: "Support and strengthen the sovereignty and independence" of the states in the region, "reduce terrorist threats," "expand and maintain support for stability in Afghanistan," "encourage connectivity between Central Asia and Afghanistan," "promote rule of law reform and respect for human rights," and "promote United States investments in and development of Central Asia."[65] Since 2015, Washington has held annual meetings between the US secretary of state and the foreign ministers of regional states under the C5 + 1 format. Under the Biden administration, secretary of state Blinken has aimed to revitalize a Central Asia strategy, yet the region has not transformed into a priority for US foreign policy goals. The absence of a comprehensive and coherent American strategic outlook toward Central Asia is quite paradoxical, given the importance that Russia and China—two official strategic competitors of the United States—attach to the region.

CONCLUSION

This chapter has argued that Russia's aspiration and attempts to build a Eurasian regional order has resulted in a greater regional dis-order. This is an outcome of the mismatch between the dominant worldview in Moscow that sees Russia as a traditional great power with a privileged sphere of influence in Eurasia and regional realities. Russia has made peaceful change in Eurasia unthinkable with its own coercive hegemonic moves, and yet blamed the United States and Europe for it. Russia's coercive strategy in the region has pushed regional states away from pursuing a true alliance with Russia. The war in Ukraine has resulted in a greater skepticism toward Russia among the authoritarian leaders of the region. Since the beginning of the invasion, Central Asian states have been in an ever-stronger search for diversifying foreign partners. China's growing economic power as well as bilateral and multilateral forms of cooperation in Central Asia have increased its appeal for regional governments. Democratic nations of the region, on the other hand, have become more pro-Western and strive harder to join the EU and even NATO, in the case of Georgia and Ukraine.

The Russian style of great power nationalism and search for regional hegemony carry significant lessons for other countries with similar aspirations. Most importantly, it demonstrates the dangers of coercive hegemony, which borderlines imperialism. Instead of pulling regional countries to its orbit, Russia has consistently constituted a source of threat for the sovereignty of smaller powers in Eurasia and pushed them away. While it currently looks like a far-fetched scenario, similar forms of nationalism and extreme centralization of domestic political power can result in war-making based on occupation in other regions of the international system. It is not difficult to foresee that the war in Ukraine will be a long-lasting one with devastating consequences for the regional economies and societies. Russia's isolation from the Western-led global economic system with the sanctions will push it toward greater cooperation with China, and to some extent India and other BRICS countries. Russian political elites see the decline of the liberal international order as a positive development for Russia, China, and the so-called Greater Eurasia. However, Russia lacks the material capability and the soft power to create a new order. All in all, the age of global disorder and the New Cold War that the Russian political elite has been long waiting for have arrived, but Russia has entered it in a weaker position due to its own foreign and security policy practices. In the age of the New Cold War, the Eurasian region is moving further away from achieving peaceful change.

NOTES

1. President of Russia, "Interview Given by Dmitri Medvedev to Television Channels Channel One, Rossia, NTV," August 31, 2008, http://en.kremlin.ru/events/president/transcripts/48301.
2. On Russia's search for status in world politics, see Deborah Welch Larson and Alexei Shevchenko, *Quest for Status: Chinese and Russian Foreign Policy* (New Haven, CT: Yale University Press, 2019).
3. On great power nationalism, see Juliet Johnson and Seçkin Köstem, "Frustrated Leadership: Russia's Economic Alternative to the West," *Global Policy* 7, no. 2 (2016): 207–216; Seçkin Köstem, "Different Paths to Regional Hegemony: National Identity Contestation and Foreign Economic Strategy in Russia and Turkey," *Review of International Political Economy* 25, no. 5 (2018): 726–52.
4. Vladimir Putin, "Rossiya na Rubezhe Tysyacheletiy," *Nezavisimaya Gazeta*, December 31, 1999.
5. Putin, "Rossiya na Rubezhe."
6. For example, see Sergei Lavrov, "Russia's Foreign Policy in a Historical Perspective," *Russia in Global Affairs*, no. 2. (April/June 2016), https://eng.globalaffairs.ru/articles/russias-foreign-policy-in-a-historical-perspective/.
7. Sergei Lavrov, "Containing Russia: Back to the Future?," *Russia in Global Affairs* 6, no. 4 (October/December 2007).
8. President of Russia, "Address by the President of the Russian Federation," March 18, 2014, http://en.kremlin.ru/events/president/news/20603.
9. Alexander Libman and Anastassia Obydenkova, "Regional International Organisations as a Strategy of Autocracy: The Eurasian Economic Union and Russian Foreign Policy," *International Affairs* 94, no. 5 (2018): 1049–52.
10. Anne Clunan, "Historical Aspirations and the Domestic Politics of Russia's Pursuit of International Status," *Communist and Post-Communist Studies* 47, no. 3–4 (2014): 287.
11. Vladimir Putin, "On the Historical Unity of Russians and Ukrainians," July 12, 2021, http://www.en.kremlin.ru/events/president/news/66181.
12. Sergei Karaganov, "The New Cold War and the Emerging Greater Eurasia," *Journal of Eurasian Studies* 9, no. 2 (July 2018): 92.
13. Alexander Cooley, "Ordering Eurasia: The Rise and Decline of Liberal Internationalism in the Post-Communist Space," *Security Studies* 28, no. 3 (2019): 588–613.
14. Gregorio Bettiza and David Lewis, "Authoritarian Powers and Norm Contestation in the Liberal International Order: Theorizing the Power Politics of Ideas and Identity," *Journal of Global Security Studies* 5, no. 4 (October 2020): 559–77.
15. Andrei Tsygankov, "Russia, Eurasia and the Meaning of Crimea," *Europe-Asia Studies* 74, no. 9 (2022): 1569.
16. Tsygankov, "Russia, Eurasia."
17. Irina Busygina and Mikhail Filippov, "Russia, Post-Soviet Integration, and the EAEU: The Balance between Domination and Cooperation," *Problems of Post-Communism* 68, no. 6 (2021): 477.
18. Johnson and Köstem, "Frustrated Leadership."
19. Rilka Dragnewa and Christopher Hartwell, "The Crisis of the Multilateral Order in Eurasia: Authoritarian Regionalism and Its Limits," *Politics and Governance* 10, no. 2

(2022): 95–105; Alexander Libman and Anastassia Obydenkova, "Regional International Organisations as a Strategy of Autocracy: The Eurasian Economic Union and Russian Foreign Policy," *International Affairs* 94, no. 5 (2019): 1037–58.
20. Dragnewa and Hartwell, "The Crisis of."
21. Alexander Libman, "Does Integration Rhetoric Help? Eurasian Regionalism and the Rhetorical Dissonance of Russian Elites," *Europe-Asia Studies* 74, no. 9 (2022): 1575.
22. Libman, "Does Integration Rhetoric," 1578.
23. For a detailed analysis of Russian political elite's discourse on regional integration, see Libman, "Does Integration Rhetoric."
24. On Russia's perception of the Belt and Road Initiative and the rise of China as a global player, see Alexander Lukin, *Russia and China: The New Rapprochement* (Cambridge, UK: Polity Press); Alexander Lukin and Dmitry Novikov, "Sino-Russian Rapprochement and Greater Eurasia: From Geopolitical Pole to International Society?," *Journal of Eurasian Studies* 12, no. 1 (January 2021): 28–45.
25. Yaroslav Lissovolik, "A Geographical Case for the 'One Belt, One Road' and the Eurasian Economic Union," Valdai Club, May 29, 2017, https://valdaiclub.com/a/highlights/a-geographical-case-for-the-one-belt-one-road/.
26. Janko Scepanovic, "Institutions, Cooperation and Hegemony: A Comparative Analysis of Russia's Cooperative Hegemonic Strategy in Central Asia's Key Institutional Frameworks," *Asian Security* 17, no. 2 (2021): 236–61.
27. Diana T. Kudaibergenova and Marlene Laruelle, "Making Sense of the January 2022 Protests in Kazakhstan: Failing Legitimacy, Culture of Protests, and Elite Readjustments," *Post-Soviet Affairs* 38, no. 6 (2022): 453.
28. "Dushanbe Accuses Bishkek of Violating Cease-Fire Deal Along Tajik-Kyrgyz Border," RFERL, October 19, 2022, https://www.rferl.org/a/kyrgyzstan-tajikistan-border-csto-peacekeepers/32091251.html.
29. On military bases in Central Asia, see Alexander Cooley, "International Ordering and Great Power Competition: Lessons from Central Asia," Brookings Institute, Policy Briefing, February 2023.
30. Seçkin Köstem, "Managed Regional Rivalry between Russia and Turkey after the Annexation of Crimea," *Europe-Asia Studies* 74, no. 9 (2022): 1657–75.
31. Köstem, "Managed Regional Rivalry," 1669–1772.
32. President of the Republic of Azerbaijan, "Declaration on Allied Interaction between the Republic of Azerbaijan and the Russian Federation," February 22, 2022, https://president.az/en/articles/view/55498.
33. "Armenia Refuses to Host CSTO Exercises," Eurasianet, January 10, 2023, https://eurasianet.org/armenia-refuses-to-host-csto-exercises.
34. On Russia's changing position in the Karabakh conflict, see Cenap Çakmak and M. Cüneyt Özşahin, "Explaining Russia's Inertia in the Azerbaijan-Armenia Dispute: Reward and Punishment in an Asymmetric Alliance," *Europe-Asia Studies* 75, no. 6 (2023): 972–88.
35. Cooley, "Ordering Eurasia."
36. Ibid., 590.
37. Ibid.
38. Valentina Feklyunina, "Soft Power and Identity: Russia, Ukraine and the 'Russian World(s),'" *European Journal of International Relations* 22, no. 4 (2016): 783.

39. The Ministry of Foreign Affairs of the Russian Federation, "The Concept of the Foreign Policy of the Russian Federation," March 31, 2023, https://mid.ru/en/foreign_policy/fundamental_documents/1860586/.
40. David G. Lewis, "Geopolitical Imaginaries in Russian Foreign Policy: The Evolution of 'Greater Eurasia,'" *Europe-Asia Studies* 70, no. 10 (2018): 1612–37; Andrej Krickovic and Igor Pelliciari, "From 'Greater Europe' to 'Greater Eurasia': Status Concerns and the Evolution of Russia's Approach to Alignment and Regional Integration," *Journal of Eurasian Studies* 12, no. 1 (2021): 86–99. Seçkin Köstem, "Kennan Cable No. 40: Russia's Search for a Greater Eurasia: Origins, Promises, and Prospects," Wilson Center, February 2019, https://www.wilsoncenter.org/publication/kennan-cable-no-40-russias-search-for-greater-eurasia-origins-promises-and-prospects.
41. Andrej Krickovic, "Russia's Greater Eurasia Project as a 'Third Way' Alternative to Western Liberal Order," in *Non-Western Nations and the Liberal International Order: Responding to the Backlash in the West*, eds. Hiro Katsumata and Hiroki Kusano (London: Routledge, 2023), 115–36.
42. Gregorio Bettiza, Derek Bolton, and David Lewis, "Civilizational and the Ideological Contestation of the Liberal International Order," *International Studies Review* 25, no. 2 (June 2023): 22.
43. Marie Dumoulin, "Steppe Change: How Russia's War on Ukraine is Reshaping Kazakhstan," *European Council on Foreign Relations Policy Brief*, April 2023, https://ecfr.eu/publication/steppe-change-how-russias-war-on-ukraine-is-reshaping-kazakhstan/.
44. Busygina and Filippov, "Russia, Post-Soviet Integration," 483–84.
45. Ninety-three members voted in favor of the resolution, fifty-eight members abstained, and twenty-four members voted against it. See United Nations Digital Library, "Suspension of the Rights of the Russian Federation in the Human Rights Council," April 7, 2022, https://digitallibrary.un.org/record/3967950.
46. United Nations Human Rights Council (A/HRC/51/L.13), September 29, 2022, https://ap.ohchr.org/documents/dpage_e.aspx?si=A/HRC/51/L.13.
47. Council of the European Union, "Ukraine," accessed September 2, 2023, https://www.consilium.europa.eu/en/policies/enlargement/ukraine/.
48. Council of the European Union, "Georgia," accessed September 2, 2023, https://www.consilium.europa.eu/en/policies/enlargement/georgia/.
49. BBC, "NATO, Warm Words but a Diplomatic Reality Check for Ukraine," July 12, 2023, https://www.bbc.com/news/world-europe-66183066.
50. Radio Free Europe/Radio Liberty, "Neutral Moldova Vows 'Intensified, Accelerated Cooperation' with NATO," accessed September 2, 2023, https://www.rferl.org/a/moldova-neutrality-nato-european-union-constitution/32500369.html.
51. Lucan A. Way, "The Rebirth of the Liberal World Order," *Journal of Democracy* 33, no. 2 (April 2022): 5–17.
52. Financial Times, "Ukraine's Counteroffensive against Russia in Maps: Latest Updates," accessed April 29, 2024, https://www.ft.com/content/4351d5b0-0888-4b47-9368-6bc4dfbccbf5.
53. Morena Skalamera Groce and Seçkin Köstem, "The Dual Transformation in Development Finance: Western Multilateral Development Banks and China in Post-Soviet Energy," *Review of International Political Economy* 30, no. 1 (February 2023): 176–200.
54. Janko Scepanovic, "The Sheriff and the Banker? Russia and China in Central Asia," War on the Rocks, June 13, 2022.

55. Scepanovic, "The Sheriff and the Banker?"
56. Marcin Kaczmarski, "The Asymmetric Partnership? Russia's Turn to China," *International Politics* 53 (2016): 415–34.
57. Deborah Welch Larson, "An Unequal Partnership of Equals: China's and Russia's New Status Relationship," *International Politics* 57 (2020): 790–808.
58. Maia Nikoladze, Phillip Meng, and Jessie Yin, "How Is China Mitigating the Effects of Sanctions on Russia?," The Atlantic Council, Econographics, June 14, 2023, https://www.atlanticcouncil.org/blogs/econographics/how-is-china-mitigating-the-effects-of-sanctions-on-russia/#:~:text=China%20is%20mitigating%20the%20impact,an%20alternative%20currency%20for%20transactions.
59. For the details of the plan, see Ministry of Foreign Affairs of the People's Republic of China, "China's Position on the Political Settlement of the Ukraine Crisis," February 24, 2023, https://www.fmprc.gov.cn/mfa_eng/zxxx_662805/202302/t20230224_11030713.html.
60. David Cadier, "Eastern Partnership vs. Eurasian Union? The EU-Russia Competition in the Shared Neighborhood and the Ukraine Crisis," *Global Policy* 5, no. S1 (2014): 76–85.
61. The European Union, "Eastern Partnership," March 17, 2022, https://www.eeas.europa.eu/eeas/eastern-partnership_en.
62. Anna Caprile and Jakub Przecatznik, "Armenia and Azerbaijan: Between War and Peace," The European Parliament, Briefing, June 2023, https://www.europarl.europa.eu/RegData/etudes/BRIE/2023/747919/EPRS_BRI(2023)747919_EN.pdf.
63. European Commission, "The EU and Central Asia: New Opportunities for a Stronger Partnership," Brussels, May 15, 2019, https://www.eeas.europa.eu/sites/default/files/joint_communication_-_the_eu_and_central_asia_-_new_opportunities_for_a_stronger_partnership.pdf.
64. On American strategy toward the region before the war in Ukraine, see Andrew C. Kuchins, "What Is Eurasia to US (the U.S.)?," *Journal of Eurasian Studies* 9, no. 2 (July 2018): 125–33.
65. U.S. Department of State, "United States Strategy for Central Asia 2019–2025: Advancing Sovereignty and Economic Prosperity," February 2020, https://www.state.gov/wp-content/uploads/2020/02/FINAL-CEN-Strategy-Glossy-2-10-2020-508.pdf.

CHAPTER 11

Conclusion

Rethinking Great Powers, Regions, and Peaceful Change in the New Cold War Era

Andrej Krickovic and Jaeyoung Kim

We find ourselves in a new era of intense geopolitical competition between great powers that can be characterized as the New Cold War.[1] Over the last decades, observers have warned that deteriorating US-Russia and US-China relations would inevitably culminate in this kind of outcome.[2] Critics questioned the appropriateness of applying the Cold War analogy to these growing tensions[3] and were hopeful that a return to great power competition could still be avoided.[4] Nevertheless, the Russian invasion of Ukraine serves as a kind of tipping point. It has severed almost all constructive relations between Russia and the United States and its Western allies, trapping the two sides into a seemingly intractable and brutal conflict.[5] It also draws attention to the growing intensity of economic and security competition between China and the United States. Despite China's claims of neutrality, they find themselves on opposite sides of the Ukraine conflict. However, the US-China relationship has its own dynamics that cannot be reduced to their respective relations with Russia. The tensions between the United States and China are growing acutely in geopolitical flashpoints such as the Taiwan Strait, the South China Sea, and the Korean Peninsula, and specific issue areas such as advanced technologies and global supply chains.

The chapters in this volume offer a nuanced examination of the emerging New Cold War from global and, perhaps more significantly, regional perspectives. The authors recognize that, despite some similarities, most notably in the major "great power" actors involved, the New Cold War plays out under very different political, economic, and social circumstances. As Paul and Kornprobst point out in the introductory chapter, the "old" Cold War was defined by a bipolarity of power and ideology between the United States and the Soviet Union and their respective alliances, which made it difficult for even the key third parties (such as China and India) to maintain their independence and refrain from choosing sides. Intense ideological rivalry has yet to emerge in the New Cold War. As Ho, Pu, and Larson explore in their contributions to this volume, the New Cold War's protagonists are motivated more by nationalist grievances and their related status concerns than by a desire to promote universalistic ideologies. Although ideology continues to be an important factor in regional competition, as Balzacq and Grantseva demonstrate in their chapter, it primarily serves as a tool of influence and epistemological point of reference great powers look to in formulating their regional grand strategies.

It is unlikely that the New Cold War will be either bipolar or multipolar. While contending coalitions are emerging, they are not as tight or cohesive as they were in the past. China does not necessarily support all of Russia's objectives in Ukraine, and US allies in Europe are reluctant to get involved in the emerging US-China confrontation. Nor does a classical multipolar system, dominated by several great powers, seem to be emerging. As a result of globalization, international and societal actors (including non-state actors) are entangled in intricate and overlapping relationships of complex interdependence across a wide range of issues (economic, technological, biological, and ecological). Power has become more diffuse throughout the system, empowering an ever-larger number of states and non-state actors.[6] Regional actors, including middle powers and small states, now have more latitude in pursuing "geopolitical promiscuity," developing beneficial relationships with all the great powers, even as the conflict between the great powers intensifies.[7]

We concur with Paul and Kornprobst that the context in which the New Cold War is occurring can best be understood in terms of Acharya's concept of "multiplex world order" (further developed in Pardesi and Acharya's chapter in this volume and vividly illustrated by their case study of the Indo-Pacific). A multiplex order is a world where the power to "break and make order" is dispersed and fragmented among a variety of actors, and multiple, interacting, and overlapping orders coexist.[8] These may be relatively comprehensive, such as the "liberal" order comprising the United States and its Western allies. Or they may be specific to certain issue areas, for example, regional and transregional agreements on trade (such as Regional Comprehensive Economic Partnership, Comprehensive and Progressive

Trans-Pacific Partnership, and Indo-Pacific Economic Framework)[9] or subregional institutions that manage environmental and resource issues (such as the Mekong River Commission). Like viewers visiting a multiplex cinema, international actors can pick and choose the particular orders they want to participate in according to their preferences and interests. While the chapters in this volume do not all explicitly embrace multiplexity, their rich and nuanced analysis alerts us to the complex dynamics that shape regional politics in the New Cold War.

Against this backdrop, three major themes emerge. Firstly, the chapters all highlight the importance of regions as a level of analysis in world politics. Not only will the New Cold War rivalries be contested at the regional level, but regions will increasingly be the locus of order-making in international politics. Secondly, regional actors exercise a great deal of agency and influence. Both in material terms—that is, in the foreign policy strategies they adopt to adjust to regional power dynamics[10]—and in their ideational capabilities—that is, their capacity to influence the norms of regional governance and define regional identities and boundaries.[11] Finally, regions vary greatly in their potential for peaceful change, with some regions inclined toward maximalist forms of peaceful transformation while others struggle to maintain minimal peace and are in danger of sliding toward violent confrontations and war.[12]

The chapters in this volume demonstrate that standard realist (distribution of power), liberal (democratic peace and economic independence), or constructivist (the emergence of regional security communities) explanations do not adequately account for these variations. Instead, peaceful change at the regional level will hinge on various complex and interrelated factors. The chapters raise several pivotal questions: Will great powers be able to assert their normative authority by getting other states to accept their ideological discourses[13] and the legitimacy of their claims to spheres of influence?[14] Will secondary states mitigate great power competition by strengthening multilateral institutions and establishing the norms of open and inclusive regional governance?[15] Can great powers and lesser states find ways to enhance their status that do not provoke zero-sum status conflicts?[16]

Drawing on the insights that the previous chapters provide on these issues, we argue that the New Cold War struggle, waged under conditions of multiplexity, prompts us to rethink such key International Relations (IR) concepts as great powers, regions, and change. Great power is traditionally understood as a category of powerful states possessing capabilities above all other states in the international system. Their position in the international power hierarchy endows them with attendant global interests, provoking competition between them for power, status, and other resources.[17] However, in the emerging multiplex world, where power and influence are more evenly diffused throughout the system, the advantages and capabilities enjoyed by great powers over other international actors are significantly reduced. Great powers struggle to assert their dominance and authority even over secondary and lesser states while expending much "blood and treasure" and alienating other states in the process. Despite high costs and diminishing returns, they continue to try and assert their dominance and compete for influence and status. This behavior cannot be solely attributed to the pursuit of material interests and privileged status warranted by their power capabilities. It should also be understood in terms of their imperial legacies and reimagined or self-ascribed civilizational identities.

Regions have been understood as the "backyards" of great powers or "battlegrounds" where they compete.[18] The great power-centered views of regions often ignore the complex web of political, economic, and societal relationships that constitute regions and the critical role that secondary states play in regional politics. Hegemonic stability theories suggest that regional hegemons are key players in securing regional peace and stability. Yet, recent developments in Europe and Asia suggest that regions with tight security blocs led by great powers (such as NATO) are less peaceful than regions with looser security arrangements where secondary states maintain greater flexibility. This does not mean, however, that we should downplay the role of structural factors in shaping regional outcomes. The diverging power trajectories of great powers—Russia's decline and China's rise—have shaped the strategies these powers use to assert their regional status but also how other regional states engage with them.

The sheer complexity and interconnectedness of challenges faced by the emerging multiplex world force us to rethink the concept of change in IR. The study of change has focused on systemic change—that is, hegemonic transitions through conflict and war within the existing system.[19] Recent scholarship shifts its focus to peaceful change—be it a minimalist one, which implies the absence of interstate war, or maximalist one, which implies "the achievement of sustained non-violent cooperation for creating a more just world order."[20] The deteriorating security situation and danger that the New Cold War may turn "hot" focuses our attention on minimalist peaceful change. Nevertheless, the increased severity of mounting anthropogenic challenges demands that we look beyond minimalist change and begin to consider possibilities for maximalist change if we are to effectively address the global problems that threaten the survival of humanity.

Moreover, multiplexity will make complex, overlapping, and constantly evolving regions the primary locus for order-making in world politics, opening up new possibilities and opportunities for transformational change.

RETHINKING "GREAT POWERS"

The way the discipline of IR tends to conceptualize "great powers" may not fully capture the nature of the relationships between the major protagonists—the United States, Russia, and China—or their rhetoric and behaviors in the New Cold War era. Great powers are traditionally defined by their size and material capabilities. The term implies that these actors stand above others in terms of military and economic strength.[21] Their power preponderance makes them conceive themselves and be recognized by others as the bearers of special rights, privileges, and responsibilities related to the management of international order.[22] Great powers can define their interests beyond local or regional concerns, use a broader range of policy options, and interact more frequently with their peers than with weaker and smaller states.[23] During the old Cold War, the traditional notion of great power politics (rooted in the experience of post-Westphalia Europe) did not fully capture the realities of bipolarity and ideological rivalry between the United States and Soviet Union, leading scholars to make a further distinction between great powers and superpowers.[24]

The more diffuse nature of power in a multiplex world forces us to question the utility of this materialist notion of great powers. It alone cannot explain why US-Russia and US-China relations are becoming more conflictual and intractable. Escalating tensions in these two dyads cannot be reduced to zero-sum competition for security or material gains because they also involve struggles to defend and restore less tangible elements of what each actor regards as indivisible, nonnegotiable, or legitimate, whether it be identity, normative values, tradition, or sphere of influence. Understanding the intensity of resurging great power conflicts requires us to recognize the trajectory through which these principal actors have emerged as central players in world politics and to pay attention to how they mobilize and are shaped by their imperial pasts.[25]

An alternative framework for the New Cold War should consider the imperial legacies of its protagonists. In the modern international system, great powers have historically been imperial states, and colonialism was its key building block. Similarly, given the history of the United States, Russia, and China, we argue that their rivalries can be understood as a clash between incumbent and former empires or between empire-like states. As an analytical concept, empire is a polity that puts other polities under its direct or indirect control, defines relations with different subordinates on different terms, and forges a hub-and-spoke structure with those subordinates linked to the center but little connection between subordinates themselves.[26] Historically, imperial China had claimed itself as the center of the universe in premodern East Asia. Russia was another empire, first under the Czarist rule and less explicitly during the Soviet era.[27] The debate about US hegemony has revealed that the United States is an empire—or at least retains many empire-like characteristics.[28]

Russian and Chinese leaders are increasingly turning to their countries' imperial past both as a source of inspiration to frame assertive and aggressive grand strategies and as a means to legitimize them.[29] These leaders believe their countries are not the same as other nation-states subject to the principle of sovereign equality but the heirs to long imperial traditions. In light of these traditions, China and Russia are willing to proactively intervene in neighboring states as they aspire to build alternative orders, at least regionally, based on their country's identity, vision, and influence. However, the United States, the incumbent empire that has enjoyed a hegemonic position in the global system for decades, is unwilling to accommodate their assertiveness. It is unprepared to cede influence and status to these upstarts in key regions such as Europe and Asia. As Wivel argues in this volume, building and maintaining the spheres of influence remains an important constitutive practice in regional and international politics, even though it clashes with norms of sovereignty and noninterference and thus remains contested by different actors.

As was the case during the old Cold War, the materialist conceptualization of great power does not fully account for the ideological and discursive dimensions of the New Cold War. Rather than accepting ideology as simply a post hoc justification for actions to advance material interests, Balzacq and Grantseva's chapter explores the role of ideology in shaping Russian, Chinese, and US grand strategies toward Central Asia. While their motivations may not be primarily ideological, the discursive moves underlying these ideologies decisively shape the form that competition takes. If so, it may be fruitful to examine the content of ideologies held by the key players in the New Cold War.

To frame and legitimize their actions, great powers are also increasingly relying on civilizational discourses that portray themselves as the bearers of distinctive civilizations. The mobilization of imperial and cultural history to glorify; the self-perception of oneself as a symbolically and materially powerful player; and the belief that shared identities, norms, and practices exist beyond national boundaries provide a fertile ground for the rise of civilizationalism.[30] Unlike the old Cold War's universalistic and inclusive ideologies of liberalism and communism, civilizationalism is exclusivist and has less appeal to lesser states, even when they share ethnic or cultural ties with the "civilizational power." As Köstem observes in his chapter, Russia's efforts to promote a civilizational identity centered on the Russian language and culture (the so-called "Russian World") have found few takers among the post-Soviet states, who see them as a vehicle for Russian domination, and completely fell flat in Ukraine.

The civilizational turn in the last few years not only reflects the growth of scholarly interest in non-Western actors and regions but also constitutes a political backlash against the United States–led liberal international order.[31] With the end of the old Cold War, the liberal order that constituted and regulated relations between the United States and its Western partners evolved into a global order that required all states to fulfill certain liberal "standards of civilization." These included democracy, universal human rights, free-market capitalism, and liberal internationalist and cosmopolitan worldviews. While claiming to be universal, these standards have been heavily influenced by the Western cultural and intellectual experience, particularly the influences of Christianity and the Enlightenment.[32] Unsurprisingly, US and Western universal claims and demands generated discontent and grievance among those non-Western states and societies labeled as illiberal and thus "uncivilized."

With the mounting crisis of the liberal international order, some dissident powers are beginning to conceive of themselves as civilizational states and are mobilizing civilizational discourses to legitimize their resistance against liberalism and US hegemony. Köstem and Larson's chapters show that Russian ruling elites increasingly rely on the civilizational discourse in their efforts to arrest Russia's decline and restore its status and geopolitical influence.[33] Russia's self-identification as the bearer of Eurasian civilization is grounded in the sense of resentment, betrayal, and insecurity following the collapse of the Soviet Union. Faced with the yawning discrepancy between their aspiration to preserve Russia's great-power status and its weakening power, Russian elites gradually turned to Eurasian civilizationalism because it can be used as a discursive weapon in its challenge against US hegemony and serves as an ideological anchor that supports its efforts to build an integrated Eurasian space under Russia's leadership.[34] Ukraine holds a special place in this identity narrative as a cradle and indispensable part of Russian civilization.[35] Losing influence over Ukraine would not only be a blow to Russia's status as a regional power but would also threaten its ontological security (i.e., its sense of identity and self-understanding).[36] Köstem notes that given Russia's lack of economic dynamism and its stagnant model of political governance, these civilizational appeals fail to resonate with audiences outside Russia, forcing Russia to fall back on coercive and violent methods to realize its aspirations for regional dominance and global status.

While Russia's civilizational narrative reflects its anxiety about decline, the Chinese civilizational narrative reflects its growing confidence and optimism in the future, as well as its determination to once and for all arise from the "century of humiliation" it suffered at the hands of European imperialism.[37] According to this narrative, there are multiple paths to modernity, and China has successfully pioneered its own as a civilizational state that combines the strengths of the Western nation-state model with its indigenous cultural traditions. The Chinese civilizational narrative emphasizes the value of Chinese culture, which strives for community, harmony, and justice while embracing differences. Chinese culture and tradition thus provide an alternative vision to the liberal international order, which is flawed by the individualism, conflicts, and imperialism that is inherent to it.[38]

Pu finds that China, in contrast to Russia, has taken a more nuanced and multidimensional approach toward enhancing its status and realizing its regional ambitions. China's Belt and Road Initiative (BRI) is paving the way for a new, Chinese-led trans-regional order that connects Asia, Africa, and Europe through infrastructure, trade and investment networks, policy coordination, and people-to-people exchange.[39] Ho argues that Beijing is now using this initiative to expand its economic interests and minimize US influence, with the ultimate goal of building a Sinocentric regional order across Eurasia. The BRI has a civilizational dimension, as the Chinese government frames it as a moral project to promote an alternative vision and values to those comprising US hegemony, as well as the restoration of the ancient Silk Road that fostered economic, social, and cultural interactions between China and its neighbors.[40] However, in dealing with recalcitrant or uncooperative neighbors, China readily turns to coercive diplomacy, economic sanction, and even the threat of military force.[41] This kind of behavior ultimately undermines its civilizational appeal and leads regional states to hedge and balance against growing Chinese power.[42]

Civilizational discourse is also gaining wider currency in the United States, though the implications for US foreign policy are still unclear. The nature of US and Western civilizational identity and the role that the United States should play in the world are highly contested in a bitterly polarized domestic political environment. US proponents of liberal internationalism continue to believe that Western civilization has evolved into a global, universal civilization and that the United States has to defend and promote liberal democracy, capitalism, and individual freedoms beyond its borders. According to Larson, the United States fiercely resists China and Russia's claims to privileged interest in their regional neighborhood and maintains that smaller states have the right to choose their own foreign policies and domestic systems. It sees itself as the indispensable outside power working to maintain regional order and stability. Russia and China (as well as many observers in the Global South) view US selective efforts to defend the rights of smaller states with suspicion and believe that the United States is simply pursuing these goals to preserve its global hegemony and spheres of influence.[43]

However, growing income inequalities, economic dislocations (especially of erstwhile privileged groups), and the issue of illegal migration give rise to fears about the demise of Western cultural identity and have fueled the rise of a more particularistic brand of civilizational populism in the United States. A new form of civilizational discourse portrays the pure people and their way of life as threatened by a comprador elite beholden to multinational corporations and "globalist" interests.[44] Those who advocate for a return to a purer form of US identity support isolationism and disengagement with the rest of the world. As Larson notes in her chapter, this represents a dramatic change from the Cold War and immediate post–Cold War periods, when the Republicans and the Democrats were united in their commitment to maintaining US global hegemony.

The United States, China, and Russia are not alone in embracing imperial and civilizational narratives to return to their past glory. Emerging and regional powers are also getting into the act. India under Modi and the BJP (Bharatiya Janata Party) promote Hindu civilizationalism, while Erdogan's Turkey has embraced a neo-Ottoman identity that justifies its efforts to increase its influence in the Middle East, Caucuses, and Central Asia. This summoning and mobilization of imperial legacies and civilizational identities are making contemporary great power conflicts, which otherwise might be subject to peaceful diplomatic settlement, more intense and intractable. More often than not, these conflicts entail not only competition for security and economic gains but also the struggle for status. As Larson notes in this volume, increased status is a psychological need that can override material concerns. Status competition is more intense and unpredictable than the balance of power dynamics because it is subjective and based on perception. On the other hand, Pu argues that status competition between great powers does not always have to be zero sum. Status-seeking can benefit regional order and stability when great powers look to enhance their status through economic means or by providing regional public goods.

However, it is unclear if great powers can overcome zero-sum competitions when their competition for influence and status is intertwined with imperial legacies and civilizational discourses. More research should be conducted to unpack and examine the content of these identities and discourses and how they shape great power behaviors, including those for status-seeking. Many experts argue that this turn toward civilizationalism is primarily rhetorical and does not reflect a genuine ideological or normative commitment among its proponents.[45] Nevertheless, civilizational discourses shape great power conflicts, making them further intractable. Great powers can become entrapped by narratives of their own making, which essentialize images of the other and erect imaginary but insurmountable barriers that prevent dialogue and compromise.

RETHINKING "REGIONS"

Focusing on the New Cold War struggle between great powers also risks neglecting many of the complexities and nuances addressed in the rich and diverse scholarship on regionalism. Rather than looking at regions as the "backyards" of great powers, it is more appropriate to conceptualize them as the clusters of proximate states that are "interconnected in spatial, cultural, and ideational terms in a significant and distinguishable manner."[46] Major IR paradigms—realism, liberalism, and constructivism—have offered unique perspectives to unpack regions and regional orders, each focusing on the distribution of material capabilities, the role of international institutions, regime type, and economic interdependence, and the sharing of norms and identities. Some scholars who do not align themselves with any single paradigm have proposed eclectic perspectives emphasizing the domestic-international interaction[47] or the sequence between realist structural and systemic preconditions (geopolitical imperatives), liberal processes (the spread of democracy, economic interdependence, and the creation of regional institutions), and constructivist outcomes (the development of a security community).[48] More recent studies, such as Pardesi and Acharya's chapter in this volume, emphasize the fluidity and diversity of forms that regions and regionalism take. Regions are dynamic, political constructions that are continually being reconstituted and reformed, overlapping with other regional, subregional, and transregional structures.[49]

The literature on regionalism informs us of the critical role that lesser states and non-state actors play in shaping regional orders. Historically, the expansion of ASEAN, the OAU (Organization of African Unity), the ECOWAS (Economic Community of West African States), and the LAS (League of Arab States or Arab League) demonstrated that secondary states can develop regional identities and multilateral mechanisms to address regional problems without the leadership of dominant powers. In their chapter, Brawley and Paquin demonstrate that middle powers and small states such as Poland, Iran, and the two Koreas exert a great deal of agency. They are prodding, engaging, and hedging against different sides and thus decisively shaping regional outcomes. Pardesi and Acharya argue that secondary states can significantly shape regional ideational structures and the norms for regional governance. Weaker states in Southeast Asia are proactively shaping the normative order in the Indo-Pacific. They promote open and consensual norms associated with the "ASEAN way," preventing the rise of hegemonism and great power conflicts in the newly emerging region.

While regional politics has become more complex and pluralistic, we should not forget that great powers have defined the boundaries of regions that exist today and that they continue to exert their influence and pursue their ambitions at the regional level. However, contrary to the expectation of realists,[50] great power hegemony has not necessarily contributed to regional stability. The preceding chapters demonstrate that great power conflicts in Europe and Asia are taking very different forms. For instance, Larson, Pu, and Köstem emphasize that conflicts in Europe resemble the old Cold War, with polarization between antagonistic blocs growing more salient. The same is not true in Asia, where tight inter-bloc polarization has yet to emerge. Ho, Aggarwal and Reddie, and Pardesi and Acharya argue that, despite geopolitical and ideological competitions between great powers, high levels of intraregional interdependence and cooperation in Asia allow room for the agency of secondary states.

Unlike in Europe, where major powers such as Germany, France, and the United Kingdom heavily depend on the security umbrella provided by the United States and NATO, weaker and smaller states in Asia are trying to exhibit greater autonomy in addressing potential security threats engendered by China's rise. On the one hand, they welcome the continued US security presence in the region, even going so far as to participate in security projects such as the AUKUS (Australia, the United Kingdom, and the United States) and the Quad. On the other hand, unlike US allies in Europe, US partners in Asia are reluctant to fully commit themselves to United States–led efforts to contain China. They recognize the benefits of continued economic engagement with China and are wary of replicating the acrimonious experience of NATO-Russia relations. Therefore, they avoid forming a NATO-like alliance structure in Asia, preferring less polarizing, multilateral, and open approaches to addressing regional security issues.

Secondary states may enjoy a great deal of agency in a multiplex world, yet their responses to regional security challenges are still heavily influenced by structural factors. Although Russia and China are often grouped together as revisionist great powers, it should be noted that, in terms of power trajectories, Russia is declining whereas China is (at least for now) rising. Weaker and smaller states in Asia are trying to mitigate conflicts with China because it is a valuable partner for their economic growth. In contrast, a declining Russia cannot provide European states with economic benefits that would entice them away from the orbit of Euro-Atlantic structures. Nor does Russia's stagnant political and economic model hold much normative appeal beyond radical right-wing circles. Unable to effectively use the kind of constructive status-seeking strategies described in Pu's chapter, Russia falls back on coercion, spreading conflict and instability throughout the continent. By contrast, China has exercised more self-restraint because it is still an ascending power and thus has more to lose than gain from antagonizing its neighbors.[51]

The current divergence between Europe and Asia may not hold in the long run. Despite the best efforts of secondary states in Asia, volatile flashpoints such as the Taiwan Strait, the Korean Peninsula, and the East and South China Seas could drag this region into open conflict. There is also a growing concern that China's economic growth is slowing down and that China may soon enter a phase of stagnation. If so, China may become an anxious declining power like Russia and opt for increasingly coercive and destabilizing regional policies.[52]

Structural forces, operating at both the regional and global levels, will continue to shape regional outcomes, even as power and authority become more diffuse and decentralized under multiplexity. Therefore, future research on regions and regional orders should develop more complex and nuanced frameworks for examining structural effects on regional politics that move beyond the standard theories of balancing or hegemonic stability. Existing approaches to studying power shifts tend to focus on the rise of emerging great powers and their disruptive impact on the existing orders. More attention needs to be paid to the decline of established powers and its consequences, especially the behaviors of declining powers as well as the ways in which other states engage with them.[53] Furthermore, as Pu, Larson, and Aggarwal and Reddie suggest in this volume, structural analysis should also move beyond their traditional focus on security and take more seriously the aspirations of declining powers to preserve their status and privileges as a key driving force at the regional and global levels.

RETHINKING "CHANGE"

The resurgence of great power conflicts in the New Cold War era and the structural conditions surrounding them prompt us to rethink the concept of "change" in international politics. In the study of change, IR scholars have primarily focused on change in the context of conflict and war rather than examining how change can come about peacefully and without resorting to violent conflict.[54] In recent years, a growing body of scholarship has looked to put the study of peaceful change at the center of the discipline.[55] Their efforts have made much progress in alerting us to the significance of historical instances of peaceful change, examining various conditions and mechanisms conducive to it as well as its relationship to more well-studied phenomena such as globalization and democratization.

The literature has also contributed to our understanding of the different forms peaceful change may take, which can be conceived of as lying on a spectrum. While the minimalist variants of peaceful change involve "change in international relations and foreign policies of states, including territorial or sovereignty agreements that take place without violence or coercive use of force," the maximalist variants bring "transformational change that takes place non-violently at the global, regional, interstate, and societal levels due to various material, normative and institutional factors, leading to deep peace among states, higher levels of prosperity and justice for all irrespective of nationality, race or gender."[56]

Given that sovereign states, and great powers in particular, still remain the principal actors in world politics, it might seem that minimalist peaceful change achieved through their policies and interactions is a necessary condition for maximalist peaceful change. However, the relationship between minimalist and maximalist peaceful change is not always so straightforward. For instance, Wivel's chapter suggests that peaceful change can be achieved when great powers establish their own spheres of influence in and around the regions where they are located and respect the other's regional hegemony. Pu's chapter stresses that minimalist peaceful change is possible when great powers perceive status as a club good and treat each other as members and potential partners within the exclusive elite club. However, these strategies for minimalist peaceful change satisfy only a handful of great powers, while diminishing the potential of maximalist peaceful change. While great powers enjoy privileged positions by establishing and respecting spheres of influence, weaker and smaller states in each sphere might have to risk subordination, domination, and even a new form of colonialism. The positional-good strategy has a similar problem. During the Concert of Europe, Britain, Russia, Austria, Prussia, and France established themselves as the "powers of the first order," a unique and superior status with the special responsibility to maintain order in Europe.[57] While these great powers enjoyed privileges and peace among themselves, weaker and smaller states endured political interference and military interventions committed by great powers in the name of preserving order in Europe.

The previous chapters in this volume can contribute to the existing literature by examining how New Cold War rivalries impact peaceful change at the regional level. Wivel finds that the establishment of spheres of influence, as an ordering principle, could help maintain minimal peace between great powers as long as they respect the other's regional hegemony. As noted above, however, Wivel acknowledges the spheres of influence can reduce the potential for maximalist peaceful change. Ho is more skeptical, casting doubt on the possibility that the spheres of influence can contribute to minimal peace. She emphasizes that the United States and China are pursuing overlapping and competing spheres of influence in Asia, making the existing minimal peace more precarious.

Larson, Köstem, and Pu all see status competition as the primary threat to minimal peace established in Eastern Europe in the post–Cold War era. Nevertheless, Pu remains optimistic that status-seeking will not disturb the minimal "cold" peace in East Asia as long as status-seekers stick to nonconflictual and non-zero-sum strategies for enhancing their status. As noted earlier, he highlights that status competition can be mitigated when they perceive status as a club good. In their chapters, Balzacq and Grantseva (chapter 4) and Brawley and Paquin (chapter 5) shed light on the agency of secondary states, holding out the possibility that they will be able to mitigate the effects of great power's strategic and ideological competition in their regions, thereby maintaining minimal peace and preventing the outbreak of war.

However, it is worth noting that the return of great power conflict and the New Cold War are only one aspect of the challenges we are encountering today. While the quest for power, status, and privileges is still a main thrust of international politics, we are now undergoing fundamental transformations resulting from various activities that are aimed to bring more efficiency, security, and prosperity to humankind but paradoxically are generating unpredictable (and potentially disastrous) consequences that disrupt material, normative, and ideological foundations of the current international order.

The acceleration of climate change and the outbreak of COVID-19 indicate that great power conflicts in the coming decades will unfold against a completely different environmental background. Despite their numerous ostensible differences, climate change and the global pandemic share much in common.[58] They are both anthropogenic crises that are attributed to and spread and amplified by human activities, many of which are part of the capitalist mode of economic growth. Increased economic interconnectivity allowed the COVID-19 pandemic to spread rapidly worldwide, causing shutdowns and curfews in many countries. Moreover, these problems are marked by the inequitable distribution of responsibilities and consequences. Many developing countries now suffer from abnormal weather conditions and sea-level rise that are the result of massive consumption of fossil fuels in the developed regions over the past decades.

Technological innovations are also restructuring the geopolitical landscape of the New Cold War era. Historically, technological change was a key driver of the rise and evolution of the modern international system.[59] During the old Cold War, the development of nuclear weapons and technologies contributed to peaceful change by forcing nuclear powers to exercise mutual restraint. Nuclear deterrence continues to restrain the New Cold War protagonists today. However, as explored by Aggarwal and Reddie in this volume, they are competing to control new technologies and adopting competitive geo-economic strategies that threaten to erode economic interdependence. Technological innovations are affecting human security as well.[60] The digitalization of economic, social, and political processes aggravates inequalities between those who can take advantage of emerging techniques and those who cannot. The establishment of data surveillance regimes by states and corporate actors is another source of threat to human security and dignity. The remarkable growth of artificial intelligence and advances in biotechnology add to growing unpredictability and uncertainty. These developments will reshape world politics and the foundations of human society in ways that are difficult to foresee, adding to our anxieties about the future survival of humanity.

The interplay between power shifts, normative and ideological contestations, anthropogenic crises, and technological innovations suggests that the New Cold War might be a harbinger of more fundamental changes that require us to develop alternative, maximalist visions for peaceful change in world politics. Most chapters in this volume approach the problem of peaceful change from a minimalist perspective. This is understandable considering the high level of current animosity between great powers and the rising threat of military conflicts such as the Ukraine War. Pardesi and Acharya's chapter is an exception. They hold out the hope that the transition from unipolarity to multiplexity creates conditions for maximalist peaceful change and the establishment of more representative, consensual, and legitimate forms of regional and global orders. They argue that an ideologically pluralistic and decentralized Southeast Asia provides a more promising model for change than an ideologically homogenous and hegemonically liberal Europe, which before the Ukraine War was often touted as the region that had come closest to achieving maximalist peaceful change.[61]

Multiplexity establishes less coercive and more consensual global governance structures, giving actors the freedom to pick and choose the particular orders (global, trans-regional, regional, and subregional) they want to participate in. However, it is unclear how such a decentralized and multilayered order will be able to address humanity's existential problems, which are global in nature and require intense coordination of the entire global community. A multiplex world may be freer and more consensual but also more atomized and fragmented. What will be the glue that maintains the cohesion necessary for relevant actors to address mounting global challenges? Future studies of multiplexity will need to devote more attention to the issue of how actors can maintain solidarity and cooperate under such fluid and complex conditions. A truly inclusive and consensual multiplex order would be endowed with a great deal of legitimacy. Perhaps states will develop such a strong normative commitment to multiplexity that they will be willing to set aside their differences and sacrifice for the greater good. This is one plausible argument. However, it requires much further theorizing about the mechanism through which decentralized and consensual governance structures induce actors to set aside their narrow interests and cooperate with each other, as well as empirical research that examines how multiplex orders address actual real-world problems.

CONCLUSION

The growing intensity of geopolitical conflict between the United States, Russia, and China, which is currently felt most acutely at the regional level, seems to signal a return to traditional great power politics. However, the New Cold War is happening under very different political, social, and economic contexts at both the global and regional levels. The chapters in this volume contribute to our understanding of how great power conflicts are taking place under the conditions of multiplexity, offering complex and nuanced analyses that move beyond the standard realist, liberal, and constructivist approaches. They draw our attention to the increased importance of regions as the locus of order-making in world politics, the growing agency of secondary states in shaping regional and global outcomes, and the dramatically diverging conditions and possibilities for peaceful change in different regions.

In doing so, the authors also push us to rethink how we conceptualize some of the discipline's most fundamental concepts, such as great power, regions, and change. First, great powers cannot simply be treated as nation-states that possess greater power and capabilities than others. The status of great powers is as much a product of enduring ideational factors as their material capabilities. In particular, the United States, Russia, and China, the protagonists of the New Cold War, are former or incumbent empires that often mobilize and internalize civilizational discourse to legitimize their ambitions and interests beyond their territories as nation-states. Future research should examine the ways in which these imperial and civilizational identities and discourses influence the behaviors of great powers and the competition between them.

Second, regions are more than just the backyards or battlegrounds of great powers. Region-making is not exclusively reserved for great powers because weaker and smaller states can often play a leading role. Regions have political, economic, and societal underpinnings but can be redefined and reformulated contingent on the needs of the actors that comprise them. Despite the greater agency afforded to lesser states, structural factors continue to shape state behaviors, though often in ways not predicted by traditional, security-focused, balance of power or hegemonic stability approaches. Finding more nuanced and innovative ways to incorporate structural factors into the study of regional politics could yield a deeper understanding of regional outcomes and the challenges different regions face.

Finally, the unintended consequences of economic growth, mass consumption, and technological innovations now pose a new challenge to the nature of the existing international system itself. Moreover, the growth of multiplexity opens up new windows for transformational change. Therefore, we should develop alternative, broader perspectives about change that include but are not confined to power transition and minimalist peaceful change. Moreover, additional research should be done into how fragmented and decentralized forms of multiplex governance can establish the solidarity and cohesion needed to address global problems.

While great power conflict will continue to shape regional and global outcomes, focusing exclusively on it distracts us from more profound changes to international politics and prevents us from finding ways to address the existential challenges to humanity. Taking a cue from the chapters in this volume, IR scholarship must continue to move beyond the established approaches and paradigms, even as the increased geopolitical conflict of the New Cold War seemingly validates them. Doing so will require creativity, flexibility, and open and honest debate. Rethinking key concepts, such as great power, regions, and change, is a good place to begin this long and arduous process.

NOTES

1. See T.V. Paul and Markus Kornprobst's Introductory Chapter in this volume.
2. Robert Legvold, *Return to Cold War* (Cambridge, UK: Polity Press, 2016); Sergey Karaganov, "The New Cold War and the Emerging Greater Eurasia," *Journal of Eurasian Studies* 9, no. 2 (2018): 85–93. Hal Brands and John Lewis Gaddis, "The New Cold War: America, China, and the Echoes of History," *Foreign Affairs* 100, no. 6 (2021): 10.
3. Andrew Monaghan, "A 'New Cold War'? Abusing History, Misunderstanding Russia," Chatham House, May 22, 2015; https://www.chathamhouse.org/2015/05/new-cold-war-abusing-history-misunderstanding-russia; Thomas J. Christensen, "No New Cold War: Why US-China Strategic Competition Will Not Be Like the US-Soviet Cold War," Asan Report, Seoul, September 2020, http://en.asaninst.org/contents/no-new-cold-war-why-us-china-strategic-competition-will-not-be-like-the-us-soviet-cold-war/.
4. G. John Ikenberry, "The End of Liberal International Order?," *International Affairs* 94, no. 1 (2018): 7–23; Odd Arne Westad, "The Sources of Chinese Conduct: Are Washington and Beijing Fighting a New Cold War?," *Foreign Affairs* 98, no. 5 (2019): 86–95.
5. Michael Kimmage and Maria Lipman, "Will Russia's Break with the West Be Permanent?," *Foreign Affairs*, June 19, 2023, https://www.foreignaffairs.com/united-states/putin-will-russia-break-west-be-permanent-kimmage.
6. T.V. Paul, "When Balance of Power Meets Globalization: China, India and the Small States of South Asia," *Politics* 39, no. 1 (2019): 50–63.
7. Dmitri Trenin, "Flexible Relationship of Cooperation," Carnegie Endowment for International Peace, accessed August 25, 2023, https://carnegiemoscow.org/2012/06/06/flexible-relationship-of-coopration-pub-48522.
8. Amitav Acharya, "After Liberal Hegemony: The Advent of a Multiplex World Order," *Ethics and International Affairs* 31, no. 3 (2017): 271–85.
9. For a discussion of these overlapping regional trade initiatives, see the Aggarwal and Reddie chapter in this volume.
10. In this volume, Brawley and Paquin present a detailed neoclassical realist analysis of the different strategies smaller regional states can adopt.
11. See Pardesi and Acharya in this volume.
12. Drawing on Paul's definitions of these concepts, the distinction between "minimalist" and "maximalist" peace will be described in greater detail in the sections that follow.
13. See Balzacq and Grantseeva's chapter.
14. See Wivel's chapter on "spheres of influence" in this volume.
15. See Ho and Pardesi and Acharya for a discussion of the role of secondary powers and smaller states in Asia.
16. See the Pu, Larson, and Köstem's chapters for a discussion of status-seeking and status competition.
17. Kenneth N. Waltz, *Theory of International Politics* (Reading, MA: Addison-Wesley, 1979).

18. John J. Mearsheimer, *The Tragedy of Great Power Politics* (New York: Norton, 2001).
19. Robert Gilpin, *War and Change in World Politics* (Cambridge: Cambridge University Press, 1981); Graham T. Allison, *Destined for War: Can America and China Escape Thucydides' Trap?* (Boston: Houghton Mifflin Harcourt, 2017).
20. For important recent scholarship on peaceful change, see T.V. Paul et al., eds., *The Oxford Handbook of Peaceful Change in International Relations* (Oxford: Oxford University Press, 2020); Markus Kornprobst and T.V. Paul, eds., "Globalization, Deglobalization and the Liberal International Order," special double issue, *International Affairs* 97, no. 5 (2021); Kai He, T.V. Paul, and Anders Wivel, eds., "International Institutions and Peaceful Change," special issue, *Ethics & International Affairs* 34, no. 4 (2020): 457–59; Bhubhindar Singh, "Special Issue on the 'Sources of Peace and Peaceful Change in East Asia,'" *The Pacific Review* 35, no. 6 (2022): 995–1009. For the distinction between minimalist and maximalist variants of peaceful change, see T.V. Paul, "The Study of Peaceful Change in World Politics," *The Oxford Handbook of Peaceful Change in International Relations*, 4.
21. Waltz, *The Theory of International Politics*; Mearsheimer, *The Tragedy of Great Power Politics*.
22. Hedley Bull, *The Anarchical Society: A Study of Order in World Politics* (London: Macmillan, 1977), 194–96, 200–218; Jack S. Levy, *War in the Modern Great Power System, 1495–1975* (Lexington: University Press of Kentucky, 1983), 16–18; Barry Buzan, *The United States and the Great Powers: World Politics in the Twenty-First Century* (Cambridge, UK: Polity, 2004), 59–63, 69–70; Mearsheimer, *The Tragedy of Great Power Politics*, 1–5.
23. Levy, *War in the Modern Great Power System*, 16–17.
24. Buzan, *The United States and the Great Powers*, 68–70; Barry Buzan, "Great Powers," in *The Oxford Handbook of International Security*, eds. Alexandra Gheciu and William C. Wohlforth (Oxford: Oxford University Press, 2018), 641.
25. Ayse Zarakol, *After Defeat: How the East Learned to Live with the West* (Cambridge: Cambridge University Press, 2010).
26. Daniel H. Nexon and Thomas Wright, "What's at Stake in the American Empire Debate," *American Political Science Review* 101, no. 2 (2007): 258–60; Joseph MacKay, "Rethinking the IR Theory of Empire in Late Imperial China," *International Relations of the Asia-Pacific* 15, no. 1 (2015): 56–58.
27. Dominic Lieven, "The Russian Empire and the Soviet Union as Imperial Polities," *Journal of Contemporary History* 30, no. 4 (1995): 607–36.
28. Peter J. Katzenstein, *A World of Regions: Asia and Europe in the American Imperium* (Ithaca, NY: Cornell University Press, 2005), 2–5; Nexon and Wright, "What's at Stake"; Daniel Immerwahr, *How to Hide an Empire: A History of the Greater United States* (New York: Farrar, Straus and Giroux, 2019).
29. Jeffrey Mankoff, *Empires of Eurasia: How Imperial Legacies Shape International Security* (New Haven, CT: Yale University Press, 2022), 60–79, 251–68; Jeffrey Mankoff, "The War in Ukraine and Eurasia's New Imperial Moment," *The Washington Quarterly* 45, no. 2 (2022): 135–41.
30. Gregorio Bettiza, Derek Bolton, and David Lewis, "Civilizationism and the Ideological Contestation of the Liberal International Order," *International Studies Review* 25, no. 2 (2023): 1–23; Christopher Coker, *The Rise of the Civilizational State* (Cambridge, UK: Polity, 2019).
31. Hiro Katsumata and Hiroki Kusano, eds. *Non-western Nations and the Liberal International Order: Responding to the Backlash in the West* (New York: Routledge, 2023),

ch. 7; Bettiza et al., "Civilizationism and the Ideological"; Markus Kornprobst and T.V. Paul. "Introduction: Globalization, Deglobalization and the Liberal International Order." *International Affairs* 97, no. 5 (2021): 1305–1316; see Balzacq and Grantseva for a detailed examination of how China and Russia have adapted their ideological discourse to confront the US liberal challenge in Central Asia.
32. Daniel H. Nexon, "Discussion: American Empire and Civilizational Practice," in *Civilizational Identity: The Production and Reproduction of "Civilizations" in International Relations*, eds. Martin Hall and Patrick Thaddeus Jackson, Culture and Religion in International Relations (New York: Palgrave Macmillan, 2007), 110–14; James Kurth, "The United States as a Civilizational Leader," in *Civilizations in World Politics: Plural and Pluralist Perspectives*, ed. Peter J. Katzenstein (London: Routledge, 2010), 41–44.
33. See also Ray Silvius, "Eurasianism and Putin's Embedded Civilizationalism," in *The Eurasian Project and Europe: Regional Discontinuities and Geopolitics*, eds. David Lane and Vsevolod Samokhvalov (New York: Palgrave Macmillan, 2015), 75–88.
34. Marlène Laruelle *Russian Eurasianism: An Ideology of Empire* (Washington, DC: Johns Hopkins University Press, 2008), 9–12.
35. Richard Sakwa, *Frontline Ukraine: Crisis in the Borderlands* (London: I. B. Tauris, 2015), 31–33.
36. Andrej Krickovic and Richard Sakwa, "War in Ukraine: The Clash of Norms and Ontologies," *Journal of Military and Strategic Studies* 22, no. 2 (2022): 89–109.
37. Wei-Wei Zhang, *The China Wave: Rise of a Civilizational State* (Hackensack, NJ: World Century, 2012), 52–69; Higgot, *States, Civilisations, and the Reset of World Order*, 51–55, 61–62; Bettiza et al., "Civilizationism and the Ideological," 19–20.
38. Yan Xuetong, *Leadership and the Rise of Great Powers* (Princeton, NJ: Princeton University Press, 2019); Tingyang Zhao, *All under Heaven: The Tianxia System for a Possible World Order* (Oakland: University of California Press, 2021).
39. Mingjiang Li, "The Belt and Road Initiative: Geo-Economics and Indo-Pacific Security Competition," *International Affairs* 96, no. 1 (2020): 169–87.
40. William A. Callahan, "China's Belt and Road Initiative and the New Eurasian Order," *NUPI Policy Brief*, http://hdl.handle.net/11250/2401876; Thomas Colley and Carolijn van Noort, *Strategic Narratives, Ontological Security and Global Policy: Responses to China's Belt and Road Initiative* (Cham: Palgrave Macmillan, 2022), 49–50, 53–55.
41. For more on these coercive policies, see Ho's chapter in this volume, 10–12.
42. T.V. Paul, *Restraining Great Powers: Soft Balancing from Empires to the Global Era* (New Haven, CT: Yale University Press, 2018), 119–45.
43. Walter Russell Meade, "Sanctions on Russia Pit the West against the Rest of the World." *Wall Street Journal*, March 22, 2022, https://www.wsj.com/articles/the-west-vs-rest-of-the-world-russia-ukraine-dictators-south-america-asia-africa-11647894483.
44. Bettiza et al., "Civilizationism and the Ideological," 13–16; Nicholas Morieson, "Understanding Civilizational Populism in Europe and North America: The United States, France, and Poland," *Religions* 14, no. 2 (2023): 5.
45. Laruelle, *Russian Eurasianism*.
46. T.V. Paul, "Regional Transformation in International Relations," in *International Relations Theory and Regional Transformation*, ed. T.V. Paul (Cambridge: Cambridge University Press, 2012), 4.
47. Benjamin Miller, *States, Nations, and the Great Powers: The Sources of Regional War and Peace* (Cambridge: Cambridge University Press, 2007).

48. Norrin M. Ripsman, "Two Stages of Transition from a Region of War to a Region of Peace: Realist Transition and Liberal Endurance," *International Studies Quarterly* 49, no. 4 (2005): 669–93.
49. Andrew Hurrell, "One World? Many Worlds? The Place of Regions in the Study of International Society," *International Affairs* 83, no. 1 (2007): 127–46; Amitav Acharya, "Global International Relations (IR) and Regional Worlds: A New Agenda for International Studies," *International Studies Quarterly* 58, no. 4 (2014): 647–59; Katzenstein, *A World of Regions*.
50. David A. Lake, "Regional Hierarchy: Authority and Local International Order," *Review of International Studies* 35 (2009): 35–58.
51. Andrej Krickovic and Chang Zhang, "Fears of Falling Short versus Anxieties of Decline: Explaining Russia and China's Approach to Status-Seeking," *The Chinese Journal of International Politics* 13, no. 2 (2020): 219–51.
52. Michael Beckley, "The Peril of Peaking Powers: Economic Slowdowns and Implications for China's Next Decade," *International Security* 48, no. 1 (2023): 7–46.
53. Dale Copeland has applied his dynamic differentials theory of power transitions, which focuses on the destabilizing effects of decline, to regional security. See Dale Copeland, "Realism and Neorealism in the Study of Regional Conflict," In *International Relations Theory and Regional Transformation* (Cambridge: Cambridge University Press, 2012), ed. T.V. Paul, 49–73.
54. A.F.K. Organski and Jacek Kugler, *The War Ledger* (Chicago: University of Chicago Press, 1980); Gilpin, *War and Change*; T.V. Paul, James J. Wirtz, and Michel Fortmann, eds., *Balance of Power: Theory and Practice in the 21st century* (Stanford, CA: Stanford University Press, 2004).
55. See footnote 19.
56. T.V. Paul, "The Study of Peaceful Change in World Politics," 4.
57. Jennifer Mitzen, *Power in Concert: The Nineteenth-Century Origins of Global Governance* (Chicago: University of Chicago Press, 2013), 88–91.
58. Thomas Heyd, "Covid-19 and Climate Change in the Times of the Anthropocene," *The Anthropocene Review* 8, no. 1 (2021): 23–27; Diana Stuart, Brian Petersen, and Ryan Gunderson, "Shared Pretenses for Collective Inaction: The Economic Growth Imperative, COVID-19, and Climate Change," *Globalizations* 19, no. 3 (2022): 411.
59. Anne L. Clunan, "Science, Technology, and Peaceful Change in World Politics," in *The Oxford Handbook of Peaceful Change in International Relations*, eds. T.V. Paul et al. (New York: Oxford University Press, 2021), 385–406; William Hardy McNeill, *The Pursuit of Power: Technology, Armed Force, and Society Since A.D. 1000* (Chicago: University of Chicago Press, 1982); Daniel Deudney, "Dividing Realism: Structural Realism versus Security Materialism on Nuclear Security and Proliferation," *Security Studies* 2, no. 3–4 (1993): 5–36; Daniel Deudney, "Nuclear Weapons and the Waning of the Real-State," *Daedalus* 124, no. 2 (1995): 209–32.
60. Changrok Soh and Daniel Connolly, "The Human Security Implications of the Fourth Industrial Revolution in East Asia," *Asian Perspective* 44, no. 3 (2020): 383–407.
61. For a discussion of these claims about Europe and their flaws, see Anders Wivel, "Peaceful Change in Western Europe: From Balance of Power to Political Community?," in *The Oxford Handbook of Peaceful Change in International Relations*, eds. T.V. Paul, D.W. Larson, H.A. Trinkunas, A. Wivel, and R. Emmers (Oxford: Oxford University Press, 2021), 569–83.

INDEX

Page numbers with *f* indicate figure and *t* indicate table respectively

Abe, Shinzo, 111, 178
Acharya, Amitav, 21, 240, 241
Afghanistan, 63, 225; Russian failures in, 11; Russia's army for protection borders, 85; US failures in, 6; US withdrawal from, 13
Africa, 7, 122
Aggarwal, Vinod K, 241
Air Defense Identification Zone (ADIZ), 196
Allison, Graham, 121
American telecommunications sector, 154
American World Order (AWO), 28
Andaman and Nicobar Islands, 43
anti-access and area denial (A2/AD) strategies, 37
anti-domination discourses, 83
1973 Arab-Israeli conflict, 17
Armenia, 221
artificial intelligence (AI), 122, 148, 245
Asia, 7, 170, 242; international system, 44; spheres of influence in, 244; US isolationism in, 182
Asian Infrastructure Investment Bank (AIIB), 133, 142, 196
Asia-Pacific, 142; Chinese economic influence in, 154; economic arrangements, 162; institutional arrangements with, 163; transregional regimes, 151

Asia-Pacific Economic Cooperation (APEC), 153, 198, 200
assertive regional powers, 2
Association of Southeast Asian Nations (ASEAN), 5, 13, 18, 35, 41, 181, 182, 190, 198, 241; ASEAN Outlook on Indo-Pacific (AOIP), 42; ASEAN Regional Forum (ARF), 35; East Asia Summit (EAS), 36; Treaty of Amity and Cooperation (TAC), 41
Australia, 35, 67, 106, 152, 159, 177, 179, 182; agreement with Japan, 112; high-income countries, 64; IPEF's November 2022 negotiations in, 159; nuclear-powered submarines, 179; Quad, 179
Australia, United Kingdom, and United States (AUKUS), 179, 241
Austria, 5, 244
AU-UK submarine, 179
Azerbaijan, 217, 221

balance of power, 14, 15, 170, 247
bandwagoning, 5, 12, 18, 100, 101, 214
Basic Telecom Agreement (BTA), 149
Beijing, 40, 87, 133, 198, 199
Beijing Consensus, 63
Belt and Road Initiative (BRI), 5, 7, 18, 58, 133, 142, 181, 196, 199, 214, 216, 238
Bettiza, Gregorio, 214
Bianchi, Sarah, 160

Biden, Joe, 158, 190
Biden strategy, 8
Boutros-Ghali, Boutros, 54
Brawley, Mark R., 20, 21, 241
Brazil, 1, 5, 7, 19
Brazil, Russia, India, China, South Africa (BRICS), 5, 18, 127, 214
Bush, George H. W., 31, 54, 113, 173
Buzan, Barry, 35

Cambodia, 35
Canada, 152
capitalism, 58
Central America, 17
Central Asia, 2, 8, 76, 84; ideology and grand strategy in, 83–90; regional conflict zones in, 7
China, 1, 5, 6, 8, 16, 19, 28, 35, 37, 76, 84, 85, 141, 142, 151, 154, 213, 247; control and exclusivity, 198–200; creation and militarization of, 37; culture and tradition, 238; demographic crisis looms in, 115; economic engagement with, 241; economic growth, 193, 242; economic interdependence, 134; in economic order, 8; economic power, 134; economic rise and defense spending, 178; Lancang-Mekong Cooperation (LMC), 197; maritime tactics, 180; and Mongolia, 192; of neocolonialism, 87; in regional affairs, 44; Regional Comprehensive Economic Partnership (RCEP), 156–58; in regional forums, 189; regional military power, 133; regional order, 177, 191–94; regional role, 189; region's economic architecture, 190; rise of, 7; Sino-centric collective identity, 200–202; Sino-Centric Hierarchical Order, 195–98; sphere of influence, 21, 194–95; strategy, 39–40; trading partners, 18; US-China economic interdependence, 18; Xiangshan Forum, 197
China-ASEAN Free Trade Area (CAFTA), 192
China-Central Asia Natural Gas Pipeline, 223
Chinese Communist Party Congress, 8
Chinese invasion of Taiwan, 180
Chirac, Jacques, 176
Christianity, 237
Chung Hee, Park, 107
civilizational discourses, 239–40
climate change, 244, 245
Clinton, Bill, 173
Clinton, Hillary, 206
Clunan, Anne L., 214
coercion, 189
Cold War, 9, 15, 75, 81, 122, 170, 172, 205, 237, 239, 245; technological innovation, 20; US-Soviet rivalry in, 121
Collective Security Treaty Organization (CSTO), 173, 211
Colombia, 154
colonialism, 7, 16
commercial liberalism, 15
Committee on Foreign Investment in the United States (CFIUS), 144
Commonwealth of Independent States (CIS), 84, 173
community of common destiny (CCD), 202
competition *See* great powers
Comprehensive and Advanced Partnership Agreement (CEPA), 224
Comprehensive and Progressive Agreement for Trans-Pacific Partnership (CPTPP), 142, 150
Comprehensive and Progressive Trans-Pacific Partnership (CPTPP), 154
Concert of Europe, 53
Congress of Vienna, 11, 53

constructivism, 16
Cooley, Alexander, 214
Costa Rica, 154
COVID-19 pandemic, 244, 245
Cox, Michael, 32, 62
Creating Helpful Incentives to Produce Semiconductors and Science Act of 2022 (CHIPS Act), 147
critical perspectives, 16
CSTO, 212
Cuba, 5, 56
Cuban Missile Crisis, 5, 176
cultural diversities, 16
Cultural Revolution, 192
cybersecurity markets, 146
Czarist rule, 236

data localization, 160
decolonization, 6
Deng, Xiaoping, 87, 192
Deutsch, Karl, 17
digital commerce and trade, 151
digital economy agreements (DEAs), 160
digital innovation, 1
distribution of identity, 16
domestic markets, 147
domestic-market trade subsidies, 144
Doshi, Rush, 121
Dragnewa, Rilka, 215
Duda, Andrzej, 110
Duterte, Rodrigo, 179

East Asia, 13, 20, 36, 111–14, 134, 136, 141, 177–82; and Collapse of Soviet Union, 107–8; and Nixon's Guam doctrine, 105–7; power transition in, 14; sphere of influence, 190; state of cold peace in, 122; US alliance system in, 172; US engagement in, 97
Eastern Europe, 17, 61, 109, 172, 173
Eastern Partnership (EaP), 222

e-commerce, 154, 156
Economic Community of West African States (ECOWAS), 241
economic policy, 162
economics, 33
economic statecraft: beyond-the-border measures, 150–51, 151f; domestic structure, 147–48; economics of innovation, 143; five-factor model, 145–49; international regime characteristics, 149; market characteristics, 146–47; security objectives, 143; systemic characteristics, 148–49; technological characteristics, 148
Ecuador, 154
Egypt, 11
English school, 16
Eurasia: peaceful change in, 212; regional economic order, 215–16; regional normative order, 219–20; regional order in, 213; regional security order, 217–19; Russia's historical leadership role in, 213; Russia's Invasion of Ukraine and regional order in, 220–22; Ukraine conflict in, 122
Eurasian Economic Union (EAEU), 85, 173, 211, 212
Euro-Atlantic, 65, 67, 69
Europe, 2, 8, 16, 17, 44, 53, 122, 141, 170, 171, 242
European right, 68
European Union (EU), 28, 67, 97, 109, 149, 190, 211, 212; EU-Central Asia summits, 225
external balancing, 100, 111, 114
external power, 172

Fernandez, Jose, 159
Finland, 5, 65, 175
First World War, 54
foreign direct investment (FDI), 223

Foreign Investment Risk Review Modernization Act (FIRRMA), 144
foreign policy, 61–63, 189
foreign policy executive (FPE), 99–100
France, 39, 112, 176, 241
Franco-German relations, 3
free and open Indo-Pacific (FOIP) strategy, 178
Freeden, Michael, 78
free-market capitalism, 237
free trade agreements (FTAs), 141

G-20, 5, 18, 127
General Assembly, 4
geographic proximity, 56
geopolitical imperatives, 240
Germany, 30, 127, 175, 176, 241
Gerring, John, 83
Gilpin, Robert, 128
Global Financial Crisis, 7, 193, 215
globalization, 2, 28
global powers, 2, 39, 98, 125, 133, 171
Global South, 61; economic and social development in, 18; proxy wars in, 6
Google, 159
Gramscian notion, 32
grand strategy, 77; in Central Asia, 83–90; policies in, 82t
Grantseva, Vera, 21, 232
Great Britain, 179
Greater Eurasian Partnership (GEP), 216
Greater Mekong Subregion (GMS), 197
great powers, 1–3, 124, 135, 233, 235–40, 243, 247; of Asia, 44; capitalism *vs.* communism, 4; China's geopolitical and geostrategic interests, 58; conflicts and regional orders, 10t; democracy and authoritarianism, 4; distribution of power, 14; hierarchies and hegemonic orders, 16; ideological constituents of *See* ideology; international crises, 4; in international politics, 9; International Relations (IR), 76; liberal international order's claim, 55; in military realm, 5; non-great power strategies, 11–13; nuclear weapons, 3; peaceful change in regions, 17; political interference and military interventions by, 244; and regional orders *See* regional orders; in regional transformation, 16; regions and regional orders, 6; rights and obligations, 53–54; role of, 15; sovereign equality and territorial integrity, 9; spheres of influence *See* spheres of influence; in status competition, 135, 136; Trump's national security strategy, 8; United States and China, 61–63

Haass, Richard, 31, 83
Harris, Kamala, 177
Hartwell, Christopher, 215
hegemonic orders, 16
1975 Helsinki Final Act, 5
Hong Kong, 96
Hu, Jintao, 193, 195
human rights, 237
Hungarian Revolution, 54
Hungary, 68

IBM, 159
ideology, 76; conceptualizing, 77–79; external manifestation of, 78; and grand strategy in Central Asia, 77, 83–90; policies and regional orders, 79–83; and power distribution, 91; United States, 232
Ikenberry, John, 54, 171
illiberal political system, 127
India, 1, 5, 7, 11, 16, 19, 28, 32, 35, 67, 180, 204; in economic order, 8; naval logistics agreements with Vietnam

and Singapore, 43; trading with Russia, 13; United States and, 38
Indian Ocean, 29
Indonesia, 1, 5, 19, 41, 196; Belt and Road Initiative (BRI) in, 196; influence on AOIP, 42; Sulu-Sulawesi Sea Patrols (SSSP), 42
Indo Pacific Economic Framework (IPEF), 142, 150
Indo-Pacific region, 2, 8, 14, 29, 66–68, 133, 241; America's power and position in, 39; non-hegemonic, decentered, and open regional order in, 30; sphere of influence, 64; strategy, 38; US-China contest in, 40; US-China maritime contest, 37; US networking, 170
Inflation Reduction Act (IRA), 147
1996 Information Technology Agreement, 149
institutional change, 151f
institutional membership, 36
internal balancing, 100, 114
international institutions, 5
international leadership, 128
international politics, 243, 244
international regime characteristics, 149
International Relations (IR), 13–14, 76, 233
international status competition, 124
International Telecommunications Union (ITU), 142
intraregional conflict, 205
investment policy, 144–45
Iran, 85
Iraq: alliance against Israel, 105; Bush's 2003 invasion of, 98; US failures in, 6, 11; US interventions in, 6; US war against, 176
Israel, 11; Hamas's terrorist attack on, 4; October 2023 Hamas attack on, 17
Israeli-Palestinian conflict, 6

Jaishankar, S., 180
Japan, 28, 32, 37, 57, 104, 106, 111, 113, 127, 152, 177–80, 182, 190; agreement with Australia, 112; bilateral security treaty, 111; foreign policy, 106; Legislation for Peace and Security, 112; US-Japan defense treaty, 111
Jervis, Robert, 83
Jonathan, Paquin, 20, 21, 241

Kausikan, Bilahari, 201
Kazakhstan, 76, 84, 196, 217, 221; Chinese factories in, 88; involvement in EAEU, 86; Kazakhstani-Chinese benefits, 87; mass media in, 86; NGO external funding in, 89; oil pipelines network, 86; Open Democracy, 90; Russian-speaking populations in, 86; Russia's strategy, 84
Kennedy, Paul, 76
Khrushchev, Nikita, 176
Kim, Jaeyoung, 22
Komorowski Doctrine, 109
Korea, 122
Korean Peninsula, 242
Korean War, 191
Kornprobst, Markus, 189
Köstem, Seçkin, 21, 237, 238, 244
Krauthammer, Charles, 31
Krickovic, Andrej, 22
Kyrgyzstan, 221, 225

Laclau, Ernesto, 78
Lake, David, 98
Lancang-Mekong Water Resources Cooperation, 197
Laos, 35, 40, 204
Larson, Deborah W., 237, 242, 244
Latin America, 6
Lavrov, Sergei, 98
League of Arab States or Arab League (LAS), 241

Lebanese political crisis, 81
legitimacy, 32
Lemke, Douglas, 14
Lewis, David, 214
liberal democracy, 64, 66
liberal hegemony, 28, 29
liberal institutionalism, 15
Liberal Internationalism 3.0, 54
Liberal International Order (LIO), 28, 97–99
liberalism, 16, 237
liberal processes, 240
Libman, Alexander, 215
Lincoln, Abraham, 61
Lower Mekong Initiative (LMI), 204
Lukashenko, Alexander, 110
Lurong, Chen, 160

Mackinder, Halford J., 59
Macron, Emmanuel, 176
Malacca dilemma, 37
Malacca Straits Patrols (MSP), 42
Malaysia: general election in, 199; security cooperation with, 112; Sulu-Sulawesi Sea Patrols (SSSP), 42
Manchin, Joe, 158
Mao, Zedong, 87, 192
Marcos, Ferdinand, 179, 182
maritime attacks, 42
market access, 191
market-based system, 115
market dynamics, 145
market economy, 58
martial law, 54
Martin, Lisa, 98
Marxism-Leninism, 61
May negotiations, 159
Medvedev, Dmitri, 173, 211
Mekong River Commission (MRC), 197
Mekong-U.S. Partnership, 204
Mexico, 152

Middle East, 2, 6, 8, 13, 97, 104, 115; regional conflict zones in, 7; Soviet Involvement in, 104–5
military capability, 206
military force, 134
military interventions, 7
military power, 33, 61, 127, 128
Milner, Helen V., 79
Mitsubishi F-2s, 112
Modi, Narendra, 180, 239
Monroe Doctrine, 64, 206
Moscow, 109, 216
multiplexity, 6, 22, 29
multiplex worlds, 29
mutually assured destruction (MAD) doctrine, 122
Myanmar, 35

Nakasone, Yasuhiro, 106
Nasser, Gamal Abdel, 104
2008 NATO summit, 173
neoclassical realist (NCR) framework, 96–99
neoliberals, 147
neomercantilism, 58
new arms race, 3
New Cold War, 19, 22, 61, 96, 114, 115, 121, 124, 205, 214, 226, 231–36, 240, 243–45, 247; and Cold War, 4–5; interstate and intrastate conflicts in, 3; for regional orders, 2; Russia-Ukraine conflict, 130–31; security and economic rivalries, 1; status politics, 122–24; technological innovations, 245
New Development Bank, 141–42
New Eurasian project, 84
New Zealand, 35
Nixon, Richard, 106, 192
Nixon's Guam doctrine, 97, 105–7
non-great power strategies, 11–13
non-state actors, 2
normative leadership, 36

North America, 53
North American Free Trade Agreement (NAFTA), 149
North Atlantic Treaty Organization (NATO), 7, 38, 44, 67, 114, 122, 172, 179, 211, 212, 241; 2016 Warsaw Summit, 110; declarative policy, 175; Eastern European and Baltic states in, 9; economic interdependence and trade, 175; Finland, 65; membership to Ukraine, 174; members of, 175; NATO-Russia relations, 241; NATO Summit, 222; Russia's rights to exercise, 53; Sweden, 65; Western coalition in, 176
North Korea, 108; international law, 113; nuclear program, 111; socio-political constraints, 112
nuclear deterrence, 113
1968 Nuclear Nonproliferation Treaty, 113
nuclear-powered submarines, 179
nuclear weapons, 3, 113, 135

Obama, Barack, 63, 111, 115, 173, 178
1Malaysia Development Berhad (1MDB), 199
open regionalism, 44
Organization for Democracy and Economic Development, 89
Organization for Security and Cooperation in Europe (OSCE), 173
Organization of African Unity (OAU), 241
organized hypocrisy, 64
Orwell, George, 3

Pakistan, 11
Pardesi, Manjeet S., 21, 240, 241
Pashinyan, Nikol, 217
Paul and Kornprobst, 232
Paul, T.V., 189

peaceful change, 2, 17, 243, 245; AWO, 43; historical instances of, 243; and regional orders, 13–18
Pearl Harbor attack, 125
Peloponnesian War, 53
Pence, Mike, 199
People's Republic of China (PRC), 191
Philippines, 42, 57, 66, 132, 177, 178, 180
Pillsbury, Michael, 121
Poland, 68, 108, 110, 176
political cohesion, 100
political community, 78
political discourse, 58
political liberalism, 68
Pompeo, Mike, 205
postcolonial politics, 82
power asymmetries, 33
power transitions, 16
Prague Spring, 54
Prayut O-Cha, 200
proxy wars, 6
Putin, Vladimir, 7, 9, 53, 96, 109, 134, 170, 171, 174–77, 181, 211, 213, 223
Pyongyang, 113

Quadrilateral Security Dialogue (Quad), 5, 30, 38, 42, 112, 179, 190, 204, 241
Quinn, Adam, 62

Razak, Najib, 199
Reddie, Andrew W., 20, 241
regional actors, 20, 22
regional agency, 19
Regional Comprehensive Economic Partnership (RCEP), 5, 141, 150, 156–58
regional economic order, 215–16
regional hegemony, 14, 211
regional identities, 241
regional leadership, 129
regional normative order, 219–20

regional orders, 12, 16, 129, 170, 182; East Asia, 105–108, 111–14; Eastern Europe, 108–11; empirical findings and predictions, 114–15; empirical section, 104; neoclassical realist (NCR) framework, 97–99; and peaceful change, 13–18; power transitions, 172; second-tier states'strategies, 99–102, 102*t*, 103*t*; Soviet Involvement in the Middle East, 104–5; strategic interaction, 102–4

regional politics, 241, 242

regional security order, 217–19

regional states, 40; China's reemergence, 193; in East Asia, 136; economic relations with China, 135; peaceful orders, 17; strategies, 12*t*; trading partner for, 178

regional trade agreements, 151

Richards, A. I., 77

Risse, Thomas, 98

Roosevelt, Franklin D., 177

Russia, 1, 3, 4, 6, 8, 28, 32, 35, 36, 76, 84, 247; annexation of Crimea, 212, 214; economic and security goals, 85; military and foreign policy doctrines of, 9; NATO troops and weapons, 174; oil and gas reserves, 96; political and economic model, 242; in regional affairs, 9; in regional geopolitical crises, 212; regional intervention, 7; Russia-Georgia war, 109; Russian invasion of Ukraine, 68, 172, 231; Russian-led regional order, 85*f*; Russian offensive against Ukraine, 7; Russian war against Ukraine, 176; Russia's invasion of Georgia, 173; Russia's invasion of Ukraine, 129, 170, 171, 179, 212, 220–22; Russia-Ukraine conflict, 130–31; Russo-Georgian war in 2008, 131; territorial disputes with Japan, 113; trading with India, 13; against Western influences, 111

Saudi Arabia, 1, 5, 81

Scholz, Olaf, 175

secondary states, 12

Second World War, 3, 37, 54

Security Council, 4, 17

security dilemma, 126

Selina, Ho, 241

Serbia, 85

Shambaugh, David, 203

Shanghai Cooperation Organisation (SCO), 5, 18, 133, 217

Silk Road Economic Belt, 216

Singapore, 85, 147

Sino-American rivalry, 36

Sino-Russia relationship, 122

Sino-Soviet Treaty, 191

Sino-US relationship, 136

small-and medium-sized enterprises (SME), 153

social cohesion, 81, 100

social order, 75

Solomon Islands, 64, 66

South Africa, 1, 19

South Asia, 2, 6, 13, 129

South China, 170

South China Sea, 18, 37, 96, 178, 198

Southeast Asia, 6, 17, 35, 44, 181, 203, 246; foreign direct investment for, 190; weaker powers of, 30; weaker regional powers in, 30

Southern Africa, 6, 17

South Korea, 104, 106, 107, 113, 147, 154, 177, 182, 193

Soviet-Afghan War, 127

Soviet Union, 1, 3, 84, 122, 173, 191–92, 206, 232

sphere of influence: in East Asia, 190, 204; in Eastern Europe, 173

spheres of influence, 53, 54, 190, 204, 206; analytical notion and political discourse, 56; Eastern Europe in, 173; foreign policy doctrine, 56; foreign-policy maker, 57; of geographic proximity, 56; geopolitical neighborhood of state, 56; global political space, 55; horizontal repertoires of expectations, 63–65; international formations, 57; in international relations, 56; international system into, 56; peaceful change in, 57–60; political communities, 53; small states and middle powers, 56; states' expectations of, 55; United States and China in, 61–63; US Chinese rivalry in, 55; vertical repertoires of expectations, 66–68
Spykman, Nicholas, 59
state actors, 2
state intervention, in markets: investment policy, 144–45, 146f; trade policy, 143–44
status competition, 183, 239; China and Cold Peace in East Asia, 131–35; Russia-Ukraine conflict, 130–31; status politics and New Cold War, 122–24; in world politics, 124–29
status politics, 121
structural analysis, 242
structural forces, 242
subversion, 81
Sudan, civil war in, 4
Suez Canal, 105
Sulu-Sulawesi Sea Patrols (SSSP), 42
Summit for Democracy, 63
Sweden, 65, 175
Switzerland, 5
Swope, Bernard, 3
Syria, 7, 13; and Yemen conflicts, 57; Russian actions in, 57
Syrian war, 81

tacit agreement, 3
Tai, Katherine, 158
Taiwan, 65, 69, 114, 154; IPEF framework, 159; Japan's tacit support for, 107; military conflicts in, 19, 134; territorial disputes and, 194
Taiwan Strait, 190, 242
Tajikistan, 85, 221
technological innovations, 247
telecommunications, 153
Thailand, 66, 177
Theory of International Politics, 59
Thierry, Balzacq, 21, 232
Tillerson, Rex, 64
Timor-Leste, 64
Tingley, Dustin, 79
Tokyo, 111–12
trade policy, 143–44
Transatlantic Trade and Investment Partnership (TTIP), 141
Trans-Pacific Partnership (TPP), 141, 150, 152
2006 Trans-Pacific Strategic Economic Partnership (P4), 152
Treaty of Amity and Cooperation (TAC), 36
Trump, Donald, 63, 110, 113, 114, 154, 177, 178, 182, 204
Tsygankov, Andrey, 214
Turkey, 11, 19
Tusk, Donald, 176
Tuvalu, 64

Ukraine, 4, 7, 9, 13, 17, 67, 69, 154, 237; 2014 Maidan Protests in, 173; European Peace Facility fund, 176; rival blocs and deterrence, 173; Ukraine war, 121, 172, 245; US funding for Ukraine aid, 177; US interest in democracy, 173
Umarov, Temur, 87
UN Human Rights Council, 221
United Arab Emirates, 1

United Kingdom, 19, 38, 112, 241
United Nations (UN), 221; UN Charter, 4, 7, 174; United Nations Security Council (UNSC), 54, 127
United States, 1, 3, 6, 7, 8, 15, 16, 19, 28, 32, 33, 35–37, 44, 65, 68, 76, 84, 96, 122, 127, 142, 151, 154, 177, 179, 189–91, 206, 213, 247; alliance network, 115; civilizational discourse, 238; civilizational populism in, 239; Cold War geopolitical priorities, 172; for defense and predictable trade relations, 171; economic engagement and NGO funding, 90; economic liberalism, 66; foreign policy, 63, 225, 238; global economic policy, 141; globalization, 8; global leadership, 136; hegemony, 7, 32, 236; leadership role in NATO, 177; leadership to regional orders, 171; liberal hegemony theory, 171; liberal international order, 237; Najib's relations with, 199; National Intelligence Council (NIC), 30; national security strategy, 178; for regional hegemony, 190; rise of India, 38; sphere of influence, 57; United States' Monroe Doctrine, 54; US-China relations, 32, 65, 121, 180, 231, 235; US Cold War foreign policy, 62; US-EU sanctions on, 224; US-Japan defense treaty, 111; US-Korea Free Trade Agreement (KORUS), 153; US-Mexico-Canada Agreement (USMCA), 149
Uruguay, 154

Vietnam, 35, 85, 122, 132, 178
Vietnam War, 127, 192

Vinod K. Aggarwal, 20, 21, 242, 245
violence: independence, peace, and limitation of, 34; in Middle East, 15; Russia's military actions, 13; in South Asia, 15
von der Leyen, Ursula, 97

Wæver, Ole, 35
Waltz, Kenneth, 59, 65
Wang, Yi, 158
Warsaw, 114, 115
Warsaw Pact, 173
Warsaw Summit, 110
Wendt, Alexander E., 78
West Africa, 15
Western cultural, 237
Western Europe, 57, 172
Western Pacific, 29
Wilson, Woodrow, 62
Wivel, Anders, 190
world politics, 128
World Trade Organization (WTO), 142
World War I, 205
World War II, 6, 127, 175, 176, 191

Xi, Jinping, 1, 8, 87, 96, 98, 134, 180, 181, 193, 200, 201, 223
Xiangshan Forum, 198
Xiaoyu, Pu, 242, 244

Yang, Jiechi, 195
Yanukovych, Viktor, 173
Yeltsin, 9, 213
Yemen, 13
Yemeni conflict, 81
Yew, Lee Kuan, 37
1973 Yom Kippur War, 105
Yugoslavia, 67

Zelensky, Volodymyr, 222

CONTRIBUTORS

AMITAV ACHARYA is the UNESCO chair in Transnational Challenges and Governance and distinguished professor at the School of International Service, American University, Washington. His books include: *Re-imagining International Relations* (Cambridge 2022, with Barry Buzan); *The Making of Global International Relations* (Cambridge 2019: with Barry Buzan); *Constructing Global Order* (Cambridge 2018); *The End of American World Order* (Polity 2014, 2018); *Why Govern? Rethinking Demand and Progress in Global Governance* (editor, Cambridge 2016); and *The Making of Southeast Asia* (Cornell 2013); and *Whose Ideas Matter* (Cornell 2009). His essays have appeared in *International Organization, International Security, International Studies Quarterly, Journal of Asian Studies, Foreign Affairs, Journal of Peace Research, International Affairs, Perspectives on Politics,* and *World Politics*. He is the first non-Western scholar to be elected (for 2014–2015) president of the International Studies Association (ISA). He has received three ISA Distinguished Scholar Awards.

VINOD K. AGGARWAL is a distinguished professor and Alann P. Bedford Professor of Asian Studies, Travers Department of Political Science; affiliated professor at the Haas School of Business; director of the Berkeley Asia Pacific Economic Cooperation Study Center (BASC); and fellow, Public Law and Policy Program, Berkeley Law, at the University of California at Berkeley. He is also editor-in-chief of the journal *Business and Politics*. Aggarwal is a permanent member of the Council on Foreign Relations. He has published over twenty-one books and 160 articles and book chapters. He has two forthcoming books: *Great Power Competition and Middle Power Strategies* and the *Oxford Handbook on Geoeconomics and Economic Statecraft*. His current research examines comparative regionalism in Europe, North America, and Asia, industrial policy, and the political economy of high-technology economic statecraft. Dr. Aggarwal received his BA from the University of Michigan and his MA and PhD from Stanford University.

THIERRY BALZACQ is a professor of political science at Sciences Po ("exceptional class") and professorial fellow at CERI-Sciences Po, Paris. He was the 2022/2023 Susan Strange Professor in the Department of International Relations at the London School of Economics and Political Science (LSE) and George Soros visiting chair and distinguished visiting professor in the Department of Public Policy at Central European University in Vienna (Spring 2022). He has published over fifteen books in English and French, including *The Oxford Handbook of Grand Strategy* (Oxford University Press, coedited with Ronald R. Krebs, 2021), *Comparative Grand Strategy: A Framework and Cases* (Oxford University Press, coedited with Peter Dombrowski and Simon Reich, 2019). He coedits the Oxford Studies in Grand Strategy book series. He is currently working on two books.

MARK R. BRAWLEY primarily focuses on the politics of trade and monetary relations but is also interested in areas where political economic issues and security concerns collide. He is the author of several books and numerous articles. His most recent publications include "Principles, Personalities, or Trade? Explaining Taft's 1911 Prosecution of U.S. Steel," *Journal of Antitrust Enforcement* 10, no. 4 (2022), and "Britain's Trade Liberalization in the 1840s: A Defensive Neoclassical Realist Explanation," *Foreign Policy Analysis* 18, no. 4 (2022).

VERA GRANTSEVA has been an associate professor at Higher School of Economics St. Petersburg since 2017. She served as international relations expert at St. Petersburg City Administration from 2008 to 2016. She defended a thesis of candidate of science in international relations at St. Petersburg State University in 2016 on Russian soft power. She is currently a PhD candidate at Sciences Po Paris.

SELINA HO is an associate professor in international affairs and co-director of the Centre on Asia and Globalisation, Lee Kuan Yew School of Public Policy, National University of Singapore. She researches Chinese politics and foreign policy, with a focus on how China wields power and influence via infrastructure and water disputes in Southeast Asia and South Asia. Selina is the author of *Thirsty Cities: Social Contracts and Public Goods Provision in China and India* (Cambridge University Press, 2019), coauthor of *Rivers of Iron: Railroads and Chinese Power in Southeast Asia* (University of California Press, 2020), and coeditor of *The Routledge Handbook of China-India Relations* (2020). She has published widely in peer-reviewed journals, including

International Affairs, Chinese Journal of International Politics, and *Journal of Contemporary China,* among others. Selina received her doctorate from The Paul H. Nitze School of Advanced International Studies (SAIS), Johns Hopkins University.

JAEYOUNG KIM is an assistant professor of political science at San Diego State University. He recently completed his PhD in the Department of Political Science at McGill University, in Montreal, Canada. His areas of research are status politics and international order with a regional focus on contemporary and historical East Asia.

MARKUS KORNPROBST is a professor of political science and international relations at the Vienna School of International Studies. His research appears in leading journals in the field such as the *European Journal of International Relations, International Affairs, International Organization,* and *International Theory.* He has coedited six books, coauthored *Understanding International Diplomacy* (Routledge, 2013, 2018, 2025), and authored *Irredentism in European Politics* (Cambridge University Press, 2008) as well as *Co-managing International Crises* (Cambridge University Press, 2019). He is coeditor of the *Routledge New Diplomacy Series,* leads the Peaceful Change Working Group at the Austrian Research Association, and serves as the regional director Africa of the *Global Research Network on Peaceful Change.* His current research projects deal with processes of global and regional ordering, peaceful change, arms control, digital international relations, and global health.

SEÇKIN KÖSTEM is an assistant professor of international relations at Bilkent University in Ankara, Turkey. He received his PhD from McGill University in 2016. In fall 2018, he was a George F. Kennan Fellow at the Kennan Institute in Washington, DC. Köstem has been a visiting researcher at Columbia University's Harriman Institute, New York University's Jordan Center, King's College London's Russia Institute, and the Moscow State Institute of International Relations (MGIMO). He is currently an editor of *Review of International Political Economy.* His research focuses on the political economy of Eurasia, regional and rising powers, and Russian-Turkish relations. He is coeditor of *Turkey's Pivot to Eurasia: Geopolitics and Foreign Policy in a Changing World Order* (Routledge, 2019). His articles have been published in journals such as *Review of International Political Economy, Foreign Policy Analysis, Cambridge Review of International Affairs, Europe-Asia Studies, Third World Quarterly,* and *Global Policy.*

ANDREJ KRICKOVIC is an associate professor of international studies at Xi'an Jiaotong-Liverpool University, in Suzhou, China. His primary areas of research are IR theory and international security with an empirical emphasis on Russian and Chinese Foreign Policy. His articles have been published in leading journals such as *International Studies Review*, *The Chinese Journal of International Relations*, *International Politics*, and *Post-Soviet Affairs*.

DEBORAH WELCH LARSON is a research professor of political science at the University of California, Los Angeles. Her research interests include status concerns, Russian and Chinese foreign policies, and the liberal world order. Her publications include *Origins of Containment: A Psychological Explanation* (Princeton University Press, 1985); "Status Seekers: Chinese and Russian Responses to U.S. Primacy," *International Security* 34, no. 4 (Spring 2010): 63–95 (with Alexei Shevchenko); and *Quest for Status: Chinese and Russian Foreign Policy* (Yale University Press, 2019) (with Alexei Shevchenko).

MANJEET S. PARDESI is an associate professor of international relations in the Political Science and International Relations Programme, and Asia Research Fellow at the Centre for Strategic Studies at Victoria University of Wellington. He is the coauthor of *The Sino-Indian Rivalry: Implications for Global Order* (with Sumit Ganguly and William R. Thompson, Cambridge University Press, 2023). His articles have appeared in *European Journal of International Relations*, *Security Studies*, *Survival*, *Global Studies Quarterly*, *Asian Security*, *Australian Journal of International Affairs*, and *International Politics*.

JONATHAN PAQUIN is a professor of political science at Université Laval in Quebec City, Canada. He has written numerous articles on foreign policy and international relations, including in *International Studies Quarterly*, *Foreign Policy Analysis*, and *Cooperation and Conflict*. He recently coedited *America's Allies and the Decline of US Hegemony*, Routledge, 2020; and coauthored *Foreign Policy Analysis: A Toolbox*, Palgrave Macmillan, 2018. Jonathan Paquin received a PhD in political science from McGill University and was a Fulbright visiting scholar and resident fellow at the School of Advanced International Studies (SAIS, Johns Hopkins) in Washington, DC. Paquin was also Fulbright Canada Research Chair in Humanities and Social Sciences at the Citadel in Charleston, South Carolina. He is currently codirector of the Network for Strategic Analysis, which is funded by the Canadian Department of National Defence.

T.V. PAUL is a Distinguished James McGill Professor in the Department of Political Science at McGill University, Montreal, Canada and a fellow of the Royal Society of Canada. He served as the president of the International Studies Association (ISA) for 2016–2017. He is the founding director of the *Global Research Network on Peaceful Change* (GRENPEC). Paul is the author or editor of twenty-four books, coeditor of four special journal issues, and author of over eighty scholarly articles/book chapters in the fields of international relations, international security, and South Asia. He is the author of the books: *The Unfinished Quest: India's Search for Major Power Status from Nehru to Modi* (Oxford University Press, 2024); *Restraining Great Powers: Soft Balancing from Empires to the Global Era* (Yale University Press, 2018); *The Warrior State: Pakistan in the Contemporary World* (Oxford University Press, 2013); *Globalization and the National Security State* (with N. Ripsman, Oxford University Press, 2010); *The Tradition of Non-use of Nuclear Weapons* (Stanford University Press, 2009); *India in the World Order: Searching for Major Power Status* (with B. R. Nayar, Cambridge University Press, 2002); *Power versus Prudence: Why Nations Forgo Nuclear Weapons* (McGill-Queen's University Press, 2000); and *Asymmetric Conflicts: War Initiation by Weaker Powers* (Cambridge University Press, 1994). He is the lead editor of the *Oxford Handbook of Peaceful Change in International Relations* (Oxford University Press, 2021). Paul currently serves as the editor of the Georgetown University Press book series: *South Asia in World Affairs*. For more, see: www.tvpaul.com.

XIAOYU PU is an associate professor of political science at the University of Nevada, Reno. He is a member of the Public Intellectuals Program of the National Committee on United States-China Relations (NCUSCR). He has also received fellowships from the Inter-American Dialogue in Washington, DC, Fundação Getulio Vargas (FGV) in Brazil, and the China and the World Program at Princeton University. He is the author of *Rebranding China: Contested Status Signaling in the Changing Global Order* (Stanford University Press, 2019). His research has appeared in *International Security*, *International Affairs*, *The China Quarterly*, and *Chinese Journal of International Politics*. He serves on the editorial boards of *The Chinese Journal of International Politics* and *Foreign Affairs Review*. He received his PhD from Ohio State University.

ANDREW REDDIE is an associate research professor of public policy at the University of California, Berkeley's Goldman School of Public Policy. He works on projects related to cybersecurity, nuclear weapons policy, wargaming, and emerging military technologies. He is also the founder and faculty director for the Berkeley Risk and Security Lab. His work has appeared in *Science*, *The Journal of Peace Research*, *The Journal of Cyber Policy*, and the *Bulletin of the Atomic Scientists*, among other outlets, and has been variously supported by the Founder's Pledge Fund, Carnegie Corporation of New York, MacArthur Foundation, and the U.S. Department of Energy's Nuclear Science and Security Consortium.

ANDERS WIVEL is a professor of international relations in the Department of Political Science, University of Copenhagen. He has published widely on foreign policy, small states in international relations, and power politics and IR realism. His academic articles have been published in, for example, *International Affairs*, *International Studies Review*, *International Relations*, *Cambridge Review of International Affairs*, *Cooperation and Conflict*, *Journal of International Relations and Development*, *Ethics and International Affairs*, and *European Security*. His most recent books are *Oxford Handbook of Peaceful Change in International Relations* (Oxford University Press, 2021, coedited with T.V. Paul, Deborah W. Larson, Harold Trinkunas, and Ralf Emmers) and *Polarity in International Relations: Past, Present, Future* (Palgrave, 2022, coedited with Nina Græger, Bertel Heurlin, and Ole Wæver).